Development and Disparities

DEVELOPMENT AND DISPARITIES

Experiences from Southern India

KALIPADA DEB

RAWAT PUBLICATIONS
Jaipur and New Delhi

ISBN 81-7033-672-4

Published by
Prem Rawat for ***Rawat Publications***
Satyam Apts., Sector 3, Jain Temple Road, Jawahar Nagar, Jaipur - 4 (India)
Phone: 0141 651748 / 657006 Fax: 0141 651748
e-mail : rawatbooks@pinkline.net

Delhi Office
G-4, 4832/24, Ansari Road, Daryaganj, New Delhi 110 002
Phone: 011-3263290

Typeset by Rawat Computers, Jaipur
Printed at Nice Printing Press, New Delhi

Contents

IV
The Economy of Karnataka

V
The Economy of Kerala

VI
Summing Up

Preface

The prime target of any development effort must be the removal of poverty among the masses, while pursuing overall growth. Extreme inequality of income can never be in the long-run interest of a nation, as the saying goes: 'Poverty anywhere is a danger to prosperity everywhere.' If some people are wallowing in riches, while a vast majority steeped in poverty and ignorance, this is bound to breed violence and disorder. The strategy of growth must, therefore, incorporate strong measures for bringing about equitable distribution of income and wealth among the people.

India's economic growth is ostensibly based on this principle. The preamble to the Constitution of India itself promised to the people: "Justice, social, economic and political; Liberty of thought, expression, belief, faith and worship; Equality of status and of opportunity; and to promote among them all; Fraternity assuring the dignity of the individual and the unity of the Nation..." The Directive Principles of State Policy contain a variety of assurances in these directions. For example, Section 43 states:

> "The state shall endeavour to secure, by suitable legislation or economic organisation or in any other way, to all workers, agricultural, industrial or otherwise, work, a living wage, conditions of work ensuring a decent standard of life and full enjoyment of leisure and social and cultural opportunities..."

Similarly, Section 46 states:

> "The state shall promote with special care the educational and economic interests of the weaker sections of the people, and, in particular, of the Scheduled Castes and the Scheduled Tribes, and

shall protect them from social injustice and all forms of exploitation."

Such pronouncements were there in the plan and other documents also. The First Five-Year Plan underscored the need for changing the socio-economic framework in order to "accommodate progressively fundamental urges which expressed themselves in the demands for the right to work, the right to adequate income, the right to education and to a measure of insurance against old age, sickness and other disabilities" (p.8). The document of the Second Five-Year Plan was also no less progressive; it expressly incorporated the objective of bringing a socialist pattern of society in the country.

What happened to these lofty objectives ultimately? How much has been achieved after five decades of development efforts? Did the government try its utmost to provide the basic necessities of life to each and every person and reduce the regional imbalance in development? This study makes an in-depth analysis of these questions.

India is a vast country with wide regional variations in resource endowment. The study is, therefore, approached on a regional basis, divided into the following five regions: (1) *The Northern Region*, comprising the states of Haryana, Himachal Pradesh, Jammu & Kashmir, Punjab and Rajasthan and the union territories (UTs) of Chandigarh and Delhi; (2) *The Southern Region*, comprising the states of Andhra Pradesh, Karnataka, Kerala and Tamil Nadu and the UTs Lakshadweep and Pondicherry; (3) *The Eastern Region*, comprising the major states of Bihar, Orissa, West Bengal and Assam, seven smaller states and two UTs; (4) *The Western Region*, covering Gujarat, Maharashtra and Goa and two UTs; and (5) *The Central Region*, comprising the states of Uttar Pradesh and Madhya Pradesh.*

Region-wise, the most developed is the Southern Region, and it has been selected first in order to see how a relatively developed region tackled the problem of disparities. This will be followed by the most backward region, the Eastern Region, and then the most heavily populated region, the Central Region. It is proposed to have five volumes in all.

This volume is divided into six parts, comprising 19 chapters in all. The first part is introductory and has two chapters. It deals with the nature of government the country has had, the constitutional

---

* Position before the constitution of three new states, namely, Uttranchal, Chattisgarh and Jharkhand.

rights and obligations of the states, and the nature of economic planning carried out. The second chapter provides an outline of the nature of development achieved in each of the southern states over the past half-a-century. The focus is on the growth of income and economic diversification, the level of consumption expenditure and reduction in poverty, the state of the social sector, and regional disparities in development.

The following four parts are on each of the four southern states, namely, Andhra Pradesh, Tamil Nadu, Karnataka and Kerala, and the last one sums up the findings of the study. Each of the parts on states has four chapters: The first one deals with the pattern of resource mobilisation and deployment; the second with the growth in agriculture and allied sectors; the third with the pattern of industrial growth; and the fourth with the specific poverty alleviation measures like wage employment and self-employment programmes and the PDS.

Some of the salient points that have emerged from the study may be noted here. On the whole, the South Indian states are in a much better position than many of the other states. Their performance is relatively poor, mainly in the area of per capita income. But even here the worst performer, Andhra Pradesh, has a level higher than in four of the large states. On poverty alleviation and in some of the social indicators of development their position is better than many other states.

Among the southern states, there is wide variation in performance, with Andhra Pradesh having the worst and Kerala the best. Andhra's only notable success is in reducing absolute poverty. In recent years, the proportion of population below the poverty line has been the second lowest here. In the social sector it has a very poor performance, as in case of growth of income. The literacy rate here is significantly below the national average. In reducing regional imbalance also its record is very poor.

Kerala has a very low per capita income---much below the national average. But, the level of consumer expenditure here is higher than in most of the states, largely due to the remittances from abroad. In poverty alleviation also its performance is one of the best. Kerala's best record is, however, in the area of social sector. It has the topmost position in literacy rate, in life expectancy and on IMR. Kerala's main problems are low growth in both agriculture and industry and acute unemployment.

Tamil Nadu, despite being the most industrialised state in the

Southern Region, has a very poor record in reducing absolute poverty. There are as many as seven major states with large proportion of population below the poverty line. The consumer expenditure in rural areas here is much below the national average. Regional disparity in development is too high, with industries concentrated in a few districts. The position of the social sector here is, however, much better than in many of the states.

Karnataka's relative position is also not good although the per capita income here has the highest growth. The monthly consumer expenditure here is not only lower than the national average, it is also lowest among the southern states. In reducing absolute poverty also its performance has not been satisfactory, and the regional imbalance in development continued to be glaring. In the social sector, however, the situation is better than the national average.

In resource mobilisation none of the states performed well. The per capita budgetary receipt in recent years has been less than the national average in three of them; only Tamil Nadu barely exceeded it. There is ample scope for larger resource mobilisation in each of the states. The deployment of funds also left much to be desired. The per capita plan expenditure is very low in each of the states, and the backward districts did not receive due attention.

In the completion of this work my debt is indeed very extensive. I have collected data from different government departments, research institutes and universities, and in the process many people came forward to help me. Among the institutes, particular mention may be made of Centre for Development Studies, Thiruvananthapuram, Institute for Social and Economic Change, Bangalore, Madras Institute of Development Studies, Chennai, and the Universities of Osmania, Kerala, Madras, Bangalore and, of course my own North Bengal. Among the government departments at Hyderabad, particularly helpful were the Directorate of Economics and Statistics, the Directorate of Economic Planning and the PRI and RD and the Fishery Departments ; at Thiruvananthapuram, the State Planning Board; at Chennai, the State Planning Commission; and at Bangalore, the Directorate of Economics and Statistics and the Planning Department of the Government of Karnataka.

Due to lack of space it is not possible to acknowledge my debt individually to all the people who helped me in different ways. The range is very wide, from railway stations to guest houses and a variety of persons in libraries and government offices. I express my deep sense of gratitude to everybody. To name a few persons here: at Hyderabad: Professor V. Surender of Osmania University, Dr. T. Koteswara Rao, Director, Directorate of Economics and Statistics, Smt. Sarwaja Rao, Director, Department of Planning, Sree K. L. Narayana, Addl. Secretary, Department of PRI and RD and Sree O. Bhavani Shanker, Addl. Director, Fishery Department; at Chennai: Sree P. Prabakaran, Secretary, Planning and Development Department, Sree K.V. Paleanidurai, Member, Planning Commission, the Librarian T. S. Ramakrishna, District Planning Officer Ahdul Azeez and the Agricultural Economist Dr. C. Sekhar, Dr. Paul P. Appasamy, Director, Madras Institute of Development Studies, and Professor D. Amarchand of Madras University; at Thiruvananthapuram: Sree V. Ramakrishnan, Librarian and Dr. Chandan Mukherjee, Director, at the Centre for Development Studies, Dr. T.M. Thomas Isaac, Member, Dr. (Mrs.) P. Sukumari, Agronomist, Mrs. P. Jayasree Thankom, Senior Librarian and the Special Officer Sree A. S. K. Nair at the State Planning Board, and Dr. N. C. Pillai, UGC Professor and Professor K. Sasikumar, at Kerala University, at Bangalore: Professor M. V. Nadkarni, Professor Abdul Aziz, Dr. S. N. Sangita and Dr. N. Sivanna at Institute for Social and Economic Change, and Professor K. Eresi, Professor K. Aswathappa and the Librarian Dr. M. Anjanappa at Bangalore University.

It is needless to add that the work atmosphere in the North Bengal University here---while otherwise it may be deprecated—was an important contributor to the completion of my work. I thank the university, and my department in particular, for making it possible to complete the work in the short time that I did. I also express a deep sense of gratitude to the library staff of the university for the assistance I received. Finally, no word is adequate to express the debt to my wife, Kalpana, without whose cooperation the work would not have been possible.

Kalipada Deb

I

Introduction

1

The Constitution and Pattern of Planning

The Southern Region of India is comprised of four states, viz., Andhra Pradesh, Karnataka, Kerala and Tamil Nadu, and two union territories, viz., Pondicherry and Lakshadweep. Being parts of the Indian Union, their powers and obligations are governed by the Constitution of India, which came into force on 26 January, 1950. The constitutional provisions made economic planning an imperative necessity, and the Government of India introduced five-year plans from 1951. Here, we give a brief look first, into the salient features of the Constitution having a bearing on economic activities, and secondly, on the nature of economic planning carried out in the last half-a-century, as a backdrop to our main theme of discussion.

Constitution: Salient Features

The Indian Constitution looks like a propaganda material. It promises to the people almost all the good things in this world. The preamble to the Constitution says, it wants "to secure to all its citizens:

Justice, social, economic and political;

Liberty of thought, expression, belief, faith and worship;

Equality of status and of opportunity; and to promote among them all

Fraternity assuring the dignity of the individual and the unity of the nation."

The Directive Principles of State Policy, which are not justiceable include, among others, the following important provisions:

Section 39 states: "The state shall, in particular, direct its policy towards securing—

(a) that the citizens, men and women equally, have the right to an adequate means of livelihood;

(b) that the ownership and control of the material resources of the community are so distributed as best to subserve the common good;
(c) that the operation of the economic system does not result in the concentration of wealth and means of production to the common detriment;
(d) that there is equal pay for equal work for both men and women;
(e) that the health and strength of workers, ... and the tender age of children are not abused and that citizens are not forced by economic necessity to enter avocations unsuited to their age or strength;
(f) that children are given opportunities and facilities to develop in a healthy manner... and that children and youth are protected against exploitation and against moral and material abandonment..."

Section 41 calls for making "effective provision for securing the right to work, to education and to public assistance in cases of unemployment, old age, sickness and disablement, and other cases of undeserved want." The state was "to provide, within a period of ten years from the commencement of this Constitution, for free and compulsory education for all children until they complete the age of fourteen years" (Section 45). Special attention was to be given to "the educational and economic interests of the weaker sections of the people, and, in particular, of the Scheduled Castes and the Scheduled Tribes" (Section 46). The question of protecting the environment was also not neglected. Section 48a states: "The state shall endeavour to protect and improve the environment and to safeguard the forests and wild life of the country." Decentralisation of power to the village panchayats for enabling them "to function as units of self-government" is stated in Section 40.

All these provisions in the Constitution appeared as precursor to the establishment of a socialist society. To emphasise this aspect, even the preamble to the Constitution was altered in 1976 from "Sovereign Democratic Republic" to "Sovereign Socialist Secular Democratic Republic". However, all these high objectives remained totally unrealised and the Constitution had to be amended 79 times in the last 50 years.

Neither the Central Government was strong enough nor the states had the wherewithal to implement the provisions. Apparently the structure was of a federal type, but the historical background made the Constitution-makers swing towards a strong Centre. The system came to be described as quasi-federal. The Constitution guarantees the existence of state but the Central Parliament can create new ones, abolish existing ones, or alter the boundaries simply by majority vote. Presently, there are 28 states and seven union territories in the country. The states are of extremely disparate size. The smallest state, Sikkim, is with 0.3 per cent of population of the largest one, Uttar Pradesh (undivided).

The Constitution divides legislative powers into three groups: Union, State and Concurrent. The longest and most important is the Union List, with 97 items. The State List has 66 items, of which 30 deal with ordinary police functions and 22 with taxation, leaving 14 items on 'development'. Most of the powers are, however, hedged about with qualifications, and in certain circumstances the Centre may override state powers. The Concurrent List, containing 47 items, has 'economic and social planning' and trade, and repeats industry but, where there is conflict, laws passed by the Central Parliament prevail over those passed by the states.

At the executive level also there are decided constitutional limits to provincial autonomy. The source of executive authority is the state Governor, appointed by the President. This power is normally exercised by the provincial council of ministers but the Governor has important discretionary powers : he initiates the process of forming a ministry and has the power to declare that no ministry is possible; he may 'reserve' bills passed by the provincial assembly for presidential consideration; and he has the right to advise the President to assume the government of the state. The actual administration of the state is in the hands of the all-India services, and the Chief Secretary, the most senior administrative officer in the state, may find himself subjected to a division of loyalties.

The distribution of taxes also disadvantages the states: whereas the Centre enjoys the most important and growing sources of revenue the states depend on three limited sources: their own powers of taxation specified in the Constitution, a share of centrally raised taxes and grants-in-aid on the recommendations of the Finance Commission, and the plan allocations. The main taxes available to the states are highly inelastic and the states came to rely mainly on commodity taxation in the form of sales tax on items of mass consumption. This is regressive, politically unpopular, and not much revenue can be collected.

The Finance Commission, appointed by the President every five-year is a quasi-judicial body whose findings are usually accepted by the Centre. It recommends how centrally collected resources should be distributed between the Government of India and the states, how the states' share should be distributed among them, and what principles should govern the allocation of grants-in-aid to individual states. The Commission's recommendations are limited to just over one-third of all the resources transferred from the Centre to the states.

The Planning Commission is a non-statutory body concerned with plan as opposed to revenue expenditure. In practice this is an ambiguous and unreal distinction which has led to strained relations between the two Commissions and much discontent in the states. The Planning Commission transfers resources to the states in two forms: Central investment for projects of all-India significance and central assistance for approved local projects. Increasingly, the latter has been in the form of loans which have come to dominate the total transfer of resources. In consequence the states have run deeply into debt. By the early 1970s many states were compelled to take recourse to unauthorised overdrafts from the Reserve Bank of India to avoid 'bankruptcy'.

This brief description of the Centre-State relations, however, somewhat exaggerates the degree to which the autonomy of states is curbed by the Centre. The centre depends on the states to a large extent for the implementation of its policies as well as for execution of the duties reserved for the states. Relations actually vary from time to time and from state to state depending on many political factors including the unity and standing of the Central Government and the strength and determination of the state or states concerned. Unbroken Congress rule at the Centre and in the states during the first two decades after Independence led to even more centralisation than what the constitution visualised. Anti-Congressism in the eighties and growth of coalition governments in recent years brought a significant change in the situation. Overall, even after so many amendments Indian Constitution continues to be a matter of great controversy, and there is presently a strong demand for its thorough overhaul. A recent background paper of the Union Law Ministry has listed the following items, among others, for review:

(i) Fundamental Rights, Directive Principles and Fundamental Duties.

(ii) Zones of silence, vagueness and uncertainties (Articles 73, 74, 102, 191, 163, 164, 167, 35).

(iii) Abuse, misuse of power and constitutional accountability (i.e., who is a public servant, corruption in high places and abuse of power, Lok Pal and Lok Ayukta, Parliamentary Committee).
(iv) Stable, effective and clean government: electoral reform, representation in legislative bodies; delimitation of committees; switch to presidential form of government, expanding/limiting powers of the President.
(v) Centre-state relations, inter-state disputes and states' reorganisation.
(vi) Role of bureaucracy and need for neutrality (quoted in *The Statesman* 2000 a).

Economic Planning

Given the socialistic pronouncements in the Constitution, there was need for tight economic planning so that the resources were utilised in the best possible manner. There was need for extracting the surpluses available with the richer section of population with a strong hand and deploying them for the benefit of weaker sections. The manpower available had to be organised properly for best possible utilisation. There was need for a severe curb on ostentatious consumptions. All these required a very strong government, and probably not of the federal type as the resource availability and ability to implement the plans varied greatly. There were some inherent contradictions between the economic objectives and the means contemplated.

Resource Mobilisation and Deployment

As the required nature of government was not there, it was futile to expect that the laid down objectives would be fulfilled. The people who came to power were born and brought up under feudal or a capitalistic system, and without a strong leader it was unexpected of them to bring a socialist type of economy. Ostentatious living became the order of the day (Deb 1982).The education system continued to be the same colonial pattern. There was no attempt to mould the man to suit the needs of the new economic philosophy as expressed.

Mobilisation of savings was far from what was required and the labour resources continued to remain highly underemployed. Gross domestic saving as percentage to gross domestic product remained less than 15 till the end of sixties and rose to 20.0 during 1980-83 and 23.5 during 1993-98 (GOI 1975, 1985; CMIE 1999a). There was absolutely no concerted efforts to utilise the labour resources. Unemployment and poverty in the rural areas continued unabated at least till the end of seventies. Underutilisation of capital was also not negligible. The production capacity of many of the public sector plants remained highly underutilised. The extent of wastage of resources belied that the government was really for developing the economy. The atmosphere in government offices and the pace in implementation of projects showed a clear lack of any sense of time.

The scope of public sector activities itself was limited. Its share of total investment in the economy never exceeded 50 per cent. Agriculture and small-scale industries remained largely beyond its control. The banking system continued to be run in the traditional way at least for two decades, and in recent years also the changes were not of the nature and magnitude required. Naturally, therefore, the resource deployment was often not in accordance with the set priorities. The public sector plan expenditure itself was very small from the angle of requirements, and the situation was made worse by huge leakages of funds.

During the First Plan, beginning in 1951, a total of only Rs. 1,960 crores was spent, and it was mainly a putting together of some on-going schemes and projects. From the Second Plan, the outlays increased rapidly reaching Rs. 15,779 crores during the Fourth Plan (1969-70 to 1973-74), Rs. 109,292 in the Sixth Plan (1980-81 to 1984-85) and Rs. 434,100 crores in the Eighth Plan (1992-93 to 1996-97). The per capita plan outlay increased from Rs. 46.52 during the Second Plan to Rs. 120.52 during the Fourth, Rs. 709.30 during the Sixth Plan and Rs. 1,679 during the period from 1990-91 to 1994-95. All these were, however, in terms of a greatly depreciated rupee -- between 1961-62 and 1995-96 prices had risen by more than five items.

Among the states, there were great variations in the level of plan expenditure. During the Second Plan, while Punjab had a per capita expenditure of Rs. 133.33 for Uttar Pradesh it was only Rs. 30.76. In the Fourth Plan, Jammu & Kashmir had as much as Rs. 343.08 as against Rs. 72.78 in West Bengal. During 1990-95, the highest was in Orissa, at Rs. 2,689, and the lowest in Bihar, at Rs. 566.[1]

In the formulation and implementation of plans there were many deficiencies. The planning continued to be a top-down process, despite plenty of talks on decentralisation of power. Even the State governments are not adequately consulted in plan formulation. The Planning Commission and the concerned central ministries had a dominating role until recently. In fact, until 1993-94, the sectoral and sub-sectoral requirements were worked out in the meetings of working groups set up in the Planning Commission (CMIE 1997a). At the same time, there had been scrutinising of the plan schemes in great detail and ear-marking of the outlays. This left little room for discretion with the state government. Below the state level there was hardly any planning exercise. Even today district planning remains far from adequate, not to talk of block-level planning. The plans, therefore, were often not based on genuine local needs.

Achievements

This nature of economic planning could not bring any appreciable growth in income, nor could it reduce regional disparities noticeably. The per capita income (at 1980-81 prices) was only a little more than doubled over the entire period of nearly five decades-rising from the annual average of Rs. 1,136 during 1950-53 to Rs. 1,486 during 1970-73 and Rs. 2,539 during 1993-96. The aggregate of net national product, however, had a much faster growth-rising from the average of Rs. 41,503 crores during 1950-53 to Rs. 227,846 crores during 1993-96 (GOI 1975, 1998), that is 5.5 times, which was eaten away by the rapid growth in population. There was no appreciable reduction in acute poverty. The proportion of population below the poverty-line (based on calorie consumption only) in rural areas rose to 57.15 per cent during 1968-71 from 46.48 during 1951-53. In the following years it declined and touched the lowest of 34.30 in 1989-90; during 1991-94, however it again rose to 39.88 (Sen 1996). The proportion of households with monthly per capita expenditure of less than Rs. 300 was as much as 69 per cent in rural areas even in 1993-94 (NSSO 1998b).

State-wise, there was wide variation in performance. As evident from Table 1.1, per capita net SDP during 1960-63 averaged only Rs. 223 in Bihar as against Rs. 418 in Maharashtra. The disparity widened over the years. During 1990-93 the highest was in Punjab, at Rs. 3,809, and the lowest in the same Bihar, at Rs. 1,133. Percentage of rural population below the poverty-line was as much as 90.8 in Kerala in 1961-62 against the lowest of 13.3 in Rajasthan. After more than a decade, in 1973-74, although the highest level came down, the lowest increased noticeably and so also the average for all-India. In this year, West Bengal had 73.2 per cent of its rural population below poverty-line and the lowest at 28.2 per cent in Punjab. After another two decades, in 1993-94, Punjab had only 12.5 per cent below the poverty-line as against 58.0 in Bihar. In certain states the proportion in total population was higher than in rural areas.

In the social sector, performance in education was distressingly poor. In 1991, the country was still burdened with an illiterate population of 47.8 per cent of the total, and for females at 60.6. The level of female illiteracy in Rajasthan was as much as 79.2 per cent. Percentage of children not attending school in rural areas of the country in 1987-88 stood at 53.2 for the age-group 5-9. Among the states, Bihar had 73.1 per cent not going to school. The infant mortality rate in 1992-93 stood at as much 78.5 per thousand in the country, and varied between 112.1 in Orissa and 14.6 in Mizoram. The control over population growth, which is an essential requirement in any development effort, was a total failure. The increase in population per decade was 24.80 per cent in 1961-71, rising from 21.51 in 1951-61. In the following decades there were only nominal declines.

The infrastructural situation continued to vary widely from state to state. An index of infrastructure development prepared for 1992-94 by using 13 indicators and taking the all-India average equal to 100, placed Madhya Pradesh in the lowest position with 74.6 and the highest at 191.5 in Punjab. There were eight states with the index number at less than 100 (Table 1.1). The proportion of households with electricity averaged only 50.9 per cent in 1992-93, and varied between 92.0 in Punjab and 16.6 in Bihar (IIPS 1995).

This level of economic performance clearly shows that the socialistic pronouncements were merely a vote-catching device. The leadership in general, neither had the desire nor the ability to implement them. Even the communist parties rarely exerted pressure in the right direction.

The democratic façade of the state itself was utterly sham. With so many political parties contesting the elections and the turn out of votes rarely exceeding 50 per cent, the government formed never represented the majority of population .The maximum of voters secured by any party in power so far is 27.8 per cent of total electorate in 1971 (Baruah and Kumar 1979), and then there was the all-pervading corruption. Recently C.R. Irani had commented thus on the situation in the country: "No democracy can survive with the level of corruption and disrespect for the law prevalent in India.... abuse of power was 'inherent in our system'. In fact, we seem to thrive on such abuse... We have one law for the rich and one for the poor" (*The Statesman* 2000: 6).

This is the national background in which the South Indian economies progressed since *Independence*. The object of this study is to make an in-depth analysis of their performance vis-a-vis other states. Apart from sectoral analysis, regional disparities within a state have been given special focus. In the following chapter, a general survey has been made of the pattern of growth in the four states, viz., Andhra Pradesh, Tamil Nadu, Karnataka and Kerala separately; the union territories have been excluded because of their small size.

Table 1.1

State-wise Trend in NSDP, Population below Poverty-Line and Infrastructure

States	*Per Capita Net State Domestic Product (Annual Averages)*[a]			*% Rise between 1960-63 & 1990-93*
	1960-63	*1980-83*	*1990-93*	
Andhra Pradesh	331	1494	1736	424.5
Assam	350	1291	1883	438.0
Bihar	223	882	1133	408.1
Gujarat	402	2027	2497	521.1
Haryana	371	2414	3401	816.7
Karnataka	312	1639	2191	602.9
Kerala	292	1470	1875	542.1
Madhya Pradesh	279	1329	1634	485.7
Maharashtra	418	2445	3428	720.1
Orissa	240	1197	1442	500.8
Punjab	401	2799	3809	849.9
Rajasthan	285	1261	1839	545.3
Tamil Nadu	357	1555	2148	501.7
Uttar Pradesh	252	1311	1585	529.0
West Bengal	399	1593	1989	398.5
All-India	315	1671	2213	601.3

% of Rural Population Below poverty-Line[b]				*Infrastructure Development Index (All-India = 100) 1992-94 (average)*[c]
1961-62	*1973-74*	*1983*	*1993-94*	
62.1	48.4	26.5	15.9 (22.2)[d]	96.0
47.7	52.7	42.6	45.0 (40.9)	79.6
37.4	63.0	64.4	58.2 (55.0)	82.2

Contd...

Contd...

19.1	46.4	29.8	22.2 (24.2)	122.6
-	34.2	20.6	28.0 (25.0)	140.7
26.9	55.1	36.3	29.9 (33.2)	96.5
90.8	59.2	39.0	25.8 (25.4)	155.1
25.8	62.7	48.9	40.6 (42.5)	74.6
61.0	57.7	45.2	37.9 (36.9)	107.0
43.9	67.3	67.5	79.7 (48.6)	97.1
14.0	28.2	13.2	11.9 (11.8)	191.5
13.3	44.8	33.5	26.5 (27.4)	82.1
55.2	57.4	54.0	32.5 (35.0)	143.6
18.1	56.5	46.5	42.3 (40.8)	103.3
44.1	73.2	63.1	40.8 (35.7)	94.3
38.0	56.4	45.6	37.3 (36.0)	100.0

Sources: CMIE 1992, 1997b; GOI 1996a; Dandekar and Rath 1971; Krishanan 1992; GOA 1998.

Notes: a: for 1960-63 in current prices, and for the other two periods at 1980-81 prices.
b: based on the minimum diet of 2,250 calorie in case of 1961-62 and 2,400 for other years.
c: the index is based on the following 13 indicators: per capita electricity and petrol consumption, villages electrified, railway route length per '000 sq. km., handling capacity of major parts, gross irrigated area as percentage of gross cropped area, bank branches per lakh of population, post offices per lakh of population, telephone lines per 100 persons, primary schools per lakh population, hospital beds per lakh population, and primary health centres per lakh population.
d: figures in parentheses refer to rural and urban areas combined.

Note

1. Calculated from relevant five-year plan documents using the population estimates of Reserve Bank of India (RBI 1970, 1983, 1991, and 1999).

2

The Southern Economies: An Overview

The southern states together account for roughly a quarter of the country's population, i.e., 196 million out of 846 million (1991 census) and around one-fifth of the total geographical area, i.e., 635,780 sq. km., out of 3,287,782 sq. km. These states have some special characteristics. They are all maritime states with long coastlines, and get a substantial portion of their rainfall in winter months. Ethnically, the people here are largely of Dravidian stock and culturally quite different from the rest of India.

Below we give a brief look into the nature of economic performance of each of these states over the last five decades. The focus will be on the broad parameters like per capita income, economic diversification, status of the social sector, regional disparity and the extent of acute poverty. Detailed analysis of the problem areas has been made in the parts devoted to each of the states.

Andhra Pradesh

The state of Andhra Pradesh was created in October 1953 out of the Madras state by putting together eleven districts of the latter. In November 1956, on the recommendations of the State Reorganisation Commission, nine districts under the Nizam's dominion were added to it. Presently, the state has 23 districts. Andhra is the fifth largest state in India, both in area and population. It consists of three distinct regions: (1) coastal region made up of nine districts, (2) the interior region, consisting of four districts collectively known as Rayalaseema, and (3) Telangana region with ten districts. The northern area of Andhra is mountainous with an annual rainfall of 110 to 125 cm. As one goes further south, the rainfall comes down to 50 cm annually.

Income Growth and Diversification

The growth in state domestic product of Andhra was quite low. The NDP recorded an increase of only 81 per cent between 1980-81 and 1995-96, from Rs. 8,191 crores to Rs. 14,826 crores, as against 122 per cent for all-India, from Rs. 110,340 crores to Rs. 245,104 crores (at 1980-81 prices). The relative share of Andhra consequently declined from 7.4 per cent to 6.0 (GOA 1998).

The growth in per capita income was still lower due to higher growth in population. There was a 26 per cent rise between 1960-63 and 1980-83 , and by 1993-96 another 32 per cent. Over the entire period of three-and-half decades, it could not be even doubled – the annual average rising from Rs. 1,185 during 1960-63 to Rs. 1,968 during 1993-96 (at constant prices). Andhra's position in relation to all-India showed a continuous decline over the years. Whereas during 1960-63 its average was 105.1 per cent of the latter, in 1980-83 it came down to 89.4 and further to 78.6 per cent during 1990-93. Most of the major states had recorded a higher growth in per capita income than Andhra's.

In economic diversification also Andhra's performance was poor. As evident from Table 2.1, although the share of primary sector in total NDP declined substantially, the growth in secondary sector was

Table 2.1

Trend in Net Domestic Product of Andhra by Industry of Origin[a]

(percentages)

Industry	*1960-61*	*1980-81*	*1990-91*	*1995-96*
Primary	61.8	43.9	37.9	37.3
Agriculture	59.6	40.5	35.2	34.6
Secondary	10.7	19.0	20.9	16.3
Manufacturing	7.0	12.2	13.0	9.5
Construction	3.2	5.1	5.0	4.9
Tertiary	27.5	37.0	41.2	46.4
Trade, hotels, etc.	11.1	13.5	14.7	22.1
Transport, storage, etc.	4.3	6.0	6.1	4.7
Finance and real estate	5.1	7.3	10.6	9.8
Public administration	2.4	3.9	5.0	5.4
Total NDP	100.0 (1892)	100.0 (8191)	100.0 (13164)	100.0 (14826)

Source: Calculated from GOA 1986, 1997, 1998.

Notes: a: for 1960-61 at 1970-71 prices, and for the remaining years at 1980-81 prices. Figures in parentheses are total value of NDP in Rs. crores.

low. In fact, it recorded a decline in the latest year, from 20.9 per cent in 1990-91 to 16.3 in 1995-96. Within the secondary sector, the share of manufacturing in NDP rose to 13.0 per cent in 1990-91 from 7.0 in 1960-61 but it was down to 9.5 in 1995-96. The fall in primary sector's share was made up largely by the tertiary sector. The latter's share in NDP increased from 27.5 per cent in 1960-61 to 37.0 in 1980-81 and then to 46.4 in 1995-96. In the tertiary sector, the share of trade, hotels and restaurants was doubled over the period.

In relation to all-India, Andhra's position was quite depressing. During 1994-97 the share of agriculture in the former's domestic product was only 26.9 per cent as against 35.9 in Andhra. In manufacturing also, the all-India level was much higher than Andhra's -- the former's being 21.3 per cent and the latter's 10.2 in 1994-97. Among the southern states, Andhra's position was the worst; all the other states had higher proportion of SDP from manufacturing (RBI 1998, 1999).

Table 2.2

State-wise Trend in Percentage of Non-Agricultural Workers in Rural Workforce

States	*1961*	*1971*	*1981*	*1991*	*1993-94*[a]
Andhra Pradesh	17.8	17.3	17.0	20.9	24.4
Karnataka	11.7	15.5	15.4	16.1	21.2
Kerala	39.7	38.0	42.3	44.0	46.8
Tamil Nadu	17.9	19.1	18.3	24.6	36.0
Madhya Pradesh	9.0	9.4	10.4	13.3	12.8
Maharashtra	10.1	12.7	13.6	22.1	24.7
Orissa	12.9	14.9	14.9	18.4	21.3
Bihar	13.1	10.4	12.6	12.9	18.0
Gujarat	11.8	14.1	17.4	23.3	28.9
Haryana	16.3	21.5	21.2	27.7	39.1
Punjab	23.9	20.5	21.1	25.2	31.9
Rajasthan	9.0	12.6	12.9	18.6	30.4
Uttar Pradesh	12.8	12.3	12.9	15.9	23.7
West Bengal	20.3	18.2	21.8	26.4	35.3
All-India	14.3	15.2	15.8	20.2	25.9

Source: Unni 1991; GOI 1993; NSSO 1995a.

Note: a: refer to men only.

As regards the trend of employment in non-agricultural occupations, its share in total rural workforce showed a decline till 1981; only in the nineties there had been a considerable growth, as evident from Table 2.2. Even then, the proportion in 1993-94 was lower than the all-India average; there were as many as eight major states employing a higher proportion in non-agriculture.

Poverty Trend

Although Andhra's position on income growth was quite dismal, in alleviating poverty its performance was appreciable. As is evident from Table 1.1, since early eighties, there was a great improvement in the situation. The proportion of rural population below the poverty-line came down to only 26.5 per cent in 1983 and further to 15.9 in 1993-94, from as much as 62.1 per cent in 1961-62. In the latest year, its position was second only to Punjab. For rural and urban areas combined,

Table 2.3

State-wise Position of Per Capita Monthly Consumption Expenditure and Pattern of Household Asset-Holding (1992)

States	MPCE				Asset-Holding (Rural)	
	Rural (Rs.)	Urban (Rs.)	% of rural pop. with MPCE of		Av. value per household (Rs.)	% of hhds. with less than Rs. 20,000
			less than Rs. 180	Rs. 385 & above		
Andhra Pradesh	241.6	369.1	36.1	8.9	58175	44.5
Karnataka	222.6	360.7	41.1	6.2	107150	19.9
Kerala	342.6	404.8	19.3	26.7	181534	12.1
Tamil Nadu	237.6	447.4	41.5	10.6	61978	45.2
Madhya Pradesh	241.3	362.8	47.3	7.5	93062	28.2
Maharashtra	250.5	462.2	37.3	12.1	92890	29.5
Orissa	223.9	465.0	48.5	9.4	45733	40.4
Assam	215.2	403.2	36.9	4.2	60087	29.7
Bihar	196.3	287.5	55.9	4.7	97900	27.8
Gujarat	261.9	388.1	28.6	14.0	102942	16.7
Haryana	368.2	356.0	11.7	42.5	337619	10.6
Punjab	395.6	461.5	6.2	33.6	328671	9.9
Rajasthan	280.5	375.4	26.5	15.8	158809	11.8
Uttar Pradesh	231.5	317.4	46.0	10.2	139233	14.8
West Bengal	244.8	418.9	31.0	9.0	61881	35.7
All-India	247.2	399.0	38.6	14.0	107007	27.0

Source: NSSO 1995b, 1998.

the percentage of population below the poverty-line stood at 22.2 in 1993-94, declining from 48.9 in 1973-74; the proportion at the national level stood at 36.0 per cent in the latest year (GOI 2000).[1]

As the poverty-line is based on calorie intake only, it is necessary to have a look at the total consumption expenditure. As evident from Table 2.3, in 1992, per capita monthly consumption expenditure (MPCE) in Andhra stood at Rs. 241.6 in rural areas and Rs. 369.1 in urban areas, and both the figures were less than the all-India average. There were seven states ahead of Andhra in rural areas and nine in urban areas. Percentage of rural population with MPCE of less than Rs. 180 was 36.1 in Andhra, and this was higher than the levels in six of the major states. The proportion with higher level of expenditure was also low here. Those with MPCE of Rs. 385 and above constituted only 8.9 per cent in Andhra as against the all-India average at 14.0 per cent.

In household asset-holding Andhra's position was very dismal. In 1992, the average value of asset per household in rural areas came to only Rs. 58,175, which was the lowest among all the major states except Orissa. The percentage of rural households with asset-holding of less the Rs. 20,000 was as much as 44.5 in Andhra, which was the highest among all the states except Tamil Nadu (Table 2.3).

Education and Health Facilities

The quality of life of a people greatly depends on the level of education, and health facilities available. Proper education is required even for spending ones income in a way as to derive maximum satisfaction from it. Availability of proper health facilities indirectly adds to the income of a person. In both the areas, however, Andhra's performance was very dismal.

Looking to bare literacy, the percentage of literate in Andhra had always been less than the all-India average. In 1961, for Andhra it was 21.2 per cent as against 24.0 for all-India. After two decades, in 1981, these were, respectively, 29.9 and 36.2 per cent. Substantial progress took place in the following decade, but then also it remained much below the all-India average, being at 44.1 and 52.2 per cent, respectively. The female literacy rate increased at a faster rate, rising from 12.0 per cent in 1961 to 20.4 in 1981 and 32.7 in 1991. These were, however, significantly less than the all-India averages. Andhra's performance in literacy was worst among the southern states (Table 2.4).

At a slightly higher level, the educational scene was more distressing. In 1992-93, in the population aged 6 and above, 9.9 per cent were

Table 2.4

State-wise Position on Schooling and Health Facilities and their Effects

States	Availability of school within the habitation (percentage of rural population covered, 1994)		School facilities and effects					
	Primary	Upper primary	% of students receiving free/ concessional rates[a]		Pupil-teacher ratio at primary level (rural) 1994	% of children not attending school in 1987-88[b]	Literacy rate	
			Books and/or stationery	Midday meals			1961	1991
Andhra Pradesh	92.4	43.0	20.5	5.2	49.8 (49.2)[h]	45.7 (36.7)[f]	21.2 (12.0)[g]	44.1 (33.7)[g]
Karnataka	91.1	60.9	70.6	22.4	38.0 (59.6)	46.1 (29.5)	25.4 (14.2)	56.0 (44.3)
Kerala	76.7	50.5	1.9	26.2	31.0 (30.9)	15.2 (15.2)	46.8 (38.9)	89.8 (86.9)
Tamil Nadu	77.2	35.4	70.7	81.5	37.9 (43.2)	18.6 (17.6)	31.4 (18.2)	62.7 (52.3)
Madhya Predesh	84.7	31.4	22.2	6.3	42.9 (31.8)	64.6 (37.7)	17.1 (6.7)	44.2 (28.4)
Maharashtra	90.6	61.1	6.8	9.1	33.4 (36.1)	40.6 (18.5)	29.8 (16.8)	64.9 (50.5)
Orissa	76.1	34.2	5.6	9.0	37.4 (30.9)	49.7 (30.4)	21.7 (8.6)	49.1 (34.4)
Bihar	77.1	27.1	1.5	0.5	50.2 (43.6)	73.1 (48.7)	18.4 (6.9)	38.5 (23.1)
Gujarat	97.1	76.8	22.8	64.4	33.3 (38.9)	42.0 (24.3)	30.5 (19.1)	61.3 (48.5)
Haryana	94.5	64.7	4.1	1.8	48.9 (41.9)	42.6 (18.7)	-	55.8 (40.9)
Punjab	90.8	45.4	10.4	0.8	43.5 (22.3)	36.9 (19.2)	24.2 (14.1)[e]	58.5 (49.7)
Rajasthan	85.4	47.0	3.4	4.7	39.0 (29.9)	62.5 (41.2)	15.2 (5.8)	38.5 (20.5)
Uttar Pradesh	60.5	21.7	0.4	0.6	44.3 (28.9)	62.2 (38.7)	17.6 (7.0)	41.6 (26.0)

Contd...

Contd...

West Bengal	61.2	14.2	59.4	18.5	45.3 (33.7)	57.1 (32.3)	29.3 (17.0)	57.7 (47.2)
All-India	77.8	37.0	-	-	40.9 (35.8)	53.2 (32.5)	24.0 (12.9)	52.2 (39.4)

Health Facilities and their Effects

Population per hospital (in '000) 1996-97	*Population per bed (1996-97)*	*Life expect. at birth (years) 1988-92*	*Infant mort. rate (rural)*	
			1969	*1990-92*
219.3	2122	60	129	76
154.0	892	62	110	83
206.1	1035	71	57	17
152.6	1224	62	113	67
209.7	2471	53	n.a.	118
116.7	689	63	107	67
190.4	2508	55	n.a.	124
306.2	2959	58	82[d]	74
17.1	609	60	165	74
228.7	1595	63	80	75
103.8	863[c]	67	98	61
220.1	1313	56	169	88
17.9	2035	55	179	103
182.3	1063	61	n.a.	71
-	-	59	140	86

Source: Visaria 1993; NCERT 1998 : I, IV; GOI 1963, 1972, 1993, 1995, 1998: I.

Notes: a: at primary level in 1986-87. b: in the age-group 5-9. c: relates to 1995-96. d: relates to 197. e: includes Haryana. f: figures in parentheses here refer to the situation in 1992-93 for the age group 6-14. g : formal literacy rates. h: relates to upper primary. n.a.: not available.

with middle school completed, marginally above the all-India average, 9.4 per cent. For females, the figures were respectively, 7.9 and 6.9 (IIPS 1995). The proportion of children in the age-group 5-9 not attending school in 1987-88 was 45.7 per cent in Andhra. This was higher than the level in six of the major states although less than the national average. In the age-group 6-14 it was 36.7 per cent in 1992-93 as against the all-India average at 32.5. For female, the proportions were respectively, 45.2 and 41.1 per cent (Table 2.4).

As regards educational facilities, Andhra's situation was very poor. The pupil-teacher ratio in rural areas has been one of the highest both at the primary and upper primary levels. In 1994, at primary level it stood at 49.8, which was second highest among the major states and much higher than in other southern states (Table 2.4). In the same year, 36 per cent of the rural primary schools in Andhra had only one teacher and 1,341 were without any teacher at all. As regards midday meals -- an important instrument for attracting students to schools – the coverage was very low, being only 5.2 per cent of students as against 81 per cent in neighbouring Tamil Nadu. In supply of books and stationery also the coverage was much lower than in the neighbouring states (Table 2.4).

On the availability of schools, however the situation was not so bad. In 1993-94, 92.4 of the population had a primary school section within the habitation as against only 77.8 per cent for all-India. On upper primary, the proportions were respectively, 43.0 and 37.0 per cent. The secondary schools were available within a distance of 2 km. for 47.9 per cent of the population in Andhra Pradesh as against 45.4 per cent at the national level.

In the provision of health facilities, Andhra's performance was very poor. Population covered per hospital in 1996-97 was as much as 2.19 lakhs, which was much higher than in most of the major states. In population per bed also the picture was similar, as may be seen from Table 2.4. As regards provision of drinking water, percentage of households with pump/pipe water was only 63.4 in 1992-93 and it was exceeded by as many as nine major states (IIPS 1995).

In this situation, it was no wonder that the life expectancy at birth was relatively low in Andhra, being at 60 years and exceeded by as many as seven of the major states. Death rate and infant mortality rate (IMR) were also relatively high. During 1990-92, annual death rate per thousand population stood at 10.0, which was higher than the levels in other southern states. On IMR the situation continued to be depressing, despite significant improvement over the years. During 1990-92, it stood at 76 per thousand live births in rural Andhra, higher than the level in eight of the major states (Table 2.4).

It is well-known that control over population growth is highly correlated with education and health facilities. Naturally, therefore, Andhra's performance in population control was very unsatisfactory. The decennial growth in population accelerated from 20.9 per cent during 1961-71 to 23.1 during 1971-81 and 24.2 during 1981-91. None of the major states recorded such a continuous rise. Further, while in the earlier decades Andhra's growth rates were lower than the national average, in the Latest one it was higher (CMIE 1996a).

Intra-State Disparities

Whatever the relative position among the states, within the state also there were wide differences among the regions in levels of development. We look here into the position of some of the elements.

First we consider the level of urbanisation, which is an important indicator of development. It is evident from Table 2.5 that in a good number of districts the growth in urbanisation was quite low. In 1991, percentage of urban population was less than 20 in eight of the districts. The growth over the last three decades were very low in some of the districts with low urban population. In Nalgonda it increased from 9.31 per cent in 1961 to 11.87 per cent in 1991 and in strikakulam from 8.74 to 12.50; one district, Mahaboobnagar, even recorded a retrogression. On the other hand, Visakhapatnam with 18.09 per cent urban population in 1961 raised it to 39.83 in 1991.

As regards economic diversification, the proportion of non-agricultural workers declined in a majority of the districts, including some of the very backward ones. In Mahaboobnagar, it was from 15.2 per cent in 1961 to 10.8 in 1991, in Nalgonda from 17.2 to 14.2 and in East Godavari from 18.5 to 14.4. The availability of electricity, which promoted non-agricultural activities, varied widely from district to district. Per thousand persons in rural areas it was available to less than 300 in four of the districts in 1991 as against with more than 500 persons in five districts (Table 2.5).

In literacy rate, despite substantial improvement, the disparity continued to be wide. In 1991, it was only 29.6 per cent in Mahaboobnagar as against more than 50 in three districts. The female literacy was only 18 per cent in Mahaboobnagar, 19 in Medak and 21 in Adilabad and Nizamabad in the same year as against above 40 in four districts. The IMR, reflecting largely the availability of health facilities, also varied greatly. In rural Andhra, it was above 100 in four of

Table 2.5

District-wise Disparity in Andhra's Development

Districts	% of urban pop. to total pop.		% of literate population		IMR[a] (rural)	Electricity[b]	% of non-agrl. workers in total pop.	
	1961	1991	1961	1991	1991	1991	1961	1991
Srikakulam	8.74	12.50	15.71	36.22 (23.5)	104	275	13.9	16.0
Vizianagaram	-	17.22	-	34.19 (22.5)	131	267	-	17.3
Visakhapatnam	18.03	39.83	17.15	45.51 (34.6)	98	272	15.0	19.1
East Godavari	18.53	23.80	26.00	48.79 (42.3)	77	326	18.5	14.4
West Godavari	15.87	20.71	30.76	53.38 (47.0)	73	345	15.1	14.2
Krishna	23.51	35.82	31.15	53.16 (45.5)	54	346	16.2	16.4
Guntur	20.83	28.89	27.66	46.35 (35.8)	54	341	18.2	14.9
Prakasam	-	16.45	-	40.30 (27.1)	68	349	-	12.9
Nellore	11.0	23.79	21.13	47.76 (37.0)	68	427	16.7	16.1
Chittoor	11.47	19.80	20.94	49.75 (36.4)	56	524	11.9	14.7
Cuddapah	13.20	24.03	21.75	48.12 (32.3)	55	563	15.7	15.7
Anantapur	17.40	23.49	20.61	42.18 (27.6)	98	526	12.5	14.0
Kurnool	19.23	25.83	21.41	39.97 (26.0)	101	415	13.3	13.0
Hyderabad	62.18	100.00	35.05	71.52 (63.6)	-	-	23.6	27.2

Contd...

Contd...

Rangareddy	-	47.22	-	49.07 (36.9)	76	437	-	19.4
Mahaboobnagar	14.04	11.12	13.46	29.58 (18.0)	102	284	15.2	10.8
Medak	7.73	14.47	14.05	32.41 (19.2)	72	425	13.1	12.2
Nizamabad	14.51	20.26	14.33	34.18 (21.3)	65	563	17.8	18.5
Nalgonda	9.31	11.87	14.11	38.00 (24.9)	77	424	17.2	14.2
Adilabad	15.49	23.12	11.72	32.96 (20.6)	71	327	15.7	15.6
Karimnagar	7.06	20.55	12.89	37.17 (23.4)	47	620	21.6	17.8
Warangal	14.10	19.39	15.37	39.30 (26.1)	86	434	16.2	14.0
Khammam	12.14	20.13	15.23	40.50 (30.5)	73	323	14.0	13.1
State Average	17.44	26.89	21.20	44.09 (29.2)	71	398	16.2	15.7

Source: GOA 1972, 1997.

Notes: a : Per thousand live births.
b: availability in rural areas per thousand persons.
Figures in parentheses are female literacy rates.

the districts – Vizianagaram, Srikakulam, Mahaboobnagar and Kurnool – as against less than 60 in five districts (Table 2.5).

While the reasons behind the poor performance of Andhra have been analysed in detail in chapters three through six, we may note here a general problem, political instability, that might have affected the growth of the state. Andhra Pradesh was ruled by the Congress Party since its formation till 1982, and in this 29 years the state had seen eleven chief ministers, that is, an average of two-and-a-half years for each.

Almost everything in this period came to be decided in New Delhi. To please the party's high command even transfers and promotions of middle ranking officials were referred to the national capital by the nominated CMs. The party was voted to power because there was no other alternative (Pinto 1999).

Tamil Nadu

Tamil Nadu has a very ancient history that goes back to some 6,000 years. The state represents the nucleus of Dravidian culture in India, which antedates the Aryan culture in India by almost a thousand years. When India became free the old Madras province, comprising Tamil Nadu and Andhra Pradesh and part of Kerala continued as the state of Madras. The first division of the state came in 1953 when Andhra was created, and then came the reorganisation under the State Reorganisation Act 1956. With the reorganisation, the state lost the Malabar district and the Kasargod taluk of South Kanara district to the newly formed state of Kerala, while Madras gained some areas from the Trivandrum and Quilon districts of Kerala. Madras also lost some parts of South Kanara and Coimbatore districts to the new Mysore state. Some further changes came in April 1960 with exchange of areas with Andhra Pradesh. The name of the state was changed to Tamil Nadu in January 1969.

Physiographically, the state can be divided into two natural divisions: (1) the eastern coastal plain, and (2) the hilly region along the north and the west. The coastal plain is usually subdivided into the coromandel plain, the alluvial plain of the Kaveri delta, and the dry southern plains. Along the whole length of the western part, at a distance from the sea varying between 80 and 160 km., runs the range of the Western Ghats, averaging 1,220 meters above the sea level.

Income Growth and Diversification

Tamil Nadu's economic performance appears to be better than most other states, although it depends largely on the period chosen. Over the entire period of three decades, 1960-93, its per capita NSDP increased 502 per cent, which was lower than the all-India average, being 601 per cent. If the period since 1980-83 is considered, then however the growth appears better, being 38.1 and 32.2 per cent, respectively. Tamil Nadu's per capita income was higher than the all-India average during 1960-63 but lower in the following two periods, 1980-83 and 1990-93. As compared to other southern states, its position was best in the first period and inferior to Karnataka in the following two periods. Among all the major states, its position was generally the sixth (Table 1.1).

A more detailed picture of the trend in Tamil Nadu's per capita income is presented in Table 2.6. In recent years, in relation to all-India average its situation has improved considerably. Till 1989-90, Tamil Nadu's per capita income was always lower than that at the national level but in the last five years it became higher.

Table 2.6

Trend in Per Capita Income of Tamil Nadu Relative to National Income (in Rs. at constant 190-81 prices)

Year (1)	*Tamil Nadu (2)*	*India (3)*	*Col. (2) as % to col. (3) (4)*	*Year (1)*	*Tamil Nadu (2)*	*India (3)*	*col % 2 as % to col (3) (4)*
1980-81	1498	1630	91.9	1989-90	2094	2157	97.1
1981-82	1640	1692	96.9	1990-91	2235	2222	100.6
1982-83	1527	1690	90.4	1991-92	2268	2175	104.3
1983-84	1582	1790	88.4	1992-93	2355	2243	105.0
1984-85	1758	1810	97.1	1993-94	2551	2334	109.3
1985-86	1798	1841	97.7	1994-95[a]	2767	2449	113.0
1986-87	1755	1871	93.8				
1987-88	1837	1901	96.6				
1988-89	1987	2059	96.5				

Source: GOT 1998.

Note : a : revised estimate.

The growth in total NSDP of the state was substantial over the years. At constant 1980-81 prices, it increased from Rs. 7,218 crores in 1980-81 to Rs. 12,411 crores in 1990-91 and then to Rs. 16,031 crores in 1995-96, that is, a growth of 122 per cent over the entire period.

Tamil Nadu's share in national income, however remained static at 6.5 per cent (GOI 1998).

In economic diversification, Tamil Nadu's performance is one of the best. The relative share of primary sector in NSDP declined from 49.1 per cent in 1960-61 to 25.9 in 1980-81 and 20.4 in 1996-97. During 1990-94, the average for primary sector came to 24.3, in which agriculture and allied activities contributed 22.8 per cent. The share of secondary sector in this period was 29.7 per cent, in which manufacturing provided 21.4 and construction 6.5. The contribution of tertiary sector was the balance of 45.9 per cent, and in it trade, hotels and restaurants provided 16.1 per cent, followed by finance, insurance, real estate, etc., which provided 12.7 per cent (GOT 1998, 1972, 1997).

In employment also, naturally, there was a significant diversification. The proportion of non-agricultural workers in rural workforce rose to 36.0 per cent in 1993-94 from less than 20 till early eighties. There were only two states with higher proportion than Tamil Nadu's (Table 2.2). The share of agriculture and allied activities in total employment declined to 61.5 per cent in 1991 from 64.4 in 1971. The gain to manufacturing sector was, however, not much. Although it rose to 15.2 per cent in 1981 from 13.4 in 1971, the 1991 census found it at 14.0 per cent. Trade and commerce raised its share to 8.7 per cent from 7.8 over the period, and services to 10.2 per cent from 9.3 (GOT 1998).

Poverty Trend

The economic growth and diversification in Tamil Nadu did not have much impact on the poverty situation, particularly in the rural areas. The per capita monthly consumption expenditure in rural Tamil Nadu stood at only Rs. 237.60 in 1992, which was much lower than the all-India average. Percentage of rural population with MPCE of less than Rs. 180 was as much as 41.6 here. The situation in urban areas was, however, much better. The MPCE in 1992 stood of Rs. 447.40, which could be exceeded by only three states -- Orissa, Maharashtra and Punjab (Table 2.3).

In this situation, it was not surprising that the population below poverty-line always remained high here. For the rural population , it rose to as much as 57.4 per cent in 1973-74 and even in 1983 it stood at 54.0. These were much above the all-India average. Only the latest estimate, for 1993-94, found to be less than the all-India level, being at 32.5 and 37.3 per cent, respectively. It was, however, still higher than the levels in seven of the major states (Table 1.1). In the urban areas also, the proportion of poverty-line population in Tamil Nadu was very high. All the estimates since 1973-74 found it to be higher than the all-India average, with the last one recording 39.77 and 32.36 per cent, respectively.[2]

The situation on asset holding by rural households was very depressing. In 1992, the average value per household came to only Rs. 61,978 as against the all-India average at Rs. 107,007. The percentage of households with asset value less than Rs. 20,000 was as much as 45.2 which was the highest among all the states (Table 2.3).

Education and Health Facilities

In the social sector, however, Tamil Nadu's position was very good. In education, even in 1961 its literacy rate was significantly higher than the all-India average, being 31.4 and 24.0 per cent, respectively; for females, these were 18.2 and 12.9 per cent. Only one state, Kerala, was ahead of it. After three decades, in 1991 , its literacy rate rose to 62.7 per cent, with females at 52.3. The relative position has, however, worsened; there are now two states ahead of it, Kerala and Maharashtra (Table 2.4). At higher levels also the situation is similar. For middle school completed, the proportion in Tamil Nadu was 21.1 per cent in 1992-93 as against 9.4 at the national level. For females, these were respectively, 10.1 and 6.9 per cent (IIPS 1995).

The educational facilities have been one of the best. The pupil-teacher ratio at primary level in rural areas was found to be 37.9 in 1994 which was next only to Kerela and much above the All-India average. Percentage of schools with more than five teachers was 12.0 here as against 5.4 at the national level. At upper primary, however the situation was quite gloomy, as may be seem from Table 2.4. On the availability of schools within the habitation the position was relatively poor. It was below the national average. However, with regard to provision of midday meals and supply of books, etc. Tamil Nadu's position was the best. In 1986-87, 81 per cent of the students of primary level were covered by the midday meal scheme. consequently, percentage of children not attending school in Tamil Nadu was very low. In the age-group 5-9 it was 18.6 in 1987-88 as against 53.2 at the national level. Even in the age-group 6-14, these were respectively, 17.6 and 32.5 per cent in 1992-93.

In the provision of health facilities also Tamil Nadu's position was not bad. As regards availability of hospitals, there was one hospital per

1.53 lakhs population in 1996-97. This was a lower level of coverage than in nine of the major states and lowest among the southern states. Population per bed was also not high -- at 12.24 lakhs, it was lower than in seven of the major states. As regards drinking water facility, percentage of households with pump/pipe water was 74.5 in 1992-93 as against 68.2 for all-India; there were five states with better coverage (IIPS 1995).

All these were reflected in the health situation of the state. Life expectancy at birth stood at 62 years during 1988-92 which was higher than the position in eight of the major states (Table 2.4). On IMR the situation was still better. At 67 per thousand live births during 1990-92, there were only two states Kerala and Punjab in better position. It is necessary to note however, that the incidence of tuberculosis is very high in Tamil Nadu; at 703 per lakh population it is the second highest, next to Rajasthan (IIPS 1995).

In controlling population growth, Tamil Nadu's performance is second only to Kerala. The decennial population growth rate here declined continuously from 22.3 per cent during 1961-71 to 17.5 during 1971-81 and 15.4 during 1981-91. The rural birth rate in Tamil Nadu stood at only 21.1 during 1990-92 as against the all-India average at 31.1 and the lowest of 18.4 in Kerala. The effective couple protection rate here stood at 28.2 in 1980 and increased to 57.1 in 1990 as against the all-India level rising from 22.3 to 43.3 (GOI 1996b).

Intra-State Disparities

Regional disparities in Tamil Nadu are no less than that in Andhra Pradesh. The district-wise position on some of the variables is presented in Table 2.7. With regard to economic diversification, there is wide variation from district to district. The proportion of main workers engaged in manufacturing, including household industry, was less than 10 per cent in as many as eleven districts as against more than 20 in five districts. The per capita consumption of power was less than 200 units in 1993-94 in five districts, with Pasumpon recording only 20 units, as against the state average at 347. The disparity in level of economic activity was reflected also in per capita bank credit deployment. It was less than Rs. 1,000 in four districts as against Rs. 9,043 in Coimbatore and Rs. 6,081 in Nilgiri, leaving aside Madras with an incomparable figure. Bank deposit per capita also varied widely, between Rs. 965 in Thiruvannamalai and Rs. 7,242 in Coimbatore. The credit-deposit ratio was less than 50 in five districts as against

Table 2.7

District-wise Disparities in Tamil Nadu's Development

Districts[a]	*% of main workers engaged*[a] *in manufacturing*[b] *1991*	*Per capita consmn. of power (Units) 1993-94*	*Bank credit per capita (Rs.) June-end 1995*	*Deposit pre capita*[c] *(Rs.)*	*% of rural hbtns. fully covered by water supply*[c]	*Literacy rate 1991*	*IMR (rural) 1991*
Madras	24.21	741	31585	27192	-	81.6 (74.9)[d]	-
Chengalpattu	23.00	281	1811	2715	47.5	66.4 (55.2)	74
North Arcot	17.86	287	1495	1796	54.4	60.9 (48.6)	75
Dharmapuri	5.04	245	1043	1160	61.9	46.0 (34.2)	81
Thiruvannamalai	6.89	229	922	965	49.7	53.1 (39.7)	77
South Arcot	5.90	182	883	1397	47.7	58.6 (45.2)	90
Villupuram	3.56	-	-	-	-	48.4 (35.4)	-
Salem	19.05	251	2020	3004	53.2	53.3 (41.4)	76
Periyar	16.19	398	2395	3479	46.1	53.8 (41.6)	99
Nilgiris	6.44	2302	6081	3924	43.7	71.7 (61.5)	71
Coimbatore	26.51	719	9043	7242	48.9	66.3 (55.7)	69
Dindigul-Anna	7.90	408	1707	1843	31.5	56.7 (43.9)	93
Tiruchirapalli	10.90	264	1890	2726	49.9	61.2 (48.9)	76
Thanjavur	8.04	123	1265	2561	34.7	65.9 (54.8)	58

Contd...

Contd...

Nagapattinam	4.61	-	-	-	26.8	66.2 (54.8)	-
Pudukkottai	7.18	109	879	1360	45.4	57.6 (43.6)	69
Pasumpon	6.74	20	1329	2755	45.1	63.0 (49.7)	81
Madurai	10.84	266	2496	2697	44.1	66.4 (54.7)	74
Kamarajar	27.13	480	2717	2282	39.1	62.9 (50.2)	99
Ramanathapuram	6.14	288	677	1612	32.1	61.6 (48.7)	77
Chidambaranar	17.55	485	2149	2860	49.7	73.0 (64.6)	87
Tirunelveli	23.54	294	1187	2427	-	65.6 (54.2)	107
Kanniyakumari	10.82	86	1327	2955	25.9	82.1 (78.4)	49
Tamil Nadu	14.02	347	-	-	46.1	62.7 (51.3)	77

Source: GOT 1997; Rajan and Mohanchandran 1998.

Notes : a: names of nine districts have been changed, and presently there are 29 districts.
b: including household industry.
c: data relate to 1994-95.
d: in parentheses are female literacy rates.

more than 100 in four, with Coimbatore recording 155.

In the area of health facilities also the situation was similar. Taking IMR as a proxy, in the rural areas it varied between the highest of 107 per thousand live births in Tirunelveli in 1991 and the lowest at 49 in Kanniyakumari. Even in the provision of drinking water the disparity was substantial. Percentage of rural habitations fully covered was 61.9 in Dharmapuri as against only around 26 in Kanniyakumari and Nagapattinam. With regard to literacy, the variation was between 46.0 and 81.6 per cent, with that for females varying between 34 and 78 (Table 2.7).

Karnataka

Karnataka is the eighth largest state of India with a population of around 45 million (1991 census) and an area of 191,791 sq. km. Until November 1973, it was known as Mysore as the old kingdom formed the nucleus of the new state formed after independence. The area under the state changed three times – in 1950, 1953 and 1956. The first change added 80 sq. km. to the existing area of 76,296 sq. km. The second in October 1953, brought the Bellary district of Madras State (excluding some taluks) under it and resulted in an increase by 9,897 sq.km. Finally, under the State Reorganisation Act a large area was added to it from the Bombay State, princely state of Hyderabad and the old Madras Presidency, in addition to the whole of 'Part C' state of Coorg.

Physiographically, the state can be broadly divided into two regions: (1) the coastal region, and (2) the Karnataka plateau. The coastal region has a length of about 400 km., broken into two parts – the plains and the Western Ghats. The plateau region is divided into the Malnad and the Maidan. The former overlaps into the Ghats reaching the heights of 1,500 to 1,800 metres. It is more rugged with a number of hills and receives larger amount of rainfall. Karnataka forms a part of the Deccan Plateau and is almost wholly composed of hard, compact, crystalline rocks. This circumstance, along with the climate – an average rainfall of only 600 mm – makes a greater part of the state semi-arid.

Income Growth and Diversification

Karnataka's performance in growth of SDP appears to be the best among the southern states. Over a period of three decades, 1960-63 to 1990-93, its per capita income recorded an increase of 603 per cent, rising from Rs. 312 to Rs. 2,193, which was higher than the all-India average and highest among the southern states. However, the amount of per capita income remained less than the national average, as may be seen from Table 1.1.

If only the last one-and-half decade is considered, then the growth appears quite low. The per capita income registered an increase of only 62.3 per cent between 1980-81 and 1994-95, rising from Rs. 1,520 to Rs. 2,467. In relation to the national per capita, Karnataka's level rose to the maximum of 104.0 per cent in 1991-92 and at the minimum 89.3 per cent in 1985-86 (Table 2.8). As regards total SDP, it increased by 109.9 per cent in this period -- from Rs. 5,587 crores in 1980-81 to Rs. 11,728 crores in 1994-95 -- as against 131.4 per cent in national income (at constant prices). Consequently, Karnataka's share in the latter declined to 4.58 per cent from 5.05.

Table 2.8

Trend in Per Capita Income of Karnataka
(At constant 1980-81 prices)

Year	*Per capita income (Rs.)*	*As % to national income*	*Year*	*Per capita income (Rs.)*	*As % to national income*
1980-81	1520	93.3	1989-90	2056	95.3
1981-82	1582	93.5	1990-91	2039	91.8
1982-83	1586	93.8	1991-92	2262	104.0
1983-84	1663	92.9	1992-93	2272	101.3
1984-85	1751	96.7	1993-94	2407	103.1
1985-86	1644	89.3	1994-95	2467	100.7
1986-87	1764	94.3			
1987-88	1853	97.5			
1988-89	1978	96.1			

Source: GKT 1997; GOI 1998.

In economic diversification there has been considerable progress in Karnataka. The share of primary sector in NSDP declined from 57.5 per cent in 1960-61 to 46.0 in 1980-81 and further to 36.0 per cent in 1994-95. For the secondary sector, the proportion increased from 16.3 per cent to 20.8 and then to 22.4 in these years, respectively. The share of tertiary sector rose to 41.6 per cent in 1994-95 from 33.2 in 1980-81 and 26.2 in 1960-61. In the latest year, agriculture contributed 34.7 per cent of NSDP, manufacturing 16.9, construction 4.0, transport, storage and communications 4.2, trade, hotels and restaurants

17.0 and banking and insurance 6.0 per cent (GKT 1997, 1972).

This diversification of economic activities was, however, not adequately reflected in employment. As evident from Table 2.2, the proportion of non-agricultural workers in rural workforce stood at only 16.1 per cent in 1991, rising from 15.5 in 1971 and 11.7 in 1961. In all the years it was lower than the national average and lowest among the southern states.

Poverty Trend

Naturally, in this circumstance, Karnataka's performance in alleviating poverty could not be satisfactory. Looking to the level of consumption expenditure, the per capita monthly expenditure in rural areas in 1992 stood at only Rs. 223, which was lower than in all the major states except two. In urban areas also the situation was not much better as may be seen from Table 2.3. At Rs. 361, all the states except three had higher levels. In the rural areas, those with MPCE of less than Rs. 180 constituted as much as 41.7 per cent, and this was higher than the level in most of the major states. The rural labour Enquiry Committee found Karnataka to be having an annual per capita total consumption expenditure of only Rs. 2,702.74 in 1993-94 for all rural labour households as against the highest of Rs. 3,994.37 in Punjab and the all-India average at Rs. 2,778.57 (GOI 1998a).

The level of household asset-holding in rural Karnataka was low. In 1992, it averaged Rs. 107,150 per household, which was slightly above the national average; there were five major states with higher values. The proportion of households with asset value of less than Rs. 20,000 was found to be 19.9 per cent, higher than the level in six of the major states (Table 2.3)

In this situation, the proportion of population below poverty-line did not show any appreciable decline. In rural areas, till early seventies, in fact there was a sharp rise in poverty-line population, the proportion rising from 26.9 per cent in 1961-62 to 55.1 in 1973-74. In the following years it declined and reached 29.9 in 1993-94; even this level is higher than in six of the major states, as may be seen from Table 1.1. In urban areas, the relative position is still worse. In 1993-94, 40.1 per cent of the population was below the poverty-line, and this was exceeded by only two of the major states.[3]

Education and Health Facilities

Karnataka's position in the area of education is not at all satisfactory. Among the southern states, in literacy rate its position was better than

Andhra only. In 1961, the percentage of literate here was 25.4, which was exceeded by five of the major states. After three decades, in 1991, the proportion rose to 56.0, but now six states were ahead of it. In female literacy, the growth in this period was from 14.2 per cent to 44.3, and the relative position was same as above. At higher levels, the situation was worse. In middle school completed, the proportion in 1992-93 was only 6.9 per cent of the population aged 6 and above, and it was exceeded by as many as 12 major states. For females, as usual, the position was worse: it was only 5.7 per cent and was exceeded by nine states (IIPS 1995).

On educational facilities however, the situation was relatively better. The pupil-teacher ratio at primary level stood at 38 in 1996-97, which was better than in eight of the major state. On the provision of mid-day meals, with 22.4 per cent of the students covered, its position was third in 1986-87. As regards the supply of books and stationery freely or at concessional rates, the coverage was nearly 71 per cent. The availability of schools within a reasonable distance was also not bad. In 1993-94, 91.1 per cent of the population had primary schools within the habitation as against 77.8 per cent at the national level. For upper primary, the proportions were, respectively, 60.9 and 37.0 per cent (Table 2.4). Despite these facilities, the percentage of children not attending school was as much as 46 in 1987-88, inferior to the position in seven of the major states. The drop-out rate was also very high. In 1996-97 it stood at 46.8 per cent in standards I-VIII (GKT 1998: 1: 305). One reason behind this situation might be that the schools here are very ill-equipped. In 1994, 29 per cent of the rural primary schools had only one teacher and the proportion with more that five teachers was 0.2 per cent. Drinking water was available in only 22 per cent of the schools (NCERT 1998: III, II). The condition of upper primary appears to be still worse. Here even the pupil-teacher ratio was very high (Table 2.4).

As regards health facilities, Karnataka presented a relatively better picture. The size of population per hospital here was 1.54 lakhs in 1996-97; there were only five states with better position. On population per bed, with 892, its position was fourth (Table 2.4). As regards drinking water facility, in 1992-93, pump/pipe water covered 75.6 per cent of households, which could be exceeded by only three states – Punjab, Maharashtra and West Bengal (IIPS 1995).

These facilities were reflected in the life expectancy at birth and on the IMR. The life expectancy in Karnataka during 1988-92 stood at

62 years, which could be exceeded by only four states. As regards IMR, in the rural areas it declined from 110 per thousand live births in 1969 to 83 during 1990-92. As many of the states recorded faster declines, Karnataka's relative position worsened over the period; there were as many as nine states with lower IMR.

In population control -- with which health situation has a strong correlation -- karnataka's performance was relatively poor. The decennial growth increased form 24.2 per cent in 1961-71 to 26.7 in 1971-81 and then declined to 21.1. Even in the last period, there were four major states with lower growth rate. The rural birth rate stood at 28.1 during 1990-92 which was the highest among the southern states. The effective couple protection rate through all methods increased from 22.3 in 1980 to 46.0 in 1990 and 52.7 in 1995. There were eight states with higher coverage in the first period, six in the second and five states in the last period (GOI 1996b).

Intra-State Disparities

The disparity in economic situation among the districts of Karnataka did not decline much over the years. In 1960-61, the lowest per capita Income was in Bidar at Rs. 199, which was only around a quarter of the level in Kodagu with highest income of Rs. 727. After two decades, in 1980-81, the lowest was 44 per cent of the highest and in 1994-95 it was 43 per cent. In relation to the state average, the lowest income in 1960-61 was only 67.2 per cent and the highest 245.6 per cent. In 1994-95, these were respectively 68.4 and 164.6. The progress in economic diversification was, however, very poor in some of the districts. In 1990-91, the share of secondary sector in NDP was less than 10 per cent in three districts -- Kodagu, Chikmagulur and Hassan -- as against the state average of 24 per cent (Table 2.9).

As regards the social sector, the disparity in literacy rates, as evident from Table 2.9, has not narrowed appreciably over the years. In 1991, while Bangalore and Dakshin Kannada had 76 per cent literate for Raichur it was only 36. In female literacy, the disparity is much wider. It was at the lowest 22.1 per cent and at the highest 68 in the same districts, respectively. On IMR also the situation was similar. The variation was between 83 per thousand birth in Bellary and the lowest at 38 in Dakshin Kannada.

A human development index, computed by using per capita income, life expectancy and total literacy, placed the lowest at only 22 per cent of the highest in 1996, the indices being 0.1872 in Raichur and

Table 2.9

District-wise Disparity in Karnataka's Development

Districts	*Per Capita Income (Rs.)*[a]			*% share of secondary sector in NDP (1990-91)*	*Literacy Rate*		*IMR*
	1960-61	*1980-81*	*1994-95*		*1961*	*1991*	*1991*
Bangalore	256	2241	13555	44.4	34.3	76.3 (68.8)[b]	51
Bangalore (R)	-	-	7519	-	-	50.2 (38.1)	-
Chitradurga	274	1740	7097	18.0	25.1	55.5 (43.4)	71
Kolar	238	920	5638	12.0	21.3	50.4 (37.7)	62
Shimoga	578	1882	9130	15.2	28.1	61.5 (51.4)	66
Tumkur	283	1255	5891	17.3	22.6	54.5 (41.9)	70
Belgaum	267	1506	8246	20.2	26.0	53.0 (38.7)	64
Bijapur	203	1071	7052	17.3	24.4	55.1 (40.1)	76
Dharwad	257	1375	7168	22.5	33.4	58.7 (45.2)	71
Uttar Kannada	577	1722	8422	24.7	33.4	66.7 (56.8)	59
Bellary	306	1637	7661	16.4	14.5	45.1 (30.5)	67
Bidar	199	1385	5865	13.6	14.7	38.5 (24.5)	67
Gulbarga	223	1435	6710	31.9	15.7	36.0 (22.1)	73
Raichur	227	1501	6293	10.8	27.5	61.0 (51.3)	67
Chikmagulur	479	1928	10594	8.2	32.3	75.9 (68.0)	38
Dakshin Kannada	357	1937	9158	31.8	24.3	56.8 (44.9)	64
Hassan	301	1425	6688	8.7	36.3	68.3 (61.2)	54
Kodagu	727	3126	12864	5.3	17.3	48.1 (36.7)	66
Mandya	258	1648	7692	10.9	21.3	47.3 (37.9)	63
Mysore	259	1651	9197	21.8	20.9	45.6 (32.0)	83
State	296	1623	8237	24.0	25.4	56.0 (49.3)	-

Source: GKT 1972,1997.

Notes: a: at current prices.
b: figures in parentheses are female literacy rates.

0.9746 in Dakshin Kannada. There were four districts – Bidar, Bellary and Kolar, apart from Raichur – with indices of less than 0.30 (Vysulu and Vani 1997).

Kerala

Kerala is the smallest among the South Indian states, with a population of around 32 million and a geographical area of 38,863 sq. km. The density of population here is the second highest, next to West

Bengal. In terms of population, Kerala is comparable with Orissa, and in area the nearest is Haryana.

When India became free, Kerala was made up of two princely states, viz., Travancore and Cochin, and Malabar which was under the direct administration of the British as a district of Madras Presidency. the Travancore and Cochin states were integrated to form Travancore-Cochin State in July 1949. But Malabar remained as part of the Madras province. When the states were reorganised in 1956, Travancore-Cochin and Malabar were united to form the state of Kerala. The territorial adjustments resulted in Kerala losing to Madras four taluks in the southern most part and one in the east, while it gained the Malabar district and the Kasargod taluk of South Kanara district. The Laccadive, Minicoy and Amindivi islands were detached from Kerala and declared a union territory.

Kerala has three natural divisions: coastal lowlands, midlands and highlands. The coastal region is alluvial and fertile and is most densely populated. The midland zone is made up of 200-600 feet high lateritic plateau, and has intensively cultivated valleys. The highland zone is wet, and naturally either forest or downland. The heavy rainfall and the steep descent to the plains offer excellent opportunities for hydro-electric generation. Kerala benefits from both the northeast and southwest monsoons, and has a higher average rainfall than any other state.

It is not only the ecological advantage, Kerala has a favourable past in terms of relations with the outside world and progressive rulers. Kerala was a major international trading centre for hundreds of years. By the time of the European Middle ages Kerala was an important entrepot connecting Europe, the middle East, South Asia and China. Kerala was exposed again and again to fairly favourable contacts from outside. The social sector of Kerala was in a much better position than the rest of India even in the 1940s, due to progressive actions from the rulers of Travancore and Cochin. As early as 1908 the Christian missionaries were running 2,198 schools in Travancore, in addition to those run by the government (Mathew 1999). Below we give a brief look into the pattern of growth in the post-Independence era.

Income Growth and Diversification

Kerala presented a very gloomy picture with regard to growth of SDP. As may be seen from Table 1.1, the per capita net SDP here increased from the annual average of Rs. 292 during 1960-63 to Rs. 1,470 during 1980-83 and then to Rs. 1,875 during 1990-93, that is, a growth of 542 per cent over the entire period as against 601 at the national level. In the last period, there were eight major states with a higher level of per capita income than Kerala's. Not only this, there was also a worsening of the relative position. Kerala's per capita was only 84.7 per cent of the national average during 1990-93, declining from 88.0 during 1980-83 and 92.7 during 1960-63. In the last three years, 1994-97, Kerala's per capita averaged Rs. 2,265 and constituted 86.5 per cent of the national level (at constant prices) (GKL 1998).

In total SDP, Kerala registered a growth of only 83.6 per cent between 1980-81 and 1995-96, from Rs. 3,823 crores to Rs. 7,018 crores, as against 116.8 per cent in national income, from Rs. 110,685 crores to Rs. 239,957 crores (at constant prices). Consequently, Kerala's share in the latter declined to 2.9 per cent from 3.5 (GKL 1998). This poor performance is due to a variety of problems being faced by the state, as will be evident from the analysis in chapters devoted to the state.

Regarding disposable income at the hands of people, however, one point needs to be clarified: It is not properly reflected in the state's per capita income. NSDP at factor cost equals gross product minus depreciation. It does not take into account the remittances of people working in other parts of India and abroad. And this is a substantial amount in case of Kerala. One estimate made a few years ago, placed the remittances by migrants at over Rs. 10,000 crores. The state's per capita income will be much higher than in most of the states, if it is adjusted for this inflow (GKL 1998).[4]

As regards diversification of economic activities, there has not been much progress in the last one-and-a-half decade. It is evident from Table 2.10 that although the share of primary sector declined from 39.2 per cent in 1980-81 to 33.4 per cent in 1994-95, for the secondary sector it was static at around 24 per cent. The fall in primary sector's share was made good solely by the tertiary sector. However, over a longer period, the change was substantial. In 1960-61, the primary sector's share stood at 56.0 per cent and in 1970-71 at 50.5; for the secondary sector, the proportion in this period increased from 15.2 per cent to 17.1 and for tertiary sector from 28.8 to 32.4 (GKL 1992).

Looking to some of the inner items, under the primary sector, all the items recorded declines in the last 15 years. For agriculture it was from 33.8 per cent of NSDP to 30.7 per cent. The fall was sharpest in case of forestry and logging, from 3.2 per cent in 1980-81 to 0.7 in

1994-95. In the secondary sector, for manufacturing the proportion rose to 15.2 per cent in 1990-91 from 13.9 in 1980-81 but declined again to 13.7 in 1994-95. Construction was the next important activity and its share remained almost static after a dip in 1990-91. In the tertiary sector, trade, hotels and restaurants continued to account for the highest proportion, although with a declining trend. The growth was highest in banking and insurance, followed by transport, etc. The relative share of the former in total NSDP rose to 8.3 per cent in 1994-95 from 7.3 in 1990-91 and 3.0 in 1980-81.

Table 2.10

Trend in Kerala's NSDP at Factor Cost by Industry of Origin (percentages based on Rs. at constant 1980-81 prices)

Industry	*1980-81*	*1990-91*	*1994-95*
Primary	39.2	36.0	33.4
Agriculture	33.8	33.5	30.7
Forestry and Logging	3.2	0.5	0.7
Fishing	2.0	1.8	1.9
Secondary	24.4	23.9	24.2
Manufacturing	13.9	15.2	13.7
Electricity	1.3	0.8	0.9
Construction	9.0	7.7	9.2
Tertiary	36.4	40.1	42.4
Transport, storage, comm.	3.6	5.6	8.8
Trade, hotels, restaurants	15.1	13.8	13.2
Banking and insurance	3.0	7.3	8.3
Real estate and dwellings	3.2	0.5	neg.
Public administration	4.0	6.2	507
NSDP	100.0	100.0	100.0
	(3822.7)	(5262.3)	(6633.7)

Source: Calculated from GKL 1998.

Note: Figures in parentheses are Rs. in crores.

As regards sectoral distribution of employment, the role of primary sector in Kerala declined noticeably. It was down to 48.0 per cent of the total main workers in 1991 from 51.7 in 1981 and 60.7 in 1961; in the latest year, the proportion for all-India was 69.4 per cent. The share of manufacturing, however, did not increase – it declined from 15.9 per cent in 1981 to 14.2 in 1991. The entire remaining burden of employment went to the tertiary sector, its share rising from

29.5 per cent to 33.8 over the period. At the national level, the proportion for tertiary sector stood at only 19.8 per cent in 1991 (GOI 1963, 1983, 1993).

Following from the above, another noteworthy feature of Kerala's employment situation is that in rural areas non-agricultural workers constituted a very high proportion. It increased from 38 per cent of the total workforce in 1971 to 44 in 1991. As evident from Table 2.2, none of the state could approach its level and the national average in the latest year stood at 20 per cent.

It needs to be noted, however, that unemployment is a big problem in Kerala. The rise in job expectations here due to the spread of education is unaccompanied by corresponding increase in employment opportunities. The unemployed in the state constitute around 10 per cent of the total unemployment in the country. Total number of work-seekers increased from 25.74 lakhs in 1985 to 32.87 lakhs in 1996. The proportion of those with educational level of SSLC and above increased from 53.05 per cent to 75.00 over the period (GKL 1998).

Poverty Trend

Despite having low per capita NSDP, Kerala's performance in poverty alleviation was remarkable. The consumption level here was one of the best. Per capita monthly expenditure in rural areas stood at Rs. 343 in 1992 which was the third highest, after Punjab and Haryana. The proportion of rural population with MPCE of less than Rs. 180 was only 19.3 per cent as against the national average of 38.6. Those with Rs. 385 and above constituted 26.7 per cent and 14.0 per cent, respectively (Table 2.3). Earlier, in 1987-88 also Kerala's MPCE was high. At Rs. 208.83, it was exceeded by Punjab and Haryana only and the national average stood at Rs. 157.66 (NSSO 1993). The Rural Labour Enquiry, 1993-94, found Kerala to be having the second highest level of consumption expenditure for rural labour households, next only to Punjab. Kerala had Rs. 3,305.68 per capita annually as against the national average of Rs. 2,778.57 (GOI 1998a). This could be possible largely because of the remittances from abroad.

These high levels of expenditure brought a sharp decline in the proportion of population below the poverty-line. In 1961-62, Kerala had the highest proportion of rural population below the poverty-line, at 90.8 per cent, against the national average 38.0. But, in 1973-74, it decreased to 59.2 per cent and further to 39.0 in 1983 and 25.8 in

1993-94. For the total population, the proportion in Kerala stood at 25.43 per cent in 1993-94 as against the national average at 35.97. There were, however, still four major states with lower levels than Kerala's.[5]

In rural asset holding also Kerala's position was very good. The average value of asset per household in 1992 was found to be Rs. 181, 534, which was significantly higher than the national average and lower than only two of the major states, Haryana and Punjab. The proportion of households with asset value of less than Rs. 20,000 was only 12 per cent in Kerala (Table 2.3).

Education and Health Facilities

The sterling performance of Kerala is in the social sector, and it greatly compensates for the inadequacies in the income sector. For better living it is not only the monetary income that is important; proper spending of money itself requires education. Similarly, health consciousness and availability of facilities reduce spendings on curing diseases. Kerala's performance in both education and health and family planning, as noted below, are worth emulating by other states in the country.

Looking first to literacy rates, it is evident from Table 2.4 that even in 1961 its level was far higher than in any other state. The all-India average for total population was 24.0 per cent as against Kerala's 46.8. After three decades, in 1991, the percentages were respectively 52.2 and 89.9. The nearest that could be reached by any state was 64.9 Maharashtra. In female literacy also the position was similar. It was 86.9 per cent in 1991 as against the national average at 39.4. It needs to be noted, however, that this achievement is based on a strong foundation laid by pre-independence governments. Kerala's literacy had always been much higher than that of India as a whole. Even in 1901 the percentages were 11.1 and 5.3, in 1931 at 21.3 and 9.5, and in 1951 at 40.5 and 16.7 respectively (GOI 1986).

At higher levels also the situation was inordinately better. In 1992-93, in the population aged 6 and above, 23.6 per cent were with primary school complete, 20.0 middle school and 14.6 per cent with high school complete. The national averages on these were respectively, 14.5, 9.4 and 10.1 per cent. On the first two stages none of the states could cross Kerala's level (IIPS 1995).

These results were largely due to the educational facilities available. As is apparent from Table 2.4, the pupil-teacher ratio at the primary level in rural Kerala was the lowest of 31.0 in 1994 as against 40.9 at the national level. At the upper primary also the situation was good. At 30.9, it was exceeded by only three states, viz., Punjab, Uttar Pradesh, and Rajasthan. Percentage of rural primary schools with more than five teachers was as much as 53.1 as against 5.4 at the national level. As regards provision of midday meals, with 26.2 per cent coverage in 1986-87 it was the third highest. During 1997, 23.75 lakh children were benefited by the programme (GKL 1998). Percentage of children in the age-group 5-9 not attending school in Kerala was the lowest of 15.2 among the major states in 1987-88. Same was the position in 1992-93 with regard to 6-14 age-group. The availability of schools in Kerala was relatively good. In 1994, 62.7 per cent of the population in rural areas had secondary schools within a distance of 2 km. (NCERT 1998: I). However, much remains much to be done even in case of Kerala. Bare literacy is not enough; the proportion with functional literacy has to be greatly increased. And then, there is need for much greater attention to the STs and SCs. The literacy rate for STs in 1991 was only 48.6 per cent and for SCs 69.4 (GKL 1998).

The growth of health facilities in Kerala was also appreciable. Number of medical institutions under allopathy increased from 490 in 1966 to 918 in 1980 and 1,310 in 1997, and of beds from 18,526 to 30,220 and 43,165 in these years, respectively. In the rural areas, number of primary health centres increased from 299 in 1986 to 956 in 1997, and of beds from 2,880 to 5,100. The relative position of Kerala among the states was not bad. In 1996-97, the population per bed was 1,035 which was lower than in nine of the major states (Table 2.4). It is also necessary to keep in view that in Kerala Ayurveda is quite popular. In 1995-96, there were 13,600 medical practitioners, 108 hospitals, 587 dispensaries and 2,349 beds under this system (GKL 1998).

These health facilities, along with other favourable factors like level of education, quality of food and hygienic environment, have produced the highest life expectancy at birth and very low IMR. As may be seen from Table 2.4, during 1988-92 the life expectancy in Kerala stood at 71 years, which could not be reached by any other state. The situation on IMR was incomparably better. During 1990-92, it stood at 17 per thousand live births as against the all-India average at 86. In 1995, the proportions were, respectively, 16 and 74 (GKL 1998).

In controlling population growth, Kerala's performance was the best. The decennial growth rate declined from 26.3 per cent during 1961-71 to 19.2 during 1971-81 and 14.3 during 1981-91. In the second decade there was one state with lower growth but in the last Kerala's was the lowest. The birth rate in rural Kerala stood at 18.4 during 1990-92, which was the lowest among the states (GOI 1996b).

In was this brilliant performance in education, health and population control that prompted the Nobel laureate Amartya Sen to comment thus on Kerala's achievements: "Despite the fact that economic growth of Kerala has been sluggish.... it has been able to achieve tremendous results in important areas such as literacy, life expectancy and mortality rates. The Indian Government should try to emulate the Kerala experience" (Sen 1994).

Intra-State Disparities

Spatial disparity in development is considerable in Kerala, despite a relatively low difference in resource endowment. As evident from Table 2.11, the per capita income in 1996-97 was the lowest of Rs. 1,369 in Malappuram as against the highest at Rs. 3,617 in Ernakulam, that is, the latter was 264 per cent of the former. In 1980-81, the highest was only 193 per cent of the lowest. The growth in per capita income over the period was only 31 per cent in Malappuram as against 79 per cent in Ernakulam. This disparity is higher than that in the neighbouring Karnataka, a state much bigger and with wider intra-state differences in resource endowment. In the proportion of population below the poverty-line also inter-district disparities are wide. In 1987, while Thrissur had only 20 per cent of the population below poverty-line, for Palakkad and Malappuram it was 42 per cent.

In literacy rate, health facilities and the related variables the district-wise disparities were substantial. In 1991, the total literacy rate was 96 per cent in Kottayam as against the lowest of 81 in Palakkad. In female literacy the disparity was wider; Kottayam had 94 per cent but palakkad and Kasargod only 76. With regard to SCs, the formal literacy in 1991 varied between 47.8 per cent in Kasaragod and 77.0 in Kottayam. For STs it was between 25.1 per cent in Palakkad and 78.0 in Kottayam (GKL 1998: Appendix 9.5). As regards health facilities, number of institutions per lakh population varied between 3.6 in Kozhikode and 5.9 in Idukki. The variation in number of beds per lakh population was between 245 in Thiruvananthapuram and 64 in Kasargod, against the state average at 134. The IMR and population growth presented a very disparate picture, as evident from Table 2.11. The former varied between 31 and 58 per thousand live births in 1991, and the latter between 9.4 per cent and 33.9 per cent during 1981-91.

Table 2.11
District-wise Disparity in Kerala's Development

Districts	Per Capita Income[a]		% of pop. below poverty-line 1987	IMR[b] 1991	Population growth (%) 1981-91	Literacy rate 1991
	1980-81	1996-97				
Thiruvananthapuram	1484	2369 (59.6)[c]	32.4	31	18.1	89.2 (85.8)[d]
Kollam	1536	2270 (47.8)	30.0	47	18.3	90.5 (87.0)
Pathanamthitta	-	2463 (-)	32.0	33	9.4	94.9 (93.3)
Alappuzha	1311	2088 (59.3)	34.0	42	11.6	93.9 (91.1)
Kottayam	1452	2369 (63.2)	21.0	39	10.3	95.7 (94.0)
Idukki	1995	3002 (50.5)	25.7	56	26.6	86.9 (83.0)
Ernakulam	2017	3617 (79.3)	22.7	42	17.2	92.3 (89.3)
Thrissur	1462	2366 (61.8)	20.0	46	14.6	90.1 (86.9)
Palakkad	1307	2121 (62.3)	42.5	56	21.3	81.3 (75.7)
Malappuram	1045	1369 (31.0)	42.0	57	29.4	87.9 (84.1)
Kozhikode	1588	2217 (39.6)	33.4	50	23.2	91.1 (86.8)
Wayanad	-	3544 (-)	27.4	58	33.9	82.7 (77.7)
Kannur	1571	2327 (48.1)	24.5	42	24.3	91.5 (87.6)
Kasargod	-	2095 (-)	37.9	49	27.8	82.5 (76.3)
State	1508	2363 (56.7)	30.7	46	19.2	89.8 (86.2)

Source: GKL 1998; Kannan 1995; Rajan and Mohanchandram 1998.

Notes: a: Rs. at constant prices.
b: probability of a new born child dying before age 5.
c: figures in parentheses are percentage growth over the period.
d: female literacy.

Region-wise, Malabar continued to be very backward. A composite index calculated in early seventies, by using levels of education, health, industrialisation and economic infrastructure, showed that the 14 most developed taluks of Kerala were all in Travancore-Cochin and the 15 least developed were either in Malabar or the High Ranges (GKL 1973). The latest situation is evident from Table 2.11. Part of the reason behind this disparity is that historically there were significant social, economic and political differences between Malabar, Cochin and Travancore. Malabar was a neglected outpost of Madras, on which the British spent little beyond the requirements of law and order. In contrast, the Travancore and Cochin governments actively stimulated agriculture, commerce and industry, and founded schools, colleges and hospitals.

Summing Up

From the above survey of the situation in southern states, the following broad conclusions have emerged:

First, on the whole, all the southern states are much better placed than the average situation for India. On per capita income each of them generally had lower level than the national average. But even here, the worst performer, Andhra Pradesh, had a higher level than four of the large states -- Uttar Pradesh, Bihar, Madhya Pradesh and Orissa -- during 1990-93. In poverty alleviation, the southern states performed much better than the national average. Even the worst performer, Tamil Nadu, had lower percentage of population below the poverty-line than seven of the major states in the latest year.

Second, among the southern states, on the whole the worst performance was in Andhra Pradesh, although in bringing the population below the poverty-line it had the best achievement. Its performance in the social sector was poor, and so also in reducing regional imbalances. The literacy rate here was much lower than the national average.

Third, Tamil Nadu's performance in per capita income has improved significantly in recent years, and so also in economic diversification. The level of consumption expenditure here is one of the lowest. Inter-district disparity in development is also high. Its performance in the social sector is however, quite good.

Fourth, among the southern states, Karnataka had the best performance in per capita income. In economic diversification also its record has been appreciable. In poverty alleviation, however, its achievement was relatively low. The MPCE here was much less than the all-India average. In reducing inter-district disparity also its record was not appreciable.

Fifth, overall, the best performing state is Kerala. Its low per capita income does not truly reflect the extent of disposable income due to the big role played by remittances from outside. In poverty alleviation, its record is one of the best. The level of MPCE here could be exceeded by only two states, and the proportion of population below the poverty-line by three states. In the social sector its performance is the best. A noticeably dark spot is, however, the extent of inter-district disparity.

In the chapters that follow, the problem areas in different states have been thoroughly analysed, starting with the situation on resource mobilisation and deployment and followed by a sectoral analysis.

Notes

1. The latest estimate on poverty-line population, for 1999-2000, found the percentage in rural Andhra at 11.05 and for combined population at 15.77 (GOI 2001).
2. As per the latest estimate, for 1999-2000, the percentage of rural population below poverty-line in Tamil Nadu is 20.55 and in urban areas at 22.11; at the national level, these were 27.09 and 23.62, respectively (GOI 2001).
3. In 1999-2000, the percentage in rural Karnataka was 17.38 and in urban areas 25.25. The relative position of the latter among the states has improved noticeably (GOI 2001).
4. Since mid-seventies, remittances played a big role in Kerala's economy in influencing the labour market, consumption, savings and investment. The inflow of migrants' remittances to Kerala is divided into four phases: 1. The initial phase of steady growth between 1976 and 1979; 2. The peak phase between 1980 and 1983; 3. The declining growth between 1984 and 1990; and 4. The revival phase between 1991 and 1995. Remittances as percentage of Kerala's NDP was estimated at 20 during 1980-83 and 22.5 during 1993-95 (quoted in Prakash 1998).
5. According to the latest estimate, for 1999-2000, rural Kerala has 9.38 per cent below the poverty-line and for combined population 12.72 per cent; the latter is higher than in only two of the major states – Punjab and Haryana (GOI 2001).

II

The Economy of Andhra Pradesh

II

[illegible]

3

Resource Mobilisation and Deployment

A backward economy requires huge resources for investment in different directions. Therefore, utmost efforts are needed to mobilise all possible resources. The quantum that can be mobilised in a given situation depends primarily on the motivation of the authority. The government must have the firmness to tap all available resources and deploy them for the right purpose. This is, however, determined largely by the nature of the government – that is, whose interest it is more inclined to serve? If the government is for the richer section of population, then it will not exert itself much in larger resource mobilisation, for uplifting the condition of the masses is not its prime consideration and there is no urgency of development.

The object of this chapter is to analyse the budgetary resource mobilisation efforts of the Andhra government. The questions addressed to are: Did the government make utmost efforts to mobilise all tax and non-tax resources? How does its performance compare with that in other states? What was the role of central transfers? Were the spendings adequately development oriented and did the government sincerely try to reduce the revenue expenditure?

Resource Mobilisation

On the aggregate of budgetary resource mobilisation, Andhra's performance is quite disappointing. Between 1965-68 and 1994-97, its total receipts registered an increase of 47 times, from the annual average of Rs. 298 crores to Rs. 14,050 crores, as against 60 times for all states together. The relative share of Andhra in the aggregate for all states declined from 8.7 per cent to 6.9 over the period. The per capita total receipts in Andhra stood at only Rs. 1,962 during 1994-97, which was lowest among the southern states, and substantially lower than the all-states' average, being Rs. 2,255 (Table 3.1).

Revenue Receipts

In the total receipts, the proportion of revenue receipts, which is of particular significance, increased from 55.7 per cent during 1965-68 to 78.4 during 1975-78 but declined to 70.8 in 1994-97. Except during 1975-78, Andhra's ratio was lower than that for all states together (Table 3.1). Over the entire period, while Andhra's revenue receipts increased 60.0 times, for all states together it was 64.1 times. The per capita revenue receipts here was only Rs. 1,390 during 1994-97 as against Rs. 1,516 for all states.

Table 3.1

Trend in Budgetary Receipts of Andhra in Relation to Other Major States

(Rs. in crores)

States	*Total receipts*	*Revenue receipts*	*Total receipts*	*Revenue receipts*	*Total receipts*	*Revenue receipts*
	1965-68 (a.a.)		*1975-78 (a.a.)*		*1994-97 (a.a.)*	
Andhra Pradesh	298	166 (55.7)[b]	910	713 (78.4)[b]	14050	9952 (70.8)[b]
Assam	122	74 (60.7)	288	223 (77.4)	4711	3398 (72.1)
Bihar	229	136 (59.4)	781	537 (68.8)	5824	7404 (127.1)
Gujarat	175	129 (73.7)	702	528 (75.2)	11080	8673 (78.3)
Haryana	59[a]	40 (67.8)	340	261 (76.8)	7845	5648 (69.7)
Karnataka	207	133 (64.3)	788	611 (77.5)	10442	8378 (80.2)
Kerala	146	103 (70.5)	505	389 (77.0)	7103	5412 (76.2)
Madhya Pradesh	237	137 (57.8)	784	614 (78.3)	11133	8762 (83.8)
Maharashtra	395	275 (69.6)	1544	1196 (77.5)	22351	16968 (75.9)
Orissa	160	97 (60.6)	435	327 (75.2)	5553	3918 (70.6)
Punjab	174	111 (63.8)	488	365 (74.8)	7409	5352 (72.2)
Rajasthan	203	106 (52.2)	581	444 (76.4)	9895	7171 (72.5)
Tamil Nadu	289	186 (64.4)	844	615 (72.9)	13414	10593 (79.0)
Uttar Pradesh	427	255 (59.7)	1479	1061 (71.7)	22279	14879 (66.8)
West Bengal	246	182 (74.0)	916	653 (71.3)	11022	7489 (67.9)
All States	3429	2142 (62.5)	11939	8969 (75.1)	180727	137308 (76.0)

Contd...

Contd...

Growth in receipts (no. of times) 1965-68 to 1994-97		*Per capita receipts[c] (Rs.) 1994-97*	
Total	*Revenue*	*Total*	*Revenue*
47.1	60.0	1962	1390
38.6	45.9	1921	1386
25.4	54.4	621	789
63.3	67.2	2477	1939
33.0	141.2	4322	3112
50.4	63.0	2161	1733
48.7	52.5	2232	1700
47.0	64.0	1535	1208
56.6	61.7	2607	1979
34.7	40.4	1625	1147
42.6	48.2	3399	2455
48.7	67.7	2040	1479
46.4	57.0	2290	1809
52.2	58.3	1468	980
44.8	41.1	1501	1020
52.7	64.1	2255	1516

Source: RBIFA 1967, 1968, 1978; CMIE 1999b.

Notes: a.a.: annual average; a: average for 1966-68.
b: revenue receipts as percentage to total receipts.
c: based on average population of 1994 to 1996.

Tax Revenue

In the aggregate of revenue receipts, the share of tax revenue increased over the years and correspondingly that of non-tax revenue declined. The share of tax revenue stood at the average of 60.6 per cent during 1965-68, increased to 66.2 during 1975-78 and 69.0 during 1994-97. Although these proportions were higher than the all-states' averages, there were a number of states with much better performance, as evident from Table 3.2. The growth in tax revenue here was only 68 times as against 72 times for all states together; all the other southern states had a faster growth.

In the tax revenue, the relative share of Andhra's own collection declined noticeably over the years. It was only 64.2 per cent during 1994-97 as against 73.3 during 1965-68. All the other southern states had registered increases in their share of own tax collection. During

1994-97, there were nine major states with OTR contributing a larger share than Andhra's. The growth in OTR was only 60 times here as against 67 times for all the states together (Table 3.2). Thus, the effort at tax collection was very low in Andhra and the state's dependence on central taxes was high.

Table 3.2

Trend in Tax and Non-Tax Revenue of Andhra vis-a-vis Other Major States

(Rs. in crores)

States	*1965-68 (a.a.)*		*1994-97 (a.a.)*		*Growth (no. of times)*	
	Tax rev.	*Non-tax*	*Tax rev.*	*Non-tax*	*Tax rev.*	*Non-tax*
Andhra Pradesh	100.6 (60.6)[a]	65.4	6871 (69.0)[a]	3080	68.3	47.1
Assam	34.0 (45.9)	40.1	1670 (49.1)	1727	49.1	43.1
Bihar	89.4 (65.7)	46.2	5471 (73.9)	1934	61.2	41.9
Gujarat	80.0 (62.0)	49.3	6475 (74.7)	2198	80.9	44.6
Haryana	22.6 (57.5)	17.4	2436 (43.1)	3212	107.8	184.6
Karnataka	72.4 (54.4)	61.0	6547 (78.1)	1831	90.4	30.0
Kerala	59.7 (58.0)	43.8	4399 (81.3)	1012	73.7	23.1
Madhya Pradesh	80.2 (58.5)	56.3	5732 (65.4)	3029	71.5	53.8
Maharashtra	202.1 (73.5)	72.7	12592 (74.2)	4376	62.3	60.2
Orissa	37.0 (38.1)	59.9	2479 (63.3)	1439	67.0	24.0
Punjab	64.7 (58.3)	46.1	3126 (58.4)	2225	48.3	48.3
Rajasthan	55.8 (52.6)	49.8	4234 (59.0)	2936	75.9	59.0
Tamil Nadu	122.4 (65.8)	64.0	8892 (83.9)	1702	72.6	26.5
Uttar Pradesh	153.0 (60.0)	102.4	10573 (71.1)	4306	69.1	42.1
West Bengal	130.4 (71.7)	51.7	6119 (81.7)	1370	46.9	26.5
All States	1294.3 (60.4)	848.2	93224 (67.9)	44084	72.0	52.0

State's OTR		*Tax Efforts*		*State's ONTR*		*Growth (no. of times)*	
1965-68	*1994-97*	*1967-68*	*1994-97*[c]	*1965-68*	*1994-97*	*OTR*	*ONTR*
73.7 (73.3)[b]	4410 (64.2)[b]	19.47	625 (32.1)[d]	39.3 (60.0)[e]	1587 (51.5)[e]	59.8	40.4
23.3 (68.6)	701 (42.0)	18.66	291 (15.6)	60.0 (15.0)	328 (19.0)	30.1	54.7
58.1 (65.0)	2020 (36.9)	12.06	217 (18.0)	24.9 (53.3)	984 (50.9)	34.8	39.5
60.0 (75.0)	5377 (83.0)	29.59	1226 (41.4)	29.1 (59.1)	1554 (70.7)	89.6	53.4

Contd...

Contd...

17.0 (75.3)	2067 (84.9)	28.95	1167 (40.3)	12.9 (73.7)	2931 (91.3)	121.6	227.2
54.1 (74.7)	5110 (78.1)	23.28	1079 (46.3)	33.1 (54.3)	1142 (62.4)	94.5	34.5
45.6 (76.3)	3360 (76.4)	27.44	1120 (40.8)	17.9 (41.0)	482 (47.6)	73.7	26.9
56.2 (70.1)	3497 (61.0)	16.94	494 (29.2)	34.5 (61.2)	1789 (59.1)	61.6	51.2
156.4 (77.4)	10701 (85.0)	36.50	1270 (34.8)	46.3 (63.7)	3144 (71.8)	69.0	67.1
22.1 (59.6)	1131 (45.6)	19.44	336 (17.3)	24.7 (41.3)	581 (40.4)	51.2	23.5
51.9 (80.2)	2662 (85.2)	37.46	1249 (33.3)	33.9 (73.6)	1909 (85.8)	51.3	56.3
40.2 (72.0)	2721 (64.3)	19.50	576 (29.5)	23.8 (47.8)	1638 (55.8)	67.7	68.8
94.6 (77.3)	6989 (78.6)	29.37	1210 (41.2)	39.4 (61.6)	839 (49.3)	73.9	21.3
102.1 (66.7)	5551 (52.5)	14.60	376 (25.8)	55.5 (54.2)	1869 (43.4)	54.4	33.7
97.9 (75.0)	4041 (66.0)	26.30	561 (21.3)	30.1 (58.3)	362 (26.4)	42.5	12.4
943.5 (72.9)	63567 (68.2)	21.92	706 (32.2)	455.1 (53.7)	22699 (51.5)	67.4	49.9

Source: As in Table 3.1; and RBI 1970.

Notes: a: figures in parentheses here are percentages of total revenue receipts.
b: percentages in relation to total tax revenue.
c: state's OTR during 1994-97 divided by the estimated population of 1994.
d: growth in number of times between 1967-68 and 1994-97.
e: percentages in relation to total non-tax revenue.
OTR: own tax revenue; ONTR: own non-tax revenue.

The contribution from central taxes increased from the annual average of Rs. 26.83 crores during 1965-68 to Rs. 129.38 crores during 1975-78 and then to Rs. 2,462 crores during 1994-97, that is a growth of 92 times over the entire period. The transfer to all the states together, on the other hand, increased 85 times in this period, from Rs. 350.8 crores to Rs. 29,657 crores (Table 3.4). In the aggregate of tax transfer, Andhra's share rose to 8.30 per cent from 7.64.

In order to find out the areas that need attention, we give a brief look into the changes in tax structure over the years. It is clear from Table 3.3 that the state's tax structure continued to be very narrow. In the total of OTR, two taxes, sales tax and state excise, together contributed as much as 80.2 per cent during 1988-91, rising from 71.4 during 1975-78 and 60.0 during 1965-68. It was only in the last few years there has been a decline in their share -- contributing 74.8 per cent during 1994-97. And this came due to a drastic fall in the revenue from state excise; the share of sales tax in fact rose further to 70.4 per cent from 52.9 during 1988-91.

Table 3.3

Changes in the Structure of Tax and Non-Tax Revenue of Andhra

(Rs. in lakhs)

Items	*1975-78 (a.a.)*	*1988-91 (a.a.)*	*1994-97 (a.a.)*
Total Own Tax Revenue	33501 (100.0)	237095 (100.0)	440989 (100.0)
Taxes on profession etc.	-	2288 (1.0)	5203 (1.2)
Land revenue	3002 (9.0)	3013 (1.3)	6190 (1.4)
Stamps and registration fees	1870 (5.6)	12223 (5.2)	35814 (8.1)
Urban immovable property tax	33 (0.1)	257 (0.1)	1666 (0.4)
Sales tax	14978 (44.7)	125338 (52.9)	310245 (70.4)
State excise	8936 (26.7)	64681 (27.3)	19509 (4.4)
Taxes on vehicles	3033 (9.1)	18257 (7.7)	45681 (10.4)
Taxes on goods etc.	-	533 (0.2)	55 (neg.)
Entertainment tax	1629 (4.9)	4630 (2.0)	3962 (0.9)
Taxes and duties on electricity	21 (neg.)	3659 (1.5)	5148 (1.2)
Total Own Non-Tax Revenue	12494 (100.0)	78684 (100.0)	158683 (100.0)
Interest receipts	6436 (51.5)	47602 (60.5)	77006 (48.5)
Dividend and profits	50 (0.4)	130 (0.2)	547 (0.3)
General services	961 (7.7)	4138 (5.3)	9540 (6.0)
Social services	1343 (10.7)	4681 (5.9)	6443 (4.1)
Education, etc.	-	2272[a] (2.9)	2277 (1.4)
Medical, pub. health, etc.	-	1165[a] (1.5)	1420 (0.9)
Economic services	3704 (29.6)	22133 (28.1)	65146 (41.1)
Forestry and wildlife	1747 (14.0)	6104 (7.8)	12117 (7.6)
Irrigation	99 (0.8)	2942 (3.7)	9523 (6.0)
Power	334 (2.7)	2600 (3.3)	1278 (0.8)
Industries	180 (1.4)	5247 (6.7)	32577 (20.5)

Source: As in Table 3.1; and RBIFA 1991, 1992.

Notes: a: average for 1989-91.

Among other taxes, the relative contribution of land revenue recorded a drastic decline over the years – from 14.6 per cent of total OTR during 1965-68 to 9.0 during 1975-78 and to a little more than one per cent in recent years. From entertainment tax, there was an absolute fall in collection in recent years. As against an annual average of Rs. 46 crores during 1988-91, in 1994-97 it contributed only Rs. 40

crores; the relative share fell from 4.9 per cent during 1975-78 to less than one per cent in 1994-97. There are, however, a few items showing a significant growth in recent years, as may be seen from Table 3.3. The contribution of taxes on vehicles rose to 10.4 per cent of total OTR during 1994-97 from 7.7 during 1988-91, and of stamps and registration fees from 5.2 to 8.0 over the same period. The taxes on electricity, on profession, etc., on urban immovable property and on goods and passengers have also shown increases in recent years but their contribution is still very insignificant.

The potential for raising tax revenue is substantial. The tax efforts of the government have been one of the lowest. The per capita OTR of Andhra was only Rs. 625 during 1994-97 as against the highest of Rs. 1,270 in Maharashtra and the all-India average at Rs. 706. The growth over the years has been very low (Table 3.2).

There could be not only increase in the rates but also better collection from the existing ones. The scope for raising the tax rates is there in at least four of the items: taxes on profession, calling etc., stamp and registration fees, land revenue and entertainment tax. The collection from the first one can be considerably increased as the ceiling on profession tax has been raised to Rs. 2,500 from Rs. 250, by a constitutional amendment. The level of tax arrear in Andhra is one of the highest. At the end of March 1990, it stood at Rs. 461.02 crores, the second highest among all the states. At the end of 1992-93, the arrear on sales tax alone stood at Rs. 435.9 crores (RBIFA 1992; GOA 1997).

Non-Tax Revenue

The contribution of non-tax revenue to the total revenue of Andhra has been quite low. During the three time periods considered it was always lower than that for all the states together. In the total revenue, its share decreased from 39.4 per cent during 1965-68 to 33.8 during 1975-78 and then to 31.0 during 1994-97; for all states together, the proportions were respectively, 39.6, 36.9 and 40.1 per cent. The NTR in Andhra had a growth of only 47 times over the entire period as against 52 times for all states. In relation to the other southern states, however, Andhra's position was significantly better (Table 3.2).

In the non-tax revenue, a very large share came from the Central government, the problem in which has been discussed later. Here we look into the state's own NTR. In the total of NTR, ONTR's contribution declined from 60 per cent during 1965-68 to 52 per cent by mid-seventies and has remained at around the same level since then. The growth in ONTR of Andhra between 1965-68 and 1994-97 was only 40 times as against 50 times for all states together. Among the southern states, however, its performance was the best (Table 3.2).

As regards the composition of Andhra's ONTR, it has changed significantly in recent years. Until recently, as evident from Table 3.3, more than half of it came from interest receipts. The proportion rose to 60.5 per cent in 1988-91 from 51.5 during 1975-78, but in 1994-97 it was down to 48.5. The relative contribution of social services has also declined from 10.7 per cent during 1975-78 to 4.1 during 1994-97. The potential for raising resources here is however, not negligible, particularly from the richer segment of users.

Among other items, contribution from economic services has shown a rapid rise. Its relative share went up to 41 per cent during 1994-97 from 28 per cent in 1988-91. This growth was almost solely due to the rapid rise in receipts from industry. Its relative share in total ONTR rose to 20.5 per cent in 1994-97 from a mere 1.4 during 1975-78. The contribution from forestry and wild life, on the other hand, was halved over the period, declining from 14 per cent to 7.6. From power also there was a sharp drop in contribution, from 2.7 per cent to 0.8. The share of irrigation has, however, risen significantly, from only 0.8 per cent of the total during 1975-78 to 6.0 in 1994-97 (Table 3.3).

The growth in receipts from general services and dividend and profit were quite low. The former increased 10 times and the latter 11 times over the period of two decades as against 13 times in the aggregate of ONTR. The relative contribution of general services was down to 5.3 per cent in 1988-91 from 7.7 per cent in 1975-78, and rose marginally to 6.0 in 1994-97. The most distressing performance was in dividend and profit. It contributed only 0.3 per cent of the total during 1994-97 and this was obtained with a total investment in public sector undertakings of Rs. 8,258.6 crores at the end of 1991-92. The operating surplus of PSUs in relation to total investment averaged only 6.0 per cent during 1989-92. The savings after tax was (-) Rs. 224.57 crores in 1991-92, rising from (-) Rs. 85.53 crores in 1989-90 (GOA 1993). The State Electricity Board of Andhra Pradesh, with huge investment, had a rate of return on capital without subsidy of (-) 32.70 per cent in 1994-95 (APSEB 1998). It is needless to add that there is immense scope for raising revenue here.

Central Transfers

In both tax and non-tax revenue, central transfers constituted a large proportion. The total transfer to Andhra Pradesh from the Centre increased from the annual average of Rs. 53 crores during 1965-68 to Rs. 253 crores during 1975-78 and then to Rs. 3,955 crores in 1994-97, that is a growth of 75 times over the entire period; the aggregate of transfer to all states in this period increased 69 times. Andhra's relative share in the total transfer increased from 7.1 per cent to 7.7 in this period. The per capita transfer to Andhra stood at Rs. 548 during 1994-97 as against the average of Rs. 567 for all states. Among the southern states, it received the highest per capita in this period. In the total revenue of the state, central transfer constituted 39.7 per cent during 1994-97, rising from 35.5 during 1975-78 and 31.9 during 1965-68. There were six major states in 1994-97 with a higher level of dependence on central transfers (Table 3.4).

In the total transfer to Andhra, tax transfer accounted for more than half, and increased from 50.6 per cent during 1965-68 to 54.0 during 1975-78 and 62.3 in 1994-97; the remaining transfers were in the form of grants and other contributions. The growth in grants, etc., to Andhra was 57 times over the entire period as against 54 times in that to all states. However, the proportion of grants in the total transfer to Andhra was always lower than that in the aggregate of transfer to all states (Table 3.4).

In the total grants, the share of non-plan grant has shown a rising tendency in recent years. The average for 1994-97 came to 32.5 per cent as against 24.2 per cent during 1988-91. Earlier, however, sometimes the proportion was still higher. For example, during 1975-78, the average came to 44.7 per cent. In the non-plan grants, statutory grants constituted the overwhelming proportion; during 1994-97 it averaged 78.6 per cent. As regards grants for state plan schemes, its share in the aggregate of grants averaged 28.2 per cent during 1994-97 as against 30.4 during 1975-78. The growth in grants for centrally sponsored schemes was particularly rapid -- the relative share rising to 32.9 per cent from 18.5 over the period -- and it has been a subject of criticism in recent years.[1]

On the central transfers, there is not much that a state can do to raise its share. The major medium of statutory resource transfer to states is the two divisible taxes, income tax and excise duties, levied by the Centre. The proportion to be transferred to the states and the basis of transfer are decided by the Finance Commission (FC). As

Table 3.4

Trend in Central Transfers to Andhra vis-a-vis Other Major States

(Rs. in crores)

States	1965-68 (a.a.)				1975-78 (a.a.)				1994-97 (a.a.)			
	Tax transfer	Grants etc.	Total transfer	as % to total rev. of state	Tax transfer	Grants etc.	Total transfer	as % of total rev. of state	Tax transfer	Grants etc.	Total transfer	as % to total rev. of state
Andhra Pradesh	26.8 (50.6)[b]	26.2	53.0 (13)[c]	31.9	136.5 (54.0)[b]	116.2	252.8 (52)[c]	35.5	2462 (62.3)[b]	1493	3955 (548)[c]	39.7
Assam	10.7 (23.8)	34.1	44.8 (32)	60.5	44.1 (33.4)	88.2	132.3 (70)	59.2	970 (40.8)	1405	2375 (1003)	69.9
Bihar	31.2 (59.4)	21.4	52.6 (10)	38.7	176.9 (67.2)	86.3	263.2 (39)	49.0	3451 (78.4)	950	4401 (467)	59.4
Gujarat	20.0 (49.8)	20.1	40.1 (17)	31.1	87.6 (62.6)	52.4	140.0 (45)	26.5	1097 (630)	644	1741 (393)	20.1
Haryana[a]	5.6 (54.9)	4.6	10.2 (11)	25.4	25.7 (49.7)	26.0	51.7 (43)	19.9	370 (56.8)	281	651 (386)	11.5
Karnataka	18.3 (39.6)	27.9	46.2 (17)	34.7	92.0 (66.6)	46.2	138.1 (41)	22.6	1437 (67.6)	689	2126 (440)	25.4
Kerala	14.1 (35.4)	25.8	40.0 (21)	38.8	65.3 (47.4)	72.6	138.0 (56)	35.5	1039 (66.2)	530	1569 (493)	29.0
Madhya Pradesh	24.0 (52.3)	21.9	45.8 (12)	33.5	129.5 (65.5)	68.0	197.5 (42)	32.2	2235 (60.6)	1240	3475 (507)	41.2
Maharashtra	45.6 (63.4)	26.4	72.0 (16)	26.2	170.1 (73.5)	61.4	231.5 (40)	19.4	1891 (58.4)	1232	3123 (368)	18.5
Orissa	15.0 (29.9)	35.1	50.1 (25)	51.6	65.4 (37.4)	109.7	175.1 (71)	53.5	1348 (58.9)	940	2288 (668)	58.4
Punjab	12.8 (51.4)	12.1	25.0 (19)	22.5	39.9 (46.7)	45.6	85.5 (49)	23.4	465 (59.5)	316	781 (398)	14.6

Contd...

Contd...

Rajasthan	15.6 (37.5)	26.0	41.6 (18)	39.3	79.4 (42.4)	108.1	187.5 (61)	42.2	1514 (53.8)	1298	2812 (589)	39.2
Tamil Nadu	27.8 (53.1)	24.6	52.4 (14)	28.2	129.4 (71.7)	51.1	180.5 (41)	29.3	1902 (68.8)	863	2765 (474)	26.1
Uttar Pradesh	51.0 (52.1)	46.9	97.8 (12)	38.4	273.8 (61.5)	171.7	445.6 (43)	42.0	5022 (67.3)	2437	7459 (503)	50.1
West Bengal	32.5 (60.2)	21.6	54.1 (13)	29.7	146.5 (59.3)	100.6	247.1 (47)	37.8	2079 (66.7)	1007	3086 (425)	40.8
All States	350.8 (47.2)	393.1	743.9 (15)	34.7	1699.7 (52.6)	1534.7	3234.4 (51)	36.1	29657 (58.1)	21385	51042 (567)	32.8

Source: As in Table 3.1.

Notes: a: average for 1966-68.
b: percentage of total transfer.
c: per capita transfer in Rs., based on population estimates for 1969, 1976 and 1995, respectively.

regards grants, it is provided both through the awards from FC and by the Planning Commission; the major portion has been coming from the latter.

There has been many changes in the basis for tax transfer. The proportion of income tax to be shared increased gradually from 55 per cent under the first FC (1952-57) to 85 per cent in the seventh and remained at the same level in the following three FCs, covering the period till 1994-95. The tenth FC (1995-2000) reduced the proportion to 77.5 per cent on the consideration that the Centre, being the authority levying and administering it, should have a "tangible interest in the yield". As regards excise duties, the proportion to be shared was 20 per cent during the periods of fourth through sixth FC covering all the commodities. Earlier, the proportion was higher but the commodity coverage lower. From the seventh FC the sharable proportion began to be increased – doubled to 40 per cent in this FC, 45 per cent in the eighth through ninth FC II and then to 47.5 in the tenth FC.

The criteria for sharing of the taxes also changed from period to period. For income tax, the state's contribution, population, per capita income, specific indicators of backwardness, poverty criterion and tax efforts were used with varying weightage from time to time. Till the eighth FC, only two criteria, population and contribution, were used. The former accounting for 80-90 per cent of the distribution. From the ninth FC I, the weightage for population was reduced to 22.5 per cent and then to 20 per cent in the tenth FC. Per capita income distance criterion became the most important factor determining the allocation among the states. The weightage on it rose to 60 per cent by the tenth FC. The criteria for allocation of excise duties also changed over the years, and almost in the same manner as in case of income-tax sharing. Population continued to be the overwhelming factor till the sixth FC.

In grants, the statutory portion – which increased from 11.2 per cent of total grants to Andhra during 1991-94 to 25.5 per cent during 1994-97 – was generally for specific purposes. For example, the sixth FC (1974-79) provided it for two purposes: (i) to help state governments upgrade their essential administrative and social services, and (ii) to cover deficits on non-plan revenue accounts, deficits which remained after redistribution of central taxes. As regards plan grants, till the end of sixties its distribution was by and large of ad hoc nature, and were not helpful in any way in bringing balanced growth. The states were also not happy with the system. From the Fourth Plan, specific criteria were laid down for allocating plan grants, on the basis of what came to be known as 'Gadgil Formula'. The criteria laid down were as follows:

(1) The requirements of special category state like Assam, Jammu & Kashmir and Nagaland should first be met out of the total pool of central assistance.
(2) The balance of the central assistance be distributed among the remaining states on the following basis:
   (a) 60 per cent on the basis of population;
   (b) 10 per cent on the basis of per capita state income, going only to the states with income below the national average;
   (c) 10 per cent on the basis of tax effort;
   (d) 10 per cent on the basis of spill-over into the Fourth Plan of major continuing irrigation and power projects;
   (d) 10 per cent for special problems of individual states.

This formula was modified once on the eve of the Sixth Plan and again in October 1990.

There is much that can be said on the above basis of transferring resources to the states, and the pace at which greater rationality was introduced. But, the fact remains that no individual state could change the system to its favour. Therefore, for raising larger revenue a state has to rely mainly on its own tax and non-tax revenues.

The urgency of taking measures for increasing the revenue receipts of Andhra may be gauged from the fact that there was a rapidly widening gap between revenue receipts and revenue expenditure. From a surplus of Rs. 80 crores during 1975-78, the adverse balance rose to the annual average of Rs. 491 crores during 1988-91 and then to Rs. 1,556 crores during 1994-97. The revenue expenditure had to be increasingly financed by capital receipts, which is fraught with grave consequences for the future.

We have noted earlier some of the ways in which the state can increase its revenue considerably, here we may give some idea about the potential at the level of panchayat raj institutions. In the second largest and relatively developed district of Andhra, Guntur, the collection from gram panchayats through taxes totalled only Rs. 190.93 lakhs in 1994-95, a per capita receipt of Rs. 4.65. The realisations from panchayat property stood at a mere Rs. 89 lakhs; there are 960 gram panchayats in Guntur. In the grand total of receipts for all panchayats, government grants constituted 60 per cent (GOA 1995).

Capital Receipts

The growth of capital receipts in recent years was very rapid. As against only a 49 per cent rise between 1965-68 and 1975-78, from the annual average of Rs. 132 crores to Rs. 197 crores, in the following two decades it multiplied 21 times – reaching Rs. 4,098 crores during 1994-97. The pattern of growth in capital receipts in the last two decades is presented in Table 3.5.

Table 3.5

Trend in Capital Receipts of Andhra Pradesh

(Rs. in crores)

Items	*1975-78 (a.a.)*	*1985-88 (a.a.)*	*1994-97 (a.a.)*
Total Capital Receipts	196.5 (100.0)	877.8 (100.0)	4098.2 (100.0)
1. Internal debt	30.3 (15.4)	191.7 (21.8)	619.1 (15.1)
(i) Market loans	24.2	170.8	509.7
2. Loans from the Centre	11.6 (56.8)	448.7 (51.1)	1593.4 (38.9)
(i) State plan scheme	79.3	256.9	938.8
(ii) Non-plan	26.0	163.9	477.2
3. Recovery of loans and advances	19.2 (9.8)	45.9 (5.2)	1350.6 (33.0)
4. Small savings, PF etc.	6.2 (3.2)	80.4 (9.2)	244.5 (6.0)
5. Deposits and advances	27.0 (13.7)	125.2 (14.3)	363.3 (8.9)

Source: RBIFA 1978, 1987, 1988; CMIE 1999b.

There has been some significant changes in the components of capital receipts. The share of loans from the Centre in total capital receipts declined from as much as 56.8 per cent during 1975-78 to 38.9 per cent during 1994-97. On the other hand, the contribution from recovery of loans and advances rose to 33.0 per cent from 9.8, over the same period. The share of internal debt increased from 15.4 per cent in 1975-78 to 21.8 during 1985-88 but in 1994-97 it contributed only 15.1 per cent. The small savings, PF etc., and deposits and advances also had a similar trend. The contribution from the first one rose to 9.2 per cent of the total during 1985-88 from 3.2 during 1975-78 but in the following period it declined substantially.

Looking to some of the inner items, in the loans from the Centre, the share of state plan schemes declined from the average of 71 per cent during 1975-78 to 57 per cent during 1985-88 and remained at around the same level in the following years. The share of non-plan loans, however, recorded a substantial rise over the years, contributing

36 per cent of total during 1985-88 and 30 per cent during 1994-97 as against 23 per cent in 1975-78. In internal debt, market loans continued to account for the overwhelming proportion.

Pattern of Expenditure

The growth in budgetary expenditure of Andhra Pradesh has been relatively low. Over the entire period of three decades, 1965-68 to 1994-97, it multiplied 48 times – from the annual average of Rs. 301 crores to Rs. 14,342 crores – as against 52 times for all the states together. The per capita expenditure of Andhra increased 26.5 times in this period – from Rs. 75 to Rs. 2,000 – as against 28.2 times for all states, from Rs. 70 to Rs. 1,972. In the latest period, there were eight major states with higher levels of per capita expenditure than Andhra's (Table 3.6).

The level of expenditure is, however, not so important as its pattern. It is necessary to know whether there was scope for economy in expenditure, and whether the priorities were in keeping with the broader interests of the state. First, we look into the revenue expenditure, then into the capital expenditure, and finally a brief analysis of the Plan expenditure.

Revenue Expenditure

Apparently the growth in revenue expenditure of Andhra is excessive. Over the period of three decades, it multiplied 66 times, from the annual average of Rs. 174 crores during 1965-68 to Rs. 11,507 crores during 1994-967, as against only 48 times in total expenditure, as noted earlier. The relative share of revenue expenditure in the total consequently rose to 80 per cent from 58 over the same period. However, in relation to the position of other states, this is not a very disappointing picture. The growth in revenue expenditure for all states together in this period was 67.5 times, and there were as many as nine major states with higher growth than Andhra's. The average share of revenue expenditure in total was also higher for all states, being 63 per cent during 1965-68 and 82 during 1994-97 (Table 3.6).

As regards the composition of revenue expenditure, the first noticeable thing is that the relative share of development expenditure has shown a decline in recent years. From the average of 70 per cent during 1975-78 it rose to 72 during 1988-91, but in 1994-97 it was down to 68 per cent. This is, however, much above the all states' average; the proportion in the latter in the latest period being only 54.0 per cent.

Table 3.6

Trend in Budgetary Expenditure of Andhra vis-a-vis Other Major States

(Rs. in crores)

States	*1965-68 (a.a.)*		
	Revenue expend.	*Capital expend.*[d]	*Total expend.*
Andhra Pradesh	173.6 (57.6)[c]	127.7 (42.4)f	301.3 (75)[e]
Assam	84.1 (68.2)	39.3 (31.8)	123.3 (89)
Bihar	144.1 (54.3)	121.4 (45.7)	265.6 (51)
Gujarat	127.9 (69.9)	55.1 (30.1)	182.9 (77)
Haryana[a]	35.1 (58.6)	24.8 (41.4)	59.9 (67)
Kerala	98.9 (67.7)	47.3 (32.3)	146.2 (76)
Madhya Pradesh	146.3 (71.0)	59.8 (29.0)	206.1 (56)
Maharashtra	271.3 (67.9)	128.4 (32.1)	399.8 (88)
Orissa	100.4 (63.7)	57.3 (36.3)	157.8 (80)
Punjab	101.3[b] (57.7)	74.3 (42.3)	175.6 (134)
Rajasthan	117.1 (58.0)	84.9 (42.0)	202.0 (86)
Tamil Nadu	191.4 (65.5)	100.8 (34.5)	292.2 (79)
Uttar Pradesh	252.4 (58.9)	176.4 (41.1)	428.2 (52)
West Bengal	185.9 (74.1)	64.3 (25.9)	250.2 (62)
All States	2185.4 (62.8)	1294.0 (37.2)	3479.4 (70)

1994-97 (a.a.)			*Growth in Expenditure (no. of times)*		
Revenue expend.	*Capital expend.*[d]	*Total expend.*	*Revenue expend.*	*Capital expend.*[d]	*Total expend.*
11507 (80.2)[c]	2835 (19.8)[f]	14342 (2000)[e]	66.3	22.2	47.6
3473 (82.3)	746 (17.7)	4219 (1714)	41.3	19.0	34.2
8147 (89.3)	979 (10.7)	9126 (962)	69.3	38.2	59.9
8858 (80.8)	2105 (19.2)	10963 (2458)	174.8	33.2	116.2
6134 (88.2)	824 (11.8)	6958 (3851)	66.6	20.5	48.3
8649 (83.0)	1766 (17.0)	10415 (2168)	59.6	22.1	47.5
5894 (84.9)	1047 (15.1)	6941 (2246)	64.7	25.6	53.4
9467 (86.1)	1529 (13.9)	10996 (1524)	64.9	35.3	55.4
17609 (79.5)	4527 (20.5)	22136 (2577)	46.0	17.5	35.6
4617 (82.2)	1002 (17.8)	5619 (1640)	61.2	15.5	41.9

Contd...

Contd...

6201 (84.3)	1151 (15.7)	7352 (3404)	66.9	26.7	50.0
7835 (77.6)	2263 (22.4)	10098 (2095)	58.5	19.0	44.9
11203 (85.4)	1919 (14.6)	13122 (2251)	68.9	24.0	50.5
17387 (80.4)	4235 (19.6)	21622 (1440)	47.7	32.2	43.7
8873 (81.1)	2068 (18.9)	10941 (1493)	67.5	25.6	51.9
147465 (81.6)	33171 (18.4)	180636 (1972)			

Source: As in Table 3.1

Notes: a: average for 1966-68.
b: includes Haryana for 1965-68.
c: revenue expenditure as percentage to total expenditure.
d: refers to total disbursement.
e: per capita expenditure based on population estimates for 1966 and 1995, respectively.
f: as percentage to total expenditure.

In the development expenditure, social services accounted for the lion's share -- being 60.6, 55.2 and 56.8 per cent in the periods, respectively.

In the expenditure under social services, the relative share of both education and medical and public health declined -- the former from 21.7 per cent of total revenue expenditure during 1975-78 to 15.6 per cent during 1994-97, and the latter from 9.9 to 7.2 over the same period. Nutrition, a relatively new item, has shown a rapid growth in recent years, constituting 5.8 per cent of the total during 1988-91. Although education continues to receive the highest proportion of expenditure under social services, probably the allocation to different levels is not very appropriate. The higher education, whose users are from the richer section of population, continues to be heavily subsidised. And this education has been largely of an ornamental nature, not functional to the needs of development.

The relative share of economic services has shown a rather steep decline in recent years, consequent on the growth of spendings under social services. During 1994-97, it accounted for only 29.3 per cent of total revenue expenditure as against 32.3 during 1988-91. Within economic services, the relative share of agriculture and allied sectors decreased drastically, from 43 per cent during 1975-78 to 14.6 in 1994-97. Rural development, an important segment for the weaker sections, became prominent in the eighties, but its share declined to 18.8 per cent in 1994-97 from 24.3 in 1988-91. The highest growth in expenditure was recorded by village and small-scale industries, but its relative share continued to be very low -- being only 2.0 per cent in 1994-97.

Table 3.7

Trend in the Composition of Revenue and Capital Expenditure of Andhra

(Rs. in crores)

Items	*1975-78 (a.a.)*	*1988-91 (a.a.)*	*1994-97 (a.a.)*
Total Revenue expenditure	633.2 (100.0)	4870.4 (100.0)	11506.0 (67.9)
I. Development expenditure	445.0 (70.3)	3511.7 (72.1)	7815.0 (67.9)
a. Social services	269.7 (42.6)	1939.7 (39.8)	4442.2 (38.6)
Education, etc.	137.6[a] (21.7)	977.6 (20.1)	1799.4 (15.6)
Medical and pub. health	62.4 (9.9)	299.9 (6.2)	545.6 (4.7)
Water supply and sanitation	-	102.0 (2.1)	287.8 (2.5)
Nutrition	-	11.5 (0.2)	668.0 (5.8)
b. Economic services	175.4 (27.7)	1572.1 (32.3)	3372.8 (29.3)
Agriculture and allied	75.2 (11.9)	246.0 (5.1)	493.0 (4.3)
Rural development	-	381.4 (7.8)	634.6 (5.5)
Irrigation and flood control	37.4 (5.9)	438.9 (9.0)	833.5 (7.2)
Energy	10.0 (1.6)	36.7 (0.8)	775.8 (6.7)
Village and small industry	2.0 (0.3)	46.6 (1.0)	67.7 (0.6)
Transport and communication	27.2 (4.3)	87.8 (1.8)	204.2 (1.8)
II. Non-development expenditure	173.3 (27.4)	1307.8 (26.9)	3607.4 (31.4)
a. Interest payment	54.4 (8.6)	477.5 (9.8)	1541.4 (14.5)
b. Administrative services	70.8 (11.2)	383.2 (7.9)	858.1 (7.5)
Police	32.3 (5.1)	201.0 (4.1)	505.8 (4.4)
Distt. administration	18.3 (2.9)	76.3 (1.6)	146.8 (1.3)
c. Pension	21.5 (3.4)	284.5 (5.8)	881.0 (7.7)
Capital Disbursements	315.1 (100.0)	1027.2 (100.0)	2834.8 (100.0)
I. Development expenditure	174.0 (55.2)	452.5 (44.1)	1474.0 (52.0)
a. Social services	11.3 (3.6)	43.1 (4.2)	54.3 (1.9)
b. Economic services	162.6 (51.6)	409.5 (39.9)	1419.8 (50.1)
Irrigation and flood control	57.4 (18.2)	315.4 (30.7)	669.5 (23.6)
Energy	23.8 (7.6)	12.0 (1.2)	483.0 (17.0)
Transport and communication	15.0 (4.8)	31.7 (3.1)	174.6 (6.2)
II. Repayment of loans	49.8 (15.8)	208.7 (20.3)	463.4 (16.3)
III. Discharge of internal debt	8.9 (2.8)	32.0 (3.1)	50.3 (1.8)
IV. Loans and advances by state government	81.2 (25.8)	321.6 (31.3)	829.3 (29.3)

Source: As in Table 3.1.

Note: a: includes scientific services and research.

The rapid growth in non-development expenditure prevented an adequate rise in development expenditure. The former multiplied 21 times in the last two decades – from the annual average of Rs. 173 crores during 1975-78 to Rs. 3,607 crores during 1994-97 – as against 18 times in the latter. Its share in total revenue expenditure increased from 27 per cent to 31 over the period.

In non-development expenditure, the, most burdensome item was interest payment. It accounted for 42.7 per cent of the total during 1994-97, rising from 31.4 per cent during 1975-78. The growth in interest payment in this period was 28 times – from the annual average of Rs. 54 crores to Rs. 1,541 crores. It may be noted, however, that Andhra's is not an isolated case of heavy payment on this account; rather it's position is better than that of many other states. During 1990-95, interest payment as percentage to revenue expenditure averaged 13.6 for all states as against 11.8 for Andhra. There were as many as eleven states with higher proportions (RBIFA 1998). It needs to be noted further that interest payments become a matter of concern only in a situation where the loans are not utilised for genuinely productive purposes; and this is largely the position in Andhra, as with most other states.

The second biggest item in non-development expenditure is the payment on pension. It accounted for 24.4 per cent of the total during 1994-97, rising from 12.4 in 1975-78. The growth in payments over the period was 41 times. In relation to the position in other states also Andhra's was one of the worst; in fact only Karnataka had a worse situation. Payments on administrative services too were quite high. It constituted 7.5 per cent of total revenue expenditure during 1994-97, declining from 11.2 per cent in 1975-78. The expenditure on police here accounted for nearly 60 per cent in recent years rising from 46 in mid-seventies. If one raises the question of productivity, such huge payments cannot be justified.

Capital Expenditure

It is not only that the relative share of capital disbursements in total expenditure has declined over the years, that of development expenditure in it has also declined. Capital disbursements constituted only 19.8 per cent of total during 1994-97 as against 33.2 per cent in 1975-78 and 42.4 in 1965-68. The growth in expenditure here was only 22 times over the entire period as against 48 times in total expenditure. As regards development expenditure, its share in capital disbursements was down to 44.1 per cent in 1988-91 from 55.2 in 1975-78; in the following years there were some recovery but could not reach the earlier level (Table 3.7).

In development expenditure, economic services accounted for the overwhelming proportion – as much as 96 per cent during 1994-97. In the aggregate of capital disbursements, its share stood at 50.1 per cent during 1994-97, rising from 39.9 during 1988-91. Irrigation and flood control was the most important item here. Its share rose to 30.7 per cent of total capital disbursements during 1988-91 from 18.2 in 1975-78, and declined to 23.6 per cent in 1994-97. In the recent years, energy sector has also become very important. During 1994-97, it accounted for 17 per cent of the total as against a mere 1.2 per cent during 1988-91.

Loans and advances by the state government was the next important item under capital disbursements. It accounted for 31.3 per cent of the total during 1988-91, rising from 25.8 during 1975-78; in recent years, however there has been a decline. The advances were mainly for development purposes, to the extent of nearly 95 per cent. Social services generally accounted for a quarter of it, and the balance by economic services. In the latter, power projects accounted for a very large share – to the extent of 94 per cent during 1994-97.

Repayment of loans to the Centre came next. It accounted for 16.3 per cent of total capital disbursements during 1994-97, declining from 20.3 during 1988-91. The amount of repayment, however, fluctuated widely from year to year. For example, it rose to Rs. 828 crores in 1996-97 from Rs. 294 crores in the preceding year, but declined again to a very low level in the succeeding year. The discharge of internal debt, which did not involve a very large sum, also fluctuated widely. In 1995-96, it rose to Rs. 109 crores from only Rs. 17 crores in the preceding year and declined again to Rs. 25 crores in 1996-97.

Such wide fluctuations in amount of repayments made the capital outlay to vary greatly from year to year. In the last six years, while the highest was Rs. 2,422 crores in 1995-96 the lowest stood at Rs. 131 crores in 1996-97. The annual average for 1994-97 came to Rs. 1,492 crores as against Rs. 175 crores during 1975-78, that is, a growth of 8.5 times.

Plan Expenditure

The plan expenditures under the budget came mainly from the capital account. In 1995-96, in the total of capital disbursement in Andhra, the

Table 3.8

Trend in Expenditure under Different Five-Year Plans in Andhra

(Rs. in crores)

Head of Expenditure	*II Plan*	*III Plan*	*IV Plan*	*V Plan*	*VI Plan*	*VII Plan*	*VIII Plan*[c]
Agriculture and allied	29.2 (15.5)	50.4 (14.3)	40.9 (9.1)	75.6 (7.5)	118.2 (3.6)	271.6 (4.5)	413.0 (3.9)
Animal husbandry	2.4 (1.3)	1.9 (0.5)	1.7 (0.4)	4.0 (0.4)	10.2 (0.3)	25.0 (0.4)	-
Forests	1.0 (0.5)	1.4 (0.4)	2.7 (0.6)	4.8 (0.5)	17.0 (0.5)	58.5 (1.0)	-
Fisheries	0.6 (0.3)	1.4 (0.4)	1.8 (0.4)	4.5 (0.4)	14.1 (0.4)	23.8 (0.4)	-
Rural development	-	-	-	22.4 (2.2)	186.8[a] (5.8)	504.9 (8.4)	534.0 (5.1)
Irrigation	65.5 (34.8)	121.9 (34.6)	117.8 (26.2)	442.3 (44.1)	861.3 (26.6)	1434.7 (24.0)	2500.0 (23.8)
Power	38.5 (20.4)	93.6 (26.6)	190.6 (42.5)	537.2 (53.5)	740.8[b] (22.8)	1044.3 (17.5)	3042.6 (29.0)
Industry and minerals	10.1 (5.4)	15.2 (4.3)	14.7 (3.3)	53.6 (5.3)	204.9 (6.3)	299.2 (5.0)	272.5 (2.6)
Large and medium industries	1.5 (0.8)	5.8 (1.7)	8.3 (1.8)	27.6 (2.7)	130.8 (4.0)	143.1 (2.4)	-
Village and small-scale	8.6 (4.6)	8.9 (2.5)	5.2 (1.2)	14.7 (1.5)	45.1 (1.4)	101.2 (1.7)	-
Transport and communication	9.5 (5.1)	17.0 (4.8)	28.9 (6.4)	125.7 (12.5)	230.7 (7.1)	605.5 (10.1)	1153.5 (11.0)
Social and comm. services	33.0 (17.5)	52.9 (15.0)	55.7 (12.4)	177.4 (17.7)	876.1 (27.0)	1717.9 (28.7)	2066.5 (19.7)
Education	12.4 (6.6)	21.1 (6.0)	15.4 (3.4)				
Medical and pub. health	8.4 (4.4)	12.8 (3.6)	4.7 (1.0)				
Welfare of SC, ST & OBC	4.4 (2.3)	3.6 (1.0)	7.9 (1.8)				
Grand Total	188.6 (100.0)	352.4 (100.0)	448.9 (100.0)				

Contd...

Contd...

24.0 (2.4)	105.7 (3.3)	289.8 (4.8)	313.4 (3.0)
17.7 (1.8)	54.8 (1.7)	138.4 (2.3)	183.3 (1.7)
31.3 (3.1)	164.8 (5.1)	370.8 (6.2)	450.0 (4.3)
1004.3 (100.0)	3243.6 (100.0)	5976.6 (100.0)	10500.0 (100.0)

Source: GOA 1986, 1981, 1986a: I, 1993a: 1.

Notes: a: a separate head since Sixth Plan, not included in agriculture and allied services.
b: energy since the Sixth Plan.
c: approved outlay.

plan expenditure constituted 84.1 per cent as against 66.4 in 1990-91 and 58.1 in 1975-76. In the revenue account, the proportion in these years were, respectively, 13.4, 16.9 and 11.1 per cent. Below we give a brief look into the pattern of plan expenditure in Andhra.

The plan expenditure of Andhra, as is evident from Table 3.8, increased from Rs. 189 crores during the Second Plan to Rs. 10,500 crores during the Eighth Plan, that is, a growth of around 56 times in current prices. The percentage increase over the preceding plan varied between the highest of 223.0 in the Sixth Plan and the lowest of 27.6 in the Fourth Plan. The per capital plan outlays of Andhra increased from Rs. 48.61 in the Second Plan to Rs. 96.67 in the Fourth Plan, Rs. 568.30 in the Sixth Plan and Rs. 1,523 during 1990-91 to 1994-95. These figures were lower than the all-India average in all the plans except Second Plan. In the latest period, there were nine major states with higher level of per capita expenditure than Andhra's.[2]

As regards the sectoral outlays, irrigation and flood control generally received a very high priority. Its relative share in total expenditure varied between the highest of 44.1 per cent in the Fifth Plan and the lowest at 23.8 per cent in the Eighth Plan. This level of preference is perfectly justified, given the importance of agriculture and the number of drought-prone districts in the state. However, the question remains how far appropriate the distribution of expenditure was between major, medium and minor irrigation, and among the districts on the basis of urgency of need. This has been looked into in the chapter on agriculture. The next important item was power, with the allocation varying between 53 per cent of the total in the Fifth Plan and the lowest of 17 per cent in the Seventh Plan. The investment in power multiplied 79 times between the Second Plan and the Eighth Plan as against 38 times in irrigation. In transport and communication, although the growth in expenditure was the highest, its relative share in the total was quite low. Between the Second Plan and Eighth Plan, the expenditure here increased 121 times and the relative share rose to the highest of 12.5 per cent in the Fifth Plan.

In the production sectors, the share of agriculture and allied services showed a substantial decline, from 15.5 per cent in the Second Plan to around 4 per cent in the last three plans. Fisheries, forestry and animal husbandry in it did not receive a fair treatment. The proportion for animal husbandry was less than half of one per cent in all the plans except two. In fisheries, it was never above 0.4 per cent. For industry and minerals, the proportion varied between the highest of 6.3 per cent in the Sixth Plan and the lowest at 2.6 in the Eighth Plan. The allocation for village and small-scale industries (VSI) here was very low. The growth in expenditure between the Second Plan and the Seventh Plan was only around 12 times as against 29 times in industry as a whole. Its relative share consequently declined sharply (Table 3.8).

To the social sector, the plan allocation increased noticeably only in the recent plans. Its relative share in total expenditure averaged 25 per cent in the last three plans as against 15.6 per cent in the preceding four plans. The growth in expenditure between the Second Plan and the Eighth Plan was around 63 times. Within the sector, the allocations for medical and public health and education were relatively low. The former received an average of less than 2 per cent of total expenditure in the last three plans as against around 4 per cent in the Second and Third Plans. For education, the proportion in these periods declined from more than 6 per cent to around 4 per cent. The welfare of backward classes, however, raised its share substantially in the recent plans, to an average of 5.2 per cent in the last three Plans as against less than 2 per cent till the Fourth plan. All these areas needed a much greater attention, with overriding emphasis on the rural areas.

It is not only the amount of allocation, even the quality of planning left much to be desired. Sometimes, the gap between approved outlay and actual expenditure was very wide. For example, in the Seventh Plan, in an important sector like general education the utilisation was only 69 per cent of the approved outlay – Rs. 252.6 crores out of Rs. 366.1 crores. On the other hand, in the transport sector the utilisation was 157 per cent of the outlay. In the Sixth Plan, the expenditure under industry and minerals was 194 per cent of the approved outlay.

From the above analysis it is apparent that there is substantial scope for economy in expenditure. We may note here the position of only two items: salaries and wages, and subsidies and transfer payments. Most of the government departments are overstaffed. There has been a rapid growth in number of government employees in Andhra. Between March 1982 and March 1988 it increased from 391 thousand to 502 thousand, that is, a compound growth rate of 4.25 per cent; this is in contrast to the growth of 3.62 per cent for all states (Rao 1992). If the government were interested in economy and efficiency, it could identify the surplus manpower and arrange for their redeployment through a detailed review of every activity. Secondly, a state should not go for pay revision by imitating the Centre or any other state. Propriety demands that the salary levels in government and government-aided institutions in a state be related to its SDP level.

As regards subsidies, etc., presently a wide range of social security and welfare payments such as old-age pension, widow pension, agricultural labourers pension, schemes for school children, and subsidies on food, cloth, etc., are there in Andhra. The expenditure on subsidy payments had an annual growth of 6.0 per cent during 1980-81 to 1987-88 and on transfer payments at the rate of 12.12 per cent (Rao 1992). In many of the cases the coverage is too wide and a large proportion of the beneficiaries are not really the intended vulnerable groups (Parthasarthy 1995). A careful review of the programmes and designing them to reach only the vulnerable groups would have saved a substantial amount of expenditure.

Notes

1. Administrative Reforms Committee had suggested that the assistance to such schemes should not exceed one-sixth of the assistance given to plan schemes. But it has been totally ignored. It needs to be noted that many of the centrally sponsored programmes are of dubious value, and they have distorted the state's spending priorities.
2. The population figures used in calculation relate to 1961 for the Second Plan, 1971 for Fourth Plan, 1981 for Sixth Plan and for 1990-95 estimate for 1993.

4

Agricultural Transformation

The agricultural sector is of critical importance to every developing economy as it provides food to the people, and work to a large segment of population. In the Andhra's economy this sector is particularly important as we have noted in Chapter 2; a relatively large proportion of the state's income is derived from agriculture. The object of this chapter is to analyse the pattern of growth in agriculture and allied activities over the years since independence. The study is divided into two parts: the first dealing with agriculture proper – that is, the raising of crops, and the second with the allied sectors – that is, animal husbandry, fishery and forestry. In the first part, after analysing the pattern of growth, the causative factors have been looked into.

I
Agriculture

Andhra's growth in agricultural production over the years has not been appreciable. In terms of value, over a period of two decades it increased by only 51.4 per cent – from the annual average of Rs. 895.8 crores during 1962-65 to Rs. 1356.4 crores in 1980-83; the all-India growth in this period was 54.3 per cent. However, among the southern states its performance was the best. As regards productivity, the value per hectare increased from Rs. 597.94 to Rs. 924.20 here in this period as against from Rs. 743.27 to Rs. 1,063.82 for all-India (all in constant 1970-71 prices) (Bhalla and Tyagi 1989).

In recent years also Andhra's performance was not encouraging. The index number of production for all crops averaged only 138.5 during 1994-97, with the base of triennium ending 1981-82=100. In the last six years, 1990-91 to 1995-96, Andhra had a compound annual growth of only 2.6 per cent in agriculture, which was the worst among the southern states (GOA 1999; RBI 1998).

Foodgrains

In foodgrains, the most important group of crops, Andhra's relative position has worsened considerably over the years, as evident from Table 4.1. In 1960-63, the per capita production here stood at 180.3 kg/year, which was better than the position in eight of the major states. After one decade, during 1970-73, it declined to 149.1 kg, which was much below the national average. This position is more or less continuing. During 1993-96, the per capita production in Andhra stood at 168.3 kg as against the national average at 207.7 kg.

As regards productivity, the yield per hectare increased from the average of 724 kg during 1960-63 to 766 during 1970-73 and 1,737 kg during 1993-96. In relation to other states, the latest position is much better than what existed earlier. In 1970-73, Andhra's yield rate was significantly lower than the national average but presently it is higher by 14.5 per cent. In 1970-73 there were nine states with higher yield rate than Andhra's but during 1993-96 it was only five (Table 4.1).

As regards crop-wise growth, the most important crop rice had recorded an increase of 91.5 per cent in production in the pre-green revolution period -- from the annual average of 22.7 lakh tonnes during 1949-52 to 43.5 during 1965-68. In the post-green revolution period, spanning two and half decades, the increase was by 104.9 per cent -- from 45.9 lakh tonnes during 1970-73 to 94.0 lakh tonnes during 1994-97. This is not a very remarkable increase. Moreover, there was a slackening of growth in the last one-and-half decade. The growth between 1970-73 and 1980-83 was 63.9 per cent as against only 25.0 per cent between 1980-83 and 1994-97 (Table 4.2).

Among other crops, production of jowar, bajra and ragi declined drastically in recent years. The production of Jowar in 1994-97 was less than half the level in 1980-83; for bajra it was down to one-third over the same period, and in ragi also a substantial decline. Production of maize, however, recorded a rapid rise throughout the period of more than four decades. In the pre-green revolution period, there was a five-fold rise in production and in the following three decades another four-and-half times.

In the growth of production, the contribution of acreage increase was dominant in the pre-green revolution period as against yield improvement in the post-green revolution period. In case of rice, the

Table 4.1

Trend in Production and Productivity of Foodgrains: Andhra vis-a-vis Other Major States

States	1960-63 (a.a.)		1970-73 (a.a.)		1993-96 (a.a.)		Growth (%)[c]	
	Per capita prod. kg/year	Productivity kg/ha	Per capita prod. kg/year	Productivity kg/ha	Per capita prod.[b] kg/year	Productivity kg/ha	Production	Productivity
Andhra Pradesh	180.3	724	143.1	766	168.3	1737	-6.7	139.9
Assam	136.2	874	143.2	988	146.4	1303	7.5	49.1
Bihar	159.0	749	154.4	881	139.1	1460	-12.5	94.9
Gujarat	104.8	473	135.4	755	99.8	1097	-4.8	131.9
Karnataka	164.7	5636	189.2	817	179.7	1227	9.1	128.9
Kerala	64.5	1313	63.0	1458	32.8	1900	-49.1	44.7
Madhya Pradesh	285.1	602	263.4	652	265.3	1063	-6.9	76.6
Maharashtra	166.9	525	89.9	282	145.5	897	-12.8	70.9
Orissa	228.4	843	220.5	826	218.0	1193	-4.6	41.5
Punjab[a]	340.6	892	510.4	1535	991.8	3610	191.2	304.7

Contd...

Contd...

Rajasthan	251.1	452	263.4	539	199.9	777	-20.4	71.9
Tamil Nadu	165.1	1102	169.6	1365	153.0	2187	-7.3	98.5
Uttar Pradesh	190.0	760	208.0	943	260.5	1883	37.1	147.8
West Bengal	153.2	988	170.1	1217	182.1	2023	18.9	104.8
All-India	-	-	188.9	847	207.7	1517	-	-

Source: Krishnaji 1975; CMIE 1998.

Notes: a: includes Haryana in the first two periods. b: based on population estimates for 1994. c: between 1960-63 and 1993-96.

Table 4.2

Trend in Area, Production and Yield of Major Crops in Andhra
(A: area in '000 ha, P: production in '000 tonnes, Y: yield in kg/ha.)

Crops	1949-52 (a.a.)			1965-68 (a.a.)			1970-73 (a.a.)			1980-83 (a.a.)			1994-97 (a.a.)			Growth A (%)			Growth B (%)		
	A	P	Y	A	P	Y	A	P	Y	A	P	Y	A	P	Y	A	P	Y	A	P	Y
Foodgrains																					
Rice	2300	2271	987	3287	4350	1323	3163	4586	1453	3687	7517	2040	3767	9397	2493	42.9	91.5	34.0	19.1	104.9	71.6
Jowar	2015	780	387	2491	1140	458	2649	1112	420	2128	1312	617	895	640	717	23.6	46.2	18.3	-66.2	42.4	70.7
Bajra	548	243	443	592	301	508	537	233	433	517	346	667	132	117	890	8.0	23.9	14.7	-75.4	-49.8	105.5
Maize	147	41	280	223	204	916	271	310	1147	328	700	2133	344	937	2723	51.7	397.6	227.1	26.9	202.3	137.4
Ragi	290	248	854	324	258	795	267	239	897	252	255	1013	124	151	1217	11.7	4.0	-6.9	-53.6	-36.8	35.7
Non-Food Crops																					
Groundnut	1140	1010	886	1266	829	655	1476	1102	747	1420	1143	800	2200	2127	967	11.1	-17.9	-26.1	49.1	93.0	29.5
Cotton	361	120	59	303	126	74	316	126	67	445	679	260	970	1628	287	-16.1	5.1	25.4	207.0	1192.1	328.4
Sugarcane[b]	70.4	456	6.5	448	982	2.2	124	9870	79.6	161	12540	77.8	207	15390	74.3	536.4	115.4	-66.0	66.9	55.9	-6.7
Tobacco	128	102	796	210	159	757	228	171	747	202	209	1030	144	173	1210	64.1	55.9	-4.9	-36.89	1.2	62.0
Castor	-	-	-	281	54.4	193	306	55	180												
Sosamum	-	-	-	240	45.5	189	249	39	157												
Chillies	160	101	632	173	105	607	191	128	660												
Turmeric	12.5	59.7	4776	14.9	-	-	21	46	2170												
Coconut[c]	-	-	-	33.9	-	-	38	165	4327												
Onions	17.2	160	9285	15.5	117	7548	-	-	-												
Banana	-	-	-	-	-	-	15.1	144	9527												

Contd...

Contd...

277	50	180	259	75	287	-	-	-	-15.4	36.4	59.4
174	29	167	189	42	220	-	-	-	23.2	7.7	40.1
167	168	1010	218	293	1805	8.1	4.0	-4.0	14.1	206.2	173.5
27	72	2697	54	305	5619	19.2	-	-	157.1	563.0	158.9
43	180	4133	89	1033	11619	-	-	-	134.2	526.1	168.5
16	125	7987	24	422	13573	9.9	16.9	-18.7	-	-	-
19	326	16930	42	789	18931	-	-	-	178.1	447.9	98.7

Source: GOA 1960, 1972; CMIE 1998.

Notes: a: production in '000 bales of 180 kg each.
b: yield in tonnes/ha; the production figures for first two periods are in terms of gur, and therefore not comparable with the rest.
c: production in million nuts and yield in nut/ha.
Growth A: refers to the period 1949-52 to 1965-68.
Growth B: refers to 1970-73 to 1994-97.

contribution of acreage increase in the former period was to the extent of 42.9 per cent, and of productivity 34.0 per cent. In the post-'green revolution' period, in the first decade, the growth in productivity was to the extent of 40.4 per cent as against 16.6 in acreage, and in the following years 22.2 per cent and 2.2 respectively.

In maize, however, even in the pre-'green revolution' period, the production increase was mainly due to growth in productivity, as may be seen from Table 4.2. For bajra, jowar and ragi, there were sharp declines in area in the post-'green revolution' period, and whatever growth in production came was solely due to yield improvement.

Non-Food Crops

Non-food crops occupy an import position in the agricultural economy of Andhra. In the state's total of gross cropped area, its share was 51.0 per cent in 1995-96 as against the national average of 33.50 per cent (CMIE 1999c). Among the non-food crops, in terms of area, groundnut is the most important crop. But the performance here had been dismal. In the pre-'green revolution' period, the production declined due to a sharp fall in yield rate, and in the following years also the growth was not much. Over a period of two-and-half decades, between 1970-73 and 1994-97, there was only a 93 per cent increase in production, consequent on 49 per cent rise in acreage and 29 per cent in yield rate. Cotton with the second largest acreage, however, had a magnificent performance in the post-green revolution period. There was a 13-fold rise in production, with the yield rate recording 328 per cent increase and the acreage 207 per cent.

Among other crops, sugarcane, castor, chillies, sesamum and tobacco were important. Sugarcane had a disappointing performance in the post-green revolution period. Over the entire period of two-and-half decades, there was a growth in production of only 56 per cent as against 115 per cent in the pre-green revolution period of less than two decades. The growth was solely due to acreage increase in both the periods. In castor, which had a substantial acreage under it, the growth in production was still lower, by only 36 per cent over the entire period of post-green revolution period. The acreage under it declined by 15 per cent over the period and the productivity increased by 59 per cent. Chillies recorded a noticeable growth only in recent years. In the pre-green revolution period, there was a mere 4 per cent increase in production, and even in the post-green revolution period, it was not much. Over the entire period of two-and-half decades the production was a little more than trebled, consequent on a 173 per cent increase in yield rate and 14 per cent in acreage. The other two crops with substantial acreage, sesamum and tobacco, recorded a negligible growth in production; the latter had a reduction in acreage by more than a third in the post-green revolution period.

There were a few crops with low acreage registering remarkable increases in production. The output of turmeric increased by 563 per cent between 1970-73 and 1994-97, with a 159 per cent rise in yield rate and 157 per cent in area. Coconut also had a similar growth. There was a 526 per cent rise in production with 168 per cent in yield rate and 134 in acreage. Banana was also not far behind; it had 448 per cent rise in production in this period, with 99 per cent growth in yield rate and 178 per cent in area (Table 4.2).

Regional Disparity

Andhra is a large state with wide diversity in physiographic conditions, as noted in Chapter 2. Therefore, differences in agricultural productivity are quite natural. But as human efforts can reduce its intensity, below we give a brief look into the changes that have come over the years. The analysis is based only on the most important group of crops, cereals.

It is evident from Table 4.3 that the growth in yield rate of cereals varied widely from district to district. Between 1967-68 and 1993-94, while there were five districts with more than 200 per cent growth, nine had less than 100 per cent. Most of the districts in the

Table 4.3

District-wise Disparity in Yield Rate and Provision of Facilities in Andhra

Districts	Rice		Total cereals		Net irrig.area as % to net sown area		Credit per ha.[b]
	1981-84 (av.)	1990-93 (av.)	1967-68	1993-94	1967-68	1996-97	1994-95
Srikakulam	1738	2138 (22.6)[c]	742	1948 (162.5)[c]	49.4	54.0	713
Vizianagram	1352	2236 (65.4)	-	1631 (-)	-	43.0	359
Visakhapatnam	1105	1626 (47.1)	541	931 (72.1)	37.0	36.0	1147
E. Godavari	2332	2254 (-3.3)	1436	2988 (108.1)	60.4	64.6	2348
W. Godavari	2690	2637 (-2.0)	1713	3200 (86.8)	72.6	76.2	2705
Krishna	2102	2683 (27.6)	1455	2898 (99.2)	63.3	63.9	3057
Guntur	2459	3020 (22.8)	1052	3243 (208.3)	27.7	54.2	653
Prakasam	2162	2553 (18.1)	-	2351 (-)	-	35.0	541
Nellore	1890	2401 (27.0)	782	2896 (270.3)	40.8	80.2	440
Chittoor	2022	2278 (12.7)	1098	2134 (94.4)	34.8	36.4	551
Cuddapah	2121	2764 (30.3)	891	2601 (191.9)	27.2	35.0	725
Kurnool	1861	2496 (34.1)	531	1460 (175.0)	8.5	19.0	392
Anantapur	1969	2302 (16.9)	477	1507 (215.9)	10.0	15.0	580
Mahaboobnagar	1636	2112 (29.1)	572	912 (59.4)	11.5	19.1	371
Nalgonda	2346	2647 (12.8)	565	2218 (292.6)	14.8	39.3	868
Rangareddy	1682	2277 (35.4)	740[a]	1198 (61.9)	14.6[a]	20.9	294
Khammam	1890	2215 (17.2)	689	2091 (203.5)	18.3	42.7	275
Medak	1785	1930 (8.1)	901	1457 (61.7)	22.1	30.1	399
Warangal	1793	2266 (26.4)	778	2017 (159.3)	27.0	62.5	163
Karimnagar	2167	2573 (18.7)	938	2599 (177.1)	25.9	69.6	689
Nizamabad	2183	2250 (3.1)	1526	2075 (36.0)	41.4	59.3	423
Adilabad	1461	1414 (-3.2)	687	1321 (92.3)	6.1	11.9	255
State	2093	2392 (14.3)	877	2179 (148.5)	27.2	40.3	785

Source: GOA 1972, 1997, 1999; CMIE 1996b.

Notes: a: relates to Hyderabad.
b: from primary agricultural credit societies, based on net sown area of 1993-94.
c: figures in parentheses are percentage growth over the period.

latter had very low productivity in the initial year. There was hardly any reduction in disparity over the years. The highest yield in 1967-68 was 359 per cent of the lowest, and in 1993-94 it was 356.

If only the period since 1980s is considered, the situation appears worse. Between 1981-84 and 1990-93, the productivity growth in rice was negative in three districts, one of which was a backward district, as against the highest of 65.4 per cent in Vizianagram. Almost all the districts in Telangana had a very low growth in productivity. The difference between the highest and lowest yield in this period was reduced from 143.4 per cent to 113.6 (Table 4.3).

Poor performance in rice was not always compensated by better performance in other crops. In jowar, during 1990-93, as against the state's average yield of 710 kg/ha and the highest of 1,151 kg in Kurnool, Nalgonda had 418 kg, Mahboobnagar 560 and Adilabad 586. A decade earlier, during 1981-84 also these districts had low yield rate. Against the state average of 631 kg, they had 342, 465 and 464 kg, respectively.

A faster growth in agricultural production required further increase in acreage and/or in productivity. In the following section, we look into the prospects in these areas. Acreage increase is possible only if there is availability of cultivable land, and therefore, a brief look first into the pattern of land use in Andhra.

Pattern of Land Use

It is evident from Table 4.4 that the proportion of reporting area available for cultivation in Andhra is relatively low. It increased from 56.5 per cent of the total in 1970-71 to 60.8 in 1992-93, both of which are lower than that for the country as a whole. In 1992-93, eight of the major states had higher proportions under cultivation. However, the position on per capita land under cultivation was not so bad. At 0.25 ha, it was higher than the national average and below only five of the major states.

The scope for further increase in area under cultivation is quite limited. Forests, accounting for the next highest area, cannot be reduced on environmental considerations. The proportion under non-agricultural use has risen over the years, and it is above the national average. But any reduction in it is unlikely due to population pressure and increasing industrial demand. The culturable waste land is presently only 7.7 lakh hectares, constituting 2.8 per cent of the total reporting area, which is well below the national average. Nevertheless, some land from here may be brought under cultivation.

Another way of augmenting land is to raise the cropping intensity, which is relatively low in Andhra. The grass cropped area here increased from 112.3 per cent of the net area in 1971-72 to 115.2 in 1981-82 and 122.6 in 1995-96; the all-India average in the latest year

Table 4.4
Pattern of Land Use: Andhra vis-a-vis Other Major States

States	*Reporting area 1992-93 (lakh hects.)*	*Land under cultivation*			*% of area under forest*		*% under non-agrl.use*		*Culturable waste 1995-96, (lakh hects.)*	*Gross cropped area (lakh hects.)*	
		per capita 1992-93[a]	*% of reporting area*		*1973-74*	*1995-96*	*1970-71*	*1992-93*		*1971-72*	*1995-96*
			1970-71	*1992-93*							
(1)	*(2)*	*(3)*	*(4)*	*(5)*	*(6)*	*(7)*	*(8)*	*(9)*	*(10)*	*(11)*	*(12)*
Andhra Pradesh	274.1	0.25	56.5	60.8	23.0	22.41	7.7	8.8	7.7 (2.8)[c]	126.5 (112.3)[e]	130.4 (122.6)[e]
Gujarat	188.2	0.32	66.0	70.2	8.3[b]	10.03	4.1	6.0	19.8 (10.5)	104.8 (107.4)	100.8 (104.9)
Haryana	43.8	0.23	85.3	86.8	2.7	3.90	7.0	7.3	0.3 (0.8)	50.5 (141.5)	59.7 (166.6)
Karnataka	190.5	0.31	65.2	73.3	15.1	16.07	5.0	6.3	4.4 (2.3)	109.9 (106.4)	119.6 (114.8)
Kerala	38.9	0.08	59.2	62.9	27.3	27.85	7.1	7.8	0.9 (2.3)	29.6 (135.3)	30.7 (135.4)
Madhya Pradesh	443.4	0.39	49.8	57.6	32.4	33.08	4.7	5.5	15.3 (3.4)	208.9 (113.2)	250.4 (126.8)
Maharashtra	307.6	0.29	67.6	73.3	17.4	17.16	2.8	3.7	9.8 (3.2)	181.1 (106.3)	213.3 (119.1)
Orissa	155.4	0.28	49.0	56.3	39.2	36.75	6.4	5.0	5.4 (3.5)	68.7 (119.2)	96.7 (155.7)
Punjab	50.3	0.21	85.0	84.6	2.8	5.70	8.3	8.2	0.3 (0.5)	57.2 (140.4)	77.5 (187.3)
Tamil Nadu	130.1	0.15	63.2	65.2	15.4	16.48	11.5	14.4	3.0 (2.3)	76.4 (120.4)	62.7 (117.3)
W. Bengal	88.5	0.09	65.8	67.1	13.4	13.76	14.6[d]	18.4	1.1 (1.2)	71.7 (133.0)	89.7 (164.3)
All-India	3050.0	0.23	58.5	64.2	21.6	22.57	5.4	7.2	146.4 (4.8)	1651.9 (118.2)	1865.6 (131.2)

Source: CMIE 1996b, 1999c.

Notes: a: on the basis of 1991 population. b: relates to 1972-73. c: figures in parentheses are percentages in relation to reporting area. d: relates to 1980-81. e: as percentage to net cropped area.

stood at 131.2, and the highest of 187.3 in Punjab. The gross cropped area of Andhra increased by a measly 3.1 per cent between 1971-72 and 1995-96 as against 12.9 per cent in all-India (Table 4.4).

It is not only that there is much scope for raising the gross cropped area, the productivity of land can also be raised through larger and better utilisation of inputs. All these, however, require motivational changes on the side of farmers, and here the government has a big role to play. We give a brief look into the landholding pattern and the availability of some of the important inputs and infrastructure.

Landholding Pattern

Whether the land cultivated by a farmer is owned by him or held under lease is an important consideration in making investment in the land. Similarly, the size of landholding determines whether he can be a full-time farmer. Very large holdings also have certain diseconomies. Then there is the question of whether all the lands are held in one let, or scattered in different parcels. Under the latter situation there will be problems in the way of proper utilisation of the land.

The situation as existed in rural India, including Andhra Pradesh, after independence was one of high concentration of land ownership. Andhra's situation was the worst among all the states. Here top 20 per cent accounted for 83 per cent of the area in 1953-54 and top one per cent 24.45; the bottom 40 per cent had only 1.02 per cent. The national averages were respectively, 77.4, 18.4 and 0.36 per cent (NSSO 1957).

The land reform policy of the country was concretised during the first-year plan. Agrarian classes were classified into intermediaries, large owners, small and medium owners, tenants-at-will and landless workers. Special emphasis was given on the abolition of intermediaries, enactment of radical tenancy laws and resumption of cultivation based on peasant proprietorship. The need for providing a ceiling and lower limit to agricultural lands was also recommended.

Tenancy Reform

The land tenure systems in Andhra Pradesh differed as between Telangana, Andhra and the scheduled areas. Telangana, which represented mainly the former state of Hyderabad, had *jagirdari* and *inamdari* systems. The jagirs and inams were free grants or sub-grants from the state with the right to collect and appropriate land revenue. By mid-fifties all the jagirs and most of the inams in Telangana were abolished.

In the scheduled areas, which were formerly part of the Madras state and comprised of East Godavari, West Godavari, Vizag and Srikakulam districts, all the rights and powers of the intermediary landlords were abolished by the Madras Estates (Abolition and Conversion into Ryotwari) Act, 1948. In 1969, further regulations were promulgated for the abolition of certain *mahalwari* and *multadari* tenures. In the rest of Andhra also most of the intermediaries were abolished by extending the Act of 1948 and passing another Act in 1956. In all, about 3.87 million hectares of land had vested in the state (Haque and Sirohi 1986: 31). The process of implementation of the legislations, however, took a long time.

As regards security of tenure, the progress in Telangana was better than in the Andhra region. The Andhra Pradesh (Telangana Area) Tenancy and Agricultural Lands Act, 1950, as amended in 1954, provided that (i) certain tenants who had held land for six years on specified dates and tenants holding from substantial holders would be given the status of protected tenants and land held by them become non-resumable; (ii) ordinary tenants were to have a minimum term of lease; (iii) all voluntary surrender of tenancies were to be verified by *Mamlatdar*; (iv) there would be a right of purchase of non-resumable lands upto a certain limit; and (v) there would be *suo moto* transfer of ownership to protected tenants in respect of non-resumable lands. As a result of implementation of this Act, 13,611 protected tenants were declared owners by mid-eighties.

In the Andhra region, the Andhra Pradesh (Andhra Area) Tenancy Act, 1956, as amended in 1974, provided that tenancy would continue, subject to the landlord's right of resumption upto two-third of the ceiling area, the tenant being left with an area not less than one-half of that held by him prior to resumption. But the law did not provide for conferment of ownership right on tenant except through exercise of the right to purchase the land when the landlord intended to sell it. Another drawback was that its implementation rested with the civil courts and not with the revenue administration. Moreover, the Act came into force only from July 1980.

In entire Andhra Pradesh, as on January 1999, there were 1.07 lakh tenants conferred ownership rights or rights protected involving an area of 5.95 lakh acres. Andhra's was the lowest achievement among the major states, and in the all-India total number of such tenants its share was a mere 0.86 per cent (GOI 1999).

The tenancy reform legislation had relatively less loopholes in

Telangana, and the implementation was better. This was primarily because the tenants were more consciously organised here. Besides wide publicity of the legislation in intelligible form, there were legal aids, tenant organisation's representation on tribunals and vigilance in the maintenance of records to make the legislation more effective.

However, on the whole, these Acts often gave protection mainly to the rich peasants. The large farmers had a relatively greater share in the total leased-in area of the state. In 1970-71 medium and large farmers (those with 4-10 hectares and above 10 hectares) together accounted for 59.0 per cent of the total leased-in area, and their share rose to 61.8 per cent in 1976-77. For those with less than 2 hectares, on the other hand, the share declined from 20.8 per cent to 18.3 in this period (Haque and Sirohi 1986: 137). A large number of marginal and small farmers lease out to big and medium farmers because of their low resource base and other adverse circumstances, and they could rarely benefit from the tenancy reform. Moreover, even in the Telangana region it has been found that tenants on oral contracts formed the main group accounting for over 75 per cent of the leased-in area in wet land zone and over 98 per cent in dry land zone (George and Rao 1979: 18). Had the provisions of the law been effectively implemented, there would have been very limited leasing practices now. But, the NSS 48th round found 14.11 per cent of the total number of holdings with leased-in area; of the total area, leased-in constituted 9.57 per cent (NSSO 1997).

As regards rent, the First Five-Year Plan had recommended that it should be so fixed as to leave an adequate margin for the actual cultivators after covering the cost of cultivation and other risks. It was expected to be within one-fourth or one-fifth of the produce. On the basis of the recommendations, different states made legal provisions for regulation of rent. In Andhra Pradesh, for the Andhra region it was fixed at 25 to 30 per cent of produce, and in Telangana region one-fourth to one-fifth of produce or 3-5 times the land revenue. However, in actual practice the rent continued to be far higher, and this was partly because the crop-sharing system itself was not very popular here. In 1992, leasing out for fixed money was found to be accounting for 25.9 per cent of the total area, and 26.8 per cent on fixed produce basis; the proportion at the national level were respectively, 19.0 and 14.5 (NSSO 1997).

The question of rent regulation is, however, not so important as the conferment of ownership right on the tenants, as the ultimate objective was to abolish the system of tenancy. Moreover, in the absence of absolute security of tenure, it is doubtful that any rent regulation measure can ever be effective. The predominance of oral contracts nullified any effective regulation of rent. The insecurity of tenure thus continued to be a stumbling block in the way of raising the productivity of land.

Land Ceiling and Surplus Distribution

Land is a basis for entitlement to a good number of things in rural areas, including social status. Therefore, for reducing rural inequity imposition of land ceiling and distribution of the surplus was a critical necessity. This was particularly important in Andhra, because the proportion of households owning no land was relatively high here. In 1953-54, 30.33 per cent of the households in Andhra were not owning any land as against 23.09 at the national level (NSSO 1957).

However, the imposition of ceiling and distribution of the surplus land was far from satisfactory here, as in case of most other states. At the beginning, the ceiling was fixed at a very high level – at four-and-half times the family holding[1], that is, 27 to 324 acres. Moreover, there could be additional one family-holding for every member in excess of five. After 1973, there was a drastic reduction in the ceiling. For a family of up to 5 persons, it was fixed at 10.18 acres in case of irrigated land with two crops a year, and 15 to 27 acres for irrigated land with one crop a year. These ceilings were revised upward subsequently. The present ceilings are 4.05 to 10.93 hectares (10 to 27 acres) for irrigated land and 14.6 to 21.85 hectares (36.1 to 54 acres) in case of unirrigated land.

The surplus available could not be large. This was not only because the ceilings were high, the enactment of legislations were preceded by a great deal of debate and consequent publicity. All prudent land-owners took steps in good time to distribute the surplus land among their relatives, friends and dependents, and sometimes even among fictitious persons. And then many categories of land were exempted from the ceiling laws, including plantations, sugarcane farms, cooperative gardens, tank fisheries, land held by cooperative societies, by religious, charitable and educational institutions, by an industrial or commercial undertaking, and by specialised farms, among many others. These exemptions gave rise to the problem of ceiling evasion through changing the classification of land.

Land that could be taken possession of from the declared surplus on the basis of 1973 ceilings was quite meagre. Area declared surplus till 1982 was 879,601 acres (i.e., 355,970 hectares), of which only

444,874 acres were taken possession of, and out of it 315,568 acres were distributed to 215,377 beneficiaries (Deb 1986). With the upward revision of ceiling subsequently, the amount of declared surplus came down to 320.3 thousand hectares till September 1998, of which 258.6 thousand were taken possession and 233.7 thousand distributed. Total number of beneficiaries came to 5.29 lakhs with per capita benefit at 0.44 hectare. In the all-India total number of beneficiaries at 55.37 lakhs, Andhra's share was 9.56 per cent (Deb 1997).

That the surplus land could be much more is evident from the persisting concentration of land-ownership in Andhra. In 1971-72, the top 20 per cent households accounted for 75.43 per cent of the total area, and after one decade, in 1982, also it remained at almost the same level -- 75.42 per cent. For top 10 and 5 per cent, there were increases in land-ownership in this period: for the former from 56.16 per cent to 56.83 and for the latter from 39.84 to 40.79. For the bottom 40 per cent, on the other hand, the proportion declined from 1.09 to 0.57. Andhra had one of the highest level of concentration in 1982: the all-India average for top 20 per cent of households stood at 73.19 per cent, for top 10 per cent at 53.78 and for top 5 per cent 37.55. It has been estimated that 13.83 lakh hectares of surplus land could be found in Andhra if the ceiling was fixed at 8 hectares (Sharma 1994).

The land reform measures have brought significant changes in the pattern of operational holdings, as evident from Table 4.5. The proportion of marginal holdings (upto 1 ha) in the total number increased from 47.3 per cent in 1970-71 to 48.6 in 1981-82 and then to as much as 59.3 in 1991-92. Their proportion in area in these years were, respectively, 9.3, 10.2 and 17.5 per cent. The marginal holdings include a large number of sub-marginal ones. For raising their productivity, there is need for cooperativisation, but the progress here is very limited. At the and of June 1978, there were only 1,680 joint farming societies with a membership of 108,511, covering 83,822 hectares, and 910 collective farming societies with a membership of 53,030 and an area of 46,367 hectares (NABARD 1984). Due to lack of resources and the organisation to carry on production, marginal holdings are leasing out land on a large scale. The proportion of marginal holdings leasing-in was no more than 10 per cent in 1992 (NSSO 1997).

The small farms in Andhra had a substantial growth over the years. Between 1970-71 and 1991-92, their share in area was doubled, from 11.7 per cent to 23.3, and in number of holdings from 19.1 per cent to 21.4. No other southern states, or even the national average had such a rapid growth in small farms. The growth in semi-medium holdings was also large. The area under them increased from 21.9 per cent to 26.2 per cent of total, although their share of holdings declined from 18.2 to 13.2 per cent over the period. Leasing-in of land was substantial in both these categories. The proportion of holdings reporting leasing-in in 1992 was 20.53 per cent in case of small farms and 20.93 for semi-medium (NSSO 1997). As regards large holdings, their relative share in total number declined from 3.47 per cent in 1970-71 to 0.81 in 1991-92, and in area from 25.75 per cent to 9.40 per cent. The proportion of holdings leasing-in was, however, highest here, at 21.95 per cent in 1992. The decline of large holdings in Andhra was much faster than at the national level (Table 4.5).

Table 4.5

Changes in Percentage Distribution of Operational Holdings and Area Operated by Size Categories: Andhra vis-a-vis other States

Year/ State	*Marginal (upto 1 ha)*		*Small (1-2 ha)*		*Semi-medium (2-4 ha)*		*Medium (4-10 ha)*		*Large (10 ha & above)*	
	No.	*area*	*No.*	*area*	*No.*	*area*	*No.*	*area*	*No.*	*area*
Andhra										
1970-71	47.3	9.3	19.1	11.7	18.2	21.9	11.9	31.3	3.47	25.75
1981-82	48.6	10.2	22.1	15.4	15.5	21.1	10.8	30.2	2.92	23.10
1991-92	59.3	17.5	21.4	23.2	13.2	26.2	5.4	23.5	0.81	9.40
Karnataka										
1970-71	28.8	5.1	22.8	10.7	25.4	23.0	17.6	34.3	5.40	26.95
1981-82	38.4	5.8	22.5	13.2	22.2	24.1	13.2	32.7	3.65	24.14
1991-92	49.7	9.6	20.3	15.4	18.0	25.2	9.8	30.8	2.28	19.04
Tamil Nadu										
1970-71	60.1	21.9	21.3	22.7	13.2	27.3	4.9	21.7	0.58	6.30
1981-82	71.4	22.4	16.7	26.7	8.3	25.4	3.3	20.7	0.28	4.84
1991-92	77.2	28.9	14.1	28.1	6.6	24.7	1.8	13.2	0.27	5.86
Kerala										
1970-71	86.2	40.0	8.9	24.7	3.7	20.1	1.1	12.3	0.10	2.86
1981-82	88.9	45.4	7.3	24.1	1.3	18.5	1.1	10.1	0.07	2.93
1991-92	91.6	53.3	5.9	23.4	2.0	14.9	0.5	8.1	0.01	0.36
India										
1970-71	45.8	9.2	22.4	14.8	17.7	22.5	11.1	30.5	3.08	22.98
1981-82	56.0	11.5	19.3	16.6	14.2	23.5	8.6	30.1	1.89	18.21
1991-92	62.8	15.6	17.8	18.7	12.0	24.1	6.1	26.4	1.33	15.20

Source: NSSO 1997 (48th Round).

Irrigation Facilities

This is the first prerequisite for growth in agricultural productivity. Dependence on rain water brings great uncertainty in production, and deters farmers from making any substantial investment. Andhra's performance in provision of irrigation facility was, however, not satisfactory. The net irrigated area as percentage to the state's cropped area, as evident from Table 4.6, increased from 27.2 per cent in 1961-62 to 34.9 in 1975-76 and 38.8 in 1995-96.[2] In comparison with the position of other states, this was not a totally disappointing performance. In the recent years, there were only four states with higher proportion of irrigated area than Andhra's.

Among the crops, foodgrains were the main beneficiary from the irrigation facility. The proportion of area under foodgrains irrigated rose to 65.7 per cent in 1996-97 from 42.2 during 1970-73 and 37.6 during 1960-63. Among the states, Andhra's position was fourth in 1992-93 in covering the foodgrains area. Within foodgrains, however, rice and wheat were far ahead of other crops. In 1996-97, rice had 95.5 per cent of its area irrigated and wheat 74.9 per cent as against 33.5 in maize, 26.0 in ragi and a negligible 2.1 in jowar. In non-food crops, the irrigated area in 1996-97 was only 17.6 per cent of the total cropped area.

As regards the sources of irrigation, noticeable changes have taken place over the years. In 1956-57, canals accounted for 44.7 per cent of the total net irrigated area, followed by tanks 41.2 and wells 11.2. In 1980-81, the share of both canals and wells increased while that of tanks declined: canals contributed 48.9 per cent, tanks 26.0 and wells 22.4. Wells increased its share further to 39.3 per cent in 1996-97, while both canals and tanks registered declines – the former to 37.1 per cent and the latter to 19.2 per cent. The decline of tanks was largely due to the growth of tube-wells in the changed socio-economic situation. It may however, be noted that the wells are still less popular in Andhra than in many other states. In 1995-96, wells accounted for 40.16 per cent of total net irrigated area in Andhra as against the national average of 55.68 per cent (GOA 1999, 1998; CMIE 1999c).

On the exploitation of irrigation potential Andhra's performance has been appreciable. The potential created in major and medium irrigation till 1991-92 was 34.1 lakh hectares against the potential of 50 lakh hectares, that is, 68.2 per cent. This was much higher than the all-India average and better than in nine of the major states (Table 4.6). In minor irrigation, however, the performance was relatively low. The potential created till 1990-91 was only 67.1 per cent of the ultimate potential as against the national average of 88.0. An important factor behind this low level of exploitation is inadequate public sector outlay on minor irrigation. In the total expenditure under irrigation and flood control, it constituted only 8.5 per cent in the Sixth Plan and 12.4 per cent in the Seventh Plan.

Table 4.6

Trend in Irrigation Facilities Against the Potential: Andhra vis-a-vis Other Major States

States	Net irrigated area as % to cropped area				Major and medium irrig. (in '000 ha)	
	1961-62	1975-76	1992-93	1995-96	Ultimate potential	Created till 1990-91
Andhra Pradesh	27.2	34.9	38.5	38.8	5000	3411 (68.2)[b]
Bihar	17.5	29.8	46.7	50.3	6500	2749 (42.3)
Gujarat	7.3	15.0	27.6	31.2	3000	1319 (44.0)
Haryana	-	50.3	75.6	78.0	3000	2066 (68.9)
Karnataka	7.3	15.3	20.3	22.1	2500	1497 (59.9)
Kerala	20.3	9.2	14.9	15.1	1000	669 (66.9)
Madhya Pradesh	4.8	8.8	24.4	30.0	6000	2288 (38.1)
Maharashtra	5.8	11.0	13.7	14.3	4100	2035 (49.6)
Orissa	18.9	19.2	32.8	33.7	3600	1472 (40.9)
Punjab	38.4[a]	73.8	93.3	92.9	3000	2702 (90.1)
Rajasthan	12.3	17.1	26.4	31.6	2750	2028 (73.7)
Tamil Nadu	42.2	46.7	46.4	49.1	1500	1471 (98.1)
West Bengal	20.5	19.4	35.8	35.0	2300	1746 (75.9)
All-India	16.9	-	35.2	37.6	58465	32802 (56.1)

Minor irrigation ('000 ha)		% of area under foodgrains irrigated[c]		
Ultimate potential	Created till 1990-91	1960-63	1970-73	1992-93
4200	2817 (67.1)[b]	37.6	42.2	70.9
5900	4608 (78.1)	20.5	25.7	51.6
1750	1878 (107.3)	8.9	12.4	35.5
1550	1502 (96.9)	-	-	97.4
2108	1399 (66.6)	10.8	14.3	27.9

Contd...

Contd...

1100	498 (45.3)	43.0	52.9	39.4
4200	2500 (59.5)	5.1	7.7	33.2
3200	2426 (76.8)	6.2	4.9	17.2
2300	1204 (52.3)	21.7	24.9	34.7
3550	3256 (91.7)	34.4a	58.6a	95.9
2400	2331 (97.1)	12.1	14.5	54.1
3800	2694 (70.9)	24.0	23.1	24.6
55047	48420 (88.0)	-	-	49.6

Source: CMIE 1999c, 1996b; GOI 1964; Deb 1997.

Notes: a: including Haryana.
b: figures in parentheses are percentages in relation to potential.
c: covers only four major cereals (rice, wheat, jowar and maize).

Whatever the performance in the state as a whole, regionally there was wide disparity in the provision of irrigation facility. In 1996-97, net irrigated area as percentage to net sown area was 56.2 in Coastal Andhra, as against 36.6 in Telangana and 23.1 in Rayalaseema. Four decades earlier, in 1956-57, the disparities were much less – the proportions being, respectively, 25.1, 31.5 and 17.9 per cent. The neglect of Rayalaseema is particularly striking because it gets the lowest amount of rainfall. During 1989-90 to 1993-94, the average annual rainfall here varied between 579 and 814 mms as against 876 to 1,577 in coastal Andhra and 782 to 1,344 mms in Telangana (GOA 1997).

District-wise, even in the coastal Andhra, as evident from Table 4.3, there was a great variation in the facility. The highest proportion of area irrigated stood at 80.2 per cent in Nellore in 1996-97 as against the lowest of 35.0 in Prakasam. In Telangana, while Adilabad had only 11.9 per cent of the area irrigated, for Karimnagar it was 69.6. The growth in irrigated area was not always in keeping with the urgency of need. In 1967-68, Kurnool had only 8.5 per cent of its net sown area irrigated, but over the following three decades, ending in 1996-97, its irrigated area increased only 80.0 per cent. On the other hand, Khammam with 18.3 per cent of its area irrigated in 1967-68 had the highest growth of 154.4 per cent.

Although the situation in Telangana has improved considerably over the years, it is necessary to mention here the extent of its deprivation. About 79 per cent catchment of Godavari in Andhra is located in northern Telangana and the remaining in coastal Andhra. Similarly,

69 per cent of the catchment of Krishna in Andhra is in southern Telangana against 18 per cent in Rayalaseema and 13 per cent in coastal Andhra. But the major beneficiary from both the rivers is coastal Andhra. Telangana faces drought conditions on an average once in two-and-half years. The two districts of Mahboobnagar and Nalgonda form the drought core of Telangana and they are located entirely in Krishna basin. The river waters dispute tribunal allocated 800 TMC ft of Krishna water to Andhra. This water is exhausted because of major projects besides medium and minor irrigation. From the major projects coastal Andhra got 56 per cent of water, Rayalaseema 17 per cent and Telangana 27 per cent. The colonial and post-independent policy initiatives always favoured the downstream coastal region at the instance of the influential caste, class and regional leadership of coastal Andhra (Simhadri 1997).

Provision of Inputs and Credit

For raising the productivity of land different types of inputs need to be used at the right time in right proportion. This requires the availability of appropriate infrastructure, and resources at the disposal of farmers. On the side of government, there has to be proper extension services and availability of credit from the banks at the right time. Then there is need for proper distribution network to make the inputs available at appropriate places. There also has to be proper marketing facilities – like arrangements for warehousing, transportation, availability of regulated markets and support prices – to serve as incentive toward larger production. Due to lack of space, our attention is focused on only some of these issues.

Use of Inputs

On high-yielding variety (HYV) seed, it is well known that they were not available for all the important crops according to requirements. Even certified seeds in required quantities could not be had in all parts of the state at the right time. Inadequate availability of breeder and foundation seeds often stood in the way of increased production of certified seeds. It is, therefore, no surprise that the area under HYV was relatively low in Andhra. The proportion of gross cropped area covered by it stood at 34.7 per cent during 1994-97 as against the national average of 39.2 per cent, and the highest at 71 per cent in Punjab. The growth in area under HYV between 1987-90 and 1994-97 was a negligible 6.6 per cent as against 25.3 at the national level (Table 4.7). The gap between target and achievement on area coverage was substantial in recent years. In 1995-96, while the target for five major cereals was 53.12 lakh hectares the achievement came to only 36.87 lakh ha (GOA 1998).

Table 4.7

Trend in Use of Some of the Inputs in Andhra Pradesh vis-a-vis Other Major States

States	Area under HYVs (lakh ha.)		% increase in area	Consumption of fertilisers per hectare (in kg)			
	1987-90 (a.a.)	1994-97 (a.a.)		1966-67	1975-76	1990-91	1995-96
(1)	(2)	(3)	(4)	(5)	(6)	(7)	(8)
Andhra Pradesh	42.41	45.20 (34.7)[a]	6.6	17.5	31.1	133.3	138.0
Bihar	44.30	61.60 (61.5)	39.1	9.0	12.5	56.8	73.9
Gujarat	22.50	23.10 (22.9)	2.7	6.5	14.7	64.9	70.6
Haryana	25.80	28.20 (47.2)	9.3	3.3	18.8	128.3	124.5
Karnataka	19.90	39.33 (32.9)	97.6	7.9	20.2	66.3	75.3
Kerala	2.23	2.43 (7.9)	9.0	21.5	21.6	84.4	66.8
Madhya Pradesh	55.24	76.63 (30.6)	38.7	0.8	5.1	35.4	33.3
Maharashtra	68.95	82.03 (38.5)	19.0	7.3	13.6	66.4	64.4
Orissa	21.20	31.03 (32.1)	46.4	3.6	6.5	20.9	24.4
Punjab	49.71	54.70 (70.6)	10.0	16.3	51.7	171.2	165.8
Rajasthan	26.74	33.07 (16.8)	23.7	1.2	4.4	28.9	33.4
Tamil Nadu	25.99	30.07 (48.0)	15.7	22.0	39.2	115.1	105.6
West Bengal	31.64	45.50 (50.7)	43.8	7.1	17.4	90.3	97.7
All-India	584.31	732.23 (39.2)	25.3	-	17.1	72.4	75.7

			Pumpsets/tubewells energised[c]		Per capita consumption of elect. in agriculture (kwh) 1993-94
1996-97	1997-98	1995-98 (average)	1968-69	1995-96	
(9)	(10)	(11)	(12)	(13)	(14)
135.6	129.9 (4.2)[b]	134.5	123	1643 (12.6)[d]	133.81
78.4	85.9 (6.9)	79.4	50	267 (2.7)	16.10
80.7	101.9 (6.9)	84.4	42	569 (5.6)	200.21

Contd...

Contd...

127.5	140.4 (7.5)	130.8	45	407 (6.8)	227.15
69.1	92.8 (4.6)	79.1	92	1015 (8.5)	130.38
61.2	71.6 (3.3)	66.5	14	305 (9.9)	8.66
38.9	48.9 (9.6)	40.4	25	1131 (4.5)	81.21
62.3	75.3 (5.5)	67.3	125	2026 (9.5)	107.44
25.09	30.1 (4.6)	26.8	1	69 (0.7)	10.25
155.8	169.6 (3.3)	163.7	59	710 (9.2)	300.86
35.6	40.0 (9.1)	36.3	18	515 (2.6)	78.72
126.2	150.4 (3.8)	127.4	410	1529 (24.4)	99.02
99.9	108.8 (6.3)	102.1	1	101 (1.1)	11.15
76.7	86.8 (5.1)	79.7	1089	10276 (5.5)[e]	79.62

Source: GOI 1983; RBI 1996, 1999; GOA 1997; CMIE 1999c, 1999d; Deb 19987: 94-95.

Notes: a: figures in parentheses here are percentages in relation to gross cropped area of the state in 1995-96.
b: growth in number of times between 1975-76 and 1997-98.
c: cumulative total in thousand numbers.
d: number of pumpsets per 100 hectares of gross cropped area.
e: relates to 1993-94.

For the negligible growth in area under HYV, in addition to non-availability of seeds for certain crops, probably an important reason was the non-realisation of expected yield. For example, in rice, the average yield for HYV in Andhra in 1990-91 came to 2,091 kg per hectare as against the all-India average at 2,192 kg and the highest of 3,725 kg in Tamil Nadu. It appears that even some of the non-HYV seeds gave better return than the HYV, for the overall average of yield in rice stood at 2,392 kg in that year (CMIE 1996b). The only plausible reason behind this situation is that the right practices could not be followed by the farmers in many parts of the state.

As regards use of fertilisers, it is necessary to keep in view that nutrient management is a complex task, particularly in areas with large scale illiteracy and poverty. Efficient use of fertilisers involves problems in the areas of soil testing facility, suitable nutrient carrier, methods of application, timing of application, accounting for residual effects, proper phasing within a cropping system, water management, complementary use of legumes, of farmyard manures, reduction in losses from soil, etc.

Despite the complexities involved, from the all-India perspective, Andhra has probably not done badly here. The consumption of fertilizer per ha increased from 17.5 kg in 1966-67 to 31.1 kg in 1975-76 and

138 kg in 1995-96; in the following two years, however, there were declines, as may be seen from Table 4.7. The annual average consumption during 1995-98 came to 134.5 kg/ha. Andhra's consumption level had always been higher than the all-India average. In 1995-96, only Punjab was ahead of it and in 1997-98 three states were ahead.

As regards the use of alternative or complementary types of nutrients, probably not much progress has been made. The experience with biological nitrogen fixers has not been happy. Despite having good potentialities, farmers are still not convinced of the effect of bio-fertilisers. Its consumption in Andhra was no more than 200 tonnes in mid-nineties against the potential demand of around 5,000 tonnes (Deb 1997: 98). On the use of green manure or of compost no data are available, but presumably there has not been any noticeable progress.

In plant protection measures, as in case of chemical fertilisers, Andhra appears to be in a better position than most other states. In the all-India total consumption of pesticides at 80,684 tonnes in 1994-95, it accounted for 16.11 per cent, the highest among all the states. On other methods of plant protection – like use of predators and parasites, of herbicides and mechanical devices – no reliable data are available. But increasing use of pesticides is fraught with dangers like contamination of soil, air and water, besides affecting the crop plants and produce. From the Seventh Plan onward, therefore, there has been an emphasis on integrated pest management, with less reliance on prophylactic treatment.

On the use of implements and machinery, we look at the situation in two time points: 1966 and 1994. The net sown area per plough increased marginally over the period, from 3.45 ha to 3.47 ha. Thus a large number of farmers remained without any plough of their own. The proportion of iron ploughs in the total number, however, increased significantly, from 1.65 per cent to 12.9. The growth in number of water pumps was also rapid. The sown area per pump declined from 128 hectares to 9.42 hectares. The proportion of electric pumps in total number increased from 47.2 per cent to 84.9 per cent. As regards tractors, in 1966 there were one tractor per 395 hectares and the use rose to one per 182 ha in 1994 (GOA 1999).

In relation to the position in other states, Andhra presents a mixed picture. As evident from Table 4.7, in 1995-96, Andhra had 12.6 pumpsets per 100 ha and there was only one state with a larger number. In tractors, however, Andhra's position was very low. In

1990-91, it accounted for only 2.77 per cent of the total number of tractors in the country as against 23.45 per cent in Punjab. The compound annual growth in number of tractors between 1979-80 and 1990-91 was 12.3 per cent in Andhra, which was below the national average (CMIE 1996b).

One measure of the extent of mechanisation in agriculture is the use of electricity, and here Andhra's position was not bad. In 1993-94, per capita consumption of electricity in agriculture here stood at 133.81 kwh, which was significantly above the all-India average, and could be exceeded by only three of the major states (Table 4.7). This, however, entailed the highest payment of subsidy to agricultural consumers among the southern states. The effective subsidy to agricultural consumers increased from Rs. 726 crores in 1992-93 to Rs. 2,167 crores in 1997-98 (CMIE 1999d).

Bank Credit

Bank credit is a critical element in raising the use of different inputs in agriculture, given the low level of own resources with a majority of farmers. Credit is required both for working capital and long-term investment. If the organised institutions do not come forward with easy credit facilities, growth in agricultural production is bound to suffer. Below we give a brief look into the provision of credit by different institutions.

The most important organisation for providing credit in rural areas is the cooperative credit institutions. It is a three-tiered system, with primary agricultural credit societies at the base. Number of PACS in Andhra, including Farmers' Service Societies, totalled 4,656 in 1994-95, with a membership of around 123 lakhs. Their paid-up capital in this year totalled Rs. 172.69 crores and working capital Rs. 1,562 crores. This was a significant improvement over a period of around three decades; in 1967-68, there were 15,329 PACS and multipurpose societies, with a membership of around 19 lakhs, and the paid-up capital at only Rs. 6.7 crores.

The loans advanced by PACS and multi-purpose societies registered a 34-fold rise between 1967-68 and 1995-96, from Rs. 24 crores to Rs. 820 crores; the per hectare loans rising from Rs. 21 to Rs. 629 – that is, 30 times. Andhra's performance in relation to other major states was appreciable, as evident from Table 4.8. The growth in loans issued per hectare was 386 per cent here between 1981-82 and 1992-93 as against 243 per cent for all-India. The amount of loans outstanding at the end of March 1993 constituted 12.3 per cent of all-India total, which was the third largest – after Maharashtra and Kerala.[3]

Table 4.8

Trend in Credit to Agriculture from the Banking System: Andhra vis-a-vis Other Major States

States	*Primary Agrl. Credit Societies*			*RRBs' agrl. advcs. outst.*		*SCBs' agrl. advcs. Outstanding[d] (1996)*	
	Loans issued per hectare (Rs.)		*Amount out-standing (Rs. crores) March 1993*	*As % to total March 1996*	*Per ha (Rs.)*	*Rs. crores*	*As % to state's total*
	1981-82	*1992-93*					
Andhra Pradesh	85	413 (385.9)[b]	1256 (12.3)	54.1	409	3525 (12.8)	21.2
Bihar	24	99 (312.5)	201[a] (2.0)	32.3	229	1040 (3.8)	20.4
Gujarat	122	473 (287.7)	729 (7.1)	67.3	106	1521 (5.5)	11.5
Haryana	220	541a (145.9)	410 (4.0)	54.1	194	904 (3.3)	23.1
Karnataka	92	213 (131.5)	394 (3.8)	55.1	396	2366 (8.6)	15.4
Kerala	373	4918 (1218.5)	1495 (14.6)	43.7	501	1259 (4.6)	14.6
Madhya Pradesh	61	110c (80.3)	565 (5.5)	49.9	112	1713 (6.2)	20.3
Maharashtra	134	206 (53.7)	1555 (15.2)	54.4	69	2877 (10.5)	4.3
Orissa	67	54 (-)	131 (1.3)	42.8	177	601 (2.2)	20.5
Punjab	386	803 (108.0)	554 (5.4)	51.2	80	1753 (6.4)	21.1
Rajasthan	51	112 (119.6)	284 (2.8)	53.7	98	1181 (4.3)	22.5
Tamil Nadu	112	741 (561.6)	1156 (11.3)	33.4	69	3839 (14.0)	13.1
Uttar Pradesh	71	296 (316.9)	1223 (11.9)	46.9	285	2594 (9.4)	20.4
West Bengal	56	121 (116.1)	214 (2.1)	24.9)	134	989 (3.6)	5.8
All-India	98	336 (242.9)	10245 (100.0)	46.2	187	27488 (100.0)	10.7

Source: NABARD 1987: I; RBI 1996, 1998, 1997.

Notes: a: data relate to 1991-92.
b: figures in parentheses here are percentage increases over the period.
c: data relates to 1990-91.
d: direct and indirect finance for agriculture and allied activities as on 31.3.1996.

District-wise, however, there were wide disparities in provision of credit. In 1994-95, loans issued per hectare was as much as Rs. 3,057 in Krishna district as against Rs. 163 in Warangal and less than Rs. 500 in ten districts. In the Telangana region, most of the districts received very low credit. The average for the region came to Rs. 412 as against Rs. 1,355 in coastal Andhra and Rs. 535 in Rayalaseema (Table 4.3).

The PACS were heavily biased against the weaker sections. In

1981-82, those owning land up to one hectare received only 17.1 epr cent of total agricultural advances. Although this was higher than the all-India average, there were six states with higher shares going to marginal farmers. The position of tenant cultivators was still worse. Only 0.7 per cent of total advances went to them in that year as against the all-India average at 1.4 per cent (Deb 1988).

For providing long-term credit to agriculture, there are Land Development Banks in the cooperative credit structure. Due to lack of recent data, we may note here the situation in early eighties. At the end of June 1982, there were 218 primary land development banks (PLDBs) in Andhra, constituting a quarter of all-India total. Their membership totalled 13.60 lakhs, of which 11.42 lakhs were regular. The PLDBs' loans outstanding on that date stood at Rs. 234.35 crores, constituting 21.6 per cent of all-India total. The loans advanced during 1981-82 was Rs. 56.25 crores. No other state could reach this level of business (Deb 1988).

The performance of commercial banks was also much better here than in most other states. The outstanding advances of all scheduled commercial banks (SCBs) to agriculture here stood at Rs. 3,525 crores at the end of March 1996, constituting 12.8 per cent of all-India total; only one state, Tamil Nadu, had a higher proportion. In the state's total of advances outstanding, agricultural advances constituted 21.2 per cent, which was nearly double the all-India average (Table 4.8).

All the above figures refer to the total of direct and indirect finance, to have a look at the position of direct finance only: at the end of June 1997, the amount outstanding to farmers on short-term loans stood at Rs. 1,789.4 crores under 17.38 lakh accounts, which were, respectively, 20.4 per cent and 22.0 per cent of all-India total. There was only one state, Tamil Nadu, with a larger amount outstanding. In the provision of loans, the marginal farmers do not appear to have received their due share. In the total amount outstanding they accounted for only 29.9 per cent and in number or accounts 36.9 per cent.

The district-wise disparity in provision of credit by SCBs appears to be much less, if Hyderabad is excluded. The per capita loans outstanding to agriculture at the end of March 1993 varied between the highest of Rs. 5061 in West Godavari and the lowest at Rs. 577 in Adilabad. Region-wise, the average for coastal Andhra came to Rs. 3,105, for Rayalaseema Rs. 1726 and for Telangana Rs. 237 against the state average of Rs. 2,454 (GOA 1997).

As regards Regional Rural Banks (RRBs), which came into existence only in 1976, their number totalled 16 with 1,123 branches in 1996. The outstanding advances of RRBs to agriculture stood at Rs. 521.04 crores at the end of March 1996, and constituted 54 per cent of their total advances. This proportion was much above the all-India average, and only three of the major states gave a larger share. The loans outstanding per hectare was more than double the all-India average (Table 4.8). It may also be noted that the C-D ratio of Andhra's RRBs was as much as 83 per cent on this date, against the national average of 53; the southern states as a whole, however, had 92 per cent.

There was wide variation in performance among the Andhra's RRBs. For example, at the end of September 1989, crop loans outstanding stood at Rs. 50.60 crores in case of Rayalaseema Grameen Bank as against only Rs. 1.20 crores in Godavari Bank and Rs. 1.80 crores in Golconda Grameen Bank. The number of accounts involved were 116,717, 2,704 and 6,597 respectively (NABARD 1989).

Other Factors

Among other production promoting factors, due to lack of data, we note here briefly the situation on only crop insurance and price trend. The Comprehensive Crop Insurance Scheme (CCI) was introduced in Andhra in 1985, that is, more than three decades after the economic planning began. This is the situation despite the fact that a large part of the state's area is drought-prone. Moreover, the coverage of the scheme is still limited. Only the farmers obtaining loans from commercial banks, cooperatives, or regional rural banks for raising paddy, wheat, millets, oilseeds and pulses can come under it. The scheme provides financial support to the farmers in the event of crop failure due to natural calamities. It is administered by the General Insurance Corporation and the risk is shared between the Centre and the State in the ratio of 2: 1.

The number of farmers covered under CCI annually varied between 4.02 lakhs in 1988-89 and 8.96 lakhs in 1987-88 in the first five years, and then declined to only 2.89 lakhs in 1990-91. In the following years there was a continuous growth from 6.49 lakhs in 1991-92 to 12.59 lakhs in 1996-97. The area covered stood at the maximum of 21.81 lakh hectares in 1987-88 and the minimum at 4.78 lakh in 1990-91; the average for last five years, 1992-97, came to 15.06 lakh hectares. The sum insured was at the lowest Rs. 10,942.79 lakhs in 1990-91 and increased continuously since then to Rs. 74,561.34 lakhs in 1996-97.

The premium collected increased from Rs. 195.95 lakhs to Rs. 1,279.14 lakhs in the last seven years. The total of compensation paid fluctuated between the highest of Rs. 1,309.35 lakhs in 1986-87 and the lowest at Rs. 75.70 lakhs in 1988-89 in the 11 years ending in 1995-96. In 1996-97, however, it touched as much as Rs. 2,754.34 lakhs. Number of farmers benefiting stood at 3.21 lakhs in 1996-97 and earlier fluctuated between 0.42 lakh in 1988-89 and 2.54 lakhs in 1986-87. In relation to the number insured, beneficiaries constituted at the highest 37.4 per cent in 1991-92 and at the lowest 9.5 per cent in 1993-94; the average for last five years came to 18.7 per cent (GOA 1998: Annexure XIII).

As regards the trend in prices, which serves as an incentive or disincentive towards larger production, the index number of wholesale prices for all agricultural commodities stood at 379.7 in 1997, with the base year of 1981-82=100. Among the commodity groups, the lowest increase was in oilseeds, the index being at 292.0, and the highest for drugs, at 524.2. sugarcane had the second highest, at 481.1, followed by pulses 435.4, fibres 408.9, fruits 403.4 and cereals 356.4 (GOA 1998: Annexure XIX).

Due to lack of proper marketing facilities, the price realisation was in general very poor, particularly in interior areas. The price support system did not operate effectively, and the availability of regulated markets was very inadequate. Even the road network was relatively poor in Andhra. The road density per '000 sq. km. was only 628 in 1995-96 as against the national average of 731 km. (CMIE 1998a).

II
Allied Activities

The activities allied to agriculture play an important role in the rural economy. They assist in making better use of some of the agricultural residues and in fuller utilisation of the land. These activities are particularly important to agricultural labourers, and marginal and small farmers as a provider of supplementary income. The important activities here include animal husbandry, fishery and forestry. Below we make a brief discussion on the position of each of them in Andhra.

Animal Husbandry

The development of animal husbandry in the country was envisaged as an integral part of a sound system of diversified agriculture. The Third Five-Year Plan stated: "Emphasis will be laid on mixed farming, a system in which crop production and animal husbandry are dovetailed for efficient and economic utilisation of land, labour and capital. The integration of farming with animal husbandry is essential for the fuller utilisation of farm bye-products, maintenance of soil fertility, fuller employment for agriculturists throughout the year and increase in rural incomes" (GOI 1961: 344). In keeping with this policy, the Andhra government took measures to develop this sector.

The growth in number of animals in Andhra, however, has not been appreciable. Total of livestock increased from 295.13 lakhs in 1956 to 315.94 lakhs in 1966 and 336.67 lakhs in 1987; in 1993, it declined to 329.11 lakhs. Thus, over the entire period of nearly four decades, there was a growth of only 11.5 per cent. In poultry, however, the growth was quite rapid, number rising from 147.37 lakhs in 1956 to 390.51 lakhs in 1987 and 498.83 lakhs in 1993 – that is, 238 per cent over the entire period. In the total of livestock, bovines accounted for 61 per cent in 1993, followed by sheep 24 per cent and goats 13 per cent (GOA 1971, 1997). As bovines account for a large majority of the livestock, we make a detailed analysis of its position.

Cattle and Buffalo Development

Bovines are kept for the dual purpose of draught power and milk. The cattle among them are kept mainly for draught power and the buffaloes for milk. Both cattle and buffaloes live mainly on dry fodder derived from straws of cereals and millets and from plant residues of legumes, and green fodder from fodder crops, grasses from forest land, pastures, permanent fallows and cultivable waste. They are sometimes fed with inferior pulses like horsegram and various oilcakes as major sources of protein.

Most of the cattle breeds in India are draught breeds. Their milk yield is as low as half a litre to one-and-half litre per day. As the demand for milk increased due to growth of human population and rising income, it became necessary to introduce high-yielding milch animals, and this was achieved mainly through increase in the number of milch buffaloes. Efforts to increase the milk yield of Indian cows through cross-breeding was also made. In recent years there has been a large-scale programme for propagating the cross-bred cattle.

The Table below presents the relative position of Andhra in the growth of different categories of bovine population. In both cattle and buffaloes, Andhra registered a lower growth than at the national level. Number of cattle here increased by only 32.2 per cent between 1972 and 1987, from around 94 lakhs to 124 lakhs, as against 56.2 per cent in all-India. Its relative share in all-India total consequently declined from 7.3 per cent to 6.2. In buffalo also the position was similar. The growth in number for Andhra was 84.1 per cent over the same period as against 107.1 for all-India. The relative share came down to 11.5 per cent from 13.0.

The female cattle which are kept for the purpose of getting milk, registered a very low growth in Andhra. Between 1972 and 1987, there was an increase of only 45.2 per cent as against 84.9 in all-India. The relative share of female in total number here increased from 41.3 per cent to 45.4 whereas for all-India it was from 41.8 to 49.4. In Kerala, the proportion increased from 76.7 per cent to 85.2 in this period.

Among the cattle, cross-bred still constitute a very small percentage. Their number totalled 3.90 lakhs in 1987, constituting 3.2 per cent of the state's total cattle population, and 3.4 per cent of all-India total of cross-breds. In the total of cross-bred in Andhra, females constituted 66.4 per cent, which is marginally higher than the all-India average. In most of the major states the female ratio was higher than in Andhra (Table 4.9).

Table 4.9

Growth in Different Categories of Bovine Population: Andhra vis-a-vis Other Major States

(number in '000)

States	*Cattle*				
	1972		*1987*		*% increase in total no.*
	Total no.	*Females*	*Total no.*	*Females*	
Andhra Pradesh	9363 (7.3)	3872	12375 (6.2)	5624	32.2
Bihar	11146 (8.7)	3851	20839 (10.4)	9920	87.0
Gujarat	4862 (3.8)	1797	6240 (3.1)	2732	28.3
Haryana	1665 (1.3)	717	2198 (1.1)	1178	32.0
Karnataka	7148 (5.6)	3346	10174 (5.1)	5514	42.3
Kerala	2856 (2.2)	2076	3408 (1.7)	2916	19.3
Madhya Pradesh	17463 (13.7)	7858	28549 (14.3)	13612	63.5
Maharashtra	10732 (8.4)	4526	16979 (8.5)	8147	58.2
Orissa	8445 (6.6)	3781	13636 (6.8)	6727	61.5
Punjab	2324 (1.8)	912	2830 (1.4)	1762	21.8

Contd...

Contd...

Rajasthan	8531 (6.7)	4590	10920 (5.5)	6555	28.0
Tamil Nadu	7513 (5.9)	2868	9342 (4.7)	5042	24.3
Uttar Pradesh	20390 (15.9)	6696	26320 (13.2)	10530	29.1
West Bengal	8382 (6.6)	3643	20311 (10.2)	10748	142.3
All-India	127868 (100.0)	53409	199695 (100.0)	98763	56.2

Cattle	*Buffaloes (Females)*		
Cross-bred (1987)	*1972*	*1987*	*% increase*
Females			
259 (66.4)[a]	3416 (71.8)[b]	7164 (81.8)[b]	109.7
93 (53.8)	1817 (71.7)	3528 (72.4)	94.2
132 (81.5)	2041 (97.4)	4183 (92.9)	104.9
160 (66.1)	1273 (95.4)	3155 (82.4)	147.8
596 (82.9)	1764 (85.3)	3416 (84.7)	93.7
1503 (88.4)	148 (43.0)	199 (60.5)	34.5
74 (68.5)	2505 (68.6)	4937 (77.6)	97.1
-	1844 (85.7)	3869 (81.4)	109.8
402 (71.4)	387 (38.1)	684 (45.4)	76.7
1132 (71.7)	1910 (87.7)	4945 (88.7)	158.9
63 (86.3)	2481 (94.4)	5576 (87.9)	124.7
793 (69.5)	1364 (77.5)	2629 (84.0)	92.7
918 (35.5)	6537 (80.1)	13588 (74.5)	107.9
517 (72.6)	189 (26.6)	369 (31.7)	95.2
7462 (65.4)	28612 (78.0)	60095 (79.1)	110.0

Source: GOI 1975a; CMIE 1996b.

Notes: a: as percentage to total cross-bred.
b: as percentage to total number of buffaloes.

In buffalo, the proportion of females was much higher than in cattle, higher than even in cross-breds. In 1972, females constituted 71.8 per cent of the total and increased to 81.8 in 1987. The all-India averages in these years were respectively, 78.0 and 79.1. The buffalo-cattle ratio in adult females increased noticeably in this period, from 0.83 to 1.27; the all-India averages were respectively, 0.52 and 0.61. There were, however, four major states in 1987 with proportions higher than Andhra's.

All this progress in bovine population could not bring any impressive result on milk output. The growth in milk production was no doubt substantial, but the per capita production continued to remain much below the national average. As evident from Table 4.10, between 1971-72 and 1994-95, the milk output in Andhra had a compound annual growth of 5.8 per cent as against 4.6 per cent in all-India. There were, however, seven states with higher growth rates. The per capita production of Andhra increased from 26 kg in 1971-72 to 58 kg in 1994-95; the latter was exceeded by as many as nine states.

Table 4.10

Trend in Production of Milk and Eggs: Andhra vis-a-vis Other Major States

States	*Milk Production*					*Egg Production 1993-94*	
	Total (lakh tonnes)			*Per capita (kg)*			
	1971-72	*1994-95*	*CAGR*	*1971-72*	*1994-95*	*Total (mill. nos.)*	*Per capita (no.)*
Andhra Pradesh	11.3	42.2	5.8	26.0	58.0 (123.1)[a]	4100 (16.8)	59
Bihar	17.5	32.2	2.7	31.0	34.2 (10.3)	1450 (5.9)	16
Gujarat	17.9	38.0	3.3	67.0	87.1 (30.0)	475 (1.9)	11
Haryana	15.1	38.9	4.2	151.0	221.0 (46.4)	528 (2.2)	30
Karnataka	7.6	31.1	6.3	25.9	65.0 (151.0)	1445 (5.9)	31
Kerala	2.8	21.2	9.2	13.1	69.0 (426.7)	1845 (7.5)	61
Madhya Pradesh	11.7	51.6	6.7	28.1	72.6 (158.4)	1090 (4.5)	16
Maharashtra	11.9	44.5	5.9	23.6	53.2 (125.4)	2440 (10.0)	29
Orissa	3.4	5.9	2.4	15.5	17.5 (12.9)	530 (2.2)	16
Punjab	21.4	64.0	4.9	157.4	302.0 (91.9)	2300 (9.4)	109
Rajasthan	25.4	48.4	2.8	98.4	99.7 (1.3)	340 (1.4_)	7
Tamil Nadu	9.3	39.7	6.5	22.6	67.7 (199.6)	2920 (11.9)	51
Uttar Pradesh	43.0	114.0	4.3	48.7	75.6 (55.2)	900 (3.7)	6
West Bengal	4.9	31.0	8.3	11.1	42.7 (284.7)	2550 (10.4)	36
All-India	225.0	631.1	4.6	41.0	68.9 (70.7)	24440 (100.0)	28

Notes: CAGR: Compound annual growth rate.
a: Percentage increase over the period.

Source: CMIE 1996b.

An important reason behind this low level of production is the low yield rate of milk from Andhra's cattle and buffalo. In 1987-88, for indigenous cow, milk yield here was 0.975 kg per day as against more than 2 kg in six states. For cross-bred, Andhra had 5.670 kg per day as against the highest of 7.943 in Gujarat. For buffalo, Andhra's yield was 2.008 kg a day as against more than 3 kg in most of the states.

The bovine density in Andhra was not very high, and it varied widely across districts. In 1993, cows and buffaloes in milk per thousand human population averaged only 69 in the state, and varied between the highest of 110 in Khammam and the lowest at 51 in Anantapur. Number of buffaloes in this averaged 48 and varied between 94 in Prakasam and 13 in Srikakulam. Extent of land available per thousand head of grazing livestock averaged 242.32 hectares in the state, and varied between 559.94 in Adilabad and 74.39 in Srikakulam (GOA 1996). Such wide disparities points to the extent of under-utilisation of the grazing land.

The efforts at fodder development was negligible in many of the districts. In 1993-94, out of the total area under fodder at 3.17 lakh acres, seven districts -- Guntur, Khammam, Nalgonda, East Godavari, Ranga Reddy, Prakasam and West Godavari – together accounted for 69 per cent, with the first four having 43 per cent. Three districts, Srikakulam, Visakhapatnam and Nellore, on the other hand, had a combined total of only 2,968 acres -- that is, 0.9 per cent of the total.

Poultry Development

In the development of poultry Andhra's performance was appreciable. As noted earlier, the growth in number of poultry was more than three times over the period of 1956 to 1993. Production of eggs also increased quite rapidly. Even in the last six years there was a 57 per cent rise, from 3,829 million numbers in 1990-91 to 6,027 million in 1995-96 (GOA 1998). Andhra Pradesh is the largest producer of egg in the country. In 1993-94, it accounted for 16.8 per cent of all-India total. In per capita production, however, its position was third, as may be seen from Table 4.10.

The potential for further growth is substantial, as evident from the district-wise variation in number of poultry reared. Per thousand of population, the state average in 1993 was 750, with the highest at 2,677 in Ranga Reddy and the lowest at 288 in Nizamabad; there were six districts with less than 500 poultry. The growth in number of poultry between 1966 and 1993 was only 32.1 per cent in Nellore, 51.2 in Cuddapah, 65.4 in Anantapur and 67.6 in Kurnool as against the state average at 239 per cent and the highest of 1,824 in Hyderabad/Ranga Reddy (GOA 1972, 1997).

There is still an awful lack of knowledge about poultry farming in interior areas, and farmers are often discouraged from continuing when faced with high mortality of birds. Lack of facilities for guidance, non-availability of chicks of superior birds and marketing facilities still stand in the way of expansion of activities, particularly in remote rural areas. High and rapidly rising cost of feed, which accounts for 70 to 80 per cent of total cost, is also an important obstacle.

On the demand side, there is vast potential for growth. As people's income increases there is bound to be a rising demand for eggs and meat. The per capita consumption of eggs and broilers is still very low in Andhra, or India as a whole for that matter. In late 'eighties, against the world average per capita consumption of 124 eggs and that of developing nations at 60, India's national average was only 19. In broilers, the world average was 5.9 kg and of developing countries 2.5 kg as against India's a mere 250 gms (Rao 1988).

Fishery Development

Andhra Pradesh has large fishery resources in both marine and inland areas. It has a long coastline of 974 kms with a continental shelf of 33,227 sq. kms. (GOA 1998). The inland resources comprise rivers, reservoirs, lakes, tanks, ponds and brackish water areas. The longest and broadest river of South India, the Godavari, passes through it. Then, there are Krishna, Tungabhadra, Pennar, Vamsadhara and the Nagavali, apart from many small rivers. The fishing community of the state is also quite large. In 1993, 8.72 lakh fishermen were engaged in fishing operations.

The growth in production of fish was, however, not in keeping with the resource base. During 1984-87, the annual average of fish production came to 239 thousand tonnes, constituting 8.3 per cent of all-India total (Table 4.11). After more than a decade, during 1994-97, it rose to 359 thousand tonnes, that is, a growth of only 47.7 per cent. Latest comparative data are available only for 1991-94. In this period, Andhra's share in all-India production declined to 6.4 per cent. There were as many as five states with higher shares.

As regards the composition of catches, inland fish production was generally higher than the marine catches. The former increased from an annual average of 113 thousand tonnes during 1981-83 to 205 thousand during 1995-97, that is, a growth of 81.4 per cent. The value of production was a little more than doubled even in the seven years of nineties -- rising from Rs. 311.46 crores in 1990-91 to Rs. 639.42 crores in 1996-97. The inland fish production was, however, largely concentrated in a few districts. During 1995-97, five districts -- Nellore, West Godavari, Vizianagaram, Warangal and Chittoor – together accounted for 48.8 per cent of total production. Another 31 per cent came from Mahboobnagar, Karimnagar, Visakhapatnam, Medak, Nalgonda and Anantapur combined. Thus, 11 districts out of 23, contributed 80 per cent of the inland fish production.

Table 4.11

Trend in Fish Production: Andhra vis-a-vis Other Major States

(in '000 tonnes)

States	*1984-87 (a.a.)*	*1991-94 (a.a.)*	*% increase*
Andhra Pradesh	239.1 (8.3)	284.8 (6.4)	19.1
Assam	50.2 (1.7)	140.5 (3.2)	179.9
Bihar	125.1 (4.4)	183.3 (4.2)	46.5
Goa	41.4 (1.4)	86.4 (2.0)	108.7
Gujarat	318.6 (11.1)	623.0 (14.2)	95.5
Karnataka	211.7 (7.4)	245.1 (5.6)	15.8
Kerala	357.1 (12.4)	573.2 (13.0)	60.5
Maharashtra	383.9 (13.4)	451.2 (10.3)	17.5
Orissa	104.3 (3.6)	209.4 (4.8)	100.8
Tamil Nadu	403.3 (14.0)	533.7 (12.1)	32/3
Uttar Pradesh	66.9 (2.3)	122.4 (2.8)	83.0
West Bengal	433.6 (15.1)	765.7 (17.4)	76.6
All-India	2873.1 (100.0)	4400.9 (100.0)	53.2

Source: CMIE 1996b.

Note: a.a.: annual average.

The marine fish production had a very slow growth. Between 1981-83 and 1995-97, it increased by only 23.6 per cent, from the annual average of 123 thousand tonnes to 152 thousand. The value of production in current prices was however, nearly doubled in half that period -- rising from Rs. 221.64 crores in 1990-91 to Rs. 434.95 crores in 1996-97. In the total value of fish production in 1996-97, marine fish accounted for 40.5 per cent, and in total quantum 42.3 per cent. District-wise, the production was heavily concentrated in a few of them. During 1995-97, Prakasam alone accounted for 46 per cent of the total, followed by Nellore 21.4 per cent; another 14.5 per cent came from East Godavari and Guntur, distributed almost equally.

Behind this poor performance in marine catches, inadequate development of infrastructure and low level of mechanisation were primarily responsible. Until recent years, the government's attention to fishery development was negligible. The plan expenditure on it remained less than Rs. 2 crores till the Fourth Plan, and even in the recent plans it was far from adequate for the task involved. The relative share of fishery in total plan expenditure never exceeded 0.4 per cent (Table 3.8).

Till the end of seventies almost nothing was done to increase fish production. In early eighties, there were only 800 mechanised boats operating from the Vizag port. In the Sixth Plan some important steps began to be taken for modernising the fishing. But the depth of mechanisation is still far from what is required. The major portion of marine catches comes from the narrow coastal belt upto a depth of about 60 metres. Almost the entire marine catch is still landed by 'small-scale fishermen'.

The depth zone 60-200 metres is rich in perches, ribbon fishes, threadfin breams, bulls-eyes, eels, scads and horse mackerel but it is still largely unexploited. The catch of perches declined from 3,602 tonnes in 1992-93 to 2,548 tonnes in 1993-94. Threadfins caught in 1993-94 was only 1,418 tonnes and of eels 763 tonnes (GOA 1997). The deeper waters have good resources of non-conventional fish like the drift fish, black ruff, green eye, deep sea prawns and lobsters. The oceanic waters are rich in tuna and squid resources. But all these require larger trawlers, and fishing harbours equipped with adequate infrastructural facilities.

In inland fisheries, the prospect of river water is bleak due to the excessive flow of industrial, urban and agricultural wastes into the river water, and overfishing. The construction of dams and barrages and other human interferences have also affected the productivity of water. As regards reservoir, there is wide fluctuation in production from one reservoir to another. Some of them have very low production. An important reason behind this is lack of proper stocking of fry and fingerlings. Most of the seed farms located adjacent to the reservoirs are ill-equipped to meet the demands properly.

In freshwater aquaculture, there is almost unlimited potential, provided the right steps are taken. So far the activities have been mainly of extensive nature, with average production of around 1,000 kg/ha. For raising the yield there has to be considerable improvement in management skill and in availability of seed and feed. The experience in Kolleru area with pond culture needs to be emulated. There should not be any difficulty in raising the yield rate to at least 3,000 kg/ha.

The brackish water aquaculture also needs much greater attention. Andhra Pradesh has an estimated brackish water area of 15,000 hectares, of which 8,100 ha is under culture. The estimated production from this in early nineties was 8,900 tonnes, giving an average of 1099 kg/ha (Deb 1997). Most of the farms are still following the traditional practice of culture. With modernisation, the existing productivity can be easily doubled.

Forestry

Proper management of forest is of great importance as it has to fulfil three sets of needs: (a) ecological security, (b) fuel, fodder and other domestic needs of the population, and (c) the needs of village and small-scale and large-scale industries. The 1952 National Forest Policy had recommended that the country should aim at a coverage of one-third of the total land area under forests.

The forest area in Andhra Pradesh increased only marginally over the years, from 6,117 thousand hectares in 1967-68 to 6,138 thousand in 1996-97, constituting respectively 22.3 and 22.4 per cent of the total geographical area of the state. In relation to the position in other major states, this is however, not a very disappointing picture; in 1992-93, there were only three major states with a higher proportion of area under forest (Table 4.4).

Out of the total forest area in Andhra, the Telangana region had 2,692 thousand hectares in 1996-97, that is 43.9 per cent, followed by Coastal Andhra 1,976 thousand, that is 32.2 per cent, and the rest in Rayalaseema region. As compared to 1967-68, while coastal Andhra increased its area by 25.5 per cent, for Rayalaseema there was a decline from 1,810 thousand hectares to 1,470 thousand -- that is by 18.8 per cent -- and in Telangana a marginal decline. The state has a tribal population of around 42 lakhs, constituting 6.31 per cent of the total population, who are largely dependent on the forests for their livelihood (GOA 1972,1999).

The return from forestry declined significantly over the years. Its contribution to the state's NDP was down to 0.25 per cent in 1981-82 from 0.59 in 1960-61 and 0.54 in 1970-71; in 1994-95, however, it recovered the earlier level of 0.59 per cent. In value term, there has been a significant growth in recent years. It increased from Rs. 9.81 crores in 1981-82 to Rs. 81.90 crores in 1994-95 (at constant 1980-81 prices).

In the last three years, 1993-96, in current prices, the average value came to Rs. 118.46 lakhs. In the total, the contribution of beedi leaves was 25.8 per cent in the last three years, followed by bamboo 22.4, timber 18.7 and firewood and charcoal 10.8 (GOA 1998).

Although forests' contribution in terms of moderating the climate, maintaining the soilmantle, improving soil fertility, purifying the air and in regulating the water flow in rivers and streams are enormous, the value of forest produce realised from almost a quarter of the state's geographical area is indeed low. Even the intangible benefits have declined noticeably over the years. The density of forest is greatly reduced despite some attempts at afforestation.

The quality of afforestation work done leaves much to be desired. The survival rate in many cases appears to be quite low. The areas planted with certain species upto 1993-94 were reported much higher than that upto 1996-97. For example, the areas planted with casurina was reported as 26,417 hectares in the first period but in the second it was only 17,054 hectares. Similarly, for eucalyptus these were respectively, 66,949 and 57,046 hectares. Till 1996-97, the highest acreage planted was under teak, at 91,809 hectares, followed by eucalyptus 57, 846, bamboo 26, 838 and cashew 19,668. Planting of teak was, however, confined to seven circles and of cashew mainly in three.

For the low returns from forestry the Forest Department was primarily responsible. Reserved forests accounted for 79 per cent of the total area and another 19 per cent formed protected forest. The policies laid down by the government were, however, rarely followed scrupulously and the encroachers had their way easily. The allocation of fund under different five-year plans was also very meagre until the Seventh Plan, and then there were large leakages.

The degeneration of forest was largely due to politicians and bureaucrats acting in collusion with businessmen to exploit forests for private gains. Lacking long-term control, they strive for immediate gains, which results in over-exploitation. Simultaneously, the abolition of community control and restrictions on local people's use have weakened villagers' motivation to use forest sustainably, owing to the uncertainty about whether they would be able to reap benefits in the future.

The demand on the forest is also enormous. Fuel-wood consumption is much more than the sustainable cut. Forests are a main source of fodder and non-timber forest products (NTFP), such as oils, medicinal plants, resins, dyes, fibres and leaves. Tribal population depends heavily on NTFP for income and subsistence as they have been pushed towards more and more marginal areas with low agricultural yields. Industrial and commercial demand for wood is also huge, and this is met by reserving the best forest for it. Large areas of forest have also been lost to river valley projects and setting up of industries.

The National Forest Policy, 1988, called for discontinuation of commercial exploitation of forests for/by industries; their maintenance was to be for conservation of soil and environment, and to meet the subsistence requirements of local people. In pursuance of this policy, guidelines were issued by the Centre in June 1990 to all states for adopting Joint Forest Management (JFM). The guidelines provided for participation of local people in protection and development of forests. They were to get in return a share in the final proceeds, in addition to usual rights of collection of dead wood and non-wood forest products. The programme has, however, been successful in only a few places.

Notes

1. A family holding varied from 6 acres of wet land bearing settlement taram No. I or settlement classification of 15 annas and above to 72 acres of dry land with taram above 5 and chalka soils with assessment below 8 annas (GOI 1961: 236).
2. In 1996-97, however, the proportion of irrigated area stood at only 32.8 per cent (GOA 1999).
3. The amount outstanding from PACS at the end of March 1995 was Rs. 1,656 crores and constituted 14.6 per cent of all-India total (RBI 1999: II).

5

Industrial Growth and Structural Change

Traditionally development has been synonymous with industrialisation. But in the recent decades it has been increasingly questioned. There is now a growing awareness about the cost of unrestrained industrial growth. No doubt, industrialisation of the backward economies is required but a strong cost consciousness should pervade all efforts in this direction. Destruction of environment due to non-recognition of the limits of industrialisation is already causing great human sufferings in many parts of the world.

The object of this chapter is to look into the pattern of industrial growth that has taken place in Andhra over the decades since independence. The analysis focuses on the structural changes and regional disparities, in addition to the overall growth. The causal factors have been looked into with particular reference to provision of bank finance and the infrastructural situation.

The industrial performance of Andhra has been quite dismal, particularly in recent years. The annual average growth in industrial production came to 9.90 per cent in the seventies but during the eighties it was only 6.68 per cent and further down to 2.98 per cent in the last seven years (1990-91-1996-97). The general index of industrial production (with 1970-71=100) averaged 406.7 during 1994-97 rising from 221.5 during 1980-83 and 102.7 during 1970-73. The growth in manufacturing was, however, much less. The index in these three periods were respectively, 306.2, 201.3 and 101.1 (GOA 1998). The contribution of manufacturing to the state's NDP, as noted in chapter 2, was less than half the proportion at the national level.

The provision of employment by the secondary sector as a whole was relatively low in Andhra. In 1991, its share in total employment stood at 8.83 as against the national average at 10.18. There were as many as eight major states, including the remaining southern states, providing a larger share. In 1981 also the position was similar. Andhra's secondary sector provided 10.07 per cent of total employment as against the national average of 11.30 (GOI 1983, 1993).

Below we make a brief discussion of the trend in different sectors of industry: the factory sector, village and small-scale industries and household industries.

Factory Sector

The performance of the factory sector in Andhra over a long period appears quite impressive. Between 1960 and 1994-95, as evident from Table 5.1, number of registered factories here increased 35 times – from only 472 to 16,616; for all-India, on the other hand, the growth in this period was by only 14 times. Andhra's relative share in all-India total consequently rose to 13.5 per cent in 1994-95 from 5.4 in 1960.

Table 5.1

Trend in the Growth of Factory Sector[a]: Andhra vis-a-vis Other Major States

States	*No. of Registered Factories*		
	1960	*1977-78*	*1994-95*
(1)	*(2)*	*(3)*	*(4)*
Andhra Pradesh	472 (5.4)	8931 (10.5)	16616 (13.5)
Assam	452 (5.2)	1675 (2.0)	1514 (1.2)
Bihar	257 (3.0)	4284 (5.0)	9600 (2.9)
Gujarat	771 (8.9)	9655 (11.4)	12034 (9.8)
Karnataka	437 (5.0)	5113 (6.0)	6184 (5.0)
Kerala	567 (6.5)	2888 (3.4)	4273 (3.5)
Madhya Pradesh	551 (6.3)	3556 (4.2)	4036 (3.3)
Maharashtra	1724 (19.8)	13075 (15.4)	17763 (6.3)
Orissa	98 (1.1)	1524 (1.8)	1774 (1.4)
Punjab	348 (4.0)	4713 (5.5)	6451 (5.2)
Rajasthan	106 (1.2)	2413 (2.8)	4508 (3.7)
Tamil Nadu	763 (8.8)	8713 (10.3)	18755 (15.2)
West Bengal	1373 (15.8)	5950 (7.0)	5593 (4.5)
All-India	8704 (100)	84924 (100)	123018 (100)

Column contd...

Column contd...

Fixed Capital (Rs. Crores)			*No. of Employees (in '000)*		
1960	*1977-78*	*1994-95*	*1960*	*1977-78*	*1994-95*
(5)	*(6)*	*(7)*	*(8)*	*(9)*	*(10)*
51.2 (4.0)	1029 (5.3)	24964 (9.0)	143 (4.9)	589 (8.3)	1049 (11.5)
29.6 (2.3)	308 (1.6)	1937 (7.0)	68 (2.3)	132 (1.9)	124 (1.4)
198.0 (15.4)	2266 (11.6)	14547 (5.2)	166 (5.7)	373 (5.3)	343 (3.8)
95.8 (7.4)	1710 (8.8)	27912 (10.1)	282 (9.7)	637 (9.0)	773 (8.5)
44.0 (3.4)	833 (4.3)	10080 (3.6)	110 (3.8)	360 (5.1)	467 (5.1)
27.7 (2.1)	591 (3.0)	4306 (1.6)	132 (4.5)	282 (4.0)	353 (3.9)
41.3 (3.2)	1199 (6.2)	20819 (7.5)	86 (3.0)	297 (4.2)	446 (4.9)
276.2 (21.5)	2993 (15.4)	43409 (15.6)	626 (21.6)	1243 (17.5)	1319 (14.5)
34.9 (2.7)	524 (2.7)	12399 (4.5)	26 (0.9)	122 (1.7)	194 (2.1)
27.9 (2.2)	913 (4.7)	10772 (3.9)	68 (2.3)	210 (3.0)	440 (4.8)
20.3 (1.6)	772 (4.0)	11201 (4.0)	44 (1.5)	163 (2.3)	273 (3.0)
73.7 (5.7)	1443 (7.4)	27759 (10.0)	206 (7.1)	703 (9.9)	1151 (12.6)
27.0 (21.0)	1392 (7.2)	21533 (7.8)	665 (22.9)	935 (13.2)	747 (8.2)
1286.6 (100.0)	19464 (100.0)	277645 (100.0)	2904 (100.0)	7093 (100.0)	9102 (100.0)

Value of Output (Rs. crores)			*Output per Employee (Rs. '000)*		
1960	*1977-78*	*1994-95*	*1960*	*1977-78*	*1994-95*
(11)	*(12)*	*(13)*	*(14)*	*(15)*	*(16)*
111.4 (3.2)	1983 (5.1)	37619 (7.3)	8	34	359
87.2 (2.5)	652 (1.7)	4316 (0.8)	13	49	348
245.0 (7.0)	2130 (5.5)	19169 (3.7)	15	57	559
270.5 (7.7)	4222 (10.9)	56469 (10.9)	10	66	731
91.6 (2.6)	1612 (4.1)	24498 (4.7)	8	45	524
73.4 (2.1)	1177 (3.0)	9350 (1.8)	6	42	265
77.8 (2.2)	1673 (4.3)	28783 (5.6)	9	56	646
777.3 (22.2)	9334 (24.0)	109428 (21.1)	12	75	829
35.1 (1.0)	615 (1.6)	9701 (1.9)	13	50	501
90.6 (2.6)	1483 (3.6)	22341 (4.5)	13	67	507
31.1 (0.9)	995 (2.6)	17946 (3.5)	7	61	657
223.3 (6.4)	4111 (10.6)	60319 (11.6)	11	58	524
720.4 (20.6)	4078 (10.5)	25922 (5.0)	11	44	347
3503.8 (100.0)	38868 (100.0)	517987 (100.0)	12	55	569

Column contd...

Column contd...

Fixed Capital per Employee (Rs. '000)			*Fixed Capital to Output*			*Net Value Added to Output*		
1960	*1977-78*	*1994-95*	*1960*	*1977-78*	*1994-95*	*1960*	*1977-78*	*1994-95*
(17)	*(18)*	*(19)*	*(20)*	*(21)*	*(22)*	*(23)*	*(24)*	*(25)*
3.6	17.5	238	0.46	0.52	0.66	0.21	0.20	0.20
4.4	23.4	156	0.34	0.47	0.45	0.29	0.29	0.23
11.9	60.8	424	0.81	1.06	0.76	0.25	0.19	0.23
3.4	26.9	361	0.35	0.41	0.49	0.33	0.20	0.22
4.0	23.1	216	0.48	0.52	0.41	0.29	0.25	0.24
2.1	20.9	122	0.38	0.50	0.46	0.29	0.20	0.24
4.8	40.4	467	0.53	0.72	0.72	0.27	0.21	0.21
4.4	24.1	329	0.36	0.32	0.40	0.31	0.22	0.22
13.5	43.0	640	0.99	0.85	1.28	0.24	0.27	0.21
4.1	43.4	245	0.31	0.65	0.48	0.18	0.16	0.16
4.7	47.2	410	0.65	0.78	0.62	0.28	0.19	0.20
3.6	20.5	241	0.33	0.35	0.46	0.28	0.20	0.19
4.1	14.9	288	0.37	0.34	0.83	0.27	0.23	0.21
4.4	27.4	305	0.37	0.50	0.54	0.27	0.21	0.21

Fixed Capital to Net Value Added		
1960	*1977-78*	*1994-95*
(26)	*(27)*	*(28)*
0.20	2.59	3.28
1.16	1.66	1.96
3.27	5.74	3.29
1.09	2.06	2.26
1.67	2.11	1.71
1.31	2.50	1.88
1.98	3.41	3.38
1.16	1.47	1.82
4.12	3.21	6.01
1.67	4.02	3.10
2.33	4.05	3.14
1.19	1.80	2.37
1.40	1.48	3.97
1.49	2.40	2.56

Source: GOI, 1963a, 1980, 1997.

Note: a: factories covered are those using power and employing 10 or more workers and those not using power but employing 20 or more workers.

The fixed capital in the sector had a still larger growth. From only Rs. 51 crores in 1960, it rose to Rs. 1,029 crores in 1977-78 and then to Rs. 24,964 crores in 1994-95, that is, a growth of 488 times over the entire period, as against 216 times for all-India. Andhra's relative share in all-India total of fixed capital under the factory sector rose to 9.0 per cent in 1994-95 from 4.0 in 1960. There were only three states with higher share than Andhra's in the latest year. The improvement, however, came mainly in the eighties.

The growth in value of gross output in comparison was much less. Over the entire period it increased 338 times. However, as this was more than double the growth for all-India, Andhra's relative share in total output rose to 7.3 per cent in 1994-95 from 3.2 in 1960. The most depressing performance was in employment creation. Between 1960 and 1994-95, it increased only seven times – from 1.43 lakh persons to 10.49 lakhs. This was, however, much better than that for all-India, being only three times. Andhra's relative share in all-India total of factory sector employment rose to 11.5 per cent from 4.9 over the period.

Fixed capital per employee had a phenomenal rise over the years, from Rs. 0.04 lakh in 1960 to Rs. 0.17 lakh in 1977-78 and Rs. 2.38 lakhs in 1994-95. However, Andhra's capital intensity continued to be less than that in all-India, although the margin narrowed down considerably. The growth in fixed capital per employee was not adequately reflected in the growth of output per employee. The latter had risen only 45 times over the period as against 66 times in the former. The value of gross output per employee continued to remain significantly less than the average for all-India. In 1994-95, there were only three states with lower levels that Andhra's (Table 5.1).

The net value added to output was also very low in Andhra, and declined over the years. It stood at 0.17 in 1993-94, declining from 0.21 in 1960. In 1994-95, Andhra's ratio was lower than that in as many as eight of the major states. The capital-output ratio in Andhra, both in relation to gross and net output, was very high. The fixed capital to gross output increased from 0.46 in 19860 to 0.66 in 1994-95, and it was always higher than the all-India average. In relation to net value added, the growth was still faster – rising from 2.20 to 3.28. The all-India average in the latest year was only 2.56.

For an answer to the poor technical co-efficients, it is necessary to have a look at the industrial structure of Andhra, and the characteristics of some of these industries. Although the structure has undergone noticeable changes over the years since independence, due to lack of comparable data we are looking at only the situation in the last few years.

Structural Change

In terms of value of fixed capital, important industries in the factory sector of Andhra are metal and alloys, electricity, basic chemicals, non-metallic mineral products, food products, machinery and equipment, rubber, plastics etc., paper and its products and cotton textiles. The first two together accounted for 67 per cent of the total value of fixed capital in 1993-94, as may be seen from Table 5.2. The productivity of these two industries therefore, greatly determined the overall situation of the factory sector.

The metal and alloys accounted for 35 per cent of the total of fixed capital in 1993-94 but its share in output value was only 11.1 per cent this year. The fixed capital per employee here increased from Rs. 1.13 lakhs in 1989-90 to Rs. 16.96 lakhs in 1993-94, that is, a growth of 15 times over the five-year period. The output per employee, however, recorded an increase of only 65 per cent, from Rs. 4.15 lakhs to Rs. 6.86 lakhs. The net value added to output which was already very low, became negligible in 1993-94.

The electricity industry was also not in a much better position. With 32 per cent of the total of fixed capital, its share in total output was only 13.7 per cent. The fixed capital per employee here was already nearly eight times the average for all industries in 1989-90 and it increased further. In the five-year period, the growth was 58 per cent, from Rs. 7.02 lakhs to Rs. 11.09 lakhs. The output per employee increased 167 per cent – from Rs. 2.24 lakhs to Rs. 5.99 lakhs. The net value added to output also recorded a substantial rise – from 0.20 to 0.24.

Basic chemicals and non-metallic mineral products, together accounting for 15.4 per cent of the total of fixed capital in 1993-94, did not perform so badly in terms of output. The former's share in output was higher than in fixed capital, and the latter's just equal. Fixed capital per employee was nearly trebled in case of basic chemicals and the output per employee doubled. Non-metallic mineral products had lower growth in both the variables. The former increased by only 7 per cent and the latter by 72 per cent. A noticeable feature of both the industries is that they doubled their proportion of net value added to output in this five-year period.

Table 5.2

Industrial Structure of Andhra Pradesh (Factory Sector)

Industry	*% share of total (1993-94)*			*Fixed capital per employee (Rs.'000)*		*Output per employee (Rs.'000)*		*Net value added to output*	
	Output value	*Employment*	*Fixed capital*	*1989-90*	*1993-94*	*1989-90*	*1993-94*	*1989-90*	*1993-94*
Beverages and tobacco	6.1	32.9	0.8	3.3	5.8	29.4	59.6	0.31	0.26
Food products	19.5	15.7	3.2	23.6	50.9	255.6	398.9	0.10	0.09
Electricity	13.7	7.3	32.3	701.7	1109.0	224.5	599.5	0.20	0.24
Cotton textiles	7.2	7.1	1.9	37.8	67.1	158.7	322.6	0.15	0.14
Machinery and equipment	8.5	6.3	3.1	71.9	123.5	318.7	437.1	0.27	0.22
Non-metallic mineral products	5.8	5.5	5.8	246.3	263.3	199.4	341.9	0.11	0.24
Metal and alloys	11.1	5.2	34.9	113.0	1696.5	414.7	686.1	0.10	neg.
Basic chemicals	11.6	4.7	9.6	173.3	512.7	398.9	791.4	0.12	0.25
Repair of capital goods	0.7	3.4	0.3	9.3	19.6	45.6	62.7	0.62	0.62
Paper and its products	3.6	3.3	2.0	85.4	151.3	221.6	348.7	0.20	0.23
Transport equipment	1.6	1.8	0.7	85.4	104.4	135.7	275.5	0.10	0.28
Rubber, plastics, etc.	6.4	1.7	3.1	273.7	468.8	1114.9	1242.6	0.08	0.12
Metal products	1.1	1.3	0.2	47.1	37.5	141.0	259.4	0.16	0.23
Jute textiles	0.5	1.2	0.1	12.7	18.4	65.7	134.6	0.27	0.32
All Industries	100.0	100.0	100.0	91.3	251.5	164.6	320.8	0.16	0.17

Source: For basic data: CMIE 1997b; GOI 1997.

In value of output, the most important industry in Andhra is food products. It accounted for 19.5 per cent of total output in 1993-94, declining from 23.9 per cent in 1989-90. Its share of fixed capital in the latest year was only 3.2 per cent. Over the five-year period, while fixed capital per employee here increased by 116 per cent, for output it was only 56 per cent. In net value added also its performance was very depressing; the ratio in relation to gross output declined from 0.10 to 0.09. This industry is, however, the second largest provider of employment (Table 5.2).

The lowest capital-output ratio is in beverages and tobacco. It accounted for 6.1 per cent of the total output value in 1993-94 with only 0.8 per cent of fixed capital. The net value added to output was also high here, although recorded a decline in the last five years. The most noticeable thing about this industry is, however, that it is the single largest provider of employment in the factory sector. Its share in total employment was 33 per cent in 1993-94, declining from 40 per cent in 1989-90.

District-wise Disparity

Whatever the pattern of growth in the state as a whole, district-wise there were wide disparities in the status of the factory sector. In 1995-96, in the total output from the factory sector, five districts, namely, Visakhapatnam, Ranga Reddy, Medak, East Godavari and Guntur, together contributed as much as 49 per cent, for the first two combined 27 per cent. On the other hand, there were nine districts with a combined share of only 11.1 per cent. In the total of fixed capital, Visakhapatnam alone contributed 27.3 per cent, and three more districts another 19 per cent. The proportion of district's main workers engaged in the factory sector was less than 2 per cent in as many as 13 districts, as against the highest of 26 per cent in Nizamabad. The fixed capital per employee varied between the highest of Rs. 14.33 lakhs in Visakhapatnam and the lowest at Rs. 1,300 in Nizamabad; and the output per employee between Rs. 11.45 lakhs and Rs. 30 thousand, in the same districts, respectively (Table 5.3).

Small-Scale Industries

The importance of small-scale industries (SSI) for decentralised industrialisation is well-known, and it has been emphasised in all our Plan documents. But, in actual practice, these industries did not get the due attention. In fact, till early seventies, even reliable information on this segment was not available. The first systematic data collection on SSI

Table 5.3

District-wise Disparity in the Status of Factory Sector in Andhra (1995-96)

Districts	Total Output (Rs. crs.)	Fixed Capital (Rs. crs.)	Employ-ment ('000 nos.)	Per Employee (Rs.'000)	
				Fixed Capital	Output
Srikakulam	283	128	8.8 (0.9)[a]	145	320
Vizianagaram	763	494	18.9 (2.0)	261	403
Visakhapatnam	6024	7539	52.6 (4.0)	1433	1145
E. Godavari	2458	1334	29.5 (1.8)	452	833
W. Godavari	1298	239	26.6 (1.8)	90	488
Krishna	1467	338	33.7 (2.2)	100	435
Guntur	2175	250	54.8 (2.9)	46	397
Prakasam	429	66	15.7 (1.2)	42	273
Nollore	653	406	15.2 (1.5)	266	428
Kurnool	906	387	18.0 (1.3)	216	504
Anantapur	682	207	11.9 (0.9)	174	573
Cuddapah	560	314	9.6 (1.0)	326	583
Chittoor	854	451	24.8 (1.8)	182	344
Ranga Reddy	5395	2016	94.7 (9.3)	213	570
Hyderabad	1816	306	35.3 (4.2)	87	514
Nizamabad	758	34	253.0 (25.9)	1.3	30
Medak	4864	1873	71.5 (6.8)	262	680
Mahbubnagar	653	322	10.4 (0.7)	310	627
Nalgonda	1559	880	27.0 (2.1)	325	576
Warangal	315	140	18.4 (1.4)	76	171
Khammam	556	470	9.7 (10)	482	571
Karimnagar	594	164	37.8 (2.6)	43	157
Adilabad	754	212	25.0 (2.9)	85	301
Andhra Pradesh	17408	27633	1115.7 (3.9)	248	383

Note: a: Percentage to total of main workers in the district; main workers refer to 1991 census data.

Source: GOA 1999.

started only towards the end of 1973, and even this was not comprehensive enough; some 22 industries were excluded from its purview and only the units registered with the Small Industries Development Organisation (SIDO) were covered. The survey included the units with original value of plant and machinery at Rs. 7.5 lakhs or less, and in case of ancillary units with Rs. 10 lakhs or less. Below we give a brief look into the findings of this survey.

In 1972, there were 8,091 units working in Andhra, constituting 5.8 per cent of the total number of SSI units in the country. Their share in output was, however, smaller. With the gross value of output at Rs. 85.91 crores, it was only 3.3 per cent of all-India total. There were as many as eight states with larger shares, including Maharashtra accounting for 20.3 per cent. The total of investment in fixed assets stood at Rs. 45.87 crores this year, and constituted 4.35 per cent of all-India total. The employment in SSI totalled 79 thousand, which was 4.76 per cent of all-India total. In the neighbouring state of Tamil Nadu, nearly three times this level of employment was provided by this sector.

The position of some of the technical coefficients was very depressing. The output per employee stood at only Rs. 10,920, which was lower than that in all the major states except one (Kerala). The fixed capital per employee was Rs. 5,830, and it was significantly lower than the all-India average. The capital-output ratio was as much as 0.53, and it was higher than in all but one state (Karnataka). Only the net value added to output presented a relatively better picture. At 0.34, it was higher than the levels in nine of the major states (GOI 1976: I).

For recent years, no detailed data are available. But the situation seems to have improved considerably, at least in terms of number of units and the capital base. In 1993, there were 111,082 SSI units registered with the SIDO in Andhra, rising from 25,047 in 1981. The all-India total number in 1993 was 17.72 lakhs; Andhra's share was, therefore, 6.3 per cent. There were five states with higher shares. As regards fixed capital base, presumably it has increased fast in recent years due to the emphasis on modernisation of the units.

The SSI units registered with the SIDO are larger of the small enterprises, and they generally get a better attention of the government than the smaller ones. Below we give a brief look into the smaller segments of the SSI sector. First, the status of khadi and village industries have been examined, and then a look into the household enterprises. Some overlapping of data between the two segments is not totally ruled out. The data source used for the former is Khadi and Village Industries Commission, and for the latter the NSSO survey for the period July 1989 to June 1990.

Khadi and Village Industries

For the development of Khadi and Village industries many steps were taken over the years. The Khadi and Village Industries Commission was established in 1957 with the objective of "eradicating rural unemployment and uplifting the poor". It provided a package of assistance, including financial assistance by way of grants and loans, procurement of raw-materials and their distribution, disposal of finished goods and supply of tools and equipments. State Khadi Board was also established in every state.

The allocation of finance for development of the Khadi and Village industries was, however, not appreciable. For village and small-scale industries as a whole, the relative share in total plan outlay of Andhra declined from 4.6 per cent in the Second Plan to 2.5 in the Third Plan and then to 1.2 per cent in the Fourth Plan; in the subsequent plans there was only a nominal recovery (Table 3.8).

With the resources available, the growth of the industries could not be on the expected pace. To look into the position in the last decade, the value of production of Khadi and Village industries increased from Rs. 47 crores in 1982-83 to Rs. 160 crores in 1993-94, that is, a growth of 243 per cent. As the all-India production increased at a higher rate, Andhra's relative share declined from 6.2 per cent to 5.0 per cent. In the latest year, there were five states with larger shares, as evident from Table 5.4.

In the provision of employment, Andhra presented a very depressing picture. It is one of the two major states that showed an absolute decline in employment. In the all-India total of employment provided by this sector, Andhra's share declined from 9.9 per cent in 1982-83 to 6.3 per cent in 1993-94. Production per employee also continued to be low. In 1993-94, it stood at Rs. 4,763 as against the all-India average at Rs. 6,014 and the highest at Rs. 12,040. In 1982-83, these were respectively, Rs. 1,376, Rs. 2,238 and Rs. 4,274 (Table 5.4).

As regards the composition of production, in 1993-94, khadi accounted for Rs. 19.87 crores, that is, 12.4 per cent of the total. Within khadi, cotton contributed as much as 71 per cent, followed by silk 16.4 per cent. In village industries, the important items were ghani oil, carpentry and blacksmithy, cottage leather, cane gur and khandsari, lime manufacturing, cottage pottery, bio-gas, palm gur and bamboo and cane. These nine items together accounted for 73 per cent of the total, with the share of first four at 45.6 per cent. In employment, the largest share was of palm gur, followed by carpentry and blacksmithy, cottage pottery and khadi.

Table 5.4
Trend in KVIs' Production and Employment: Andhra vis-a-vis Other Major States

States	*Production (Rs. crs.)*			*Employment (lakh no.)*			*Production per employee (Rs.)*	
	1982-83	*1993-94*	*%rise*	*1982-83*	*1993-94*	*%rise*	*1982-83*	*1993-94*
Andhra Pradesh	46.8	160.5	242.9	3.40	3.37	-	1376	4763
Assam	5.5	24.2	340.0	0.76	1.02	34.2	724	2373
Bihar	55.1	138.5	151.4	2.88	3.45	19.8	1913	4014
Gujarat	49.2	121.6	147.2	1.24	1.01	-	3968	12040
Haryana	26.6	73.9	177.8	0.64	0.83	29.7	4156	8904
Karnataka	50.0	160.6	221.2	1.17	1.72	47.0	4274	9337
Kerala	31.7	110.7	249.2	1.67	1.88	12.6	1898	5888
Madhya Pradesh	14.4	87.6	508.3	0.70	0.92	31.4	2057	9522
Maharashtra	79.7	537.3	574.2	1.98	4.81	142.9	4025	11170
Orissa	10.1	42.3	318.8	0.89	1.31	47.2	1135	3229
Punjab	29.5	124.1	320.7	1.00	1.49	49.0	2950	8329
Rajasthan	55.0	297.2	440.4	2.28	4.83	111.8	2412	6153
Tamil Nadu	116.1	454.7	291.6	5.82	10.34	77.7	1995	4397
W. Bengal	20.2	131.5	551.0	1.39	3.02	115.8	1453	4354
All-India	768.4	3204.3	317.0	34.33	53.28	55.12	2238	6014

Source: KVIC 1983, 1994.

There were a number of items with very low production levels and it points towards the potential for growth. The production of cottage soap was valued at only Rs. 1.40 lakhs in 1993-94 as against Rs. 76.88 lakhs in the neighbouring state of Tamil Nadu. In cottage soap, these were Rs. 56.05 lakhs and Rs. 863.73 lakhs in the two states, respectively, and in bee-keeping Rs. 57.87 lakhs and Rs. 538.75 lakhs. In cottage match, Andhra had a production of only Rs. 132.48 lakhs, constituting 4.0 per cent of all-India total, as against ten times this level in Tamil Nadu.

Household Enterprises

The NSSO survey covered two types of enterprises: (i) those not employing any hired worker – referred to as 'own account manufacturing enterprises (OAMEs)', and (ii) establishments employing at least one hired worker and not exceeding five – designated as 'non-directory manufacturing establishments (NDMEs)'. The combined total number of these enterprises in Andhra Pradesh in 1989-90 stood at 15.75 lakhs, that is, 18 times the number of SSI units registered with the SIDO. In the total number, rural areas accounted for 80 per cent.

Among the enterprises operating in rural areas, the share of OAMEs was 95.4 pe cent, and the balance by the relatively bigger NDMEs. Both the groups together provided employment to 21.32 lakhs, of which 95 per cent was full-time. The output per enterprise stood at Rs. 7,182 and the gross value added at Rs. 4,387, that is, 61 per cent of the farmer. The proportion of total output produced for others was 36 per cent, and therefore, for the balance market had to be found out (NSSO 1995c).

The prominent industries in rural areas in terms of number of enterprises were manufacture of wood and wood products, beverages, tobacco etc., textile products, non-metallic mineral products, cotton textiles, leather and fur products, repair services and food products. These eight industries together accounted for 85 per cent of the total. In employment also their share was similar, being 86 per cent. The largest provider of employment was wood and wood products, with 30 per cent of the total, followed by beverages etc., 17 per cent (NSSO 1995c).

In the value of output per enterprise, transport equipment and parts came first with Rs. 32,058, followed by electrical machinery etc., and manufacture of wool, silk and synthetic fibre textiles. None of these industries had important position in providing employment. In value added again the picture is changed. The gross value added in relation to output was highest in case of beverages etc., followed by machinery, machine tools etc., repair of capital goods and basic chemicals.

A comparison with the all-India situation presents Andhra in a very inferior position, as evident from Table 5.5. The value of fixed assets per enterprise in rural Andhra was only Rs. 4,135 as against Rs. 6,338 in rural India as a whole; in plant and machinery, these were respectively Rs. 969 and Rs. 1,495. The difference was wider in value of working capital. Among the southern states also its position was not good, except in relation to Karnataka.

In Urban areas of Andhra, the household enterprises were much less important. Their share in total number of enterprises, as noted earlier, was only 20 per cent. The prominent industries here were somewhat different. The largest number of enterprises was in beverages and tobacco, followed by repair services, cotton textiles and wood and wood products. The proportion of NDMEs was higher here than in rural areas, being at 16 per cent and 5 per cent respectively. Partly because of this, the output per enterprise was higher here, by as much as 153 per cent for all industries together. In gross value added, however, the urban areas' position was much worse. The GVA as percentage to output came to only 48.4 per cent on the average as against 61 per cent in rural areas.

Table 5.5

Household Enterprises in Andhra vis-a-vis Other States

States	*Rural areas*				*Urban areas*			
	Total no. of enterps. (in '000)	*Per enterprise*			*Total no. of enterps. (in '000)*	*Per enterprise*		
		Value of fixed assets (Rs.)		*Value of working capital (Rs.)*		*Value of fixed assets (Rs.)*		*Value of working capital (Rs.)*
		Total	*Plant & machin.*			*Total*	*Plant & machin.*	
Andhra Pradesh	1260	4135	969	278	312	8609	2302	650
Karnataka	600	4089	1007	140	224	13441	3867	1070
Kerala	479	5947	1808	617	97	14218	4750	1587
Tamil Nadu	753	5512	1405	176	593	12065	2463	2744
All-India	11969	6338	1495	523	3682	18690	4624	-

In urban enterprises Andhra's relative position was very much worse than the all-India average. The value of fixed assets per enterprise was only Rs. 8,609, which was 46 per cent of the all-India level. The value of working capital stood at Rs. 650, only a quarter of that in the neighbouring state of Tamil Nadu.

As regards regional disparity, some idea about it is obtained by a look at the distribution of number of electric services and the connected load for cottage industries. The relative position of Telangana has worsened noticeably over the years. In 1994, this region accounted for only 33.8 per cent of the total number of services to cottage industries and 46.1 per cent of the connected load as against 45.3 and 60.3 per cent, respectively, in 1983. Coastal Andhra, on the other hand, raised its share in number of services from 9.8 per cent to 27.1 per cent, and in connected load from 8.9 per cent to 28.5 over the same period.

Among the districts in Telangana, Adilabad continued to have the lowest number of services and the connected load, only 13 in each. Nalgonda and Karimnagar, on the other hand, together accounted for 67 per cent of the total connected load in the region in 1994. In coastal Andhra also cottage industries were concentrated in a few districts. In the state as a whole, seven districts, namely, Nalgonda, Chittoor, Karimnagar, Krishna, Kurnool, Warangal and West Godavari, together accounted for 70.2 per cent of the total number of services and 69.4 per cent of connected load in 1994; in 1983, their shares were, respectively, 79.6 and 75.1 (GOA 1986, 1997).

Industrial Sickness

On industrial sickness no comprehensive data are available. Closure of an enterprise in the SSI sector, particularly in the tiny segment, rarely attract the attention of government. Data on sickness are collected from time to time only on the large-scale sector and the modern sector of SSI. Table 5.7 below presents the situation at certain time points.

Andhra's position on sickness of large-scale units appears quite gloomy. Number of sick units[1] here increased from only 13 in June 1982 to 122 in March 1990 and then to 234 in 1996, that is, a growth of 18 times over the entire period. Neither at all-India level, nor in any other southern state such a rapid growth was recorded. In all-India, number of sick units in this period increased by only 4.5 times. Andhra's share in all-India total number rose to 12.0 per cent in 1996 from 8.4 in 1990 and only 3.0 in 1982 (Table 5.6).

Bank credit outstanding with the sick units had a faster growth. Between June 1982 and March 1996, it multiplied 32 times, from Rs. 32 crores to Rs. 1,037 crores. In the all-India total amount outstanding, Andhra's share rose to 11.8 per cent from only 1.9 per cent over the period. In the other southern states also the growth was much less (Table 5.6).

In the SSI sector, however, Andhra's situation was not so bad. Although the total number of sick units increased by 77.8 per cent between December 1985 and March – 1997 from 8,694 to 15,460 -- the relative share in all-India total declined from 7.4 per cent to 6.6 per cent, as the latter had recorded a much faster growth. Among the southern states, however, its latest position is quite gloomy. As regards outstanding bank credit with the SSI, there has been some

Table 5.6

Trend in Industrial Sickness: Andhra vis-a-vis Other States

States	Large-Scale Units					SSI Units					
	No. of units			Outstanding bank credit (Rs. crs.)		No. of units			Outstanding bank credit (Rs. crs.)		
	June 1982	March 1990	March 1996	June 1982	March 1996	Decem. 1985	March 1994	March 1997	Decem. 1985	March 1994	March 1997
Andhra P.	13	122	234	32	1037	8694	13842	15460	63	263	214
Karnataka	20	82	114	141	493	5705	15145	6937	78	204	203
Kerala	17	32	69	74	412	2378	10792	8908	46	169	168
Tamil Nadu	35	133	129	216	763	15171	8125	9809	108	428	399
Maharashtra	88	322	337	355	1689	8567	21350	19360	187	768	765
Gujarat	42	155	177	132	670	4045	7812	6510	75	235	197
All-India	435	1455	1956	1729	8823	117786	256456	235032	1068	3602	3609

Source: CMIE 1996c; RBI, 1998: II, 1999: II.

improvement recently. In the national aggregate, Andhra's share declined from 7.3 per cent in March 1994 to 5.9 per cent in 1997. Ignoring fluctuations, the growth in outstanding credit between 1985 and 1997 was as much as 239.7 per cent, slightly higher than that at the national level (Table 5.6).

Causal Factors

Behind the low industrial growth and the level of sickness, many factors have worked. It is the overall industrial environment that determines the growth of industries; and the environment is influenced by multifarious factors. Even the fact that historically Tamil Nadu had an advantage over Andhra, influences the latter's growth. The same argument applies to the differential growth in different regions of Andhra. However, the historical or natural disadvantages are not totally irremediable. With determined efforts on the part of government the situation could be greatly improved.

The determining factor in industrial growth is the attitude of the government; from this follows the right policies and their proper implementation. For adequate growth in the disadvantaged regions, the government could have diverted all its attention and larger resources towards them. Similarly, to overcome the disadvantages in relation to Tamil Nadu it could have taken appropriate policy measures. As the situation on infrastructure and availability of bank finance are two of the critical factors determining industrial growth, below we give a brief look into the pattern of development in them over the years.

(i) Economic Infrastructure

The infrastructural situation of Andhra has not been satisfactory. An index of infrastructure development, prepared by using 13 indicators, gave Andhra Pradesh a score of only 96.0 (taking all-India=100) in 1992-94. As many as nine of the major states had higher values, with Tamil Nadu having as much as 143.6 (Table 1.1). Here, however, we are looking at only two of the indicators, power and transport, as these are more directly relevant for industrial growth.

The power situation in Andhra has been quite distressing in recent years. The deficit in supply in relation to demand averaged 6.48 per cent during 1990-91 to 1995-96. Apparently the growth in supply was quite fast. The installed capacity increased from a mere 98.9 MW in 1956 to 2,298 MW in 1980-81 and 6,764 MW in 1996-97, and power generation from 7,276 MKWH to 24,698 MKWH between 1980-81 and 1996-97. But the demand increased at a faster rate. Total number of consumers stood at 98.35 lakhs in 1996-97 as against 1.49 lakhs in 1956. The per capita consumption in this period increased from 7 kwh to 371 kwh. The consumption in agriculture had a growth of more than eight times in the last 17 years, from 941 MKWH in 1980-81 to 7,835 MKWH in 1996-97, whereas for industry it was by only 2.3 times, from 2,546 MKWH to 5,889. The relative share of industry in total consumption declined from 70.0 per cent in 1960 to 54.8 in 1985-86 and then to 27.5 in 1995-96 (GOA 1998; APSEB 1998).

The power shortage has arisen mainly because of delay in completion of projects. The investment in power was also relatively low, particularly in the initial plans. The average proportion of total plan outlay going to this sector during the second through fourth plan was only 29.8 per cent in Andhra as against 38.0 per cent in Tamil Nadu. The plant load factor in Andhra is however, much higher than that in most other states. In 1994-95, it stood at 70.2 per cent as against the average for all SEBs at 55.0 per cent. The transmission and distribution losses in Andhra was also relatively low. In 1994-95, it was 18.94 per cent, lower than that in 11 of the SEBs (APSEB 1998).

As regards the transport system, road density in Andhra is very low. In 1995-96, it stood at only 628 per thousand sq. km. of area as against the all-India average at 731 km. There were as many as 11 major states with higher road length. The proportion of unsurfaced roads was also high. It stood at 41.02 per cent of the total in 1995-96, which was higher than the levels in six of the major states. Availability of motor vehicles was also low in Andhra. Vehicle density per sq. km. was only 10.18 in 1996-97 here as against the national average of 11.33 and the highest of 41.59 in Punjab. All the other southern states also had levels higher than Andhra's (CMIE 1999e). As regards railways, per thousand sq.km. it stood at only 18.44 km. in 1994-95 as against 30.78 km. in Tamil Nadu (CMIE 1998a).

District-wise, there was wide variation in the situation. On road length, while the state average stood at 534 km. per thousand sq. km. of area in 1993-94, for Kurnool it was only 411 km., Adilabad 431 km., Cuddapah 455 km. and East Godavari 471 km. The proportion of unmetalled roads was also very high in some of the districts. In Adilabad it was 53 per cent, and for Telangana as a whole 48 per cent (GOA 1997).

(ii) Bank Finance

Adequate and timely provision of finance, both for working capital and long-term purpose, is a prerequisite for growth in production, particularly in case of small-scale industries. Below we discuss first the role of commercial banks in Andhra, and then of the term-lending institutions in providing credit.

(a) Commercial Banks

The main source of working capital for industries is the commercial bank. Andhra Pradesh had 4939 offices of scheduled commercial banks (SCBs) at the end of September 1997, of which 49.6 per cent were in the rural areas and 22.8 per cent in semi-urban areas. In the total of gross bank credit, however, the rural areas accounted for only 17.4 per cent and the semi-urban areas 19.0 per cent, with the balance going to the urban and metropolitan areas (GOA 1998).

Table 5.7

Trend in SCBs Outstanding Advances to Small-Scale Industries: Andhra vis-a-vis Other Major States

(Rs. in crores)

States	*June-end 1968*	*Dec.-end 1983*	*March-end 1995*	*No. of units (in '000)*		
				December 1983	*March 1995*	*% increase*
Andhra Pradesh	3.3 (1.7)	348.9 (6.5)	1704 (5.8)	105.3	164.2	55.9
Assam	1.1 (0.6)	33.8 (0.6)	225 (0.8)	19.4	67.5	247.9
Bihar	1.6 (0.8)	139.8 (2.6)	736 (2.5)	59.6	228.4	283.2
Gujarat	14.1 (7.3)	432.5 (8.0)	1985 (6.8)	84.3	108.2	28.4
Haryana	3.8 (2.0)	214.5 (4.0)	929 (3.2)	26.5	48.0	81.1
Karnataka	12.3 (6.4)	351.3 (6.5)	1738 (6.0)	85.2	130.1	52.7
Kerala	18.8 (9.8)	217.8 (4.0)	1149 (3.9)	58.5	218.7	273.8
Madhya Pradesh	4.7 (2.5)	161.6 (3.0)	954 (3.3)	73.3	132.8	81.2
Maharashtra	45.0 (23.5)	984.9 (18.3)	5610 (19.2)	93.7	160.9	71.7
Orissa	0.8 (0.4)	64.1 (1.2)	395 (1.4)	55.3	154.2	178.8
Punjab	10.7 (5.6)	352.6 (6.5)	1540 (5.3)	52.0	110.0	111.5
Rajasthan	3.0 (1.6)	33.5 (2.5)	710 (2.4)	71.3	109.8	54.0
Tamil Nadu	26.2 (13.7)	544.1 (10.1)	3786 (13.0)	138.2	225.9	63.5
West Bengal	15.5 (8.1)	398.0 (7.4)	1984 (6.8)	102.3	616.5	502.6
All-India	191.6 (100.0)	5389 (100.0)	29175 (100.0)	1243.8	2963.5	138.3

Source: Deb 1988: Table VIII.2; RBI 1988a.

In getting working capital, the large-scale industries generally did not face any problem; rather they often got more than their genuine requirement.[2] Therefore, we focus our attention here only on the availability to the SSI sector. Table 5.8 presents the situation of Andhra vis-a-vis other major states.

The growth in SCBs' credit to the SSI sector of Andhra was quite dismal, particularly in the last decade. During 1983 to 1995, it registered an increase of only 4.9 times as against 5.4 times at the national level. Andhra's relative share in all-India total of credit declined from 6.5 per cent to 5.8 per cent. In contrast to this, the neighbouring state of Tamil Nadu raised its share from 10.1 to 13.0 per cent, and Maharashtra from 18.3 to 19.2. In the pre-nationalisation period also Andhra's position was very depressing. At the end of June 1968, it accounted for only 1.7 per cent of the aggregate of credit to SSI, which was exceeded by as many as nine states (Table 5.7).

In the number of units assisted the situation was still worse. Between 1983 and 1995, it increased by only 56 per cent as against 138 per cent at the all-India level. Andhra's relative share in total number assisted declined from 8.5 per cent to 5.5. There were only three states registering a lower growth than Andhra's.

District-wise, the provision of credit was heavily concentrated in a few of them. At the end of March 1993, in the aggregate of credit outstanding with SSIs, at Rs. 998.42 crores, five districts, viz., Hyderabad, Ranga Reddy, Guntur, East Godavari and Krishna, together accounted for as much as 68.0 per cent. On the other hand, there were 11 districts with a combined share of only 13.6 per cent. Region-wise, Rayalaseema received 7.5 per cent of the total, Telangana 57.9 per cent and Coastal Andhra 34.5. If Hyderabad and Ranga Reddy are excluded from Telangana, then for the remaining eight districts it comes to only 9.5 per cent (GOA 1997).

(b) Financial Institutions

There are a number of financial institutions providing medium and long-term credit to industries in Andhra Pradesh. At the national level, the Industrial Finance Corporation of India (IFCI) was set up in 1948, then came the Industrial Credit and Investment Corporation of India (ICICI) in 1955, the Industrial Reconstruction Bank of India in 1985, and the SCICI Ltd. in 1986. Earlier, in 1964, the Industrial Development Bank of India (IDBI) was set up as the apex institution for providing finance to industries. The Small Industries Development

Table 5.8

Trend in Assistance Disbursed by Financial Institutions: Andhra vis-a-vis Other States

States	*Per Capital Assistance Disbursed (Rs.)*							*SFC's assist. to SSI cum. till March 1994 (Rs. crores)*
	From AFI		*From AIFI cum. till March 1997*	*From SFC*		*SIDC cum. till March 1997*	*SIDBI cum. till March 1997*	
	Cum. till March 1997	*Av.for 1992-97*		*Cum. till March 1997*	*Av. for 1992-97*			
Andhra Pradesh	2192	256	2137	225	14.8	57	152	925.8 (65.5)
Karnataka	3189	429	2844	659	84.8	229	372	1365.5 (67.5)
Kerala	1364	155	1136	293	34.6	112	301	422.8 (63.1)
Tamil Nadu	3535	446	3458	370	42.0	102	204	1190.7 (64.6)
Madhya Pradesh	1545	199	1513	90	7.2	45	98	405.2 (69.4)
Maharashtra	6109	833	6192	280	36.2	178	323	1423.6 (76.9)
Gujarat	7072	961	6841	434	44.5	291	481	1387.5 (69.3)
Orissa	1184	115	1054	220	14.9	59	48	361.5 (55.0)
Punjab	2770	312	2408	343	33.9	340	75	530.9 (80.0)
West Bengal	1235	133	1202	69	5.0	42	86	343.2 (72.9)
All India	2587	347	2501	223	23.3	103	197	11867.4 (70.5)

Source: IBDI 1995, 1998.

Notes: All financial institutions (AFI) comprise six all-India development banks, three specialized financial institutions, three investment institutions, and two state-level institutions. AIFI: All-India financial institutions.

Figures in parentheses are percentages to cumulative total assistance sanctioned by the SFC.

Bank of India came in 1990 as a wholly-owned subsidiary of the IDBI. There are also three specialised financial institutions: the Risk Capital and Technology Finance Corporation Ltd., set up by IFCI in 1975, Technology Development and Information Company of India Ltd., jointly by the ICICI and the Unit Trust of India (UTI) in 1988, and Tourism Finance Corporation of India in 1989. Then there are three investment institutions: the Life Insurance Corporation of India set up in 1956, the UTI in 1964 and General Insurance Corporation of India in 1973. The state-level institutions are the State Financial Corporations (SFCs) set up in the fifties, and State Industrial Development Corporations (SIDCs) in the sixties and early seventies. All the national level institutions, except the recently set up SIDBI, are concerned with medium and large industries. At the state level, the SFC gives its major attention to the SSI sector. Table 5.8 below presents the trend in growth of assistance by all these institutions to Andhra Pradesh vis-a-vis other major states.

Andhra did not receive much attention from the financial institutions. The per capita assistance from all the institutions, covering the entire period till March-end 1997, came to only Rs. 2,192 as against the all-India average at Rs. 2,587; neighbouring Maharashtra received nearly three times this level. The trend in recent years is also similarly disappointing. The average for 1992-97 came to Rs. 256 as against Rs. 347 for all-India.

This low level of assistance was primarily because of poor performance by all-India financial institutions. The per capita cumulative from them till March 1997 was only Rs. 2,137 as against the national average at Rs. 2,501 and the highest of Rs. 6,841 in Gujarat. The SFC of Andhra Pradesh also did not perform well. The per capita cumulative total came to Rs. 225, which was nominally higher than the average for all states; the SFC of neighbouring Karnataka provided nearly three times this level. The recent trend is also very depressing. In the last five years, the per capital assistance averaged only Rs. 14.80 in Andhra as against the all-states' average of Rs. 23.30. The other state-level institution, SIDC, was also no better. The cumulative per capita assistance till March 1997 came to Rs. 57 in Andhra as against the average of Rs. 103 from all SIDCs. In the other southern states the SIDCs performed much better (Table 5.8).

As regards assistance to SSIs, the performance of Andhra's SFC was not appreciable. The cumulative total till March 1994 came to Rs. 926 crores, constituting 7.8 per cent of all-India total from SFCs; Karnataka and Tamil Nadu's shares were much higher. The relative share of SSI in the aggregate of assistance from SFC was also relatively low in Andhra. At 65.5 per cent, it was significantly lower than the average for all SFCs. The role of SIDBI too is disappointing, as evident from Table 5.8.

Apart from financial assistance, a variety of other measures were taken over the years for promoting industrial growth. But these were often not implemented with the level of sincerity required. The backward areas in particular did not get the expected attention. The District Industries Centres, set up towards the end of seventies, for development of small-scale, tiny and village industries in rural areas, diverted a large proportion of their resources towards semi-urban and urban areas. The Andhra Pradesh Small Scale Industries Development Corporation, started in 1962, also did not function properly, and presently it is proposed to be closed down.

A technical consultancy organisation, APITCO, was set up to perform a variety of functions like preparing project profiles, feasibility reports, identifying potential entrepreneurs and providing them with technical and management assistance, to undertake market surveys, export consultancy, etc. But its activities remained very limited and far from satisfactory. Six years ago, the state had projected an overall investment of about Rs. 71,000 crores in major, medium and small industries but the realisation was no more than a third of it (GOA 1998: 32).

While the measures taken often proved to be utterly inadequate, some times in the name of industrial growth bigger problems were created. WE give here examples of two industrial estates (IE) which provided a variety of facilities for attracting companies (Sarangi and Cohen 1995). The Jeedimetla IE, located about 15 km. north of Hyderabad, has become a cause of great misery to the people in the neighbourhood. The chemical and pharmaceutical factories there, numbering nearly 500, discharge unprocessed liquid waste to the poor neighbourhood which runs to the municipal sewage drain through the paddy fields. Residents surrounding the IE complain of asthma, skin diseases, spontaneous miscarriages, gastro-intestinal problems and a variety of mental disorders. All the drinking water and agricultural wells in the area are contaminated with toxic chemicals. The traditional livelihood of the people has also been severely affected. The factory emissions have burnt out the tops of toddy palms and affected the toddy tappers' only source of income. Local farmers too are economically ruined due to the drenching of croplands by toxic chemicals.

The other IE at Patancheru, also near Hyderabad, presents a worse situation. Here more than 300 factories are producing chemicals, plastics, paper, paints, meat for export etc. Effluents from these factories are routinely dumped into the river Nakavagu, which used to provide irrigation and drinking water to surrounding villages. More than 2,000 acres of farmland have been destroyed in Patancheru. Well water as far down as 140 feet is completely contaminated and unfit for consumption. Dairy farmers have had to give up this livelihood as thousands of cattle died by drinking the poisoned river water.

The government did not make any plan for dealing with the massive pollution problem. The State Pollution Control Board has neither the expertise nor the political will to adequately monitor the hazardous practices of these industries. In Jeedimetla, there were only three PCB inspectors expected to monitor 500 companies. Till early 1995, the PCB never tested the toxic wastes for their specific toxicity, and air monitoring was done at only one location in Jeedimetla and none at all in Patancheru.

Notes

1. A sick industrial company means a company (registered for not less than five years) which has at the end of a financial year accumulated losses equal to or exceeding its entire net worth.
2. For details on this, see Deb 1988: 247-50.

6

Towards Poverty Alleviation

Poverty is not only a matter of low income; it is multidimensional and a relative term. However, adequate income for a minimum level of consumer expenditure is the first essential requirement. There has to be the wherewithal for purchasing the essential food and clothing, and also for a minimum level of shelter. Poverty alleviation should be the prime objective of development in a backward economy with majority of population living in half-starved condition. Development does not mean, should not mean, giving more to those who have more.

We have noted in Chapter 2 that Andhra's performance in reducing poverty has been better than that in many other states, at least with regard to calorie intake. From early seventies, the proportion of population below poverty-line here declined at a faster rate than in the national average. With regard to per capita monthly consumption expenditure however, the position continued to be quite depressing. The proportion with Rs. 385 and above was only 8.9 per cent in 1992 as against the national average at 14.0 per cent (Table 2.3).

Poverty reduction is possible through the right pattern of growth in sectors where the poor are mostly engaged. A rapid development of agriculture and other rural economic activities would have brought a noticeable change in the poverty situation. It could have also reduced the migration to urban areas. Right type of land reforms, and proper fixation and rigorous implementation of minimum wages were the two prerequisites for poverty alleviation. There was also the need for giving special attention to the most backward areas of the state as most of the poor lived there.

We have noted in the preceding chapters the pattern of growth in Andhra's agriculture and allied activities and in the industrial sector, and how the backward regions did not get the desired attention. Here in this chapter, we look into only some of the special measures that were taken for reducing mass poverty.

The poverty situation in the country instead of being ameliorated got aggravated in the first two decades, and this compelled the government to undertake some special programmes for benefiting the poorer sections and for developing the disadvantaged areas. The measures that came up over a period of years as a result may be classified into four broad groups:

1. Wage employment programmes like the Crash Scheme for Rural Employment, National Rural Employment Programme, Rural Landless Employment Guarantee Programme, Jawahar Rozgar Yojana and Employment Assurance Scheme.
2. Self-employment programmes which included Small Farmers' Development Agencies, Integrated Rural Development Programme, Training of Rural Youth for self-employment (TRYSEM) and Development of Women and Children in Rural Areas (DWCRA).
3. Minimum Needs Programme, covering elementary education, adult education, primary health facilities, potable drinking water, etc.
4. Programmes for the development of ecologically disadvantaged areas such as the Drought Prone Areas Programme and the Desert Development Programme.

Wage Employment Programmes

The first rural employment scheme to be launched on a national basis was the Crash Scheme for Rural employment (CSRE) in 1971. This was followed by the Food for Work Programme (FWP) in 1977, after a gap of three years when there was no national programme in operation. The FWP continued till September 1980, when it was replaced by the National Rural Employment Programme (NREP). In August 1983, the Rural Landless Employment Guarantee Programme (RLEGP) was created with the objective of providing guaranteed employment of upto 100 days in a year to at least one member of every landless household. In April 1989 came the Jawahar Rozgar Yojana (JRY), and with it the NREP and the RLEGP were merged. The guarantee aspect of the latter was, however, dropped with the merger. In October 1993, as the unemployment problem continued to be acute, the Employment Assurance Scheme was introduced.

The size of all these programmes were too small to have any significant impact on the employment situation. Below we give a brief look into how some of the programmes were implemented.

Earlier Programmes

The CSRE had the objectives of: (i) generating employment at the rate of 2.5 lakh man-days (lmd) per annum in each district, and (ii) creating durable assets in consonance with local development plans. The cost of the material, equipment, etc., was not to exceed one-fourth of the total cost of project. The rate of wages was to be equal to the off-season rate for agricultural labourers and in no case to exceed Rs. 100 per month. The entire cost of the scheme was borne by the Centre and it continued till 1973-74, that is, for around three years.

Total expenditure under the scheme came to Rs. 880 lakhs in Andhra, constituting 7.3 per cent of the total for 18 states. Employment generated over the period came to 236.51 lmd and constituted 7.8 per cent of all-India total. In the works undertaken, there was an over-emphasis on road construction. In the total spending till September 1973, it accounted for 87.1 per cent, followed by minor irrigation 8.7 per cent and land development 4.2 per cent; the proportions at the national level were, respectively, 71.3, 12.8 and 15.9 per cent. The guidelines on the scheme were often violated. There was a stipulation on the minimum size of work to be undertaken but in many cases smaller works of non-durable nature were taken up in Andhra (GOI 1979).

The FWP was launched in Andhra in 1978-79 – that is, one year later than in other states – and operated in only two districts, Guntur and Medak. The programme's objective was to create employment opportunities by utilising surplus foodgrains, which were provided free of cost by the Centre. Under the programme, upto 10 tonnes of foodgrains could be allotted to the district magistrate for this purpose.

In 1978-79, employment to the extent of only 21,598 mandays were created in Guntur by spending Rs. 1.25 lakhs, and in Medak 25,360 mandays with Rs. 1.48 lakhs. The foodgrains demanded in Andhra this year could be met only to the extent of 25.2 per cent as against more than 80 per cent in most of the other states. The increase in income of selected beneficiaries as result of the programme was 97.3 per cent in Guntur but only 17.8 per cent in Medak; the number of person-days created increased by 22.6 and 5.3 per cent in the two districts, respectively (GOI 1980a).

The NREP which replaced the FWP in September 1980, came on a more stable basis. The expenditure on it was shared between the Centre and state on 50: 50 basis. The Centre's portion came in the form of foodgrains to the extent available and the balance in cash. Inter-state allocation was made on criteria related to the state's population of marginal farmers and agricultural labourers and the rural population below the poverty-line. This was the first significant programme for creating employment opportunities. During the Sixth Plan, a sum of Rs. 84.39 crores was spent on the programme in Andhra.

The impact of the programme on the employment situation was, however, very meagre. The person rate of unemployment in Andhra stood at 25.59 in 1983, which was higher than the levels in seven of the major states. The time rate of unemployment declined from 11.3 in 1972-73 to 8.63 in 1983; in the latter year, nine states had lower rates (NSSO 1987,1977)[1]. There were many deficiencies in implementation of the NREP. A study on the East Godavari district had pointed out inappropriate timing, higher material cost and unauthorised deductions by the engineering staff (AERC 1986).

Jawahar Rozgar Yojana

The JRY replaced the earlier programmes in 1989 and brought some significant changes in the policies on employment creation. The Centre's share of fund was raised to 80 per cent, and the allocation among the states was to be done on the basis of the ratio of poor in a state to the total rural poor in the country. The distribution from the state to the districts was to be done on the basis of an index of backwardness calculated as follows:

(i) 20 per cent weightage for the proportion of agricultural labourers in the total workers in rural areas;

(ii) 60 per cent weightage to the proportion of rural SC/ST population in relation to the total rural population; and

(iii) 20 per cent weightage to the inverse of agricultural productivity.

From 1993-94, it was calculated by taking into account only two criteria with equal weightage: (i) proportion of rural SC/ST population in the district, and (ii) inverse of per capita production of agricultural workers.

The JRY had two sub-schemes: (i) the Million Wells Scheme (MWS) for providing open wells free of cost to poor SC/ST small and marginal farmers and to freed bonded labourers; and (ii) the Indira Awas Yojana (IAY) for SC/ST and freed bonded labour. Of the total allocation to a state under JRY, 20 per cent was to be earmarked for the first scheme and 6 per cent for the second. A maximum of two per cent of the JRY fund could be spent as administrative cost. Of the remaining funds, 20 per cent were to be retained at the district level for inter-block/village works, and 80 per cent allocated to village panchayats on the basis of 60 per cent weightage to SC/ST population and 40 per cent to the total population of the panchayat.

In 1993-94, two more streams were introduced under JRY: an intensified JRY in 12 states with additional allocations, and another for special and innovative projects. The allocation for IAY was at the same time raised to 10 per cent of total resources under the first and second stream, and for MWS to 30 per cent of the resources. Both the schemes were extended to non-SC/ST category also. After this earmarking, at least 80 per cent of the remaining funds were now to be distributed among the village panchayats (VPs) in the district, the basis of allocation remaining the same as before.[2]

In respect of the district share of fund, the utilisation had to be as follows: (a) 35 per cent for economically productive assets, (b) 25 per cent on social forestry, (c) 15 per cent for individual beneficiaries schemes for SC/ST, raised to 25 per cent since November 1992, and (d) other works including roads and buildings 25 per cent, reduced to 17.5 per cent since November 1992. At the VP level, the only requirement was that 15 per cent of the annual allocation be spent on works directly benefiting the SCs/STs; it was later raised to 22.5 per cent.

At the village level, all plans for development were to be discussed at the gram panchayat meeting, and the gram sabha apprised of the progress in implementation at least twice a year. Contractors were prohibited in execution of works, and had to be done through the elected panchayat and its members, etc. As regards wages, at least 60 per cent of the resources were to be spent on it, and the workers paid the minimum wages fixed by the state. In the total employment, 30 per cent had to be reserved for women.

Andhra's performance in JRY, although better than in many other states, cannot be considered satisfactory. Since the inception to March 1995, 4,439 lmds were created here by spending a total of Rs. 1,336 crores. These were respectively, 8.8 per cent and 7.7 per cent of all-India total. There were only four states creating a larger number of mandays. The growth in resources utilised was 72 per cent here between 1989-90 and 1995-96 as against 61 per cent at all-India level (Table 6.1). In recent years, however, the situation in Andhra seems to have worsened considerably. In 1998-99, the target for employment creation under JRY was fixed at only 254 lmd, which was 6.4 per cent of all-India total (GOI 1999).

Table 6.1

Jawahar Rozgar Yojana in Andhra vis-a-vis Other Major States

States	*Total amount utilised 1989-95 (Rs. crores)*	*Mandays created (in lakhs) 1989-95*			*Growth in resources utilised (Rs. crores)*	
		Total	*% share of*			
			SC & ST	*Landless*	*1989-90*	*1995-96*[a]
Andhra Pradesh	1336.0 (7.7)	4439	46.3	69.1	184.2	317.1 (72)[b]
Assam	377.8 (2.2)	1024	46.4	41.1	48.0	95.8 (100)
Bihar	2514.5 (14.5)	5983	63.3	64.3	316.9	507.2 (60)
Gujarat	551.8 (3.2)	1287	65.7	32.5	80.8	113.4 (40)
Haryana	131.7 (0.8)	207	58.9	89.1	19.7	33.0 (68)
Karnataka	813.5 (4.7)	2688	40.1	38.6	109.4	219.9 (101)
Kerala	425.3 (2.4)	946	38.2	16.5	65.9	88.9 (35)
Madhya Pradesh	1733.1 (10.0)	4982	65.7	35.2	205.6	347.9 (69)
Maharashtra	1286.4 (7.4)	5123	48.9	35.7	210.6	359.5 (71)
Orissa	887.1 (5.1)	2458	67.8	19.7	104.4	246.8 (136)
Punjab	101.8 (0.6)	171	77.8	41.4	17.2	4.1 (-76)[c]
Rajasthan	813.9 (4.7)	2466	65.5	16.6	106.5	164.3 (54)
Tamil Nadu	1372.3 (7.9)	5018	52.0	79.0	201.6	363.6 (80)
West Bengal	1265.6 (7.3)	3078	49.9	60.0	199.7	261.1 (31)
All-India	17369.5 (100.0)	50280	55.6	45.5	2458.4	3966.1 (61)

Source: GOI 1991, 1996c.

Notes: a: relate to first stream only.
b: figures in parentheses are percentage increases over the period.
c: upto October 1995.

As regards the category-wise distribution of beneficiaries, the share of SC and ST in total employment was relatively low. It stood at the average of 46.3 per cent during 1989-90 to 1994-95 as against 56.6 per cent at the national level. In case of landless labourers, however, the coverage in Andhra was appreciable. It was 69.1 per cent of the total employment as against 45.5 at the national level. In providing employment to women also Andhra's position was relatively better, being at 30.3 per cent of the total as compared to all-India's 24.4.

On the nature of physical assets created, the latest data are not available but it is apparent that the emphasis differed considerably from year to year. We may note here the situation in the first two years. Number of School buildings constructed declined from 2,713 in 1989-90 to only 1,012 in the following year, and of rural roads from 6,643 kms. to 3,924 kms. The social forestry covered only 4,323 hectares with 83.43 lakh trees planted in the first year but in the second year it rose to 5,563 hectares with 516.37 lakh trees planted. In the all-India total number of trees planted, Andhra's share in these two years were respectively. Construction of sanitary latrines increased from 1,394 to 2,388 and of houses (other than those under IAY) from 147 to 513. Directly productive activities got scanty attention in these two years. Area covered by minor irrigation and flood protection works declined from 87.15 hectares to 39.80 hectares. Number of works benefiting SC/ST declined sharply from 33,511 to 14,830 (GOI 1991).

As regards the performance under MWS, between 1988-89 and 1994-95, 73,975 wells were constructed in Andhra with an expenditure of Rs. 27,576 lakhs. In the all-India total, these were respectively, 8.6 per cent and 9.3 per cent. Andhra's expenditure here was the fourth highest, after Uttar Pradesh, Bihar and Madhya Pradesh. In recent years, the relative share seems to have declined much. In 1998-99, only Rs. 3,165 lakhs were allocated for MWS, constituting 5.6 per cent of all-India total (GOI 1999).

In IAY also Andhra's performance was similar. Between 1985-86 and 1994-95, 182,207 houses were constructed with an expenditure of Rs. 21,390 lakhs, constituting respectively, 8.9 and 8.6 per cent of all-India total. Here also the relative share has declined in recent years. In 1998-99, Rs. 10,463 lakhs were allocated to it, constituting 5.6 per cent of all-India total. As regards the Operation Black Board, during 1991-92 to 1994-95, 3,810 one-room school buildings were constructed with a total cost of Rs. 3,827 lakhs. In the all-India totals, these constituted respectively 14.9 and 21.7 per cent.

In the implementation of JRY there were many deficiencies. The violation of guidelines was frequent. The first concurrent evaluation of JRY carried out during January-December 1992 found that in Andhra the wage/non-wage ratio was 55:45, and the requirement of paying the legal minimum wage was not observed. As against the minimum wage rate of Rs. 17 for unskilled workers, the wages paid to male workers were Rs. 24.06 and to females Rs. 17.78. In relation to the all-India average, while the former was higher the latter was lower (Neelakantan 1994).

On the maintenance of muster rolls, for which there was a clear stipulation in the guidelines, Andhra's record was very poor. It was not available in 27.88 per cent of the cases as against the average of 15.85 per cent in all-India. In the absence of its proper maintenance, there was a high probability of manipulation of the employment figures. There were instances of recording the payment of minimum wage even when the actual wages paid were less. Another important finding was that in a large number of cases the Annual Action Plan were not discussed in Gram Sabha meetings; it was to the extent of 38.18 per cent of Gram Panchayats.

Although the JRY was apparently a massive programme, its impact on additional employment generation was not significant. In Andhra Pradesh, the survey revealed that on an average a JRY worker could get only 4.05 mandays of employment in a month. Other members of the family got another 3.61 days of employment. Thus, the JRY could provide an average of only 7.66 days of employment in a month. This was, however, better than the all-India average, being 5.15 days.

A very disturbing feature of the implementation of JRY was that a large number of ineligible workers got selected for the works. The poverty-line income during 1991-92 was an annual family income of Rs. 6,400, and the survey found that 66.79 per cent of the workers in Andhra were from families at or above this level. At the all-India level the proportion was 56.96 per cent, and even in other southern states it was lower than in Andhra. Thus, the better performance of Andhra on some other counts was considerably diluted by this phenomenon.

Employment Assurance Scheme

The EAS introduced in October 1993, aimed at assuring 100 days of unskilled manual work to rural job seekers. A maximum of two adults per family could be employed and it was to be provided during the lean agricultural season. A new project could be started by the block-level officer for providing employment when about 10 workers demanded work. Initially, the scheme was started in a selected number of blocks in which the revamped PDS was in operation. The blocks were in the drought prone areas, desert areas, tribal areas and hill areas. The cost of the programme was borne by the Centre to the extent of 80 per cent, as in case of the JRY.

The programme's secondary objective was to create economic infrastructure and community assets. The works were to be selected on the following basis: (a) water and soil conservation including afforestation, agro-horticulture and silvipasture 40 per cent; (b) minor irrigation works 20 per cent; (c) link roads featuring in the Master Plan developed for this purpose 20 per cent; and (d) primary schools and anganwadi buildings 20 per cent.

The scheme expanded in coverage of blocks in each of the years since its launch, and presently operates in all the blocks in the country. The intensified JRY was also merged into it in January 1996.

In Andhra Pradesh, the EAS created 62.42 lmds in 1993-94 with an expenditure of Rs. 25.66 crores, and in the following year 277.24 lmds with Rs. 137.87 crores. The employment generated in 1994-95 constituted 10.1 per cent of the all-India total. In the following years, there was a substantial growth of the scheme. In 1998-99, Rs. 264.88 crores was made available for it, constituting 9.4 per cent of all-India total; there were only three states, viz., Uttar Pradesh, Madhya Pradesh and Bihar, with larger allocation for the scheme (GOI 1996c, 1999).

As regards the distribution of employment among different categories, in 1994-95, SC and ST together accounted for 59.6 per cent of the total, distributed almost equally. This was slightly above the proportion at the national level. The share of women in the total stood at 33.9 per cent in Andhra as against 30.9 at all-India level. Number of works completed in Andhra this year was 19,460, and constituted 17.0 per cent of all-India total.

All these programmes could not bring any significant change in the employment situation in Andhra. The concurrent evaluation of JRY (1992) had found that all the programmes together could provide an average of 19.43 persondays of employment in a month to a JRY worker. After the introduction of EAS it might have increased by a few more days. Andhra's relative position among the states is also not encouraging. According to the NSSO survey, participation in public works per thousand households was only 22 in Andhra in 1987-88 as against the national average of 64. In 1993-94, the figures were 46 and 59 respectively (NSSO 1998a).[3]

The growth in wage rate over the years was not appreciable in Andhra. The real agricultural wages in paddy farming, for example, increased by only 27.8 per cent between 1981-84 and 1989-92, from the average of Rs. 7.20 to Rs. 9.20. In the north coastal districts, it was by only 17.6 per cent – from Rs. 5.92 to Rs. 6.96 (Reddy 1998). If wage employment is to help substantially in reducing the poverty, there is need not only of enlarging the size of programmes but also of raising the wage rates. The rates paid presently are in fact at 'starvation' level.

From the angle of minimum food, clothing and other essential requirements for survival, the minimum wage rate should be at least five times the present level.[4]

Self-Employment Programmes

The first SEP to be launched in the country was the Agency for Marginal Farmers and Agricultural Labourers (AMFAL) in the late sixties. This was on a very small scale and did not prove to be successful. In the Fourth Plan, the Small Farmers' Development Agency (SFDA) was launched for assisting the small but potentially viable farmers. The agency was to make specific efforts to ensure that the needed inputs and credits were available to these persons. The AMFAL was merged into it in 1975. The coverage of this scheme was also limited. In 1977, the Integrated Rural Development Programme (IRDP) was launched, and from the beginning of Sixth Plan it was made a national programme. The SFDA was merged into it.

The IRDP was more specific on assisting agricultural workers and landless labourers, and tried to develop a variety of activities in different sectors. It was stipulated that 33 per cent of the beneficiaries should as far as possible be from the secondary and tertiary sectors. In identification of beneficiaries, the IRDP emphasised the family rather than the individual approach followed in case of the SFDA. The scheme is financed on 50:50 basis by the Centre and the state.

The assets provided to the selected households were financed through a mix of government subsidies and institutional credit in the ratio of 1:2 on an average. The subsidy provided on the purchase of asset was to the extent of 25 per cent in case of small farmers, one-third for marginal farmers, agricultural labourers and rural artisans, and half for SC/ST beneficiaries and physically handicapped persons. There was also a ceiling on the extent of subsidy, varying between Rs. 3,000 and Rs. 5,000, raised by Rs. 1,000 subsequently. In recent years it was stipulated that at least 50 per cent of the beneficiaries should be from SC/ST families, and 40 per cent from women. A new category of trained literate youth was also introduced recently with the admissible subsidy at 50 per cent of the project cost or Rs. 7,500 whichever is lower. Below we give a brief look into how the SFDA and IRDP were operated in Andhra Pradesh.

SFDA/IRDP

The performance of SFDA/IRDP in Andhra was quite disappointing. Out of the total of 55.18 lakh target group households in 1971-72, only 4.81 lakhs, that is, 9 per cent, could be assisted by the SFDAs during 1970-71 to 1984-85. Under the IRDP, during the Sixth Plan (1980-85) 12.16 lakh families, that is, 22 per cent of the total, were covered (Hara Gopal and Ramulu 1989).

In the selection of beneficiaries, the weakest group, agricultural labourers, was largely neglected under the SFDA. In the total number of families covered till 1978-79, their share was only 14.6 per cent as against 39.1 for small farmers and 46.1 for marginal farmers. Under the IRDP however, their coverage was better. In the total number of families assisted during the Sixth Plan, agricultural labourers constituted 36.2 per cent, marginal farmers 31.1 and small farmers 16.5.

District-wise, there was wide variation in performance. The programme itself was started very late in many of the districts. In only four districts, viz., Srikakulam, Visakhapatnam, Cuddapah and Nalgonda, it was launched in 1970-71. In six of the districts the programme was started after full one decade, in 1980-81. The proportion of target families covered till 1984-85, by both SFDA and IRDP, varied between 19 per cent in Chittoor and Mahbubnagar and 49 per cent in Nalgonda, with the state average at 31 per cent. The coverage by SFDA was at the highest 28.5 per cent in Nalgonda and at the lowest 3.4 per cent in Guntur, with the state average at 9.0 per cent; the SFDA had operated in 16 districts (Hara Gopal and Ramulu 1989).

The implementation of the scheme suffered from many deficiencies like, identification of wrong families, purchases under fictitious names, cornering of benefits by more developed blocks, etc. A study of 18 villages in Nalgonda had found the coverage of agricultural labourers at only 6 per cent of total as against 41 per cent for marginal farmers and 24 per cent for small farmers; even medium and large farmers were found to have entered to the extent of 25 per cent of the total. As regards utilisation of the scheme, as many as 42 per cent of the beneficiaries were found to be not possessing the asset. The non-possession was mainly in case of weaker groups, to the extent of 90 per cent of the agricultural labourers and 81 per cent of marginal farmers. Only three per cent of the beneficiaries had crossed the poverty line (Hara Gopal and Ramulu 1989).

In the Seventh Plan some important steps were taken to rectify the weaknesses. Much greater care was to be exercised now in the selection of beneficiaries. Provision of a total package of benefits and services was envisaged for the identified households. Special attention was to be given to improving infrastructural support and backward and forward linkages. The basis of fund allocation among the blocks was changed in this period for giving grater weightage to poverty. The situation however, did not improve much, particularly for the weakest among the weaker groups, as will be evident from the analysis below.

Table 6.2

Relative Position of Andhra on IRDP Among the Major States

States	*Coverage of Families*				*Total Fund Utilised (Rs. lakhs)*	
	Total No. (in '000)		*Percentage of SC/ST*			
	1990-91	*1997-98*	*1990-91*	*1997-98*	*1990-91*	*1997-98*
Andhra Pradesh	306.8	162.1 (9.5)	43.1	45.4	8076	11500 (42.4)[a]
Assam[b]	32.1	39.6 (2.3)	32.8	40.2	916	3561 (288.8)
Bihar	415.8	196.8 (11.5)	47.9	45.6	9949	12422 (24.9)
Gujarat	724.3	418.2 (2.4)	53.1	42.7	2341	3397 (45.1)
Karnataka	125.0	94.7 (5.5)	36.4	39.7	3077	5471 (77.8)
Kerala	60.9	44.2 (2.6)	41.1	35.2	2044	2532 (23.9)
Madhya Pradesh	344.4	138.8 (8.1)	54.3	50.8	8355	11996 (43.6)
Maharashtra	213.6	147.6 (8.6)	44.8	38.4	5692	9396 (65.1)
Orissa	145.4	75.3 (4.4)	56.4	49.0	3561	6038 (69.6)
Punjab	35.9	6.1 (0.4)	50.6	51.8	1050	572 (-45.5)
Rajasthan	135.0	60.8 (3.6)	50.6	48.0	3549	3929 (10.7)
Tamil Nadu	181.5	180.7 (10.6)	50.9	48.3	4904	9284 (89.3)
West Bengal	226.7	91.7 (5.4)	42.2	37.4	6467	4770 (-26.1)
All India	2905.3	1706.6 (100.0)	48.7	46.4	80236	110954 (38.3)

Source: GOI 1991, 1999.

Note: a: figures in parentheses here are percentage increases over the period.
b: in 1990-91, coverage of families is upto February and of fund utilised upto January.

First, the number of families covered by the programme has declined sharply in recent years. In 1990-91, it stood at around 3.07 lakhs but came down to only 1.60 lakhs in 1994-95 and in the following years also it was around the same level. Andhra's relative share in all-India total declined to 7.2 per cent in 1994-95 from 10.6 in 1990-91; in the latest year, 1997-98, however, it recovered to 9.5 per cent, as may be seen from Table 6.2. The coverage of SC/ST families continued to be below the laid-down norm. In 1994-95, it rose to 47.3 per cent from

43.1 in 1990-91 but declined again to 45.4 in 1997-98. The all-India coverage in these years were, 49.8, 48.7 and 46.4 per cent respectively. With regard to women also the norm could not be fulfilled. In 1997-98, they constituted 36.7 per cent of the total, rising from 26.6 in 1994-95 and 24.0 in 1990-91.

In contrast to the decline in number of beneficiaries, the expenditure on the programme has risen significantly. There was a 42 per cent rise over the last eight years, from Rs. 80.76 crores in 1990-91 to Rs. 115.00 crores in 1997-98. Andhra's relative share in all-India total expenditure has remained at almost the same level, slightly more than 10 per cent. There were seven major states registering a faster growth in expenditure.

In mobilisation of credit Andhra's performance was very poor. The amount of credit disbursed increased from Rs. 105.28 crores in 1990-91 to Rs. 155.73 crores in 1997-98, that is, by 47.9 per cent, as compared to 70.9 per cent at the national level. The credit-subsidy ratio here continued to be much below the all-India average. Whereas in Andhra it increased from 1.30 to 1.35 over the period, at the national level it was from 1.46 to 1.80.

The per capita investment on beneficiary has risen noticeably in recent years in order to ensure the crossing of the poverty-line. There was a 175 per cent rise in the last eight years, from Rs. 6,064 in 1990-91 to Rs. 16,700 in 1997-98. These levels were, however, lower than the all-India average, being Rs. 6,703 and Rs. 18,200, respectively.

The deficiencies noted earlier has not been totally eliminated. There are still reports of substandard assets supplied at prices higher than the market rate, inadequacy of infrastructure and aftercare support and wrong selection of beneficiaries. In order to strengthen the bargaining power of beneficiaries, the system of disbursement in cash was introduced in 1991-92, and since 1996-97 it was extended to all blocks in the country. The ceiling on permissible expenditure on infrastructure has also been raised recently to 20 per cent from 10 per cent earlier.

On the wrong identification of beneficiaries, it may be noted that this problem is largely removed now through a policy change. Although still there is a family-income ceiling of Rs. 11,000 for inclusion in the scheme, the emphasis presently is on the beneficiary having the necessary motivation and skill for taking up the project. This requirement largely removes the possibility of weaker among the target group getting selected.

TRYSEM and DWCRA

The scheme for training of rural youth for self-employment was launched in 1979 as a sub-component of IRDP, but since 1991-92 it has been treated as an independent programme. Selection for this scheme is made from families below the poverty line identified under the IRDP. The training is normally provided for six months, and the amount of stipend varies depending on the nature of training and the status of the agency. A free toolkit costing not more than Rs. 800 is given to the trainees. At least 50 per cent of the trainees have to be from SC/ST, 40 per cent women and 3 per cent from physically handicapped.

The performance of the programme varied significantly from year to year. To look at the situation in only two of the years: In 1989-90, 11,361 youths were trained in Andhra, constituting only 5.3 per cent of all-India total. In 1995-96, the number rose to 13,825 but the relative share declined marginally, to 5.2 per cent. As regards the category-wise distribution of trainees, while in 1989-90 the norms laid down could be fulfilled, in 1995-96 it fell short with regard to SC/ST. In the former year, SC/ST constituted 51.0 per cent and women 59.2 but in the latter year these were respectively, 45.8 and 44.1. As regards placement, a large number could not be absorbed in the same year. The proportion of self-employed in the total in 1989-90 was 48.7 per cent and another 10.5 per cent got wage employment. In 1995-96, the proportions were respectively 31.0 per cent and 14.8 per cent. The all-India averages on them were also not much different.

In the implementation of this scheme there was hardly any relationship between the target and the achievement. In 1995-96, while the allocation was Rs. 685 lakhs, the actual expenditure came to Rs. 1,776 lakhs; in relation to all-India total, the latter constituted 18.9 per cent. The physical performance was however, far short of the target: only 36.1 per cent could be realised (GOI 1996c).

The programme for development of women and children was also launched as a sub-scheme of the IRDP in 1982-83. In Andhra Pradesh, it was started in 1983-84 and in only three of the districts -- Adilabad, Cuddapah and Srikakulam – initially. In 1986-87, the scheme was extended to two more districts, Anantapur and Mahbubnagar. Under the programme, women members formed groups of 10 to 15 for taking up economic activities suited to their skill and aptitude.

Andhra's achievement here appears to be better than in most other states. By March 1997, 20 lakh women from below the poverty-line families had joined the self Help/DWCRA groups. Andhra accounted for one-third of the total number of groups in the country. The groups were provided with a revolving fund of Rs. 100 crore. The expenditure on the programme, however, fluctuated widely from year to year. In 1996-97, Rs. 35.45 crores was spent on it for 17,737 groups, but in the following year it was only Rs. 12.88 crores for 7,178 groups (GOA 1998).

Minimum Needs Programme

The standard of living of a family depends not on income alone but also on the quality of access to certain basic services and facilities. Although the situation in rural India was distressingly poor on all the basic services at the time of Independence, the realisation of this fact came to the government very late. It was only in the Fifth Plan that a minimum needs programme was launched in the country. And then also, the allocation of fund for it was very meagre. For the entire country the expenditure during 1974-78 came to Rs. 1,038 crores and in 1978-79 at Rs. 540 crores. In the Sixth Plan, however, the allocation was raised nearly four times, to Rs. 5,807 crores.

The MNP had the following nine components in the Fifth and Sixth Plans: (a) elementary education, (b) adult education, (c) rural health, (d) rural water supply, (e) rural roads, (f) rural electrification, (g) house sites/houses for rural landless labourers, (h) environmental improvement of slums, and (i) nutrition. Since the Seventh Plan, three more items were added: rural domestic cooking energy, rural sanitation, and public distribution system.

The trend of expenditure under MNP in Andhra Pradesh is presented in Table 6.3. In current prices, the growth in expenditure was appreciable. It increased from the annual average of Rs. 15.8 crores during 1974-80 to Rs. 173.8 crores during 1992-97, that is, 11 times. As a proportion to the aggregate of plan expenditure, however, the trend is quite disappointing. It increased from 5.0 per cent during 1974-80 to 17.0 per cent in the Sixth Plan but declined to 12.2 in the Seventh Plan and further to only 8.3 in the Eighth Plan. The MNP was to provide a minimum level of facilities after three decades of Independence, but adequate funds could not be spared for it.

Table 6.3

Trend in Expenditure Under the Minimum Needs Programme in Andhra

(Rs. in lakhs)

Head of Development	*During 1974-80*	*During Sixth Plan*	*During Seventh Plan*	*During Eighth Plan*[a]
Rural electrification	561 (5.9)	10552 (19.1)	-	-
Rural roads	412 (4.3)	1687 (3.1)	2400 (3.3)	13400 (15.4)
Elementary education	922 (9.7)	3745 (6.8)	15441 (21.3)	12745 (14.7)
Adult education	-	211 (8.4)	1089 (1.5)	5200 (6.0)
Rural health	641 (6.8)	1484 (2.7)	4946 (6.8)	3815 (4.7)
Rural water supply	2922 (30.8)	8637 (15.7)	12976 (17.9)	19902 (22.9)
Rural house sites-cum-construction	2733 (28.8)	16609 (30.1)	30026 (41.3)	21435 (24.7)
Improvement of slums	662 (7.0)	2380 (4.3)	4221 (5.8)	852 (1.0)
Nutrition	624 (6.6)	9818 (17.8)	1261 (1.7)	8572 (9.9)
Rural fuelwood plantation	-	-	299 (0.4)	968 (1.1)
Total	9482 (100.0)	55123 (100.0)	72659 (100.0)	86890 (100.0)

Source: GOA 1981, 1986, 1993a.

Note: a: approved outlay.

The distribution of expenditure over the different areas varied significantly from plan to plan. In the initial six years, rural water supply justifiably got the highest proportion of 30.8 per cent, but adult education which was of critical importance could not come into the picture even. In the following plans, the relative share of water supply declined drastically although the situation even now is far from satisfactory. Adult education received a substantial share only in the Eighth Plan. Overall, rural house sites-cum-construction schemes received the highest priority. Its relative share increased from 28.8 per cent during 1974-80 to 41.3 during the Seventh Plan and then declined to 24.7 in the Eighth Plan. Elementary education which should have received a high priority, did not get any large share until the Seventh Plan. However, the proportions are not so important, each one of them required much larger funds given the desperate situation.

Public Distribution System

The PDS could be an important instrument for poverty alleviation by making foodgrains and other essential items available to the weaker sections at reasonable prices. But this aspect did not receive any attention worth the name until recent years. In fact, it was included under the MNP only from the Seventh Plan, and the question of its proper targeting given some attention in the Eighth Plan. Lip-services on it had, however, started much earlier.

In Andhra Pradesh, the PDS was in a very bad shape until recent years. Even as late as 1988, distribution of foodgrains through fair price shops (FPS) was only 3.16 lakh tonnes, which was around one-third the level in Tamil Nadu. In 1978, government supplies as a ratio of domestic consumption of Rice worked out to a mere 1.22 per cent (Parthasarathy 1995). The per capita PDS foodgrains per poor population was one of the lowest among all the states till early eighties, as may be seen from Table 6.4, and declined from 16 kg in 1973 to 12 kg in 1978.

Table 6.4

Per capita PDS Foodgrains per Poor Population in Andhra vis-a-vis Other Major States

(in kg)

States	*1973*	*1974*	*1977*	*1978*	*1983*	*1987*	*1988*
Andhra Pradesh	16	15	15	12	65	74	47
Karnataka	22	24	55	39	43	57	47
Kerala	71	75	107	68	124	149	149
Tamil Nadu	14	18	35	22	60	68	67
Assam	31	29	48	47	65	83	68
Bihar	12	12	13	13	19	20	16
Gujarat	52	51	29	14	28	79	81
Haryana	41	36	38	47	66	38	53
Madhya Pradesh	13	9	10	9	15	28	22
Maharashtra	81	69	45	30	48	54	58
Orissa	15	20	15	13	26	23	18
Punjab	73	41	68	104	86	93	31
Rajasthan	33	19	9	19	7	75	67
Uttar Pradesh	13	15	10	18	17	16	18
West Bengal	66	56	63	51	92	55	59

Source: Geetha and Suryanarayana 1993.

The situation however, changed noticeably since 1983, with the introduction of the 'two rupees a kilo' scheme. Under it green cards were issued to the families with annual income of Rs. 6,000 and below and having upto 1.5 acres of wet land under assured water source/2.5

acres under other irrigation source/three acres of dry land under commercial crops/5 acres of land under other crops. Green card holders were eligible to draw 5 kg of rice per capita per month, subject to a maximum of 25 kg per household. The non-poor were given yellow cards and they were not eligible to draw rice. The colours of the card were subsequently changed to white and pink, respectively.

In 1985, there were 8.03 million white card holders in rural areas, accounting for 80 per cent of the total. Total number of white card holders rose to 10.7 million in 1991-92 and after a decline in the following years rose again to 11.27 million in 1996-97. Number of pink cards stood at 4.93 million in the latest year. The total off-take of foodgrains from the Central Pool rose to 18.40 lakh tonnes in 1986 from 6.26 in 1983. The quantum of rice distributed to white card holders in 1995-96 stood at 25.20 lakh tonnes. Number of FPS in rural areas is presently 32,674, out of the total of 39,648, that is, 82.4 per cent (GOA 1998).

As regards the relative position of Andhra among the major states, undoubtedly a significant improvement has taken place over the years. The per capita supply of foodgrains to poor population rose to 74 kg in 1987 from only 12 kg in 1978, and it was exceeded by five of the major states as against most of the states earlier (Table 6.4). Data for recent years on this basis are not available, but in 1993-94, the per capital PDS distribution of foodgrains in Andhra stood at 33 kg for all card-holders as against the all-India average at only 16 kg; Andhra's distribution was next only to Kerala (Mooij 1999).

Even after the changes, the PDS in Andhra suffered from many problems. A large number of non-poor could easily enter the green/white card system. In Rayalaseema area, a study under the NSS (44th round) found that the leakage of benefits to non-target group was to the extent of 24 per cent in terms of households and 21 per cent in quantity. In mid-1995, number of green/white cards was estimated to be roughly double the number of rural poor (Parthasarathy 1995).

The system also came under heavy financial pressure. The subsidy expenditure on white card holders increased from Rs. 78.69 crores in 1983-84 to Rs. 368.54 crores in 1990-91. The government was compelled to raise the price of Rice from Rs. 1.90 per kg to Rs. 3.50 in January 1992. The quantity to which the poor were eligible was also reduced to 4 kg per capita per month, subject to a maximum of 16 kg per household, raised to 20 kg subsequently. Even after this the amount of subsidy escalated to as much as Rs. 1,124.77 crores in 1995-96 (GOA 1998).

The government had to start the targeted PDS in June 1997. The annual requirement of Rice for this came to 21.60 lakh tonnes in 1997-98 but the Government of India agreed to supply at half the Central Issue Price (CIP) only 3.92 lakh tonnes. The half the CIP was fixed at Rs. 3.50 per kg, the same price at which it was sold to white card holders. The state government was permitted to add up to Rs. 50 per quintal towards transport, etc., and fix the consumer price accordingly. The budget for 1997-98 provided for a subsidy of Rs. 712.80 crores.

Ecologically Disadvantaged Areas

The regions of Andhra differ significantly in resource endowment but the efforts to reduce the imbalance in development through special measures came very late, and then also not in adequate measure. Perspective plans, covering a period of 15 years, came in 1969-70 in Rayalaseema and for Telangana and coastal Andhra in 1974-75. The backward areas were identified on the basis of certain criteria. Seventy-five taluks were delineated as drought affected, of which 33 were treated as hard-core. These taluks were mostly in Anantapur, Kurnool, Chittoor, Mahbubnagar, Cuddapah, Nalgonda and Prakasam. All the heads of departments were instructed to give priority to schemes in the drought affected areas. A special Drought Prone Area Programme was also taken up for them. Moreover, on the recommendations of the state government, 14 districts were declared by the Centre as industrially backward in 1971, for concession to be offered by all-India financial institutions. In 1973, the government of India announced a Six-Point Formula for providing a special assistance of Rs. 90 crores in the Fifth Plan for development of the backward areas. Under the programme, 52 taluks were identified in eight districts.

What effect all these had, we have noted in the preceding chapters. We may note here the magnitude of the schemes presently running. There are now three programmes in operation on area basis: (i) Drought Prone Area Programme (DPAP), (ii) Desert Development Programme (DDP), and (iii) Integrated Wasteland Development Project (IWDP). The DPAP is operating with funds provided by the Centre and the state on 50:50 basis, with the objective of drought proofing by taking up soil-land-moisture conservation, water harvesting structures, afforestation and horticulture programmes on a comprehensive micro watershed basis. The programme covered 69 blocks of eight districts in 1994-95 and was extended to 11 districts with 94 blocks in 1995-96. In 1996-97, the expenditure on DPAP came to Rs. 43.13 crores as against the target of Rs. 52.39 crores. Number of watershed targeted was 908 but only 587 could be achieved.

The DDP was launched in 1977-78, and has been in operation in 16 blocks of Anantapur district. The expenditure on the programme in 1996-97 was Rs. 5.92 crores against the target of Rs. 8.98 crores. The physical target and achievement were respectively, 106 and 96 watersheds. As regards IWDP, financed by the Waste Land Development Board of the Central Government, there are 20 projects in 13 districts under implementation. In 1996-97, Rs. 11.81 crores was spent on them against the allocation of Rs. 13.86 crores. The area targeted was 32,935 hectares but the achievement came to only 23,187 hectares (Rao 1998). In the face of rapid depletion of green cover, and vast stretches of marginal lands lying fallow, this level of activity is almost nothing for making a dent on the situation.

From the above analysis it is apparent that poverty reduction is not a matter of any great importance to the government. We conclude the chapter by citing one more instance of the callous attitude of the government towards the poor, the manner of handling the problem of tribal land alienation.

For safeguarding the interests of tribals, laws were passed prohibiting the transfer of landownership from a girijan to a non-girijan. The first one came in 1917 which allowed such transfers only with the written consent of the agent (the District Collector). The second in 1959, which withdrew the powers given to the collector, while the third in 1970 prohibited land transfers from one non-girijan to another non-girijan.

Despite the existence of these regulations, non-tribals continued to acquire land in the scheduled areas. According to a report by the department of tribal welfare, out of 18,48,000 acres of land in the agency areas, non-tribals hold 7,53,435acres, that is around 40 per cent. Non-tribal holding is 52 per cent in Khammam, 60 per cent in Adilabad and 71 per cent in Warangal (Rao 1998).

The very presence of non-tribals owning land in the scheduled areas is proof of the systematic violation of the regulations made from time to time. While during the British period the Act remained on paper only and the girijans continued to be exploited by outsiders, the record of the present government is also no better. Until the powerful Srikakulam girijan movements, the rulers conveniently forgot the existence of the laws and allowed the non-girijans to push out the girijans from their habitat. It was only after the bloody suppression of this movement, the government passed the legislation known as I of 1970. But then also, the Act remained unimplemented and the girijans had to wage many a struggle demanding its implementation.

In a blatant violation of I of 1970 regulation, a government order in 1979 permitted the non-tribals to have occupation up to 5 acres of wet land and 10 acres of dry land. This order was quashed by the High Court in 1984. But despite the court decision, non-tribals continued to occupy the lands on the strength of the above order because the revenue officials connived with the landlords (Rao 1998). Even the legal machinery dupes the girijans. Till March 1997, the settlement courts had rejected 23,531 appeals for restoration involving 1,29,845 acres; the area restored was only 1,06,315 acres and the possession given to 97,688 acres (GOA 1998). It was not infrequent that the girijans did not get any notice of the hearings at any stage before the disposal of a case.

All these are probably not unexpected from a society characterised by, as stated by the President of India on the eve of the fiftieth anniversary of the Republic, "unabashed, vulgar indulgence in conspicuous consumption from a small segment of population". He further stated: "Our giant factories rise out of squalor; our satellites shoot up from the midst of the hovels of the poor. A decade of liberalisation has completely ignored the poor and needy...." (*The Statesman* 2000).

The future of poverty alleviation in Andhra appears gloomy. The present Chief Minister, N. Chandrababu Naidu, is consciously pro-rich. All his programmes are meant for the wealthy sections. As stated by Ambrose Pinto: "His concept of development is limited to cities and towns.... The huge amounts spent on industry oriented infrastructure are normally at the cost of rural development" (Pinto 1999: 2546). The only hope is pressure from below -- probably organisations like the People's War Group. They may compel the government to provide at least palliatives.[5]

Notes

1. The person rate of unemployment is defined as the ratio of total number of unemployed to the total number of persons in the labour force, and time rate of unemployment as the ratio of total person days unemployed to the total labour force person days during the reference period.
2. Subsequently, the ratio of distribution among DRDA/ZP, intermediate panchayats and village panchayats in a district was changed to 15: 15: 70.
3. Participation is to be understood as a household of which at least one member was employed in public works for at least 60 days during a reference period of 365 days preceding the date of survey. Public works cover construction of roads, dams, bunds, digging of ponds etc., as test relief measures, national employment schemes such as NREP, RLEGP, Minimum Needs Programme etc.
4. Based on the norms laid down by the 15th Indian Labour Conference and later modified by the Supreme Court, the minimum wage should be Rs. 125 per day (Jhabvala 1998). In February 1999, the agricultural wages in Andhra varied between Rs. 40 to Rs. 75 for man and Rs. 25 to Rs. 65 for woman (GOI 1999a).
5. It may be noted here that Andhra's relative position has deteriorated considerably in recent years. The Planning Commission's estimate of percentage of population below poverty line for 1999-2000 found Andhra's position worse than in five of the major states, viz., Punjab, Haryana, Kerala, Gujarat and Rajasthan; in 1993-94, only Punjab was ahead of it (GOI 2001).

III

The Economy of Tamil Nadu

7

Resource Mobilisation and Deployment

In budgetary resource mobilisation Tamil Nadu's position has improved significantly in recent years. Out of the last six years of the nineties, it had an overall surplus position in five, and in the last three years, 1994-97, it annually averaged Rs. 292 crores. During 1988-91, on the other hand, there was an annual deficit of Rs. 68 crores (Table 7.1).

The aggregate of receipts in Tamil Nadu, however, had a relatively low growth. Between 1965-68 and 1994-97, it registered an increase of only 46 times, from the annual average of Rs. 289 crores to Rs. 13,414 crores, as against 60 times in all states together. Its relative share in the latter consequently declined from 8.4 per cent to 6.6 per cent. The per capita receipts, however, continued to be higher than the all-states' average, being at Rs. 2,290 and Rs. 2,255 respectively, during 1994-97 (Table 3.1). Below we give a brief look into how the resources were mobilised in the last three decades.

Revenue Receipts

In the aggregate of receipts, the share of revenue account increased from the average of 64.4 per cent during 1965-68 to 78.3 during 1985-88 and 79.0 during 1994-97. The growth in revenue receipts here was 57 times over the entire period as against 64 times in all the states together. Tamil Nadu's growth rate was lower than in Karnataka and Andhra. However, in the relative contribution of revenue receipts to the total, its position could be exceeded by only three states in the latest period. The per capita revenue receipts here was much higher than the average for all states (Table 3.1).

Tax Revenue

In the total revenue receipts of the state, tax revenue always accounted

Table 7.1

Trend in Budgetary Position of Tamil Nadu

(Rs. in crores)

Year/ Period	Receipts			Expenditure			Revenue deficit/ surplus	Overall deficit/ surplus
	Revenue	Capital	Total	Revenue	Capital Disbursement	Total		
1965-68 (a.a.)	186 (64.4)[a]	103	289	191 (65.4)[b]	101	292	-5	-3
1975-78 (a.a.)	615 (72.9)	229	844	632 (74.0)	222	854	-17	-10
1985-88 (a.a.)	2821 (78.3)	784	3605	2825 (77.4)	823	3648	-4	-43
1988-89	3489 (76.7)	1058	4547	3763 (81.5)	854	4617	-274	-69
1989-90	4252 (75.9)	1352	5604	4731 (83.6)	931	5662	-479	-63
1990-91	4976 (82.1)	1084	6060	5295 (86.0)	859	6154	-319	-72
1991-92	6776 (70.6)	2828	9604	8680 (90.4)	920	9600	-1904	+4
1992-93	7016 (71.2)	2842	9858	4543 (87.6)	1206	9748	-1527	+110
1993-94	8062 (79.1)	2126	10188	8758 (87.0)	1304	10062	-696	+126
1994-95	9219 (77.3)	2702	11922	9635 (84.3)	1795	11432	-416	+490
1995-96	10599 (82.0)	2331	12930	10911 (87.1)	1621	12531	-312	+399
1996-97	11961 (77.7)	3429	15390	13065 (84.8)	2337	15402	-1104	-12
1994-97 (a.a.)	10593 (79.0)	2821	13414	11203 (85.4)	1918	13122	-610	+292

Source: RBIFA 1967, 1968, 1978, 1987, 1988, 1991, 1992, 1993; CMIE 1999b, 1998c.

Notes: a.a.: annual average. a: as percentage to total receipts. b: as percentage to total expenditure.

for the major share, and increased from 65.8 per cent during 1965-68 to 78.2 during 1985-88 and 83.9 during 1994-97. The growth in tax revenue over the entire period was 73 times, from the annual average of Rs. 122 crores during 1965-68 to Rs. 8,892 crores during 1994-97, which was nominally higher than the all-states' growth. The ratio between tax revenue and NSDP in Tamil Nadu stood at 9.4 per cent during 1987-90 as against the average of 7.9 for 15 major states (GOT 1997).

In the tax revenue, the proportion of own tax revenue fluctuated between 72 and 75 per cent till early nineties and showed some improvement in the recent years. This performance was noticeably better than the average for all states; in the latter, the contribution declined from 72.9 per cent during 1965-68 to 68.2 during 1994-97. Over the entire period, the OTR increased 74 times here as against 67 times for all states together. Among the southern states, only Karnataka had registered a faster growth (Tables 7.2 and 3.2).

Table 7.2

Trend in Tax and Non-Tax Revenue in Tamil Nadu

(Rs. in crores)

Year/Period	*Tax Revenue*		*Non-Tax Revenue*	
	Total	*OTR*	*Total*	*ONTR*
1965-68 (a.a.)	122.4 (65.8)[a]	94.6 (77.3)[b]	64.0 (34.2)[a]	39.4 (61.6)[c]
1975-78 (a.a.)	470.9 (76.6)	341.5 (72.5)	144.2 (23.4)	93.2 (64.6)
1985-88 (a.a.)	2262.6 (80.1)	1677.4 (74.2)	558.2 (19.9)	246.1 (44.1)
1988-89	2717.1 (77.9)	1994.2 (73.4)	771.7 (22.1)	334.6 (43.4)
1989-90	3436.3 (80.8)	2489.0 (72.4)	815.3 (19.2)	393.0 (48.2)
1990-91	4033.1 (81.0)	3030.2 (75.1)	942.5 (19.0)	388.0 (41.2)
1991-92	4923.6 (72.7)	3734.1 (75.8)	1852.0 (27.3)	1118.5 (60.4)
1992-93	5581.9 (79.6)	4162.2 (74.6)	1434.2 (20.4)	612.8 (42.7)
1993-94	6354.0 (78.8)	4801.4 (75.6)	1707.8 (21.2)	703.9 (41.2)
1994-95	7569.2 (82.1)	5833.8 (77.1)	1650.2 (17.9)	772.7 (46.8)
1995-96	8956.8 (84.5)	7151.2 (79.8)	1642.5 (15.5)	858.4 (52.3)
1996-97	10148.9 (84.8)	7983.4 (78.7)	1812.3 (15.2)	885.4 (48.9)
1994-97 (a.a.)	8891.6 (83.9)	6989.5 (78.6)	1701.7 (16.1)	838.8 (49.3)

Source: As in Table 7.1.

Notes: a: percentage to total revenue receipts.
b: percentage to total tax revenue.
c: percentage to total non-tax revenue.

In terms of tax efforts, that is, OTR per capita – Tamil Nadu is much above the all-India average. As against Rs. 1,199 for the former during 1994-97 the latter had Rs. 706. There were only three states, viz., Maharashtra, Punjab and Gujarat, ahead of Tamil Nadu. Three decades earlier, in 1967-68, Tamil Nadu's per capita tax came to Rs. 29.37 as against the all-states' average at Rs. 21.92. The same three states were ahead of Tamil Nadu then also (Table 3.2).

The scope for further growth in OTR was substantial. The agricultural income-tax had registered an increase of only 13 times between 1960-70 and 1994-97, rising from the average of Rs. 1.49 crores to Rs. 18.73 crores. Its relative share declined from 1.8 per cent to 0.3 per cent in this period. The contribution from land revenue had a steeper fall -- from 10.7 per cent to only 0.4 per cent over the same period; the growth in collection was less than three times, from Rs. 9.05 crores to Rs. 25.16 crores. Similarly, urban immovable property tax made a contribution of only 0.2 per cent during 1994-97. Other taxes recording sharp declines in the relative share were taxes on vehicles, entertainment tax and stamp and registration fees. The taxes that have become somewhat important in recent years are taxes an goods and passengers and taxes and duties on electricity (Table 7.3).

The government relied too heavily on a few of the taxes. The share of sales tax in total OTR increased from 48 per cent during 1960-70 to 67 per cent since mid-seventies. The collection from state excise had a phenomenal growth and its relative share rose to 12.3 per cent from 0.6 over the period. Thus, these two taxes together contributed as much as 79 per cent in recent years. Including stamp and registration fees and vehicle tax, the share of these four taxes was 93 per cent of the total (Table 7.3).

As regards transfers from the Centre, its contribution to total tax revenue fluctuated quite widely. During 1975-78 the average came to 27.5 per cent but in 1994-97 it was only 21.4 per cent. The amount transferred increased from the annual average of Rs. 27.8 crores during 1965-68 to Rs. 129.4 crores during 1975-78 and Rs. 1,902 crores during 1994-97, that is, a growth of 68 times over the entire period; the aggregate of transfer to all the states had increased 84 times (Table 3.4).

Non-Tax Revenue

The growth of NTR in Tamil Nadu was very low. Over the entire period of three decades, 1965-68 to 1994-97, it increased by only 26.6 times, from the annual average of Rs. 64 crores to Rs. 1,702 crores, as against 52.0 times for all states. Its relative share in total revenue declined from 34.2 per cent to 16.1 per cent. This is a very gloomy picture in relation to the position in other states. For all the states, the average share of NTR came to 32.1 per cent of total revenue during 1994-97. Tamil Nadu's was the lowest proportion among all the major states (Tables 3.2 and 7.2).

Table 7.3

Trend in the Structure of Own Tax Revenue in Tamil Nadu

(in Rs. crores)

Items	*1960-70 (a.a.)*	*1988-91 (a.a.)*	*1994-97 (a.a.)*
Agricultural income tax	1.49 (1.8)	10.6 (0.4)	16.7 (0.2)
Land revenue	9.05 (10.7)	15.0 (0.6)	26.4 (0.4)
Stamp and registration fees	10.01 (11.8)	199.3 (8.0)	570.1 (8.2)
Urban immovable property	0.13a (0.2)	2.6 ().1)	10.4 (0.1)
Sales tax	40.70 (48.0)	1686.7 (67.3)	4648.1 (66.5)
State excise	0.55 (0.6)	293.4 (11.7)	870.8 (12.5)
Taxes on vehicles	13.18 (15.6)	193.5 (7.7)	396.7 (5.7)
Taxes on goods and passengers		5.7 (0.2)	153.1 (2.2)
Entertainment tax	4.87 (5.7)	68.1 (2.7)	102.2 (1.5)
Total (including others)	84.73 (100.0)	2504.5 (100.0)	6989.4 (100.0)

Source: GOT 1997.
Note: a: land tax only.

In the NTR, a large proportion has been contributed by grants from the Centre. As evident from Table 7.2, its relative share rose to 50.7 per cent during 1994-97 from 38.4 during 1965-68, although with considerable fluctuations. The growth of own non-tax revenue in this period was only 21 times as against 35 times in grants. The relative share of ONTR in Tamil Nadu was 49.3 per cent during 1994-97, lower than in most of the major states (Table 3.2).

There was ample scope for raising the contribution of ONTR. Receipts from dividend and profit stood at the average of Rs. 0.57 crore during 1975-78 and even during 1988-91 it was a mere Rs. 2.07 crores, constituting 0.6 per cent of total ONTR. During 1994-97, however, there was a substantial growth -- the annual average stood at Rs. 19.48 crores, constituting 2.3 per cent of the total. Even this is not very significant if the level of investment in Tamil Nadu PSUs is considered. Excluding reserves, it stood at Rs. 4,810.52 crores in 1996-97, rising from Rs. 2,529.56 crores in 1992-93 (Ambirajan 1999).

The contribution from general services, as well as social services, declined significantly in relative term. With a growth of only 6.2 times between 1975-78 and 1994-97 – from Rs. 18.1 crores to Rs. 111.7 – the relative share of general services declined to 13.3 per cent from 19.4. For social services, the decline was from 18 per cent during 1988-91 to 13.5 during 1994-97 – the collection rising from the annual average of Rs. 66.9 crores to Rs. 113.7 crores. The scope for raising revenue from certain segments of social services was enormous. The higher income groups using educational institutions and medical services could easily be made to pay much more than the cost of providing them. The fees charged to students in higher educational institutions continue to be ridiculously low.

The collection under ONTR came overwhelmingly from economic services and interest receipts. The contribution of the former increased from 40.0 per cent of the total during 1975-78 to 42.1 per cent during 1988-91, and then declined to 32.2 in 1994-97. The proportion for interest receipts in these periods were, respectively, 24.2, 23.3 and 38.6 per cent.

Within economic services, the contribution of crop husbandry declined from 13.1 per cent of ONTR during 1975-78 to 7.4 during 1994-97, and of forestry and wild-life from around 11 per cent during 1988-91 to 7.0. Irrigation, after so much of investment, contributed an average of only Rs. 6.84 crores during 1994-97, constituting 0.8 per cent of the total; during 1975-78 it provided 2.6 per cent. Industries was the only sector under economic services that raised its share substantially over the years -- from 2.5 per cent of the total during 1975-78 to around 8 per cent since the late eighties.

The contribution from dividend and profit showed an increase only in recent years. The annual average for 1994-97 stood at Rs. 19.48 crores, rising from Rs. 2.07 crores in 1988-91. The investment in public sector enterprises totalled Rs. 3,023 crores at the end of 1993-94 and the return on investment in the last two years (1992-94) averaged 1.34 per cent (GOT 1997: 114). Among the statutory bodies, the Electricity Board had incurred a total loss (commercial) of Rs. 1,454 crores in the last six years (1992-98) (CMIE 1999d).

On the central transfers to Tamil Nadu a few words need to be added. The total transfer of resources to the state increased from the annual average of Rs. 52.4 crores during 1965-68 to Rs. 2,765 crores during 1994-97, that is a growth of 53 times as against 69 times in the transfers to all states. The per capita transfer increased from Rs. 14.20 in 1965-68 to Rs. 41 during 1975-78 and then to Rs. 474 in 1994-97, that is, a growth of 33 times over the entire period; for all states together, on the other hand, it was 38 times – from Rs. 15 to Rs. 567. As percentage to total revenue of the state, central transfer constituted 26.1 during 1994-97, declining from 29.3 in 1975-78. For all states, the proportion averaged 32.8 and 36.1 in the two periods respectively (Table 3.4).

The low level of central transfer to Tamil Nadu probably cannot be rectified, so long as the criteria for transfers are not changed. But it needs to be considered how long the Centre will continue to provide unduly large funds to some of the states. For instance, Nagaland gets 90 per cent of its resources from the Centre, and even the remaining 10 per cent it finds difficult to collect.

Capital Receipts

The relative importance of capital receipts in Tamil Nadu's budgets has declined substantially over the years. In the aggregate receipts of the state it contributed around 35 per cent during 1965-68 but declined to 21 per cent during 1994-97. Excepting two other states, all had greater reliance on capital receipts in recent years. The growth in receipts over the entire period was 27 times here as against 52 times for all states together (Tables 3.1 and 7.1).

In the total of capital receipts, the lion's share was contributed by loans from the Centre. This item accounted for 52 per cent during 1965-68 and decreased to 46 during 1975-78 and 45 in 1994-97. The growth in receipts was from the average of Rs. 53.7 crores during 1965-68 to Rs. 1,265.9 crores during 1994-97, that is around 24 times. Major portion of the central loan came for state plan schemes. Its share declined from 64 per cent during 1975-78 to 57 per cent during 1988-91 and then rose to 66 during 1994-97. The next important item was non-plan loans, with its shares at 28, 37, and 33 per cent in these periods, respectively. In recent years, these loans were almost entirely from the share of small savings.

Among other items in capital receipts, as evident from Table 7.4, internal debt and recovery of loans and advances were important. The contribution from the former rose to 19 per cent during 1988-91 from 15 in 1975-78 but declined again to 16 per cent. Within it, the share of market loans was 89 per cent in 1994-97 as against 79 in 1975-78. Other important sources in recent years were loans from the LICI,

NABARD and National Cooperative Development Corporation. As regards recovery of loans, its relative share showed a significant decline, and stood at 18 per cent of total during 1994-97. The recovery from power projects was the most important source in recent years.

Table 7.4

Trend in Composition of Capital Receipts in Tamil Nadu

(Rs. in crores)

Items	*1975-78 (a.a.)*	*1988-91 (a.a.)*	*1994-97 (a.a.)*
Total capital receipts	229.3 (100.0)	1164.9 (100.0)	2820.5 (100.0)
I. Internal debt	34.6 (15.1)	219.9 (18.9)	449.1 (15.9)
(a) Market loans	27.2	190.0	399.2
II. Loans from the Centre	104.7 (45.7)	548.6 (47.1)	1265.9 (44.9)
(a) State plan scheme	67.3	315.5	831.7
(b) Non-plan	28.9	202.0	420.6
III. Recovery of loans	50.5 (22.0)	201.2 (17.3)	512.6 (18.2)
(a) Power projects	3.3	77.4	179.6
IV. Small savings	8.5 (3.7)	101.7 (8.7)	199.6 (7.1)
V. Reserve fund	13.4 (5.9)	47.5 (4.1)	89.8 (3.2)

Source: As in Table 7.1.

Of the remaining items, small savings registered a significant rise in recent years, and contributed 7 per cent of the total during 1994-97. The growth in receipts was 23.5 times over the period of two decades since 1975-78. Reserve fund showed a continuous decline in relative term, with the growth in amount at only around seven times over the period of two decades. The collection from deposits and advances, which fluctuated wildly, contributed 6.7 per cent of the total during 1994-97.

Although Tamil Nadu's reliance on capital receipts is relatively low, its outstanding liabilities are quite high. In 1997, it stood at Rs. 14,183 crores, giving a per capita liability of Rs. 2,352; this is higher than the level in two of the southern states, Karnataka and Andhra Pradesh (RBI 1999: II).

Resource Deployment

The growth of budgetary expenditure in Tamil Nadu was relatively low. Over a period three decades, between 1965-68 and 1994-97, it increased by a factor of only 45 -- from Rs. 292 crores to Rs. 13,122 crores -- as against 52 times for all the states together. The per capita expenditure in Tamil Nadu was, however, always higher than the all-states' average. During 1994-97, these were respectively, Rs. 2,251 and Rs. 1,972; there were four states with higher levels than Tamil Nadu's (Table 3.6).

In the total expenditure, the proportion of revenue expenditure increased from 65 per cent during 1965-68 to 77 during 1985-88 and then to 85 in 1994-97. In very few other states this proportion was so high; the average for all states stood at 82 per cent during 1994-97, rising from 63 during 1965-68. Below we give a brief look into the trend in composition of revenue and capital expenditure in Tamil Nadu.

Revenue Expenditure

The first striking change in revenue expenditure is the decline in share of development expenditure in recent years. It stood at 73 per cent during 1985-88, rising from 62 per cent in 1965-68, but declined to 67 during 1994-97. The growth in expenditure over the entire period was 64 times, from Rs. 117.6 crores to Rs. 7,521 crores, but in the last two decades, 1975-78 to 1994-97, it was only 17 times.

In the development expenditure, as may be seen from Table 7.5, social services accounted for the lion's share, although with a declining trend. Its share stood at 62.8 per cent during 1975-78 and 59.0 during 1994-97; in the total of revenue expenditure, it constituted respectively, 43.1 and 39.6 per cent. Very few states were spending so much on social services. In 1994-95, for example, there were only two states, viz., Kerala and West Bengal, providing a slightly higher proportion (GOT 1997).

Within social services, education accounted for around half, and recorded a growth in expenditure of 15 times in the last two decades. In the aggregate of revenue expenditure its share declined from 22.9 per cent in 1975-78 to 19.7 in 1994-97. The high level of expenditure here was reflected in its success in reducing illiteracy and improving primary education, as noted in a preceding chapter. Medical, public health and family welfare was the next important item. The growth in expenditure here was 13 times, and the relative share in aggregate of revenue expenditure declined from 11.0 per cent to 8.1 per cent over the period. Other important items were social security, nutrition, and welfare of backward classes. The share of the first one declined from 5.5 per cent during 1975-78 to 2.1 during 1994-97, with a growth in expenditure of only 6.7 times. The remaining two items received attention only in recent years (Table 7.5).

Table 7.5

Trend in Composition of Revenue and Capital Expenditure in Tamil Nadu

(Rs. in crores)

Items	*1975-78 (a.a.)*	*1985-88 (a.a.)*	*1994-97 (a.a.)*
Total Revenue Expenditure	631.9 (100.0)	2825 (100.0)	11203.5 (100.0)
I. Development expenditure	433.9 (68.7)	2055.7 (72.8)	7521.0 (67.1)
(A) Social services	272.3 (43.1)	1270.3 (45.0)	4433.9 (39.6)
(i) Education etc.	145.0 (22.9)	608.2 (21.5)	2205.9 (19.7)
(ii) Medical etc.[a]	69.5 (11.0)	285.4 (10.1)	903.9 (8.1)
(iii) Social security and welfare	35.0 (5.5)	148.1 (5.2)	235.8 (2.1)
(iv) Nutrition	-	102.0 (3.6)	366.4 (3.3)
(B) Economic services	161.6 (25.6)	785.4 (27.8)	3087.1 (27.6)
(i) Agriculture and allied	88.8[b] (14.1)	213.8 (7.6)	1087.0 (9.7)
(ii) Rural development	-	166.4 (5.9)	347.4 (3.1)
(iii) Irrigation and flood control	21.5 (3.4)	75.4 (2.7)	220.4 (2.0)
(iv) Village and SSI	7.3 (1.2)	51.9 (1.8)	207.5 (1.9)
(v) Transport and comm.	31.2 (4.9)	86.0 (3.0)	302.7 (2.7)
II. Non-development	180.3 (28.5)	700.8 (24.8)	3456.4 (30.9)
(a) Interest payment	50.0 (7.9)	222.1 (7.9)	1286.1 (11.5)
(b) Administrative services	70.0 (11.1)	249.5 (8.8)	912.4 (8.1)
Police	30.0 (4.7)	111.0 (3.9)	428.7 (3.8)
(c) Pension etc.	22.5 (3.6)	150.1 (5.3)	831.0 (7.4)
Capital Disbursement	222.0 (100.0)	823.2 (100.0)	1918.6 (100.0)
I. Total capital outlay	60.7 (27.3)	170.4 (20.7)	730.2 (38.1)
Development expenditure	58.5 (26.4)	158.7 (19.3)	703.4 (36.7)
(A) Social services	9.2 (4.2)	26.2 (3.2)	181.7 (9.5)
(B) Economic services	49.3 (22.2)	132.5 (16.1)	521.7 (27.2)
(i) Agriculture and allied	7.5 (3.4)	33.9 (4.1)	64.3 (3.4)
(ii) Irrigation and flood	22.0 (9.9)	54.5 (6.6)	62.2 (3.2)
(iii) Transport and comm.	6.8 (3.1)	26.9 (3.3)	233.5 (12.2)
II. Repayment of loans to centre	39.3 (17.7)	148.1 (18.0)	262.7 (13.7)
III. Discharge of internal debt	13.6 (6.1)	38.5 (4.7)	21.0 (1.1)
IV. Loans by state govt.	105.0 (47.3)	466.3 (56.6)	904.7 (47.2)

Source: As in Table 7.1.

Notes: a: including water supply and sanitation.
b: includes Rs. 4.12 crores for minor irrigation.

As the share of social services declined, the economic services gained. Since mid-eighties, it was receiving around 28 per cent of the aggregate of revenue expenditure as against 25.6 during 1975-78 and 24.0 during 1965-68. Within economic services, agriculture and allied sectors received the highest proportion. Its share was a little more than 50 per cent during 1975-78 and in recent years around 35 per cent. Transport and communication was the next important item, and its share declined from 19.3 per cent to around 10 per cent over the period. Irrigation and flood control also recorded a decline from 13.3 per cent during 1975-78 to 7.1 during 1994-97. Rural development, which was introduced in early eighties, received 21 per cent during 1985-88 but declined to only 11 per cent during 1994-97.

The most alarming aspect of revenue expenditure is the high growth in non-development expenditure. Over the period of two decades it registered a 19-fold rise, and the relative share rose to 31 per cent in 1994-97 from 25 per cent during 1985-88. The most rapidly growing item here was interest payment. Between 1975-78 and 1994-97, it multiplied 26 times -- rising from Rs. 50 crores to Rs. 1,286 crores -- and the relative share rose to 37.2 per cent from 27.8. Even in the aggregate of revenue expenditure it accounted for 11.5 per cent in 1994-97 (Table 7.5).

Among other items, while the relative share of administrative services declined over the period, for pension payments the growth was very rapid. The proportion for the former in non-development expenditure was 26.4 per cent in 1994-97 as against 38.8 in 1975-78; the growth in expenditure over the period was 13 times. The expenditure on pension payment, on the other hand, had a 37-fold rise in this period, and the relative share rose to 24.0 per cent from 12.5. In administrative services, the expenditure on police accounted for a very large share, rising from 42.9 per cent of the total in 1975-78 to 47.0 in 1994-97 with a growth in expenditure of 14.3 times. From the angle of productivity of the services rendered all these payments can definitely be questioned.

One aspect of revenue expenditure that often became a matter of controversy is the rapid growth in payment of subsidies to different functions. The total of annual subsidy payment increased from Rs. 396.8 crores in 1977-78 to Rs. 2,379.9 crores in 1987-88. Recoveries from social and economic services as percentage to the cost of providing them, declined from 18.4 to 8.8 over the period (Rao, 1992). In recent years, however, there has been some improvement in the situation. During 1989-95, the annual average of subsidies payment totalled Rs. 1,428.9 crores. In this total, economic services received 929.4 crores, that is 65 per cent. Within economic services, agriculture, forestry and fishing accounted for around half, and electricity, gas, etc., little more than a third. Outside economic services, social security and welfare services was the single largest item. It received an average of Rs. 442.4 crores in this period, constituting 31 per cent of the aggregate of subsidies payments (GOT 1997).

The controversy on subsidies is not limited to the amount spent, but extends to whether these payments are properly targeted. There have been allegations that the really needy were often bypassed by the system. The public distribution system, as will be noted in a subsequent chapter, has not benefited the poor much. Even in other areas, the beneficiaries were largely the not-so-poor.

Capital Expenditure

The capital expenditure in Tamil Nadu generally fell short of capital receipts by a large amount. The gap during 1994-97 annually averaged Rs. 902 crores as against only Rs. 2 crores during 1965-68 and Rs. 7 crores during 1975-78. The growth in capital expenditure was only 19 times between 1965-68 and 1994-97 as against 45 times in the aggregate of expenditure. For all states together, the capital expenditure had multiplied 26 times in this period (Table 3.6). This use of capital receipts for financing revenue expenditure amounts to depriving the future generations of their dues; the latter will be making the repayments without getting anything in return.

It was not only that the growth in capital expenditure was low, within it the proportion going for development purposes was not high. An overwhelming proportion was spent on loans by the state government, repayments to the Centre and discharge of internal debt. The share of these three items together increased from 71.1 per cent during 1975-78 to 79.3 during 1985-88 and then declined to 62 per cent in the last three years. The proportion left for development expenditure, therefore, could not be much. Of course, the loans by the state government were largely for development purposes.

The development expenditure by the state government had a growth of 12 times in the last two decades, from Rs. 58.5 crores annually during 1975-78 to Rs. 703.4 crores during 1994-97. Its relative share in aggregate of capital disbursements declined to 19 per cent during 1985-88 from 26 per cent in 1975-78 and then rose to 37 per cent in the last three years.

In the development expenditure, the share of economic services decreased to 74 per cent during 1974-97 from more than 80 per cent till late eighties. The important sectors receiving investment were irrigation and flood control, transport and communication and agriculture and allied. The share of irrigation and flood control in economic services was as much as 45 per cent during 1975-78 but declined to 12 per cent during 1994-97. For transport and communication, on the other hand, it rose to 45 per cent from only 14 per cent, over the same period (Table 7.5).

The loans by state government generally accounted for around half of the aggregate of capital disbursements, and therefore, their proper utilisation was of critical importance. The loans were overwhelmingly for development purposes -- to the extent of 95 per cent during 1994-97. In development purposes, economic services accounted for 65 per cent in the last three years as against 71 per cent during 1975-78, the balance went for social services. In economic services, power projects often accounted for the largest share, and in social services it was housing (CMIE 1999b).

Plan Expenditure

The level of plan expenditure in Tamil Nadu's budgetary expenditure was very low. It was generally around a fifth of the total as against the average of more than a quarter for all states. In the capital account, the share of plan expenditure in Tamil Nadu increased from 38.0 per cent in 1975-76 to 50.1 in 1995-96. In the revenue account, the proportion in these two years were respectively 12.7 and 17.5 per cent. Below we give a brief look into the pattern of growth in plan expenditure.

The plan expenditure of Tamil Nadu, as evident from Table 7.6, increased from Rs. 80 crores during the First Plan to Rs. 14,017 crores in the Eighth Plan, that is a growth of 175 times in current prices. If the First Plan is excluded, which was too small, the growth since Second Plan comes to 75 times. The per capita plan outlay of Tamil Nadu increased from Rs. 38 in the First Plan to Rs. 98 in the Third, Rs. 201 in the Fifth, Rs. 1,110 in the Seventh and Rs. 1,825 in the Eighth Plan. In relation to the average for all states, Tamil Nadu's per capita was lower in five of the plans -- first, fourth, fifth, sixth and eighth. The plan expenditure as percentage to the state's NSDP declined from 7.69 during 1980-85 to 5.33 during 1992-97 (GOT 1998: 11-12,575).

Table 7.6

Trend in Plan-wise Expenditure of Tamil Nadu in Different Sectors

(Rs. in crores)

Sectors	*I Plan (1951-56)*	*II Plan (1956-61)*	*III Plan (1961-66)*	*IV Plan (1969-74)*	*V Plan (1974-78)*	*VI Plan (1980-85)*	*VII Plan (1985-90)*	*VIII Plan (1992-97)*
Agriculture and allied	9.6 (11.9)	30.6 (16.3)	74.5 (21.5)	103.7 (18.6)	93.3 (11.2)	707.9 (19.4)	938.1 (14.8)	2510.7 (17.9)
Irrigation and flood	20.1 (25.1)	17.6 (9.3)	31.5 (9.1)	28.3 (5.1)	59.6 (7.3)	204.2 (5.6)	343.9 (5.4)	539.7 (3.8)
Power	30.3 (37.7)	79.1 (42.1)	119.2 (34.3)	210.0 (37.6)	259.8 (31.2)	967.6 (26.5)	1770.8 (28.0)	3115.9 (22.2)
Industry and minerals	1.5 (1.9)	14.1 (7.5)	23.7 (6.8)	33.9 (5.9)	50.6 (6.1)	293.2 (8.0)	504.8 (8.0)	1160.2 (8.3)
Transport and comm.	2.7 (3.4)	5.5 (2.9)	11.7 (3.4)	30.7 (5.5)	86.1 (10.3)	291.4 (8.0)	342.1 (5.4)	1465.5 (10.5)
Social and comm. services	16.0 (20.0)	38.0 (20.2)	80.2 (23.1)	142.8 (20.0)	237.7 (20.2)	1108.7 (19.7)	2293.3 (20.0)	5043.4 (36.0)
Grand Total (incl. Others)	80.4 (100.0)	187.8 (100.0)	347.1 (100.0)	559.0 (100.0)	833.6 (100.0)	3644.6 (100.0)	6316.1 (100.0)	14016.8 (100.0)

Source: GOT 1998: Statement I.

In the sectoral distribution of expenditure, power sector received the highest priority. The average share for it came to 32.4 per cent in the eight five-year plans, followed by social and community services 22.4 and agriculture and allied sectors 16.4 per cent. Irrigation and flood control, closely related to agriculture, received an average of 8.8 per cent, and declined sharply from 25.1 per cent in the First Plan to 3.8 in the Eighth Plan. The average share for industry came to 6.6 per cent, and of transport and communication 6.2 (Table 7.6).

To look at the growth of expenditure in some of the items: Between the Third Plan and the Eighth, while the grand total of expenditure had a 40-fold rise, for agricultural programmes it was only 34 times. Within agriculture, the expenditure on fishery had a growth of only 31 times, from Rs. 2.57 crores to Rs. 79.60 crores, and for animal husbandry 32 times, from Rs. 3.3 crores to Rs. 106.4 crores. In minor irrigation, the growth was only 8.4 times in this period -- from Rs. 22.6 crores to Rs. 190.1 crores. In village and small-scale industries, which are of critical importance for diversifying rural economic activities, the expenditure increased only 28 times, from Rs. 22.1 crores to Rs. 629.0 crores. The social and community services had registered a 63-fold rise in expenditure in this period, but medical and public health in it had only 18.5 times and in general education 15 times (GOT 1998, 1982).

Finally, a few words may be added on the status of devolution of resources to the Panchayat Raj Institutions (PRIs). Tamil Nadu's position here is relatively dismal. Not only the beginning came late, the amount provided was also low. The first step towards decentralised district planning came only in 1993-94, when it was introduced only for certain sectors involving small investments. The amount provided was very small, and declined in recent years. It increased from Rs. 20 crores in 1993-94 to Rs. 60 crores in 1996-97 but in the following two years it was down to Rs. 35 crores each. For the entire Ninth Plan the outlay has been fixed at Rs. 275 crores, and it is to cover more than two dozen activities (GOT 1998: 38-39).

Even the overall devolution of plan outlays to the PRIs was relatively small in Tamil Nadu. During the Ninth Plan, they will be getting only Rs. 7,888.75 crores out of the grand total outlay of Rs. 25,000 crores, that is, 31.5 per cent. In all the neighbouring states the devolutions are of higher order. In Andhra Pradesh, even during the Seventh Plan it was to the extent of 36 per cent of total outlay (GOA 1993a: I). This is the situation despite the Constitution's 73rd Amendment specifically providing for vesting the PRIs with powers and financial resources to enable them to function as institutions of self-government.

8

Agricultural Transformation

The economy of Tamil Nadu is much less dependent on agriculture than most other states. The proportion of SDP contributed by agriculture and allied activities was only around 22 per cent in recent years, as noted in Chapter 2. However, the well-being of a large proportion of the state's population is still dependent on the progress of this sector. In total employment its contribution was 61 per cent in 1991. In this chapter, we look into the pattern of growth in agriculture and allied activities over the last four decades or so. The analysis follows the same pattern as in Chapter 4.

I
Agriculture

The growth of agricultural output in Tamil Nadu was generally very low. Considering the recent years first, during 1991-92 to 1996-97, Tamil Nadu had a compound annual growth of only 1.4 per cent as against 3.9 per cent for all-India; the other southern states also had a much higher growth (RBI 1999: I). The index of agricultural production (with the triennium ending 1981-82=100) stood at 163.0 in 1994-95 (GOT 1997). As regards earlier years, between 1962-65 and 1980-83 the value of output of 19 major crops, according to one calculation, had a growth of only 11.8 per cent – from Rs. 732.40 crores to Rs. 818.50 crores (at constant prices). In fact, in relation to 1970-73 there was an absolute decline, the average value of output in this period being Rs. 895.85 crores (Bhalla and Tyagi 1989).

Foodgrains

The most important group of crops, foodgrains, had recorded a very poor performance. The per capita production increased by only 2.7

per cent between 1960-63 and 1970-73 and in the following period of two-and-half decades ending in 1993-96 a decrease by 9.8 per cent. The production declined from the annual average of 169.6 kg during 1970-73 to 153 kg during 1993-96. In the latest period, the all-India average stood at 208 kg and there were eight states with higher level than Tamil Nadu's (Table 4.1). Total production of foodgrains increased from the annual average of 48.4 lakh tonnes (lts) during 1956-59 to 70.3 during 1970-73, that is, a growth of 44 per cent in one-and-half decades, but in the following two-and-half decades there was a negligible 10 per cent rise, production in 1994-97 being 77.1 lts (Table 8.1) (for earlier years GOT 1972).

Table 8.1

Trend in Area, Yield and Production of Selected Crops in Tamil Nadu

Crops	*1970-73 (a.a.)*			*1980-83 (a.a.)*			*1994-97 (a.a.)*		
	A	*P*	*Y*	*A*	*P*	*Y*	*A*	*P*	*Y*
Rice	2743	5391	1963	2195	4423	1997	2149	6305	2923
Jowar	715	5233	747	619	449	727	437	415	950
Bajra	471	303	647	323	280	857	191	225	1177
Ragi	282	305	1053	215	324	1487	145	267	1850
Maize	14	15	1076	22	43	1903	54	85	1590
Arhar	86	36	410	99	44	447	107	87	806
Foodgrains	5203	7028	1350	4220	5907	1390	3824	7713	2023
Groundnut	1059	1098	1033	905	924	1007	1047	1695	1620
Sesamum	130	42	323	114	35	307	133	55	420
Coconut[a]	105	950	9120	125	1195	9500	316	3805	12091
Sunflower	78	64	820	28	13	433	38	37	963
Castor	9.5	4.0	417	15	4.6	307	36	11.2	313
Sugarcane[b]	132	10727	81250	186	17996	96	308	32110	103833
Cotton[c]	309	374	203	218	264	207	258	384	250
Chillies	80	116	1443	72	48	667	66	34	514
Coriander	32	13	410	53	21	410	34	6.8	177
Turmeric	10	36	3763	13	51	3893	16	95	5955
Tapioca	44	547	12413	50	1406	28090	75	2958	39882
Banana	46	904	19420	56	978	17457	71	3100	43414

Source: CMIE 1998.

Notes: A: area in '000 ha. P: production in '000 tonnes; Yield: in kg/ha.
a: production in million nuts, and yield in nuts/ha.
b: yield in tonnes/ha.
c: production in '000 bales.

How far the growth that took place was due to yield improvement and how far due to acreage increase? The yield per hectare in foodgrains had recorded a rise of only 98.5 per cent over a period of more than three decades – from the annual average of 1,102 kg during 1960-63 to 2,187 kg during 1993-96. The growth rate of Tamil Nadu was lower than that in six of the major states (Table 4.1). The acreage under foodgrains, as may be seen from Table 8.1, declined continuously, from the annual average of 52.0 lakh ha during 1970-73 to 38.2 lakh during 1994-97.

As regards the pattern under different foodgrains, the most important crop, rice, had registered an increase in production of 67.4 per cent between 1956-59 and 1970-73, but in the following two-and-half decades, ending in 1994-97, it was by only 16.9 per cent. The annual average production in these three time points were 32.2, 53.9 and 63.0 lts respectively. The growth in the latter period was exclusively due to yield increase as the area under rice registered an absolute decline. The acreage increased from the average of 2.27 lakh hectares during 1956-59 to 2.74 lakh hectares in 1970-73 and then declined to 2.15 lakh hectares during 1994-97. The yield per hectare increased from the average of 1,417 kg during 1956-61 to 1,963 kg in 1970-73 and then to 2,923 kg during 1994-97, that is, 38.5 per cent over the first period and 48.9 per cent in the second.

The next important crop was jowar, and the production here declined continuously from the annual average of 5.69 lts during 1956-61 to 5.33 during 1970-73 and 4.15 lts during 1994-97. The fall in acreage under it was very sharp in recent years. It was down to 4.37 lakh ha during 1994-97 from 6.19 lakh hectares in 1980-83 and 7.56 lakh hectares during 1961-66. The growth in yield rate was substantial in recent years, after recording declines till early eighties. The yield per hectare fell to 727 kg in 1980-83 from 754 kg during 1956-61, but rose noticeably to 950 kg during 1994-97.

In bajra, the fall in acreage was still sharper. During 1994-97 it stood at the average of only 1.91 lakh hectares, declining from 5.14 lakh hectares during 1956-61. The production here declined continuously, as may seen from Table 8.1, despite the growth in yield rate from 559 kg during 1956-61 to 647 during 1970-73 and 1,177 kg during 1994-97. Among other cereals, ragi recorded a sharp decline in area, and despite a rapid growth in productivity the production fell to 2.67 lts during 1994-97 from 3.24 lts during 1980-83. Maize, a minor cereal, was the only crop that gained noticeably in acreage, from only 7 thousand hectares during 1956-61 to 54 thousand hectares during 1994-97. The yield rate also showed a noticeable growth.

In pulses, the growth in production was substantial, particularly since mid-eighties. Total production rose to the annual average of 3.36 lakh tonnes during 1994-97 from 2.73 during 1984-87, 1.53 in 1970-73 and 1.07 lts during 1961-66, that is, a three-fold rise over the entire period. The area under pulses rose to 7.65 lakh hectares during 1994-97 from 5.43 during 1970-73 and 4.08 during 1961-66. The growth in productivity was substantial, particularly in recent years. In arhar, the most important crop, yield per hectare rose to 806 kg during 1994-97 from 447 kg in 1980-83 (Table 8.1).

Non-Foodgrains

Among non-foodgrains, as evident from Table 8.1, groundnut has always accounted for the largest acreage. The area under it generally varied between 9 and 11 lakh hectares. The production of groundnut showed a significant rise in recent years – the annual average being 16.95 lakh tonnes during 1994-97, rising from 9.24 lts during 1980-83. This was due to a sharp rise in yield rate – from 1,007 kg/ha to 1,620 kg/ha over the period.

Other important oilseeds in Tamil Nadu are sesamum, coconut and sunflower. The area under sesamum has remained more or less static. The average for 1994-97 came to 1.33 lakh hectares and even during 1960-63 it stood at 1.23 lakh hectares. The production showed a substantial growth in recent years, mainly due to the growth in yield rate. Coconut is the only major oilseed in Tamil Nadu recording a rapid rise in both area and productivity. The area under it registered a three-fold rise between 1970-73 and 1994-97, from 1.05 lakh hectares to 3.16 lakh hectares, and the yield per hectare increased by 32.6 per cent -- from 9,120 nuts to 12,091. Sunflower, the next important crop, had wide fluctuations in both production and productivity and the area under it declined steeply. In castor, there was a nearly four-fold rise in area but the yield rate showed a decline (Table 8.1).

The production of sugarcane in Tamil Nadu recorded an appreciable growth. Between 1970-73 and 1994-97, there was a three-fold rise, from 107 lts to 321 lts. This was primarily a product of increase in acreage. The area under it recorded a 133 per cent rise over the period, from 1.32 lakh hectares to 3.08 lakh hectares. The growth in productivity, on the other hand, was by only 28 per cent – from 81.2 thousand tonnes to 103.8 thousand tonnes.

In cotton, the crop with quite a large acreage, the performance was not at all satisfactory. The production declined from the annual average of 378 thousand bales during 1961-66 to 264 thousand in 1980-83, and then recovered to 384 thousand bales during 1994-97. The area under it declined continuously till early eighties and then recovered partially in recent years. The yield per hectare rose to 250 kg during 1994-97 from 203 during 1970-73.

Among other crops, production of chillies declined sharply over the years. After rising to the average of 116 thousand tonnes during 1970-73, from 84 thousand tonnes during 1956-61, it fell continuously to only 34 thousand tonnes during 1994-97. The acreage under it declined and so also the yield rate, as may be seen from Table 8.1. Another spice, coriander, too performed no better. The production during 1994-97 was only 6,800 tonnes, less than one-third the level reached in early eighties. There was a sharp fall in yield rate. Turmeric with a relatively small area, however, performed quite well; the production was nearly trebled in the last two-and-half decades, with a 60 per cent rise in area and 58 per cent in yield rate.

Among fruits and vegetables, banana and tapioca were particularly important. Production of banana increased from 9 lakh tonnes annually during 1970-73 to 31 lakh tonnes during 1994-97, that is, a growth of 3.4 times. This was mainly a product of yield increase, by 124 per cent over the period. The highest growth was, however, in tapioca. Production registered a more than five-fold rise, with 221 per cent growth in yield rate and 70 per cent in acreage. Onions had also recorded some increase in production. It stood at 2.66 lts during 1994-97, rising from 2.10 during 1980-83 and 1.61 during 1956-61. The area under it was nearly doubled, rising from 14 thousand ha to 25 thousand, but the yield rate declined, from 12,559 kg/ha to 10,855 kg/ha over the entire period. The production of potato decreased noticeably in recent years. It stood at the average of only 79 thousand tonnes during 1994-97 as against 95 thousand during 1980-83. This was solely due to the fall in area, from 10 thousand hectares to 4.2 thousand hectares, as the yield rate had risen from 9,500 kg/ha to 18,890 kg/ha.

District-wise Disparity

It was not only that the overall growth in agricultural production was low and crop-wise there were great variations, the performance district-wise also varied greatly. As evident from Table 8.2, the per capita production of foodgrains during 1992-94 varied between the highest of

350 kg in Nagapattinam and the lowest at 5 kg in Nilgiris. Seven districts had levels much below the state average. The yield rate of the most important crop, rice, was as much as 4,745 kg in Dindigul during 1993-95 as against the lowest of 1,797 kg in Ramanathapuram. The growth in yield rate between 1981-84 and 1993-95 was only 24 per cent in Ramanathapuram whereas in Tirunelveli, which already had a high yield, it was 95 per cent.

Table 8.2

Inter-District Variation in Foodgrains and Groundnut Production: Tamil Nadu

Districts	*Per capital foodgrains prod. (kg) 1992-94 (a.a.)*	*Yield Rate (kg/ha) in rice*			*Yield rate in groundnut 1993-95 (a.a.)*
		1981-84 (a.a.)	*1993-95 (a.a.)*	*% rise*	
Chengalpattu	1665	1681	3136	86.6	2077
South Acrot	172	2167	3076	41.9	1618
North Acrot	70	2222	2893	30.2	2184
Tiruvannamalai	125	-	2797	-	1336
Salem	106	2408	3492	45.0	1535
Dharmapuri	182	1955	3433	75.6	1683
Coimbatore	45	2756	3537	28.3	1287
Periyar	141	2667	4268	60.0	1780
Tiruchirappalli	151	1989	3489	75.4	1437
Pudukkottai	227	1734	3039	75.3	1203
Thanjavur	286	2134	2763	29.5	1486
Nagapattinam	350	-	2840	-	1733
Madurai	142	2429	3900	60.6	1490
Dindigul	141	-	4745	-	2398
Ramanathapuram	239	1452	1797	23.8	827
Kamrajar	113	-	3292	-	1470
Pasumpon	252	-	2738	-	979
Tirunelveli	183	2403	4680	94.8	2134
Chidambaranar	112	-	4048	-	1695
Nilgiris	5	1389	2095	50.8	2521
Kanniyakumari	79	2145	3825	78.3	1295
State	143	2024	3159	56.1	1621

Source: GOT 1997; CMIE 1996b.

Note: Names of some of the districts have been shortened.

As foodgrains are not grown on a significant scale in some of the districts, we look into the disparity in yield rate of the most commonly grown non-foodgrain, groundnut. The yield rate in groundnut was the highest in case of Nilgiris, at 2,521 kg/ha, in 1993-95 and the lowest in Ramanathapuram at 827 kg. Both the districts, however, had a relatively low area under the crop. Among the major groundnut-growing districts, Dindigul and North Arcot had a substantial yield, 2,398 and 2,184 kg, respectively. The largest area under groundnut in this period was in Tiruvannamalai and its yield rate was only 1,336 kg. The growth in yield in relation to 1981-84 varied greatly from district to district. While North Arcot had 119 per cent increase, for Ramanathapuram it was a mere 6 per cent.

Although the performance in agriculture depends on a variety of factors, as noted in Chapter 4, with regard to one basic factor, availability of cultivable land, Tamil Nadu's position is very unfavourable. In the total reporting area, land under cultivation constituted only 65 per cent in 1992-93, which was lower than the position in six of the major states, as may be seen from Table 4.4. The per capita availability was 0.15 hectare here, which was lower than in all the states but two. The net sown area declined from about 60 lakh hectares in the sixties to 57.6 lakh hectares in 1992-93 and stood at 59.4 lakh hectares in 1995-96. As percentage to reporting area, it was only 41.08 in the latest year as against the national average of 46.64 (GOT 1998: 44; CMIE 1999c). The proportion of land under non-agricultural use in Tamil Nadu was double that of all-India average, being 14.4 and 7.2 per cent, respectively. Culturable waste constituted only 2.3 per cent of the total reporting area in 1992-93 as against the average of 4.8 at the national level (Table 4.4).

The raising of cropping intensity which is an important means for augmenting land, has not shown any consistent improvement over the years. The gross cropped area reached the maximum of 74.56 lakh hectares in the seventies but declined to only 66.77 lakh hectares in eighties and further down to 62.7 lakh hectares in 1995-96. The cropping intensity in Tamil Nadu in the latest year came to only 117.3 as against the all-India average at 131.2 (Table 4.4).

For raising the returns from agriculture, the other alternatives are better inter-crop distribution of land and efficient and adequate provision of different inputs. On the first, probably there is much scope as a considerable acreage is devoted to low-return crops. A large proportion of the farmers are yet to be adequately commercially motivated, and the motivation depends on a variety of factors. Below we make a brief analysis of the land tenure system first, and then look into the availability of inputs and infrastructure.

Landholding Pattern

Along with other states, Tamil Nadu also took steps for abolition of intermediaries, regulation of tenancy, and ceiling on land-holdings. Starting with the Tamil Nadu Estates Act of 1948, a series of laws were enacted, through long intervals, for the abolition of various types of intermediaries. By mid-seventies, an area of nearly 3.65 million hectares got vested in the state. Apart from the long delay, the tenants in Tamil Nadu were not given the right of ownership through purchase or otherwise. Besides, the intermediary rights of *jenmies* in Nilgiri district and *sreepadam* lands in Kanniyakumari could not be abolished because of the Supreme Court's ruling.

For the protection of tenants, the Madras Cultivating Tenants Protection Act was passed in 1955. It provided for resumption by landlord for personal cultivation upto the maximum of one-half of lands leased out. Resumption was, however, not allowed if the landlord owned land exceeding 13.50 acres of wet land or was assessed under the sales tax or profession tax or income tax. Besides, the Tamil Nadu Public Tenants Act, 1961 provided that no public trust can evict its cultivating tenants except for arrears of rent, etc. There was also the provision for preparation and maintenance of a complete record of tenancy rights under the Tamil Nadu Agricultural Land Records of Tenancy Right Act, 1969.

Despite all these legislations, the tenants continued to be insecure in many parts of the state, particularly in the traditional areas. Till January 1999, number of tenants conferred ownership rights or rights protected stood at only 4.98 lakhs involving an area of 6.95 lakh acres. This performance is much inferior to the position in Karnataka, not to speak of Kerala. In the all-India total number of such tenants Tamil Nadu's share is only 4.0 per cent (GOI 1999).

As regards regulation of rent, the regulated rents in Tamil Nadu were higher than what had been recommended in the Plan documents. The latter had suggested one-fourth to one-fifth of the gross produce, but in Tamil Nadu it was fixed at 50 per cent in case of irrigated lands and 33 per cent for other areas. The actual rates of rent, however, varied not only between different regions, depending on the fertility of land, irrigation facilities and the like, but also in respect of different crops and terms of lease.

Nonetheless, over the years, significant changes took place in the extent and pattern of tenancy. The proportion of tenant holdings in Tamil Nadu declined from 24.7 per cent in 1981-82 to 15.3 in 1991-92. Even this level was much higher than the national average, or what existed in other southern states. The all-India average in these two years were 15.2 and 11.0 per cent respectively. The proportion of leased-in area in Tamil Nadu remained unchanged at 10.9 per cent in this period, and in all-India it increased from 7.2 to 8.3 per cent (NSSO 1997).

As regards the terms of lease, the proportion on fixed money increased from 19.2 per cent in 1981-82 to 32.4 in 1991-92 while that for share of produce declined from 36.5 to 16.1 per cent; fixed produce system continued to account for 20 per cent of the total. The all-India averages on them in 1991-92 were, respectively, 19.0, 34.4, and 14.5 per cent. The high proportion for fixed money system, which is disadvantageous to the lessor in a situation of rising prices, in Tamil Nadu is probably due to the fact that tenant holdings are more common in larger holdings with higher bargaining power (NSSO 1997).

As regards ceiling on landholdings, the legislation for it was passed in Tamil Nadu only in 1961, and then also it was fixed at a high level – varying between 12.14 and 48.56 hectares. This was one of the highest among the major states (Haque and Sirohi 1986: 81). Family was made the unit of application here in contrast to individuals in as many as ten states. Moreover, there was a long list of exempted categories. The exemptions gave rise to the evasion of law through changing the classification of land. In this situation, the surplus land available was very small.

The national guidelines came in 1972 and, as in other states, the government amended the ceiling law. The level of ceiling was now fixed at 4.86 to 24.28 hectares, more or less in keeping with the ceilings in other states. The surplus area was estimated at 204.40 thousand acres (82.7 thousand ha), and as of February 1984, 43.6 per cent of it was declared surplus. In most other states, the proportion declared surplus by that date was much higher – it was 100 per cent in seven states and the average for all-India came to 81.2. In taking possession, however, Tamil Nadu's position was much better. It was 92.2 per cent of the area declared surplus as against the all-India average at 69.1 (Haque and Sirohi 1986: Table 6.3). After around one-and-half decades, in September 1998, the total of land declared surplus came to 79.7 thousand hectares, of which 74.0 thousand hectares were taken possession (GOI 1999).

The surplus land was distributed among the landless and other weaker sections. The maximum eligible extent of land for assignment to a family was fixed at one-and-half acres of wet land or 3 acres of dry land. By early eighties, 24.38 thousand hectares of land were distributed to 40.5 thousand beneficiaries, giving the average of 0.60 hectare per beneficiary. After another one-and-half decades, at the end of September 1998, the total of land distributed stood at 69.2 thousand hectares to 1.83 lakh beneficiaries. The per capita benefit came to 0.38 hectare in Tamil Nadu as against the national average at 0.39 hectare (GOI 1999; Deb 1986).

Consequent upon the imposition of ceiling and distribution of surplus land there has not been much change in the concentration of land-ownership. In fact, for the bottom 40 per cent the situation worsened considerably. Their share of area declined from 0.80 per cent in 1961-62 to 0.42 in 1971-72 and then to a negligible level in 1982. Tamil Nadu's was the worst situation so far as this group is concerned; at the all-India level, the bottom 40 per cent accounted for 1.20 per cent of total land in 1982. For the top 20 per cent, the share of land declined from 83.3 per cent of the total in 1953-54 to around 77 per cent in the sixties and seventies but increased again to 79 per cent in 1982. The proportion of households owing no land declined substantially till 1971-72, from 33.6 per cent in 1953-54 to 17.0 per cent, but in 1982 it increased to 19.13 per cent. Tamil Nadu's position was the worst among the southern states, and in relation to the national average also it was very depressing – the proportion of landless in the latter being 11.33 per cent (Sharma 1994).

In operational holdings also the land concentration did not decline much, as may be seen from Table 4.5. The percentage of large holdings (10 ha and above) declined from 0.58 in 1970-71 to 0.27 in 1991-92, but their share in area did not show a clear trend and stood at 5.06 per cent in 1991-92. For medium holdings, the proportion in number declined from 4.9 per cent to 1.8 per cent over the years, and in area from 21.7 per cent to 13.2 per cent. The proportion of marginal holdings in Tamil Nadu was always much higher than at the all-India level. In the former it increased from 60.1 per cent in 1970-71 to 77.2 per cent in 1991-92 as against from 45.8 to 62.8 per cent in the latter. With such a large proportion of marginal holdings, the share in area stood at only 28.9 per cent in 1991-92, rising from 21.9 in 1971-72.

A very large proportion of holdings in Tamil Nadu is sub-marginal, that is, less than 0.50 hectare. Their share in total number of holdings in 1992 was as much as 61.2 per cent and in area a little more than 12; 43 per cent of the holdings were 0.20 hectare or less (NSSO

1997). The ability of these holdings to utilise the land properly can definitely be questioned, given the bias of our credit system and other institutional structures. There is need for cooperativisation or an appropriate system of leasing out.

In consolidation of holdings, there has been much progress in Tamil Nadu. In 1961-62, the average number of parcels for all size-classes was 4.96 and even for category 0.41 to 1.00 hectare it was 3.77 parcels. In 1982, the number of parcels were respectively, 2.54 and 2.74, and in 1992 it was further down to 1.6 and 2.1 parcels. The latest position is better than that in many other states (NSSO 1997; Thangaraj 1995).

Irrigation Facilities

Provision of irrigation facility is particularly important in Tamil Nadu because there are many districts with a very low amount of rainfall. While eight districts receive a normal rainfall of above 1,000 mm, with Nilgiris as much as 1,857, for eleven districts it was less than 900 mm, for three of them -- Coimbatore, Periyar and Chidambaranar -- less than 700 (GOT 1997: 5-18).

Irrigation facilities are, however, much better in Tamil Nadu than in many other states, and best among the southern states. Net irrigated area as percentage to the state's cropped area was 42.2 even in 1961-62. This was the highest among all the states and the all-India average stood at only 16.9. By 1975-76, it rose further to 46.7 per cent, and in 1995-96 to 49.1 per cent. Now, however, there are three states with higher proportion of irrigated area than Tamil Nadu's (Table 4.6).

Crop-wise, the proportion of area under foodgrains irrigated increased from 54 per cent till early seventies to 77 per cent in 1992-93; the all-India average in the latest year was around 50 per cent. During 1992-95, 93 per cent of the area sown by Paddy was irrigated, for Maize it was 51 per cent and Ragi 32; during 1961-66, the annual average for these crops were respectively, 92, 39 and 44 per cent. Among other crops, Sugarcane had the entire cropped area irrigated even in early fifties. For Groundnut, the irrigated area was 32 per cent of the total during 1992-95 as against 12 per cent during 1961-66, and in Cotton 36 and 27 per cent, respectively (GOT 1972, 1997).

As regards the source of irrigation, substantial changes have taken place over the years. During 1991-94, wells accounted for an average of 45.2 per cent of the total net irrigated area as against only 25.0 per cent during 1961-66. The proportion irrigated by tanks has, on the other hand, declined from 37.4 to 23.1 per cent, and by canals from 35.9 to 31.0 per cent.

Table 8.3

District-wise Disparity in Provision of Irrigation Facility, Inputs and Credit: Tamil Nadu

Districts	*Irrigated area as % to sown area*[a]	*% of area irrig. by wells (1993-94)*	*Fertiliser consump. per ha (1994-95)*	*Agrl. credit per ha*[b] *(Rs.) as at 31.3.95*
Chengalpattu	80.7 (70.1)[c]	58.6	146	455
Chidambaranar	24.9	38.8	68	288
Coimbatore	40.9 (42.8)	77.8	185	330
Dharmapuri	25.5	76.8	43	191
Dindigul	35.8	75.1	63	364
Kanniyakumari	44.1 (51.5)	3.3	148	757
Kamarajar	35.6	52.4	99	169
Madurai	57.3 (41.7)	42.1	213	410
North Arcot	49.2 (54.7)	80.7	107	428
Nilgiris	0.6	-	151	431
Periyar	52.5	37.8	123	488
Pasumpon	69.1	14.6	85	274
Padukkottai	56.4	17.2	138	351
Ramanathapuram	31.9 (40.5)	11.8	54	188
Salem	38.1 (28.7)d	86.1	56	463
South Arcot	52.9 (56.9)	68.3	188	378
Thanjavur	79.2 (70.5)	7.2	160	410
Nagapattinam	77.5	1.9	214	438
Tiruchirappalli	37.7 (41.8)	51.4	134	378
Tirunelveli	72.5 (42.9)	34.8	218	384
Tiruvannamalai	54.9	75.4	78	378
Villumpuram	-	-	94	341
State	49.5 (47.7)	48.7	125	370

Source: GOT 1997; Kurien 1981: Table 3.17.

Notes: a: refers to gross area.
b: per hectare of net sown area.
c: figures in parentheses relate to 1972-73, there were only 11 districts then.
d: Relates to undivided Salem.

District-wise, there has been wide disparity in the provision of Irrigation facilities, as may be seen from Table 8.3. Gross irrigated area as percentage to gross sown area in 1993-94 constituted more than 70 in four districts – Chengalpattu, Thanjavur, Nagapattinam and Tirunelveli – as against only 25 in Chidambaranar and Dharmapuri and a negligible 0.6 in Nilgiris. A number of districts with low irrigation facility recorded declines over the years. In Ramanathapuram, the percentage of irrigated area fell to 31.9 in 1993-94 from 40.5 in 1972-73. The quality of facility also varied greatly. Canal irrigation was a negligible source in as many as seven districts and non-existent in three. Wells and tanks, largely at private cost, accounted for an overwhelming proportion in many districts. Wells accounted for above 70 per cent of the gross area in six districts, and tanks in three. Such wide disparity in the provision of facilities cannot be explained solely by the differences in natural factors. With right initiatives from the government the disparities could be considerably narrowed.

It is, however, necessary to bear in mind that the irrigation potential of Tamil Nadu is relatively low. In major and medium irrigation the ultimate potential is only 1.5 million hectares, which is lower than in any other state except Kerala (Table 4.6). This potential was already exploited to the extent of 98 per cent by 1991-92; at the national level, the exploitation averaged only 56 per cent. In minor irrigation however, while the potential is substantial, the utilisation is relatively low. The level of utilisation till 1990-91 was 87.1 per cent, which is marginally higher than the all-India average.

The state faces a number of problems in the area of irrigation. It has no perennial water resource except the river Cauvery. But, the unsettled riparian issues with neighbouring Karnataka are affecting the area under crops and production in the delta economy, which accounts for more than 50 per cent of the total canal irrigated area. There is also the problem of proper utilisation of water in canal commands. Seepage of water due to lack of proper maintenance of channels and non-availability of water in tail-end villages continue to be severe problems.

The utilisation of groundwater also needs to be properly monitored. Easy availability of institutional finance has led to a rapid growth in number of wells and energisation of pumpsets. Number of pumpsets energised rose to 1,529 thousand in 1995-96 from 410 thousand in 1968-69. Number of pumpsets per 100 hectares stood at 24.4 in Tamil Nadu in the latest year, which is the highest among all the states and four times the national average (Table 4.7). Overexploitation of groundwater has increased significantly in recent years. Number of dark blocks rose to 97 in 1997 from 89 in 1992. Tamil Nadu presently accounts for 29 per cent of the total number of dark blocks in the country (GOT 1998: 180).

The tank system has declined but it still plays an important role in a number of districts. There are several problems afflicting this type of irrigation. Heavy silt accumulation has taken place in tank bed and in the inlet channel of many of the tanks. There are also many instances of encroachments in the catchment area, inlet channels and tank bed. And then there is paucity of funds for maintenance work. Certain institutional changes and development of the groundwater irrigation have also affected the operation of the tank system (Janakarajan 1993).

As the potential left to be exploited is very limited, the main thrust in the development of irrigation has to be on conservation and more productive use of water. There is need for evolving appropriate rain harvesting techniques and avoiding wastage of water. Conjunctive use of surface and groundwater has to be promoted. There is also need for properly integrating the water-use and land-use policies.

Provision of Inputs and Credit

The farmers' use of different inputs depends on a variety of factors like availability of the inputs at the right time and at right price, expertise for using them properly, the availability of credit at the right time, and arrangement for disposing the products at remunerative prices. Due to lack of space, we do not make any detailed analysis of the problems involved in different areas; only the growth in use of different inputs and availability of credit have been discussed, and the problems in the area of marketing just touched upon.

Use of Inputs

On the use of improved seeds, Tamil Nadu's relative position is quite good. During 1994-97, the proportion of gross cropped area covered by HYV seeds averaged 48 per cent, and it could be exceeded by only three of the major states; all the other southern states had much lower proportions. However, the rate of growth in area covered has been very low in recent years. During 1987-90 to 1994-97 it increased by only 15.7 per cent here as against 25.3 per cent at the national level (Table 4.7). In fact, there is a clear tendency of stagnation in the last few years, if not decline. In 1991-92, the area under HYV stood at 31.7 lakh hectares but touched the low of 28.7 lakh hectares in 1995-96. Crop-wise, paddy accounted for the overwhelming proportion of area under HYV. During 1992-95, it averaged 71.5 per cent. Of the total area under paddy, HYV coverage increased from 45 per cent in 1969-70 to 78 per cent in 1973-74 and 92 per cent in 1994-95. Millets accounted for the balance of area under HYV. The proportion of total area under millets covered by HYV stood at 94 per cent in 1994-95, rising from 26 per cent in 1973-74.

In the use of improved seeds, other than HYV, also the situation was not satisfactory. The quantum distributed rose to 41.0 thousand tonnes in 1992-93 from 33.7 thousand tonnes in 1990-91, but in the following years it declined, to only 30.7 thousand tonnes in 1995-96. Of the total quantum distributed, foodgrains accounted for an average of 71.4 per cent during 1993-96, i.e., 24.5 thousand tonnes out of 34.3. In non-foodgrains, oilseeds accounted for the overwhelming bulk – as much as 96 per cent during 1993-96.

Production of improved seeds often fell short of the requirement, and consequently, the replacement rate was very low in many of the crops. For example, in 1994-95 while ragi had 34.6 per cent of the total area under the crop replaced and paddy 19.6, for jowar it was only 2.1, maize 3.8 and for pulses 9.3. In non-foodgrains, seed replacement could be done in only 4.8 per cent of the area in case of groundnut and for cotton 7.9 in the same year as against 79 per cent in sunflower and 46.7 in castor (GOT 1997: S-26, 32).

As regards use of chemical fertilisers, the growth has been quite rapid in Tamil Nadu. The per hectare consumption increased from 6.18 kg in 1961-62 to 22.04 in 1966-67 and 39.2 in 1975-76. In the following years, the growth was at a much slower pace. It reached 115.1 kg in 1990-91 and 150.4 in 1997-98; the average for last three years, 1995-98, came to 127.4 kg. Tamil Nadu's consumption of fertiliser has always been far above the national average. During 1995-98 it was 60 per cent higher -- the latter being only 79.7 kg. There are presently three states – Punjab, Haryana and Andhra – with larger consumption than Tamil Nadu's (Table 4.7).

District-wise, there is great variation in consumption of fertilisers. In 1994-95, while there were three districts -- Tirunelveli, Nagapattinam and Madurai -- with per hectare consumption of above 200 kg, for nine districts it was less than 100 kg, with the lowest at 43 kg in Dharmapuri (Table 8.3). Generally, the districts with poor irrigation facility had low consumption of fertilisers.

While the use of chemical fertilisers in the state is significant, there has not been much progress in the use of alternative or complementary types of nutrients. There are 20 blue green algae production centres and six bio-fertiliser production units. But, neither their production is substantial nor any concerted efforts have been made to popularise them. On the use of green manure and compost also there has not been any noticeable progress. There is virtually no infrastructure for popularising their use. Even soil testing facilities are far from adequate. There are only 31 soil testing laboratories in the state, including 15 mobile.

As regards plant protection, there are both preventive and curative measures. But the magnitude of action varies from year to year depending on the requirement and means of the farmers. In 1994-95, the area covered under pest control stood at 55.7 lakh hectares and that treated against diseases at 25.8 lakh hectares. In 1990-91, on the other hand, these were, respectively, 61.42 and 84.08. The annual average during 1992-95 came to 53.5 and 20.5 lakh hectares. The distribution between composition of food and non-food crops in the total area treated was 62:38 during 1994-95 (GOT 1997: 34, 5-31).

Despite the hazards involved in indiscriminate application of pesticides, integrated pest management has not received much attention. The use of 'dust' declined from 0.75 lakh tonnes in 1993-94 to 0.46 lakh tonnes in the following year, and of 'liquid' from 32.67 lakh litres to 19.42 lakh litres. The consumption of technical grade material was down to 1,800 tonnes in 1995-96 from 5,000 tonnes in 1992-93 (GOT 1998: 49). The use of herbicides and natural methods are yet to get adequate attention. On parasite breeding, the focus is primarily on sugarcane and coconut, and the use of mechanical devices is almost non-existent.

On the mechanisation of agriculture, Tamil Nadu's progress is substantial. An important indicator on this is the consumption of electricity in the agricultural sector. The per capita consumption in Tamil Nadu stood at 99 kwh in 1993-94 as against the all-India average of 79.6 kwh (Table 4.7). In the total sale of power in Tamil Nadu in 1994-95, the share of agriculture was 26.8 per cent – 6,600 million units out of 24,586 million. The effective subsidy to agricultural consumers increased from Rs. 643 crores in 1992-93 to Rs. 1,394 crores in 1997-98 (CMIE 1999d). District-wise, there was extreme of variation in per capita consumption. In 1993-94, as against the state average of 347 kwh and the highest of 2,302 in Nilgiris, there were five districts with less than 200 kwh – in Pasumpon it was only 20 kwh (GOT 1997: S-101, S-103).

Among the machines used, the rapid growth in number of pumpsets/tubewells energised has been noted earlier. Other types of machines recorded a much slower growth. In number of tractors in use, the state accounted for only 0.87 per cent of the all-India total in 1990-91 as against 2.73 per cent in 1979-80. The compound annual growth in number over the period was 0.5 per cent here as against 12.7 per cent for all-India (CMIE 1996b). In plant protection equipment, number per thousand ha increased from 4.7 in 1972 to 16.5 in 1987; the all-India average in these years were respectively, 3.3. and 13.6. The use of power tiller and disc-harrow was much less here. In the former, it was 1.15 number per thousand hectares in 1987, and in the latter 0.85; the all-India averages were, respectively 1.17 and 2.63. Among bullock-operated implements, Tamil Nadu's position was relatively better in both iron and wooden ploughs. Number per thousand hectares were 91.3 and 393 respectively, in 1987 as against 65.1 and 316 at the national level (Deb 1997: Table 5.5).

Bank Credit

In the provision of credit to agriculture, Tamil Nadu's performance was significantly better than most other states. Looking to the position of SCBs first, it may be seen from Table 4.8 that in their aggregate of agricultural advances outstanding in the country in 1996, Tamil Nadu's share was 14.0 per cent; no other state could reach this level. Two-and-half decades earlier, in 1971, also its relative position was the same. The provision of short-term loans from them rose to Rs. 2,225 per hectare in 1996-97 from Rs. 185.40 in 1982-83, that is, a growth of twelve times; the all-India averages were much less, being Rs. 302 and Rs. 32 in these two years, respectively.[1]

The marginal farmers' share in SCBs' credit was also substantial, although with a declining trend. In the total of short-term loans provided, their share in number of accounts was 65.9 per cent in 1979-80 and in amount 56.3. In 1996-97, however, the proportions were much less, at 41.6 and 40.1 per cent, respectively. There was only one state, Kerala, providing a larger share to marginal farmers than Tamil Nadu's in the latest year.

As regards RRBs, it is evident from Table 4.8 that their role in Tamil Nadu was relatively insignificant. Agricultural advances outstanding per hectare came to only Rs. 69 here in 1996 as against Rs. 187 at the national level. The proportion of agricultural advances in the aggregate of advances outstanding was also very low in Tamil Nadu and showed a sharp decline in recent years, from 43.9 per cent in 1990 to 33.4 in 1996.

Cooperative credit in contrast, played a much bigger role in Tamil Nadu. Amount of loans per hectare came to Rs. 741 in 1992-93 as against the all-India average at Rs. 336. There were only two states, Punjab and Kerala, ahead of it. The increase over 1981-82 was 562 per cent in case of Tamil Nadu as against 243 per cent for all-India. The amount outstanding at the end of 1992-93 constituted 11.3 per cent of all-India total, which was exceeded by five of the major states (Table 4.8).

Tamil Nadu's PACS appear to have given relatively greater attention to the weaker farmers. In the loans and advances outstanding as on 31 March, 1996 at Rs. 1,776.60 crores, the share of those with ownership holding up to 2 hectares was Rs. 755.84 crores, that is, 42.5 per cent, for tenant cultivators, agricultural labourers and others the share was 19.2 per cent. At the national level, the proportion for the two groups were, respectively, 29.6 and 6.1 per cent (RBI 1999).

District-wise, there were wide variations in availability of credit. For example, at the end of March 1995, credit per hectare of net sown area under the Annual Credit Plan varied between the highest of Rs. 757 in Kanniyakumari and the lowest of Rs. 169 in Kamarajar, with the state average at Rs. 370. The share of agricultural credit in the total credit for the district was more than 80 per cent in case of seven district -- Villupuram, Nagapattinam, Dharmapuri, Tiruvannamalai, Thanjavur, Kanniyakumari and Pudukkottai -- as against the lowest of 19.4 in Coimbatore, and the state average at 61.5 per cent (Table 8.3).

Marketing Facilities

Regulated markets provide a number of facilities like storage, grading, standardisation, dissemination of information, etc., for enabling the farmers to realise optimum prices for their produce. But the availability of such markets in Tamil Nadu does not appear satisfactory. In 1997, there were 270 regulated markets and 15 sub-markets out of the total of 6,809 operating in the country as a whole. More than half of the regulated markets are small, that is, with receipts less than Rs. 5 lakhs. Total quantum of agricultural produce transacted in the regulated markets stood at 9.09 lakh tonnes in 1996-97, rising from 5.59 lakh in 1992-93 (GOT 1998: 93).

There are 14 market committees in the state but four of them – North Arcot, South Arcot, Coimbatore and Periyar -- together accounted for 79.4 per cent of total agricultural produce marketed, with South Arcot alone contributing 30.8 per cent in 1994-95. Four market committees – Kanniyakumari, Pudukkottai, Chengalpattu and Salem -- together, on the other hand, contributed a mere 3.0 per cent of the total (GOT 1997: 37). The disparities are not only because of lack of marketable surplus but also due to the poor quality of services provided in many of them.

In the grading of agricultural produce, the progress has been very slow. The quantum with Agmark grading increased from 3.83 lakh quintals in 1992-93 to 5.14 lakh in 1993-94 but in the following years it declined -- the average for 1994-97 came to 3.82 lakh quintals. The quantum with commercial grading increased from 59.48 lakh quintals in 1992-93 to 106.34 lakh quintals in 1996-97; the average for last three years came to 92.49 (GOT 1998: 93).

With a view to improving the withholding capacity of the farmers and to avoid distress sales, a scheme of pledge loan was introduced in recent years. Under it loan could be availed to the extent of 75 per cent of the value of agricultural produce stocked in the regulated market subject to a limit of Rs. 25,000. The scheme is in operation in 137 godowns, 98 of which are in rural areas. In 1994-95, the scheme was utilised by 4,579 farmers, with loans totalling Rs. 614 lakhs. This cannot be considered an impressive response, given the size of the problem. Probably small farmers are not coming forward to take advantage of it, and the storage facility is also inadequate.

The role of cooperative marketing is also not noteworthy. There are 113 cooperative marketing societies functioning at the primary level. The value of agricultural produce transacted by them totalled Rs. 610 crores in 1994-95, with the food group accounting for 56.3 per cent. In the food group, sugarcane alone accounted for 82 per cent; and in non-food group, cotton 77.5 per cent and oil seeds 21.3 per cent. Even in the grand total of transactions by cooperatives, these three items -- sugarcane, cotton and oilseeds -- together accounted for 89.3 per cent. Thus the spread of cooperative marketing to other commodities is very limited. Even the contribution of foodgrains in the grand total was only 4.8 per cent, valued at Rs. 29.5 crores.

The infrastructure facilities provided by the cooperatives are very inadequate. There were 5,098 godowns in 1994-95, comprised of 4,787 rural and the remaining marketing and consumer godowns. On an average, the storage capacity of a cooperative godown in the state worked out to 139 tonnes (GOT 1997).

II
Allied Sectors

Animal Husbandry

The animal husbandry sector plays an important role in Tamil Nadu's economy. In the gross value of output from agriculture its contribution is estimated at 26 per cent. The average annual growth of employment in the livestock sector during 1972-73 to 1987-88 was 4.15 per cent as against 1.1 in the agricultural sector. The livestock population of Tamil Nadu was placed at 263.66 lakh in 1989, of which cattle accounted for 35.5 per cent, buffalo 11.9, sheep 22.3 and goats 22.4. Poultry also occupies an important position, their number in 1989 being 215.70 lakh (GOT 1998: 99). We confine our analysis to only cattle and buffalo and to poultry due to their higher economic importance.

Cattle and Buffalo Development

Total number of cattle in Tamil Nadu increased from 75.1 lakhs in 1972 to 93.4 in 1987, but in 1994 it stood at 92.7 lakhs. Thus, over the entire period of more than two decades there was a growth of only 23.4 per cent.[2] The states' relative share in all-India total declined from 5.9 per cent in 1972 to 4.87 in 1987 and probably still lower in the following years. However, there has been a remarkable increase in number of female cattle, by 76 per cent between 1972 and 1987, and their relative share in the state's cattle population rose to 54.0 per cent from 38.1. In adult cattle, the sex ratio (number of females divided by the number of males) in Tamil Nadu increased from 0.79 to 1.17 in this period as against from 0.76 to 0.98 for all-India. There were four states with higher sex ratio than Tamil Nadu's in 1987 (Table 4.9).

The growth in number of buffaloes was faster than in cattle. It increased by 78 per cent over the period, from 17.6 lakhs in 1972 to 31.3 in 1987.[3] At the national level, however, the increase was faster, by 107 per cent, and consequently, Tamil Nadu's share in all-India total declined from 4.8 to 4.1 per cent. The proportion of females in total number was, however, better here than in most other states. The sex ratio for adult buffaloes in Tamil Nadu increased from 3.70 to 5.26 over the period as against from 3.64 to 3.79 in all-India (GOI 1975a; CMIE 1996b).

In cross-bred cattle, Tamil Nadu's position appears to be was better than most other states. With the total number at 7.93 lakhs in 1987, its share of all-India total was 10.0 per cent. There were only three states with higher proportions. The proportion of females in total number was, however, relatively low here. At 69.5 per cent, there were as many as eight states with higher proportions.

District-wise, there were great variations in maintenance of cattle and buffalo. The cattle density per thousand population in 1989 varied between as much as 642 in South Arcot and the lowest of 52 in Nilgiris (excluding Madras), with the state average at 167. In buffalo, the disparity was between 136 in Thanjavur and 8 in Nilgiris, with the state average at 56 (Table 8.4).

Table 8.4

District-wise Disparity in Livestock Density and in Milk and Egg Production: Tamil Nadu

Districts	*No. of cattle per '000 pop.*[a]	*No. of buffaloes per '000 popul.*	*per capita milk prod.*[b] *(1994-96)*	*per capita egg prod. (1994-96)*
Madras	6.4	7.5	13.3	1.2
Chengalpattu	160.0	72.6	72.0	22.4
North Arcot	164.7	44.0	63.0	10.2
Tiruvannamalai	296.8	41.8	86.3	7.4
South Arcot	642.3	89.4	64.5	6.0
Villupuram	-	-	80.9	8.8
Dharmapuri	213.4	45.1	53.3	40.1
Salem	159.6	115.3	94.1	471.5
Periyar	166.0	112.5	110.9	33.2
Nilgiris	52.3	7.6	43.9	1.5
Coimbatore	95.6	44.0	68.0	81.9
Tiruchirappalli	206.4	74.8	72.2	67.9
Thanjavur	465.2	136.1	77.0	9.3
Nagai-Quaid-e	-	-	77.7	9.0
Pudukkottai	396.9	97.9	102.3	16.4
Madurai	116.2	43.9	68.0	11.8
Dindigul	156.3	67.5	76.7	14.6
Ramanathapuram	201.1	26.7	72.7	13.6
Pasumpon	233.1	42.2	51.7	16.9
Kamarajar	84.9	41.5	39.8	11.6
Tirunelveli	111.9	59.2	53.0	8.9
Chidambaranar	120.8	44.3	58.7	37.7
Kanniyakumari	61.6	11.9	46.0	11.2
State	167.4	56.0	67.0	54.6

Source: Basic data from GOT 1997.

Notes: a: based on livestock census 1989 and population census 1991.
b: based on 1991 population.

The growth in milk production was substantial over the years. Between 1971-72 and 1994-95, it had recorded a compound annual growth of 6.5 per cent – production rising from 9.3 lakh tonnes to 39.7 lakh tonnes; the all-India growth in this period was at the rate of 4.6 per cent. Tamil Nadu's share in all-India production rose to 6.3 per cent in 1994-95 from 4.1 in 1971-72. In the total production of the state, cows contributed 60 per cent in 1995-96 and the balance by buffaloes; the total production of milk in this year was 37.9 lakh tonnes, of which cows provided 22.73 (GOT 1997: 45). Despite the improvement, the per capita milk production however, continued to be less than the national average – it was, respectively, 67.7 kg and 68.9 kg in 1994-95 (Table 4.10).

District-wise, as the bovine density varied greatly, so also the production of milk. The annual average of per capita production during 1994-96 was only 39.8 kg in Kamarajar (leaving aside Madras) as against the highest of 110.9 kg in Periyar and the state average at 67 kg. In the state's total production, as may be seen from Table 8.4, seven districts – Salem, Chengalpattu, Tiruchirappalli, Periyar, Coimbatore, Madurai and Villupuram – together accounted for 52.4 per cent.

Behind the low production in a number of districts, factors like inadequate availability of fodder, veterinary care, poor extension services and poverty of the farmers worked. Exotic and crossbred cattle require high quality fodder and higher investment, and the poor farmers had therefore, to go only for indigenous cows with low yield. In 1995-96, the average yield rate of milk from an indigenous cow was only 2.413 kg per day as against 5.369 for exotic and cross-bred and 3.537 kg from buffaloes.

Fodder production did not get any attention worth the name until recent years. Green fodder requirement is currently met only to the extent of around a quarter. It was only in 1995-96 that the area under fodder cultivation increased noticeably, to 6,232 hectares from 1541 int he preceding year. Number of minikits distributed rose to 9,275 in 1995-96 from 3,840 in the preceding year. There are presently 20 cattle breeding and fodder development units and 3,510 artificial insemination centres. As regards veterinary care facilities, although substantial improvement has taken place over the years, much remains to be done, particularly int he backward districts. In 1995-96, there were 2,147 veterinary sub-centres – that is an average of 74 per district, 765 dispensaries, 386 mobile dispensaries, 94 hospitals and 55 mobile veterinary units (GOT 1997: 50).

The potential for increasing milk production is substantial. The per capita production here is lower than that in seven of the major states, as may be seen from Table 4.10. On the demand side also there is no problem: the per capital consumption of milk in the state was 195 grams per day in 1996-97 as against the requirement of 284 grams. With better availability of fodder, breeding services, veterinary care, extension services and easy availability of bank credit, production of milk can be considerably raised.

Poultry Farming

In poultry farming, Tamil Nadu has made a significant progress. Egg production in the state increased from 834 million in 1980-81 to 2,551 million in 1990-91 and 3,041 in 1996-97. Tamil Nadu is the second largest producer of egg in the country, next to Andhra Pradesh. In 1993-94, its share in all-India total production stood at 11.9 per cent. In per capita term, however, two more states – Punjab and Kerala – were ahead of it (Table 4.10).

The production in Tamil Nadu is heavily concentrated in a few districts. During 1994-95, Salem alone accounted for 60 epr cent of the total and another 19 per cent came from Coimbatore and Tiruchirappally, distributed equally. The per capita production in these two years averaged as much as 471 in Salem as against less than 10 in eight districts (Table 8.4). Such wide disparity points to the potential for growth in production.

The distribution of fowls among the districts was also similar. In 1989, Salem alone accounted for 29 per cent of the total number and another 32 per cent came from Tiruchirappalli, Thanjavur, Coimbatore, Chengalpattu and Periyar combined. The improved variety of fowls was less than 10 per cent in eight districts as against 84 per cent in Madras, 78 in Salem and Coimbatore and the state average at 40. There is wide gap in yield rate of 'desi' and 'improved' birds. In 1995-96, the former had an annual yield of only 87 eggs as against the latter's 211.

The per capita consumption of eggs in Tamil Nadu is still far from the requirement. In 1995-96, it was only 55 per year as against the nutritional norm of 183. For raising consumption, production has to be increased sharply. This will require much greater attention to provision of infrastructure, extension services, and availability of improved birds. Facilities available at present are far from adequate. There are only two chick hatcheries for quality birds and 26 poultry extension centres in the state. Production of chicks by them totalled 51,146 in 1995-96, of which 16,100 were sold for rearing. There are only two poultry disease diagnostic laboratories (GOT 1997). The facilities for marketing of eggs, live birds, etc., are also not satisfactory. The Poultry Development Corporation cannot give adequate coverage to the farmers.

As regards, the plan expenditure on animal husbandry, although the growth over the years is substantial, the relative share has declined in the recent plans. The expenditure increased from Rs. 3.3 crores in the Third Plan to Rs. 9.8 crores in the Fifth Plan, Rs. 25.9 crores in the Seventh Plan and Rs. 109.2 crores in the Eighth Plan, that is 33 times over the entire period. Its relative share in the total for agricultural programmes, however, declined to around 6 per cent in the Seventh and Eighth Plans from 11.9 per cent in the Fifth Plan.

The quality of planning for the animal husbandry sector was very poor. In some of the segments the expenditure was incredibly higher than what was proposed, while in others it was the reverse. For example, during the Eighth Plan, the original allocation on cattle and buffalo development was only Rs. 29.48 crores but the actual expenditure came to Rs. 69.58 crores. On fodder and feeds development, the expenditure became 24 times the proposed outlay, Rs. 4.98 crores and Rs. 0.21 crore, respectively. On the other hand, in poultry development the actual expenditure was only 31 per cent of what was proposed -- Rs. 0.99 crore and Rs. 3.25 crores, respectively. Similarly, in an important area like extension and training these were Rs. 0.17 crore and Rs. 0.43 crore (GOT 1998: 101).

Fishery Development

Tamil Nadu has a great potential in fish production. Total length of the coast line in the state is 1,000 km with a continental shelf area of 41,412 sq. km. The sea around Tamil Nadu has a variety of fin fishes, shell fishes, aquatic plants, corals, chank and pearl oysters, which are of high export potential. There are 442 fishing villages with a population of about 5.0 lakh, of which 2.6 lakh are active fishermen. In inland fishery, the culturable water-spread area is 3.7 lakh hectares, which include large and medium reservoirs, major and minor irrigation tanks and village ponds and small tanks. There is also available about 56,000 ha of brackish water. Among the two lakh inland fishermen, about 47,000 are actively engaged in fish production (GOT 1998: 117).

The growth of fish production in the state was substantial. From the annual average of only 1.44 lakh tonnes during 1960-63 it increased to 2.51 lakh tonnes during 1965-68, 4.03 during 1984-87 and 4.49 lakh tonnes in 1994-97, that is, a growth of slightly more than three times over the entire period. Tamil Nadu's relative share in all-India production, however, declined in recent years, from 14.0 per cent during 1984-87 to 12.1 per cent in 1991-94 (Table 4.11). During 1991-97, Tamil Nadu had a compound annual growth of only 2.9 per cent as against the all-India average of 6.4 per cent (RBI 1999: I).

Although the growth in fish production was relatively low in Tamil Nadu, exports had a very rapid growth. The value of exports rose to the annual average of Rs. 657.2 crores during 1993-96, from Rs. 89.6 crores during 1987-90, Rs. 27.5 crores in 1977-80 and Rs. 1.81 crores during 1967-70. Thus, over the period of nearly three decades, there was a 363-fold rise. This growth was mainly due to a rapid rise in unit value realisation. The quantum of exports increased only five times over the period, from the annual average of 5,264 tonnes during 1967-70 to 26,738 tonnes during 1993-96. Tamil Nadu's relative share in all-India total value of export rose to 19.5 per cent during 1992-95 from only 7.0 per cent during 1967-70 (GOT 1997: 60; State Planning Commission).

Marine Fish Production

In the total production of fish, marine fisheries always contributed the major share. During 1960-63, it accounted for 66.6 per cent of the total but in 1984-87 the proportion declined to 61.5; in recent years again it has risen, to as much as 75.8 in 1994-97. The annual average of production stood at 3.40 lakh tonnes in the last three years, rising from 2.48 during 1984-87 and only 0.96 lts during 1960-63.

District-wise, in recent years, marine production came largely from five districts, viz., Ramanathapuram, Nagapattinam, Padukkottai, Chidambaranar and Kanniyakumari. Their combined share in 1995-96 stood at 78.6 per cent. In 1984-85, on the other hand, 85 per cent of total production came from four districts, namely, Kanniyakumari, Thanjavur, Ramanathapuram and Tirunelveli. Kanniyakumari's production has declined sharply over the years. In 1984-85, it alone accounted for 39 per cent of the total but in 1995-96 the share was down to only 9.5 per cent, production declining from 96 thousand tonnes to 32 thousand. Similarly, Tirunelveli's production decreased from 40 thousand tonnes in 1986-87 to only 3.7 thousand tonnes in 1995-96, and of Thanjavur from 55 thousand tonnes in 1985-86 to 10 thousand tonnes.

From the angle of natural resources available, this level of growth in production is far from satisfactory. The reasons behind the low growth are mainly use of low level of technology, inadequate infrastructural facilities and over-exploitation of in-shore waters. In the total of marine fish production, the contribution by mechanised sector declined from 59.5 per cent in 1989-90 to 51.4 per cent in 1991-92 and stood at 53.7 per cent in 1994-95. In some of the areas the technology used was very poor. For example, in tirunelveli, the entire catch in 1995-96 came from the motorised and non-mechanised sectors.

As regards infrastructure, it is not only that fish landing facilities are very poor in some of the harbours and jetties, the processing and storage facilities are also very inadequate. Apart from Chennai, no other fishing harbour has capacity for trawler landing. Nagapattinam has capacity for only 10 motorised fishing boats (MFBs) and for Cuddalore I & II stage 40 MFBs. Fish landing jetties like Kodiakarai, Rameshwaram, Mandapam and Kottaipattinam also have capacity for only 40 MFBs each. The exploitation of the continental shelf is still very low.

Inland Fishery

The growth in inland fish production was very small. It increased from the annual average of 48 thousand tonnes during 1960-63 to 1.02 lakh tonnes during 1965-68, but during 1988-91 production averaged only 80 thousand tonnes. In the following years also the recovery was small – production during 1994-97 averaged 1.08 lakh tonnes. Districtwise, it was largely confined to Thanjavur, Chengalpattu, Nagai, Madurai and South Arcot Vallalar. Their combined share stood at half of the total production in 1994-95, with the first two accounting for 23 per cent. Another six districts -- Trichy, Tirunelveli, Ramanathapuram, North Arcot, Dharmapuri and Pasumpon – together contributed 36 per cent. Thus, 50 per cent of the districts contributed 85 per cent of total production in the inland sector.

Resource-wise, the most important contributor to inland fish production is seasonal tanks and ponds, followed by major irrigation tanks, and rivers, streams, etc. These three sources together provided 88.6 per cent of the total in 1995-96, and a similar proportion in the late eighties also. However, while the production from the first two sources increased over the years, that from rivers etc., showed a decline. The relative contribution of seasonal tanks and ponds increased from 37.8 per cent in 1988-89 to 40.4 per cent in 1995-96, and for major irrigation tanks from 25.6 to 37.1 per cent over the same period. The production from rivers, etc., on the other hand, contributed only 11.1 per cent in 1995-96 as against 24.7 per cent in 1988-89, the quantum declining from 20.2 thousand tonnes to 12 thousand tonnes. The poorest performance was, however, by major reservoirs. The production rose to 3,400 tonnes in 1993-94 from 2,250 tonnes in 1988-89, but in 1994-95 it stood at only 1,465 tonnes. The production from estuaries and backwaters was also insignificant. Their contribution in the total was around 4 per cent, and the production increased from 3,000 tonnes in 1988-89 to 4,550 tonnes in 1995-96.

There are a number of reasons behind the poor performance by inland fishery. Fish seed production always fell short of the requirements. There was shortage of nursery space for fish seed rearing. Wide gap between target and achievement was a common phenomenon. At Sathiyar, for example, the target in 1994-95 was 22 lakh numbers but the achievement came to only 5 lakh; in the preceding two years, the performance was worse. The situation at Chetput, Thirukapuliyar, Poondi, Vaigai and Chesharambakkam centres were also similar (SPC).

The management of reservoirs left much to be desired. The exploitation targets often remained unrealised. In 1994-95, with regard to stocked varieties, out of 44 reservoirs only seven could achieve their targets; in most cases, the exploitation was incredibly below the target. For all the reservoirs together, with an area of 41,086 hectares, the annual average of fish caught during 1992-95 came to 801 tonnes, that is, a per hectare realisation of only 19 kg. At Veeranam, with 5,760 hectares, nothing could be produced in these three years.

That there is ample scope for increasing production, is evident from the great variation in per hectare realisations. The fish farmers' development agencies had an average yield rate of 1,358 kg in 1994-95, with the lowest at 390 kg in Periyar and the highest at 2,342 kg in Dharmapuri. In brackish water demonstration prawn farms, while the average in 1994-95 was only 149 kg, the maximum came to 729 kg per ha. What is required for larger production is better management of the water areas with higher levels of culture. Increased production must also be accompanied by better preservation and processing facilities.

For all these, greater initiative is called for from the government. It may be noted here that the growth in plan expenditure on fishery was quite low. During the Third Plan it stood at Rs. 2.57 crores and increased to Rs. 15.19 crores in the Seventh Plan and Rs. 73.44 crores in the Eighth Plan; over the entire period, the growth was thus 28.6 times as against 49.2 times in agriculture and allied services as a whole. The relative share of fishery in the total for agricultural programmes declined to only 2.9 per cent in the Eighth Plan from 9.1 per cent in the Fifth Plan. Within fishery also, the inland waters did not get their due attention. For example, during the Eighth Plan, inland fisheries received only 7.5 per cent of the total whereas marine fisheries got 48.7 per cent. The expenditure on the latter was 360 per cent of what was proposed but in case of the former it was only 72 per cent.

Forests

The forest area in Tamil Nadu has shown some increase over the years. It stood at 22.70 lakh hectares in 1994-95, rising from 19.16 in 1970-71 and 18.78 in 1959-60. In the total geographical area of the state, its share is presently about 17.5 per cent as against 14.4 per cent in 1959-60. These data, however, do not say anything about the density of the forest. Estimates indicate that the forest cover is being exploited at an appalling rate. Of the degraded forest area available for reforestation, barren lands account for 12.71 per cent and partial tree cover 53.44 per cent (GOT 1998: 131, 1972). The relative position of Tamil Nadu among the states is also not satisfactory. In 1995-96, most of the major states had larger proportion of their reporting area under forest, and the all-India average stood at 22.6 per cent (Table 4.4).

The forest area could not be maintained on a sustainable basis despite the fact that 84 per cent of it constituted reserved forests and another 10 per cent reserved land. The increasing pressure from a rising population led to deforestation and a widening gap between demand and supply of various forest products. In 1995-96, the supply of raw materials to industry stood at only 1.20 lakh tonnes as against the estimated requirement of 5.20 lakh tonnes (GOT 1997: 62-63).

A variety of measures were taken under the different five-year plans, but these were not effective enough to meet the magnitude of challenges faced. Even the very First Plan included the schemes of afforestation and plantation, improvement of forest communication and strengthening the administration. The Second Plan tried to strengthen the commercial and industrial plantation and preservation of wild life. In 1960-61, the social forestry and farm forestry programmes were initiated. During the Third Plan, a major emphasis was given to raising of quick growing species to meet the demands of wood-based industries. The area under plantation increased in each of the five-year plans. During the Fifth and Sixth Plans, a total of 3.21 lakh hectares of plantations were raised. Forestry came to be adopted as one of the priority sectors under the 20-Point Programme in the Sixth Plan. The Seventh Plan adopted the policy of "aggressive forestry". The cumulative total of afforestation covered rose to 12.13 lakh hectares in 1995-96 (GOT 1998: 131-32).

But all these proved utterly inadequate because of administrative inefficiencies. The violation of regulations on maintenance of forests was rampant. Illegal felling of trees was a common phenomenon. The allocation of fund for forestry was also not adequate from the angle of requirements, and then there were leakages to unauthorised and low priority areas.

The plan expenditure on forestry increased from Rs. 2.72 crores during the Third Plan to Rs. 11.29 in the Fifth Plan, Rs. 110.0 in the Seventh Plan and Rs. 231.3 crores in the Eighth Plan, that is, a growth of 85 times over the entire period. The relative share of forestry in the total expenditure on agricultural programmes increased from 5.3 per cent in the Third Plan to 26.6 in the Seventh Plan, but in the Eighth Plan it declined to 9.2 per cent.

Failure of the present system of forest management in protecting the forests has led the government to take some bold initiatives. The National Forest Policy 1988, as noted in Chapter 4, has brought some drastic changes in the system of forest management. Some of the actions taken in recent years are: (i) constitution of a Hill Area Conservation Authority; (ii) setting up of 21 forest stations in sensitive areas to tackle the illicit removal of forest produce; (iii) introduction of Interface Forestry Programmes as a precursor to the Joint Forest Management (JFM) programme; (iv) Tamil Nadu Afforestation Project, with full participation of local people, involving an outlay of Rs. 496 crores in the Ninth Plan; and (v) plantations differentiated on the basis of conservation oriented and production oriented programmes (GOT 1998: 133).

In the Ninth Plan (1997-2002), the outlay on forestry has been set at Rs. 815.2 crores, constituting the highest ever share of 31.3 per cent of the total for agriculture and allied services. Within forestry, the highest proportion of 23.2 per cent has been allocated to biological upgradation and ecological restoration through the JFM, followed by 19.7 per cent on comprehensive watershed development programmes and 10.1 per cent on project greening (GOT 1998: 138-39). How far effectively the funds will be utilised is, however, a big question, given the holds of vested interests and the inertia of officials.[4]

Notes

1. The loans per hectare are based on gross cropped area of 1981-82 and 1995-96 (RBI 1983, 1999).
2. In 1961, however, the total number of cattle in the state stood at 108.3 lakhs (GOT 1972).
3. Comparison with 1961, however, shows a different picture. Total number of buffaloes stood at 25.9 lakhs in that year (GOT 1972).
4. A patent example of the government's inability to safeguard the forests has been provided in recent times by the manner in which the forest brigand Veerappan was dealt with. The sandal-wood smuggler abducted the megastar Dr. Rajkumar and started dictating terms for his release, which the government was inclined to accept (The Statesman 2000b: 8).

9

Industrial Growth and Structural Change

The industrial base of Tamil Nadu was relatively strong even at the time of independence, and with measures taken in the following years it became stronger. Here, as in Chapter 5, first we look into the overall growth of the industrial sector, and then analyse the performance in different segments.

The industrial growth of Tamil Nadu has been quite impressive, except for the last few years. Between 1982-83 and 1991-92, there was an average annual growth of 6.8 per cent but in the last four years, 1992-93 to 1995-96, it was only 1.5 per cent (based on index of industrial production with 1981-82=100). In the first period, the growth in manufacturing was at the rate of 7.1 per cent but in the second it was a negligible 0.6 per cent (GOT 1997). The contribution of manufacturing to the State Domestic Product averaged 20.7 per cent in Tamil Nadu during 1994-97 as against 21.3 per cent for all-India. There were, however, only two states – Gujarat and Maharashtra – with higher contribution from manufacturing.

Tamil Nadu's relative position in all-India production of some of the industries declined substantially. In machinery other than transport, it was down to 12.0 per cent in 1992-93 from 18.0 per cent in 1982-83, in transport equipment and parts from 17.7 per cent to 15.2 per cent, in non-metallic mineral products from 12.6 per cent to 10.8 per cent and in chemicals and chemical products from 11.6 per cent to 7.3 per cent. In cotton textile, however, Tamil Nadu's share increased to 32.2 per cent from 18.8 per cent over the same period, in leather and leather products from 50.0 per cent to 53.5 per cent and in paper and paper products from 10.4 per cent to 13.3 per cent (GOT 1998: 272).

Factory Sector

The performance of the factory sector in Tamil Nadu was quite impressive. The value of output here increased from Rs. 223 crores in 1960 to Rs. 4,111 crores in 1977-78 and then to Rs. 60,319 crores in 1994-95, that is, a growth of 270 times over the period of nearly three-and-half decades. The relative share of Tamil Nadu in the all-India total rose to 11.6 per cent from 6.4. In the latest year, there were only two states-Maharashtra and Gujarat -- with higher shares than Tamil Nadu's (Table 5.1). The growth in net value added was, however, much less. It increased only 189 time over the entire period, and consequently, the ratio in relation to gross output declined from 0.28 to 0.19.

The growth in fixed capital was much higher here than at the national level. It was 377 times over the entire period as against 216 times for all-India. As the growth in output was significantly less, the capital-output ratio increased from 0.33 in 1960 to 0.46 in 1994-95. However, still it was lower than the all-India average. In relation to net value added also the pattern was similar, as may be seen from Table 5.1.

The growth in employment in comparison was negligible. It increased from 2.06 lakhs in 1960 to 11.51 in 1994-95, that is, a growth of only 5.6 times. As the growth at the national level was still lower, Tamil Nadu's relative share in factory sector employment rose to 12.6 per cent from 7.1. In the latest year, in the provision of employment it was next only to Maharashtra. It needs to be noted however, that in recent years employment increased at a much lower rate than in the earlier years. Between 1960 and 1977-78, there was an increase of 241 per cent as against only 64 per cent in the following period ending in 1994-95.

The growth in output per employee was substantial. Over the entire period, it increased 48 times which was slightly higher than at the national level. This was achieved with relatively low fixed capital per employee. The fixed capital per employee in Tamil Nadu increased from Rs. 3,600 in 1960 to Rs. 20,500 in 1977-78 and then to Rs. 2.41 lakhs in 1994-95, that is, 67 times over the entire period. At the all-India level it was 69 times, from Rs. 4,400 to Rs. 3.05 lakhs (Table 5.1).

Structural Changes

There has been a noticeable change in the industrial structure of Tamil Nadu in recent years. Looking to the output value first, as may be seen from Table 9.1, the relative share of food products, paper etc., and

Table 9.1
Industrial Structure of Tamil Nadu (Factory Sector)

Industry	*% share of total*			*Fixed capital per employee (Rs. '000)*		*Output per employee (Rs. '000)*	
	Output value	*Employ -ment*	*Fixed capital*	*1989-90*	*1994-95*	*1989-90*	*1994-95*
Cotton textiles	16.3 (14.4)[a]	18.2	10.3 (7.8)[a]	42	136	198	466
Rubber, plastic etc.	11.9 (10.8)	2.7	8.3 (6.8)	252	742	1019	2302
Food products	9.4 (11.5)	11.4	3.6 (3.6)	30	77	248	435
Machinery and equipment	11.8 (10.1)	9.3	6.7 (5.8)	56	171	248	660
Basic chemicals	10.4 (9.5)	11.1	11.2 (11.6)	102	243	214	489
Electricity	8.3 (4.6)	6.1	28.8 (43.7)	475	1120	129	698
Transport equipment	72.0 (3.3)	7.8	3.4 (5.0)	58	103	99	479
Leather, etc.	4.5 (4.2)	6.1	1.5 (1.4)	25	61	198	384
Textile products	4.2 (2.0)	9.4	2.0 (0.7)	16	51	127	235
Metal and alloys	4.4 (4.9)	2.7	4.5 (3.3)	113	404	436	856
Non-metallic min.prod.	3.0 (3.0)	3.0	2.1 (3.4)	107	168	243	534
Paper, etc.	2.5 (3.4)	3.6	14.0 (3.7)	87	954	211	371
Metal products	1.4 (1.4)	2.1	0.7 (0.9)	42	87	173	365
Total (incl.others)	100.0 (100.0)	100.0	100.0 (100.0)	99	241	253	524

Note: a: figures in parentheses refer to the position in 1989-90.

Source: CMIE 1997b; GOI 1997.

metal and alloys have recorded declines whereas cotton textile, rubber, plastic etc., machinery and equipment, transport equipment, electricity and textile products have gained substantially. The relative share of food products in total output value declined from 11.5 per cent in 1989-90 to 9.4 in 1994-95, and of paper, etc., from 3.4 to 2.5. On the other hand, the share of electricity rose to 8.3 per cent from 4.6 over the same period, of cotton textiles from 14.4 to 16.3 and textile products from 2.0 to 4.2 per cent. Presently, seven industry groups -- cotton textiles, rubber etc., machinery and equipment, basic chemicals, food products, electricity and transport equipment – together account for 70 per cent of total output; their share in 1989-90 was 64 per cent.

More significant changes have occurred in the distribution of fixed capital. In 1994-95, six industries – electricity, paper, basic chemicals, cotton textiles, rubber etc., and machinery and equipment -- together accounted for 79.3 per cent of the total. Although their share in 1989-90 was also more or less the same, within these industries a significant change has come about. While the share of electricity has declined from 43.7 per cent to 28.8 over the period, for paper etc., there was a nearly four-fold rise – from 3.7 per cent to 14.0. The paper industry is undergoing a major change in its technology. The industry's traditional raw material base is dwindling rapidly and an increasing emphasis is being placed on renewable resources.

In the provision of employment, three industries -- cotton textiles, food products and basic chemicals -- together contributed 41 per cent of the total in both 1989-90 and 1994-95. Another five industries -- textile products, machinery and equipment, transport equipment, leather etc., and electricity – together provided 38.7 per cent in 1994-95 and 37.2 in 1989-90. In the latter group, however, the shares of electricity, machinery and equipment and transport equipment declined. The electricity industry with huge investment in fixed capital provided only 6.1 per cent of total employment in 1994-95, declining from 9.1 in 1989-90. Cotton textiles continued to be the largest provider of employment, at 18 epr cent of the total in both the years. The highest growth in employment was recorded by textile products, and its share rose to 9.4 per cent from 4.0 over the period.

The growth in productivity of employees was in most cases not in commensurate with the growth in fixed capital per employee. In the paper industry, fixed capital per employee increased 11 times in this period but the growth in output was only 75 per cent. Similarly, in textile products, these were respectively, 219 per cent and 85 per cent, and in metal and alloys 258 and 96. Only two industries, electricity and transport equipment, recorded a noticeable growth in output per employee as compared to that in fixed capital. However, the former was also the only major industry registering an absolute decline in employment. It is well-known that this industry – being primarily in the public sector -- was over-manned.

Spatial Distribution

Spatially the industrial units were heavily concentrated in a few districts. In 1987-88, 68 per cent of the total output from factory sector came from five districts, viz., Changalpattu, Madras, Coimbatore, Tiruchirappalli and North Arcot; the first two contributing 42 per cent. On the other hand, eight districts – Ramanathapuram, Kanni-

Table 9.2

District-Wise Position of the Factory Sector, and of Registered SSI in Tamil Nadu

Districts	Factory sector (1987-88)				Value of output of SSI (Rs. crores)		
	Output value		Fixed capital (Rs. crs.)	No. of employees ('000)	1980-81	1987-88	% increase
	Total (Rs. crs.)	Per employee (Rs.'000)					
Madras	2706 (16.4)	152	2880 (43.6)	178.1 (20.0)	1118	1512 (16.4)	35.3
Chengalpattu	4229 (25.7)	351	936 (14.2)	120.3 (13.5)	2005	2363 (25.7)	17.9
North Arcot	1137 (6.9)	227	287 (4.3)	50.0 (5.6)	307	635 (6.9)	106.8
South Arcot	649 (3.9)	278	178 (2.7)	23.3 (2.6)	146	362 (3.9)	147.4
Dharmapuri	654 (4.0)	372	362 (5.5)	17.6 (2.0)	47	365 (4.0)	675.4
Salem	942 (5.7)	173	360 (5.4)	54.5 (6.1)	378	526 (5.7)	39.2
Periyar	235 (1.4)	155	38 (0.6)	15.2 (1.7)	130	131 (1.4)	1.0
Coimbatore	1920 (11.7)	157	378 (5.7)	122.6 (13.8)	916	1073 (11.7)	17.1
Nilgiris	248 (1.5)	234	36 (0.5)	10.6 (1.2)	134	139 (1.5)	3.6
Madurai	473 (2.9)	119	98 (1.5)	39.9 (4.5)	356	386 (4.2)	8.4
Tiruchirappalli	1233 (7.5)	270	413 (6.3)	45.6 (5.1)	436	689 (7.5)	57.9
Thanjavur	136 (0.8)	95	29 (0.4)	14.2 (1.6)	76	76 (0.8)	-
Pudukkottai	94 (0.6)	106	39 (0.6)	8.8 (1.0)	19	52 (0.6)	173.8

Contd...

Contd...

Ramanathapuram	55 (0.3)	166	9 (neg.)	3.3 (0.4)	-	30 (0.3)	-
Tirunelveli	861 (5.2)	148	337 (5.1)	58.1 (6.5)	404	481 (5.2)	19.0
Kanniyakumari	81 (0.5)	28	21 (0.3)	29.4 (3.3)	44	45 (0.5)	3.2
Pasumpon	79 (0.5)	136	25 (0.4)	5.8 (0.7)	-	44 (0.5)	-
Kamarajar	520 (3.2)	68	123 (1.9)	76.1 (8.6)	250	291 (3.2)	16.0
Dindigul	218 (1.3)	148	57 (0.9)	14.7 (1.7)	-	-	-
State	16472 (100.0)	185	6605 (100.0)	888.2 (100.0)	6768	9202 (100.0)	36.0

Source: GOT 1997.

yakumari, Pasumpon, Pudukkottai, Thanjavur, Dindigul, Periyar and Nilgiris – together had a share of only 6.9 per cent.

In fixed capital, Madras alone accounted for 43.6 per cent of the total, followed by Chengalpattu 14.2. Another five districts, as may be seen from Table 9.2, together contributed 28 per cent. Thus, seven districts, out of 19 in existence then, accounted for 86 per cent of the total. In the distribution of factories also, the situation was not much different. Four districts – Coimbatore, Salem, Madras and Chengalpattu – together contributed half of the total number.

In the total number of employees in the factory sector in 1987-88, Madras, Chengalpattu and Coimbatore together contributed 47.3 per cent, and another 32 per cent came from Kamarajar, Tirunelveli, Salem, North Arcot and Tiruchirappalli. The output per employee varied between the highest of Rs. 3.72 lakhs in Dharmapuri and the lowest at Rs. 28 thousands in Kanniyakumari (Table 9.2).

Small-Scale Industries

For the SSI sector, as noted in Chapter 5, three sources of data have to be used. For the units registered with the SIDO, generally called modern SSI, census surveys conducted at long intervals provide a reasonably reliable data. The units which are not covered by these surveys are included either in the data collected by the KVIC or by the NSSO. First, we look into the trend in modern SSI.

Modern SSI

The first census survey carried out in 1973, found Tamil Nadu to be having the largest number of units in the country. With 16,002 working units in 1972, it accounted for 11.5 per cent of the total number. In the gross value of output, however, its position was second, with 12.4 per cent of all-India total, next to Maharashtra, which had 20.3 per cent. The ratio of value-added to output here was just equal to the national average, and was lower than in as many as seven of the major states.

In the provision of employment, Tamil Nadu's position was quite good. It accounted for 13.0 per cent of all-India total number, which was second only to Maharashtra. In output per employee, however, the situation was very poor; at Rs. 14,954, it was lower than the national average – being Rs. 15,744. Of course, fixed capital per employee was also much lower here. At Rs. 5,165, it was lower than the levels in 11 of the major states. In fact, Tamil Nadu's share in total of fixed investment itself was very low, at 10.5 per cent only, which was half of that in Maharashtra. The capital-output ratio here was 0.35, lower than that in most other states.

The growth of the SSI sector in the following two-and-half decades was substantial. At the end of March 1992, there were 1,38,404 registered units, that is, a nearly nine-fold rise over 1972. The investment rose to Rs. 2,906.48 crores and the value of production to Rs. 7,612 crores, representing a growth of 26 times and 24 times, respectively. The employment, however, increased by only seven times in this period, from 2.15 lakh to 14.95 lakh persons. After another five years, at the end of March 1997, number of units rose to 2,63,845, investment to Rs. 6,395 crores, value of production Rs. 16,257 crores and employment to 25.22 lakh persons, that is, a growth of 91,120,114 and 69 per cent, respectively (GOT 1998: 231).

Looking to the latest position of some of the technical coefficients: Fixed capital per employee rose to Rs. 25,357 in March 1997, that is, a rise of 4.9 times over 1972. The output per employee had a slightly lower growth, 4.3 times – the value in the latest year being Rs. 64,461. The capital-output ratio recorded a small rise, to 0.39.

As regards industry-wise distribution of SSI units, at the end of March 1995, out of the total number of 2,07,357 units, hosiery and readymade garments accounted for 16.7 per cent, followed by food and food products 10.9 per cent, non-electrical machinery and parts 8.8 per cent, cotton textiles 8.0 per cent, metal products and parts 7.6 per cent and paper and paper products and chemicals and chemical products around 7 per cent each. Thus, these seven groups together accounted for 66 per cent of the total number of units. Another 16 per cent was contributed by rubber and plastic products, non-metallic mineral products, wood and wooden products and electrical machinery and apparatus, distributed almost equally (GOT 1997: Table 6.5).

District-wise, the distribution of industries was only slightly better here than in case of the factory sector. At the end of March 1995, three districts – Coimbatore, Salem and Chengalpattu – together accounted for 33 per cent of the total number of SSI units. Another 33 per cent came from Periyar, Madras, Madurai, North Arcot, Kamarajar and Tiruchirappalli. In value of output, the concentration was much deeper. In 1987-88, as may be seen from Table 9.2, three districts – Chengalpattu, Madras and Coimbatore – together contributed as much as 54 per cent of the total. Another quarter came from Tiruchirappalli, North Arcot, Salem and Tirunelveli combined. The reduction in concentration was insignificant over the years. Eight years back, in 1980-81, the same seven districts accounted for 82 per cent of the total output. The growth in output was very small for most of the backward districts (Table 9.2).

Khadi and Village Industries

In khadi and village industries Tamil Nadu occupies an important position. As may be seen from Table 5.4, in 1993-94 it accounted for 14.1 per cent of the all-India total value of production. There were only two states, Uttar Pradesh and Maharashtra, with higher levels. In early eighties, its share was 15.3 per cent, second only to Uttar Pradesh. The growth in production here was relatively low. At 292 per cent over the period of 12 years, it was exceeded by as many as eight of the major states.

In the provision of employment, Tamil Nadu's position was much better. In 1993-94, with 10.34 lakh persons employed in the KVI sector, it accounted for the highest proportion of 19.4 per cent of all-India total. The growth in employment here was 78 per cent between 1982-83 and 1993-94 as against 55 per cent for all-India. The productivity of the employees is, however, very low. It stood at only Rs. 4,397 per employee in 1993-94 as against the all-India average at Rs. 6,014; all the other southern states had higher levels. The growth over 1982-83 was 120.4 per cent here as against 168.7 in all-India.

As regards the composition of production, in 1993-94, khadi accounted for 15 per cent of the state's total, and the balance came from village industries. In the all-India total production of Khadi, Tamil Nadu's share was 19 per cent and in village industries 13.4. In the state's khadi production, cotton alone accounted for 57 per cent and silk 40 per cent. In the all-India total production of silk khadi, Tamil Nadu's share was 39.6 per cent and in cotton khadi 18.7 per cent (KVIC 1994).

In the village industries of the state, four items – palmgur, ghani oil, cottage leather and carpentry and blacksmithy – together contributed as much as 68.3 per cent of total production, for the first one alone 28.5 per cent. Another 16 per cent came from cottage pottery, polyvastra, processing of cereals and pulses (PCPI) and cottage match. In the all-India total production of palmgur, Tamil Nadu's share was as much as 77 per cent, in cottage match 41 per cent, in polyvastra 39 per cent, in other textiles 26 per cent and in beekeeping 25 per cent (KVIC 1994).

As regards the organisation of village industries, it was largely on the basis of cooperatives. In 1994-95, out of the total production valued at Rs. 376.16 crores, industrial cooperative societies accounted for

50.6 per cent, individual artisans 45.4 per cent and the balance by departmental units. In employment, the cooperatives accounted for 68.2 per cent and individual artisans 30.6 (GOT 1997: Table 14).

Household Enterprises

The household enterprises, as noted in Chapter 5, are defined to include only OAMEs and NDMEs, that is, those not employing any hired worker and those with not more than five workers, respectively. The number of such enterprises in Tamil Nadu stood at 13.52 lakh in 1989-90, constituting 8.6 per cent of all-India total. Of the total number, only 55.8 per cent were working in rural areas, in contrast to 76.4 per cent at the national level. In the other southern states also the proportion in rural areas were much higher (Table 5.5).

In the total employment provided by household enterprises, rural area's share was 52.8 per cent, that is, less than its share in total number of units. Industry-wise, the important provider of employment in rural areas were wood and wood products, cotton textiles, beverages, tobacco etc., textile products, rubber, plastics etc., and food products. Their combined share in this year was 75 per cent of the total, for the first three 53 per cent. The proportion of part-time employment was 11 per cent on the average, and at the highest 30 per cent in food products.

In value of output per enterprise, the most important industry in rural areas was basic metal and alloys, with Rs. 1.07 lakh, followed at a great distance by electrical machinery etc., food processing, metal products and parts and food products. The lowest output value per enterprise was in leather and fur products, at Rs. 3,811, against the average for all industries at Rs. 8,811. The urban enterprises had a much higher output per enterprise -- the average being Rs. 23,576.

The proportion of value added in output was, however, much higher in rural enterprises. The average for all industries in rural areas came to 56.9 per cent as against 38.6 per cent in urban areas. Among the industries in rural areas, it was more than 70 per cent in eight industries whereas in urban areas only three industries had this level of value added. Another point worth noting is that the proportion of output produced for other concerns was significantly higher in rural enterprises than in urban ones. The average for all industries in rural areas came to 44 per cent, and there were five industries with above 70 per cent. In urban areas, this type of production constituted only 28 per cent.

As regards the value of fixed assets per enterprise, Tamil Nadu's position was very depressing. In the rural areas it averaged only Rs.

5,512 as against the all-India average at Rs. 6,338. In value of plant and machinery, the figures were Rs. 1,405 and Rs. 1,495 respectively. The widest gap was, however, in value of working capital per enterprise, being Rs. 176 and Rs. 523, respectively. In urban enterprises, the relative position was worse. Value of fixed capital per enterprise in Tamil Nadu came to Rs. 12,065 as against Rs. 18,690 for all-India. In plant and machinery, these were respectively Rs. 2,463 and Rs. 4,624 (Table 5.5).

On the health of industrial units, as noted in Chapter 5, no comprehensive data are available. We may note here the position of only large-scale industries and the modern sector of SSI. Number of sick units in the large-scale sector of Tamil Nadu was not very high. In the three time points considered, as may be seen from Table 5.6, it stood at the highest of 133 units in March 1990, constituting 9.1 per cent of all-India total, and declined to 129 in March 1996 – 6.6 per cent of the total. The most industrialised state of Maharashtra accounted for 22.1 and 17.2 per cent of the total number of sick units on these two dates, respectively. In outstanding bank credit also the situation was similar. Between June 1982 and March 1996, the growth in Tamil Nadu was by 253 per cent as against 410 per cent at the national level.

In the SSI sector, so far as number of sick units are concerned the situation appears to have improved considerably. Number of sick units in Tamil Nadu declined from 15,171 in December 1985 to 8,125 in March 1994, and then rose to 9,809 in March 1997. In the all-India total number, the proportion was down to 3.2 per cent and 4.2 per cent respectively, from 12.9 in 1985. The outstanding bank credit with them, however, increased at a high rate. There was a nearly four-fold rise over the period, which was higher than that at the national level. Tamil Nadu's relative share in all-India total rose to 11.9 and 11.1 per cent in the later time points from 10.1 in 1985 (Table 5.6).

The most striking point that has emerged from the above analysis is the neglect of backward district and the rural areas. Industries in every sector are concentrated in a few districts and in the urban areas and their periphery. The industrial growth of a state or a district depends on a variety of factors, as noted in chapter 5. Below we give a brief look into the state of infrastructure and the provision of bank finance.

Infrastructural Situation

Overall, Tamil Nadu's position on availability of infrastructure for industrial growth appears much better than most other states. A composite index of infrastructure prepared for 1992-94, covering 13 indicators, for all the major states placed Tamil Nadu in the third position, next to Punjab and Kerala. With the base of 100 for all-India, it scored 144. However, the index included a number of items, which are not directly related to industrial growth. Below we give a brief look into the position of power and transport facility and the role of some of the promotional agencies.

Power and Transport

Adequate availability of power is a prerequisite for industrial growth, and here Tamil Nadu's position appears to be much better than most other states. Per capita consumption of power increased from 21 kwh during the First Plan period to 92 during the Third, 157 in the Fifth Plan, 295 in the Seventh Plan and then to 420 kwh in the Eighth Plan. In 1992-93, there were four states – Punjab, Gujarat, Haryana and Maharashtra -- with higher levels of consumption than Tamil Nadu's. The annual gross generation of power in Tamil Nadu increased from 1,053 million units in the First Plan to 9,453 in the Fifth Plan and then to 32,700 million units during the Eighth Plan (GOT 1997: S-104, 1998: 213). The industrial consumption of power in 1994-95 stood at 9,289 million units, constituting 40.2 per cent of the total sale of power (GOT 1997: S-101).

District-wise, however, the power consumption varied greatly. In 1993-94, against the state average of 347 kwh per capita, it was only 20 kwh in Pasumpon, 86 in Kanniyakumari, 109 in Padukkottai and 123 in Thanjavur; on the other hand, Nilgiris had 2,302 kwh, Coimbatore 719 and Chidambaranar and Kamarajar nearly 500 kwh (GOT 1997: S-103).

In road network also Tamil Nadu's position was very good. The density of roads here increased from 29.7 kms per 100 sq km in 1951 to 107.3 kms in 1991. In 1995-96, its road density was more than double that of all-India, being 158.2 kms and 73.1 kms, respectively. In April 1996, it had a total road length of 1,41,761 kms, comprised of 2,002 kms of national highways, 1,934 kms of state highways, 13,975 kms of major district roads, 39,063 kms of other district roads and 84,784 kms of other roads. Proportion of unsurfaced roads was 32.1 per cent of total here as against 44.5 for all-India (GOT 1998: 291; CMIE 1998a).

District-wise, road availability varied considerably. In 1994-95, state government roads per 100 sq km varied between the highest of 68.2 km in Kanniyakumari and the lowest of 26.2 in Tiruchirappalli, with the state average at 41.4 (GOT 1997: S-156). The road availability in many of the rural areas are far from satisfactory. Based on 1991 census, it was identified in the Eighth Plan that 377 habitations in the population category of 1,000-1,500 and 140 habitations in above 1,500 category needed to be provided with connectivity. The Ninth Plan has a target of connecting 517 villages with population above 1000 and 4,986 villages with population between 500 and 1,000 (GOT 1998: 292, 297).

Promotional Agencies

There are a number of organisations in Tamil Nadu for promoting the growth of both large and small-scale industries. The earliest to come was the Tamil Nadu Industrial Investment Corporation (TIIC), set up in 1949, for providing term loans and subscribing to share capital. In 1965 came the Tamil Nadu Industrial Development Corporation (TIDCO) for the medium and large-scale industries. Its activities included identification of projects and entrepreneurs and assisting them with licences, location, term finance etc., and also providing equity support. Then came the State Industries Promotion Corporation of Tamil Nadu (SIPCOT) for the development of major and medium industries and helping them to spread into backward areas. The schemes implemented by it over the last two-and-half decades included mainly (a) term lending with refinance from the IDBI, (b) interest free sales tax deferral/waiver, (c) state capital subsidy, and (d) setting up industrial complexes in backward areas. Over the entire period since inception it could develop only seven industrial complexes. In 1977 came the Electronic Corporation of Tamil Nadu for assisting the growth of electronic industries. The latest promotional agency to be set up is the Tamil Nadu Corporation for Industrial Infrastructure Development in 1992, with the objective of developing new industrial growth centres with fully integrated on-site and off-site infrastructure facilities.

The agencies for small-scale industries received much less attention. Presently, there are organisations like the Khadi and Village Industries Board, Tamil Nadu Small Industries Development corporation (SIDCO), TANSI, Tamil Nadu Handloom Development Corporation, Tamil Nadu Leather Development Corporation, and District Industries Centres (DICs). We give a look at the level of activities of some of them.

The KVIB provides financial and technical assistance to KVIs, and apparently its role was substantial in recent years. In 1993-94, it provided loans totalling Rs. 561 lakhs and grants to the extent of Rs. 75 lakhs. Only one state, West Bengal, had provided larger loans this year, and in grants Gujarat. Including the KVIC disbursements, the total for KVIs in Tamil Nadu came to Rs. 7.96 crores in loans and Rs. 11.89 crores in grants. No other state except Uttar Pradesh could exceed these levels.

The SIDCO, established in 1971, undertakes activities like the creation of infrastructure, distribution of scarce raw materials, supply of machinery, provision of marketing assistance, distribution of central investment subsidy in backward areas, construction and allotment of workshops and allotting plots with all basic amenities. Till the end of 1995, the corporation had provided around 3,800 worksheds in 66 locations. Among other activities, only supply of scarce raw materials was substantial. In 1994-95, its distribution was of the value of around Rs. 100 crores.

The DICs were established towards the end of seventies with the objective of providing all the services and support facilities under a single roof. However, the objectives remained far from fulfilled, and presently its activities are largely confined to registration of small-scale units, conduct of training programmes, and executing various schemes of assistance of the government. The level of DIC activities varied greatly from district to district. For example, in cottage industries, number of units registered during 1994-95 stood at the highest of 1,025 in Salem and the lowest at 81 in Villupuram. Number of units benefited by state capital subsidy and special subsidy was five or less in three districts – South Arcot, Tirunelveli and Villupuram – as against 66 in Chengalpattu alone. The amount distributed was less than Rs. 6 lakhs in four districts whereas in Chengalpattu it was as much as Rs. 1.22 crores (GOT 1997: S-82).

Most of the organisations for promoting industrial growth remained weak until recent years, particularly those serving the SSIs. The backward districts and the remote rural areas did not get any attention worth the name. Moreover, the institutions assisting the SSIs were generally biased towards the more resourceful of them; the weaker groups did not get the quality of attention required for survival and growth.

Bank Finance

Working Capital

In the provision of working capital to industries, the most important institution has been the scheduled commercial banks. The outstanding credit from them to the industrial sector stood at Rs. 8,092 crores at the end of March 1993, constituting 48.9 per cent of the total bank credit to the state. This is quite a high proportion, given the contribution of this sector to the state's domestic product. However, these credits were highly concentrated in a few districts. Madras alone accounted for 54.4 per cent of the total, followed by Coimbatore 16.2 and Chengalpattu 5.3. Thus, these three districts together appropriated as much as 76 per cent of the total, and the remaining 19 got only the balance of 24 per cent (GOT 1997: S-120).

Moreover, the beneficiaries were mainly in the large-scale sector. The outstanding credit with the SSIs increased from Rs. 26.2 crores at the end of June 1968 to Rs. 544.1 crores at December-end 1983 and Rs. 3,785 crores in March 1995, that is, a growth of 144 times over the entire period. This high rate of growth is due to the low base. The relative share of SSIs in the aggregate for industry did not increase at any noticeable rate, and in recent years it was no more than a third of the total.

Among the states, however, Tamil Nadu's SSIs do not appear to have been neglected. In the all-India total of credit outstanding to SSI, Tamil Nadu's share stood at 13.7 per cent in 1968, and after a decline to 10.1 in 1983 it rose again to 13.0 per cent in 1995. Tamil Nadu always had the second largest share, as may be seen from Table 5.7. The growth in credit was, however, very low here, both in terms of amount provided and the number of units served. The growth in the latter was by only 63.5 per cent between 1983 and 1995 as against the all-India average at 138 per cent.

Under the Annual Credit Plan of districts, which covered the RRB and cooperative credit institutions as well and provided credit solely to small and tiny enterprises, the share of industry stood at 26.8 per cent of the total at the end of March 1995, Rs. 934 crores out of Rs. 3,480 crores. District-wise, there was great variation in the share of industry. It was less than 10 per cent in eight of the districts, with Nagapattinam having only 1.7 per cent. On the other hand, in Coimbatore 75 per cent of the total went to industry, followed by 40 per cent in Chengalpattu. The gap between allocation and utilisation was very wide in some of the districts. In Kamarajar the utilisation was only 36.6 per cent, in Nagapattinam 38.1 per cent and in Tiruvannamalai 41.8 (GOT 1997: S-121).

Term Finance

In the provision of finance by term-lending institutions, like development banks, specialised financial institutions and investment institutions, the relative share of Tamil Nadu was quite high. The per capita cumulative assistance provided by all the institutions together stood at Rs. 3,535 till the end of March 1997 as against the all-India average at Rs. 2,587. Only two states, Maharashtra and Gujarat, received higher amounts. As regards the recent trend, during 1992-97 Tamil Nadu received an annual average of Rs. 446 per capita as against Rs. 347 for all-India and the highest of Rs. 961 in Gujarat (Table 5.8).

Considering only the all-India financial institutions, the per capita cumulative came to Rs. 3,485, which was 38 per cent higher than the all-India average, and could be exceeded by the same two states, Gujarat and Maharashtra. Among these institutions, the SIDBI which commenced operation only in April 1990 and provided credit to the small-scale sector, the cumulative total of per capita assistance in Tamil Nadu came to Rs. 204 till March 1997. Although this was higher than the average for all-India, there were five states with higher levels of assistance.

Among the state level institutions, the TIIC was relatively more important and it provided a major portion of its credit to the SSI. The cumulative total of per capita assistance from it stood at Rs. 370 till March 1997, and it could be exceeded by only two of the major states, Karnataka and West Bengal. The recent years' trend is also similar. The average for 1992-97 came to Rs. 42, which is 80 per cent higher than the all-India average. The TIIC's cumulative total of assistance sanctioned to SSI reached Rs. 1,191 crores till March 1994, constituting 64.6 per cent of the total. This relative share for SSI is quite low as compared to the position in other states; most of the major states provided a much higher proportion to the SSI, and the average for all-India came to 70.5 per cent. The assistance from TIDCO – going to large and medium projects – was relatively low. The per capita cumulative till March 1997 came to only Rs. 102, less than the average for all-India.

While the industrial growth of Tamil Nadu is appreciable, except for the wide inter-district disparity, it is necessary to bear in mind the practices in some of these industries. We may note here a situation in the leather industry, in which Tamil Nadu has a dominating position.

Even under the best of circumstances, tanneries can be dangerous places of work. The Factories Act, 1948, has a separate provision for tanneries, and has notified liming and tanning of raw hides and skins and processes incidental thereto as dangerous operations. Women workers are prohibited from working in certain operations. But this rule is largely violated in Tamil Nadu. The most polluting part of the operation (upto pre-tanning) is performed in premises not technically covered under the Factories Act, and most of this operation employ women and children. A survey in Dindigul had reported that women working in tanneries and allied workshops are infected not only by common tannery diseases like dermatitis, anthrax, bronchitis, tuberculosis, etc., but also have menstrual disorders and miscarriages (Nihila 1993).

While pursuing industrialisation, every government must keep a close watch on its costs. Industrial growth at the cost of human sufferings cannot be pursued for long; it is bound to have its backlash.

10

Towards Poverty Alleviation

In reducing poverty, as noted in Chapter 2, Tamil Nadu's performance was the worst among the southern states. Both in the proportion of population below the poverty-line and in per capita consumption expenditure its relative position was very depressing. Almost all the survey carried out by the NSSO found the percentage of population below poverty-line higher than the national average. It may be seen from Table 1.1 that of the four time points considered, only in 1993-94 it was lower than the all-India average.

We have observed in the preceding chapters that the development of Tamil Nadu's economy was highly concentrated in a few districts and the rural areas in general did not receive the required attention. Here, in this chapter, we look into the magnitude and manner of implementation of some of the directly poverty-alleviating measures. The focus is primarily on the schemes for employment creation, self-employment programmes, and the minimum needs programme.

Wage Employment Programmes

Wage employment is particularly important in Tamil Nadu due to the large proportion of agricultural labourers here. In the total of main workers, agricultural labourers constituted 44.73 per cent in rural areas in 1991, rising from 40.27 in 1981; the average for all-India in these years were respectively 32.17 and 30.09 per cent. The proportion of agricultural labour in the rural population with MPCE of below Rs. 190 constituted as much as 45 per cent in Tamil Nadu in 1993-94 (NSSO 1998b).

Despite the importance of wage employment, creation of employment opportunities did not get much attention from the government. Under the CSRE, which was in operation during 1971 to 1974, Rs.

8.48 crores was spent in Tamil Nadu, constituting 7.0 per cent of the total spent in 18 states in which the scheme was in operation. The employment generated came to 226.45 lakh mandays (lmd), which was 7.5 per cent of the total. Year-wise, number of mandays created declined from 84.04 lakh in 1971-72 to 78.33 in 1972-73 and then to 64.08 lakh in the last year. The employment created per household was only 101.6 mandays in a year for 1.5 persons (GOI 1979). The FWP was not implemented here. The first significant programme was the NREP launched in 1980, which was later on merged with the JRY.

The unemployment situation in Tamil Nadu continued to be one of the worst. In 1983, according to the NSS, the person rate of unemployment here stood at as much as 42.03, which was higher than in all but one state. The person rate of full employment was only 8.24, with the same relative position (NSSO 1987). Below we make a brief analysis of two of the employment programmes currently in operation – the JRY and the EAS.

Jawahar Rozgar Yojana

Under the JRY, since the inception in 1989 to March 1996, Rs. 1,736 crores was spent in Tamil Nadu, constituting 7.9 per cent of all-India total. The growth in expenditure was 80 per cent over the period, from Rs. 202 crores in 1989-90 to Rs. 364 crores in 1995-96, as against 61 per cent at the all-India level. The physical performance was also not bad. Total number of mandays created till March 1995 was 5,018 lakh mandays (lmd), constituting 10.0 per cent of all-India total (Table 6.1). In recent years, however, the size of the scheme has been considerably reduced. In 1998-99, total fund available for it was only Rs. 140 crores, constituting 6.3 per cent of all-India total, and the target for employment set at 230.4 lmd – 5.8 per cent of the total (GOI 1999).

As regards the extent of benefit to weaker sections, the position of landless workers was much better here than in most other states. In the total number of mandays created till March 1995, their share was 79 per cent as against the all-India average at 45.5. The share of SC/ST was, however, lower here than at the national level (Table 6.1).

Under the intensified JRY, launched in 1993-94, Rs. 29.03 crores was made available to Tamil Nadu in the first year but only Rs. 7.94 crores, that is, 27.3 per cent, could be spent. In the all-India total of resources utilised this year, Tamil Nadu's share was only 2.8 per cent. In the following year, however, the situation improved considerably.

Out of the available resources of Rs. 53.64 crores, Rs. 43.40 crores – that is, 81 per cent – could be utilised. Tamil Nadu's share in all-India total utilisation came to 4.8 per cent. The employment created was much above the target set, being 130.29 lmd and 87.89 lmd, respectively. The former constituted 6.3 per cent of all-India total. The next year, 1995-96, however, witnessed a sharp decline. The target itself was low, and 86.01 lmd were created by spending Rs. 30.51 crores (GOT 1997: 145).

The district-wise performance of JRY varied considerably. For example, during 1994-96, as may be seen from Table 10.1, the average number of mandays created was at the highest 85.60 lmd in Chengalpattu, a relatively developed district, and at the lowest 19.42 lmd in Kanniyakumari. While the latter is a very small district, still smaller ones like Nilgiri, Pasumpon, Pudukkottai and Chidambaranar had much higher levels of employment generation. The second stream operated in eight districts only, and 29 per cent of the mandays created during 1994-96 was in Chengalpattu, followed by Dharmapuri and Nagapattinam around 13 per cent each.

As regards the nature of assets created, as data for recent years are not available, we may have a look at the situation in earlier years. In 1989-90, the emphasis was on social forestry, rural roads, construction of village tanks and minor irrigation and flood protection works. The social forestry covered an area of 14,013 hectares, constituting 7.4 per cent of all-India total. Rural roads constructed this year totalled 7,244 kms, number of village tanks 8,001 and minor irrigation and flood control covered 2,698 hectares; in relation to the all-India total, these were, respectively, 4.0, 38.3 and 5.0 per cent. The proportion of works benefiting SC/ST was substantial in Tamil Nadu; number of works for them totalled 44,358 and constituted 9.1 per cent of all-India total this year (GOI 1991).

As regards the sub-schemes of JRY, under the MWS 28,406 wells were constructed in Tamil Nadu between 1988-89 and 1994-95, with an expenditure of Rs. 183.82 crores, constituting respectively, 3.3 per cent and 6.2 per cent of all-India total. Under the IAY, Tamil Nadu's position was much better. Between 1985-86 and 1994-95, 3,05,818 houses were constructed at a cost of Rs. 472.68 crores, constituting respectively, 14.9 per cent and 19.1 per cent of all-India total (GOI 1996c).

The implementation of JRY in Tamil Nadu suffered from many deficiencies, as in case of other states. We note here the findings of the

Table 10.1

District-wise Status of Special Poverty Alleviation Schemes in Tamil Nadu (average for 1994-96)

Districts	*Self-Employment Schemes*		*Employment Generation (lmd)*			
	IRDP (no. of beneficiaries)	*TRYSEM (no. trained)*	*JVVT*	*IJVT*	*EAS*	*Total*[b]
Chengalpattu	11,976 (2.6)[a]	1577	85.60	31.44	neg	109.5 (19.2)[c]
South Arcot	6248 (2.9)	825	60.4	11.9	"	97.4 (26.7)
Villupuram	9777 (3.5)	1084	49.6	12.6	5.0	73.9 (14.4)
North Arcot	9651 (3.2)	1009	52.1	0	7.6	65.7 (17.4)
Tiruvannamalai	4033 (2.0)	682	53.2	0	2.7	59.8 (16.7)
Salem	16412 (4.2)	1266	58.7	0	20.1	83.1 (13.4)
Dharmapuri	9508 (3.9)	1082	46.1	14.6	25.5	81.7 (22.7)
Periyar	9876 (2.5)	597	39.9	0	0	42.3 (9.4)
Coimbatore	13223 (3.8)	1124	32.8	0	6.1	46.6 (10.2)
Nilgiris	2005 (2.8)	113	42.6	0	8.1	44.8 (179.3)
Thanjavur	6152 (2.9)	803	23.9	9.3	neg	35.6 (10.3)
Nagapattinam	8527 (3.6)	875	49.6	13.8	"	81.5 (16.7)
Tiruchirappalli	15201 (3.7)	1365	69.4	0	17.4	95.1 (14.7)
Padukkottai	6770 (5.1)	533	35.2	0	11.0	42.3 (31.6)
Madurai	8432 (2.4)	790	40.0	0	0	44.4 (7.0)
Dindigul	7919 (4.5)	647	38.9	0	3.4	50.1 (13.7)
Ramanathapuram	6485 (5.7)	528	21.5	5.0	18.9	32.5 (33.4)
Kamarajar	5390 (3.4)	529	28.5	0	12.3	49.0 (20.0)
Pasumpon	5092 (4.7)	399	33.0	0	16.2	48.2 (39.2)
Tirunelveli	9537 (3.8)	919	35.1	0	1.4	38.6 (11.1)
Chidambaranar	6972 (4.8)	519	25.1	9.4	20.4	41.9 (21.7)
Kanniyakumari	8666 (5.4)	391	19.4	0	0	17.0 (9.6)
State	192558 (3.4)	17661	940.6	108.1	176.3	1281.1 (16.2)

Source: GOT 1997.

Notes: a: number of beneficiaries per '000 population.
b: for 1995-96 only, include employment under EAS.
c: persondays created per agricultural labour.

first concurrent evaluation carried out during January-December 1992.

First, the norm regarding wage/non-wage ratio and also that on wage rate were largely violated. The wage/non-wage ratio in expenditure was found to be 54:46 in Tamil Nadu against the norm of 60:40. On wage payments, the guidelines' prescription of paying the statutory minimum wage and equal wage to men and women were not followed. As against the minimum wage of Rs. 15 for unskilled workers, men were paid at the rate of Rs. 25.93 and women Rs. 16.88. Further, in the execution of works, contractors were found to have been engaged in 7.21 per cent of the cases, despite its prohibition in the guidelines.

Another glaring deficiency was the non-maintenance of muster roll, very necessary for proper assessment of progress of work, employment generation and payment of wages. The JRY guidelines had clearly stipulated its up-to-date maintenance by panchayats/executing agencies. But in Tamil Nadu muster rolls were not maintained at all as against its absence in only 15.85 per cent of cases at the all-India level. The non-maintenance encouraged manipulation of employment generation and wage payment data.

As regards the type of assets created this year, there was an overriding attention to construction of link roads. Many important sectors like social forestry, land development, flood protection/soil and water conservation works, community sanitary latrines, etc., did not get the deserving attention. On the question of quality of assets created also Tamil Nadu's position was not satisfactory. According to the survey, only 65.36 per cent of the assets were good/satisfactory as against 73.80 at the all-India level.

A very disturbing feature was that, although the programme was targeted at the poor, the beneficiaries were largely from the better-off groups. The poverty-line income during 1991-92 was an annual family income of Rs. 6,400, and in Tamil Nadu 62.95 per cent of the beneficiaries were from above this income level. The share of workers with income at Rs. 4,800 and below was only 8.5 per cent in Tamil Nadu as against 18.4 per cent at the national level.

Another serious deviation was that the Annual Action Plan was not discussed in gram sabha meeting in most of the cases. In only 36.8 per cent of the GPs surveyed it was found to have been observed as against 60.7 at the all-India level. Stranger, however, is the fact that the JRY manual itself was not available in most cases. In Tamil Nadu, it was not there in 75.8 per cent of the panchayats as against around one-third at the national level.

Even the extent of employment benefit received by a family was not substantial. A JRY worker in Tamil Nadu could get 6.44 mandays of employment under JRY and another 12.95 under other programmes, that is, in all 19.39 persondays in a month. For other members of the family the JRY could provide 1.04 persondays of work (Neelakantan 1994).

Employment Assurance Scheme

The EAS, introduced only in 1993, has the objective of providing a minimum level of assured work to rural job-seekers. As notice in Chapter 6, it was also financed by the Centre to the extent of 80 per cent. The expenditure on the scheme was very small until recently. In the first three years, 1993-96, a total of Rs. 134 crores was spent on it and 363.6 lmd created. Annually, the mandays created increased from only 10.96 lmd in 1993-94 to 141.29 in 1994-95 and 211.35 lmd in 1995-96. The fund available for the scheme has risen significantly in recent years. In 1998-99, Rs. 241.56 crores was allotted to it, constituting 8.6 per cent of all-India total (GOI 1999).

In the employment created, the share of landless workers was generally high here. In 1994-95, it stood at 84 per cent of the total as against the all-India average at 23.3. The share of women was, however, relatively low, being 30.6 per cent this year. For SC and ST, the combined share stood at 53.2 per cent as against the all-India average of 58.6 per cent.

District-wise, as may be seen from Table 10.1, during 1994-96, the EAS did not operate at all in three districts and four others had negligible levels. In the total employment created in this period, six districts -- Dharmapuri, Chidambaranar, Salem, Ramanathapuram, Tiruchirappalli and Pasumpon – together contributed 67 per cent.

The impact of the employment schemes on employment opportunities was not substantial. Through all the schemes, Tamil Nadu could create only 1,281 lmd in 1995-96. Persondays created per agricultural labourer (on the basis of number of agricultural labourers in 1991) came to 16.2. District-wise, there was too much of variation. While Nilgiri had 179.3 persondays per agricultural labourer, for Madurai it was only 7.0.

The NSSO surveys have brought out that participation by rural households in public works in Tamil Nadu is relatively low. In 1987-88, number participating per thousand households was only 34 here as against the national average at 64 households. In 1993-94, the figures were respectively 42 and 59 (NSSO 1998a). Moreover, the participation by weaker group households was found to be low in Tamil Nadu. In 1993-94, the group with MPCE of less than Rs. 190 had only 113 per thousand households as against the all-India average at 272 households. Those with MPCE of Rs. 560 and above, on the other hand, had 67 in Tamil Nadu as against 49 at the national level. The participation by SC and ST households were also relatively low. As against 75 and 88 households per thousand, respectively, at the national level, Tamil Nadu had only 49 and 29 in 1993-94.

Self-Employment Programmes

Integrated Rural Development Programme

Among the self-employment programmes launched since late sixties, the most important is IRDP. Its objective, as noted in Chapter 6, was to augment income of the identified poor families on a sustainable basis. The procedure for identification of beneficiaries and implementation of the scheme has also been described in the same chapter. Here, we first make a comparison of Tamil Nadu's performance with other states, and then look into the district-wise situation.

So far as expenditure on the programme is concerned, Tamil Nadu's position is much better than most of the other states. Between 1990-91 and 1997-98, as may be seen from Table 6.2, the expenditure here increased by 89 per cent as against only 39 per cent at the national level. Its relative share in all-India total rose to 8.4 per cent from 6.1. The number of families assisted, however, recorded a decline in recent years, after rising to 2.01 lakhs in 1994-95; in 1996-97, it stood at only 1.53 lakhs. Over the entire Eighth Plan (1992-97), 8.98 lakh families were assisted with an expenditure of Rs. 357.27 crores.

The representation of weaker groups among the beneficiaries was not satisfactory, and appears to have worsened in recent years. In 1990-91, SC/ST constituted 50.9 per cent of the total but in 1994-95 it was 47.2 and in 1997-98 at 48.0 per cent, that is, less than the norm of 50 per cent. The representation of women also had a similar trend. Their share increased to 45.2 per cent in 1994-95 from 40.5 in 1990-91 but in 1997-98 it stood at 42.5 per cent. However, all these were much better than the all-India average situation.

On the basis of land-ownership and occupation, the distribution of beneficiaries in Tamil Nadu was very much worse. According to the 50th round of the NSSO (1993-94), the agricultural labour households among the IRDP beneficiaries constituted only 62 per thousand households in Tamil Nadu as against the national average at 71; for other labour households, these were respectively 32 and 66. The representation of self-employed in agriculture was, on the other hand, as much as 102 in Tamil Nadu in contrast to 62 at the national level.

While the number of beneficiaries showed a decline in recent years, the per capita investment has recorded a significant rise. It increased from Rs. 5,996 in 1990-91 to Rs. 13,151 in 1997-98. These are, however, much less than the national average, being Rs. 6,783 and Rs. 18,200, respectively. The mobilisation of credit here was relatively low. The credit disbursed in 1997-98 totalled Rs. 144.98 crores and constituted 7.3 per cent of all-India total; in number of beneficiaries, its share this year was 10.6 per cent.

District-wise, as in most other schemes, there was wide variation in performance. As may be seen from Table 10.1, four districts, viz., Salem, Tiruchirappalli, Coimbatore and Chengalpattu, together accounted for nearly 30 per cent of the total number of beneficiaries during 1994-96. On the other hand, seven districts, viz., Nilgiris, Tiruvannamalai, Pasumpon, Kamarajar, Thanjavur, South Arcot and Ramanathapuram, had a combined share of only 18.4 per cent. Number of beneficiaries per thousand population varied between the highest of 5.67 in Ramanathapuram and the lowest at 1.97 Tiruvannamalai.

There were many deficiencies in implementation of the scheme. Number of beneficiaries crossing the poverty line was limited. Wrong identification of families was also not infrequent. There was no proper backward and forward linkages. No effective steps were taken for marketing of the products produced. The financial and physical targets for the blocks did not adequately emphasise the disparity in incidence of poverty, or the size of population. The administrative cost was also relatively high in Tamil Nadu. For example, in 1993-94, it stood at 11.8 per cent of total expenditure as against the national average at 10.5 per cent.

Some of the deficiencies are, however, sought to be removed by modifying the scheme itself. In the Ninth Plan, in order to make the programme viable and more effective, there has been a shift in strategy from individual beneficiary approach to a group or cluster approach. The investment level is to be raised substantially and development of skills given greater attention. However, the outlay on IRDP in this plan has been fixed at only Rs. 470 crores, 31.6 per cent higher than the actual expenditure in the preceding plan (GOT 1998: 159).

TRYSEM and DWCRA

The performance under both of these schemes was unsatisfactory in Tamil Nadu. The number of youths trained under TRYSEM varied widely from year to year. It was 13,252 in 1989-90 but declined to only 6,921 in 1990-91; rose again to the highest of 24,974 in 1993-94 but in 1996-97 it was down to 15,877 persons. Over the entire period of the Eighth Plan, number of youths trained totalled 1,03,378. As regards the relative position of Tamil Nadu among the states, in 1995-96 it accounted for 4.3 per cent of all-India total number. There were as many as six states with a larger number trained. The expenditure on the programme stood at Rs. 5.47 crores this year, and constituted 5.8 per cent of all-India total (GOT 1998: 155; GOI 1991, 1996c).

Among the beneficiaries, the share of SC/ST was generally very low. In 1995-96, their share in Tamil Nadu stood at only 15.1 per cent as against 46.8 per cent at the all-India level. The representation of women was also insignificant in some of the years. In 1990-91, they constituted a negligible 1.6 per cent. In 1995-96, their share stood at 44.4 per cent as against the all-India average at 46.8.

The placement of the trained youth in Tamil Nadu was very disappointing, and has shown a deteriorating trend in recent years. In 1989-90, of the total number trained, 71.2 per cent could be employed but in 1995-96 it was only 15.1 per cent. The proportion in wage employment in these two years were, respectively, 50.1 and 7 per cent.

Due to this phenomenon of a large number remaining unemployed, changes are now being made in the design, curriculum, etc., for improving the employment opportunities. During the Ninth Plan, however, the emphasis will be on activities in which the rural youths are already engaged and there is potential for skill upgradation. This strategy negates the objective of providing employment opportunity to the unemployed, and it amounts to removing the problem itself instead of solving it.

As regards the district-wise situation on implementation of the TRYSEM, it is evident from Table 10.1 that in many of the districts the number trained was insignificant. During 1994-96, the annual average came to only 113 in Nilgiris as against the highest of 1,577 in Chengalpattu. Six districts, out of 22, accounted for 42 per cent of the total number trained in this period.

The implementation of DWCRA, for women and children, was still weaker. Launched in 1982-83, it aimed to improve the status of women by providing opportunity for self-employment. The scheme is operated through formation of groups of 10 to 15 women with an identified organiser to take up the responsibility. Each group is provided with a revolving fund of Rs. 25,000 for purchasing the raw materials to start the venture. During the Eighth Plan, 8,031 groups were formed with number of beneficiaries totalling 1,41,193. There was, however, wide variation in performance from year to year. Whereas in 1992-93 4,103 groups were formed with 70,050 persons, in 1994-95 it was only 452 groups with 9,492 beneficiaries. Often the targets set could not be fulfilled.

District-wise, as in other areas, the performance varied widely. In 1995-96, for example, in Tiruchirappalli not a single group could be formed as against the highest number of beneficiaries at 2,755 in Madurai. Five districts – Madurai, Dindigul, Salem, North Arcot and Tiruvannamalai – together accounted for 57 per cent of the total number of beneficiaries. On the other hand, there were seven districts with a combined share of only 10.6 per cent.

Minimum Needs Programme

Although Tamil Nadu's position on some of the basic services was better than in many other states, it continued to be far from satisfactory. And a major reason behind this is very low allocation of fund for the MNP at least till the end of Sixth Plan. In this plan a sum of only Rs. 242 crores was provided for it, constituting 4.9 per cent of all-India total and 7.7 per cent of the state's total plan outlay. The expenditure in the Seventh Plan was, however, four-and-half times this level, at Rs. 1,089 crores – constituting 17.2 per cent of the state's total. In the Eighth Plan, the growth decelerated; only Rs. 1,578 crores, constituting 11.3 per cent of the state's total, was spent on MNP.

As regards the sectoral pattern of expenditure, in the Sixth Plan, rural roads received the highest priority, followed by rural water supply. The combined share of these two items was half of the total, with the former accounting for 29 per cent. The relative share of all the other sectors varied between 9 and 11 per cent, as may be seen from Table 10.2. A glaring deficiency was that adult education did not come into the picture even, despite its critical importance. In the Seventh Plan, the priorities were changed drastically. Nutrition, which received 11 per cent of the total outlay in the preceding plan, was now provided 46 per cent. This was followed by rural water supply 20 per cent and elementary education (including adult education) 17 per cent. Thus, these three items together received as much as 77 per cent of the total expenditure. In the Eighth Plan also the pattern was similar. The combined share of these three items rose to 79 per cent, with nutrition now accounting for 33.4 and rural water supply 25.6. It may be stated here that, in the all-India total outlay on nutrition, Tamil Nadu's share was 31.1 per cent in the Seventh Plan and 29.4 in the Eighth Plan.

Table 10.2

Plan Outlays under the Minimum Needs Programme in Tamil Nadu

(Rs. in crores)

Programmes	*Sixth Plan*[a]	*Seventh Plan*	*Eighth Plan*	*Ninth Plan*[a]
Rural roads	70.0 (28.9)	52.7 (4.8)	117.1 (7.4)	780.6 (20.8)
Rural housing	25.0 (10.3)	36.2 (3.3)	33.3 (2.1)	237.7[b] (6.3)
Elementary education	24.0 (9.9)	180.1 (16.5)	312.5 (19.8)	116.0 (3.1)
Rural health	21.8 (9.0)	51.3 (4.7)	131.3 (8.3)	255.3 (6.8)
Rural water supply	50.0 (20.7)	218.2 (20.0)	404.0 (25.6)	1853.1 (49.4)
Improvement of slums	25.0 (10.3)	11.5 (1.1)	39.5 (2.5)	-
Nutrition	26.0 (10.8)	504.1 (46.3)	527.6 (33.4)	500.0 (13.3)
PDS	-	14.5 (1.3)	6.0 (0.4)	7.3 (0.2)
Total	241.8 (100.0)	1088.9 (100.0)	1578.5 (100.0)	3750.0 (100.0)

Source: GOT 1982, 1993, 1998.

Notes: a: outlay, not actual expenditure.
b: housing facility total.

In the currently running Ninth Plan, again, the priorities have changed significantly. Rural water supply has been allotted as much as 49.4 per cent of the total, followed by rural roads 20.8 and nutrition 13.3. The large allocation to water supply is justified because even after nearly five decades of development efforts it has not been possible to provide such a basic service to all the habitations.

The relative share of rural housing, rural health, improvement of slums and the PDS was always very low. For the first one, rural housing, it declined from 10.3 per cent in the Sixth Plan to 2.1 in the Eighth Plan; only in the Ninth Plan it rose again to 6.3 per cent. This level of fund allocation was very inadequate, given the size of the problem. The total shortage of housing is currently estimated at around 13.7 lakh units; about 80 epr cent of the households cannot afford a pucca house. The fund available under the IAY is also not much (GOT 1998).

The impact of these outlays was substantial in some of the areas. We have noted in Chapter 2 the increases in literacy rate, attendance in schools and the provision of drinking water. We may have a brief look here on how the nutrition programme was managed, as it accounted for a very large share of the total expenditure.

Nutrition Programme

The scheme of mid-day meal was launched in Tamil Nadu as early as 1956, for the first time in India. However, the coverage of the scheme was very limited then. About 20 lakh children of first to eighth standard were fed for 200 days in a year (Rajan and Jayakumar 1992). In June 1982, that is, after nearly three decades, the Tamil Nadu government launched a scheme called Chief Minister's Nutritious Noon Meal Programme (CNMP), for providing noon meal of 400-odd calories to 56 lakh poor children throughout the year. It covered children in the age-group 2-10 and was served through 20,747 child welfare centres and 32,470 elementary schools. The scheme was gradually extended to cover children in urban areas, old age pensioners, ex-service men's widows and adolescent school children. By the end of 1984, the total number of beneficiaries rose to 80 lakh. The state also began to supply tooth powder, textbooks, uniforms and footwear free to all children.

The CNMP had two objectives: the eradication of malnutrition among the school children, and the promotion of universal primary education. The response to the scheme, at least initially, was impressive. According to government sources, a total of 2.6 lakh children in the age-group 6-10 were enrolled within 10 weeks of introduction of the scheme. Another report stated 70 per cent increase in enrolment within a few months, decline in drop-outs by 90 per cent and in truancy by 80 per cent (Moses 1983). Over a long period, however, the progress was not impressive. The enrolment in primary schools increased from 48.06 lakh in 1983-84 to 57.34 lakh in 1994-95, that is, by only 19.3 per cent. The drop-out rate declined from 25.20 per cent in 1985-86 to 17.65 in 1994-95 (GOT 1997). There were also reports that teachers reduced their teaching contract from five to two or three hours per day because of the pressure of supervision work (Moses 1983).

The nutritional problems in Tamil Nadu were handled by other projects also. Towards mid-eighties, all the programmes were combined into three major projects. Tamil Nadu Government's Nutritious Noon-Meal Programme (NMP), Tamil Nadu Integrated Nutritious Project (TINP) and Integrated Child Development Scheme (ICDS). The NMP has three components presently: (i) school children in the age-group 2-4 plus and takes care of nutrition, education and health care; (ii) children in the age-group 5-14 plus studying in standards I to X; and (iii) for old age pensioners, ex-service men and those eligible to draw old age pension from the government. At the end of March 1997, there were 68,745 centres administering the NMP, and the beneficiaries totalled 75.16 lakh, of whom 97 per cent were children (GOT 1998: 471).

The ICDS was introduced in 1975-76 and it provides services like supplementary nutrition, pre-school education, health check-up, immunisation, etc. The target group includes children of 0-6 age-group and expectant and nursing mothers. There are 111 ICDS projects. The TINP is also more or less concerned with the same objective. It is presently operated in 318 blocks in 19 districts.

The impact of these programmes on the nutritional status of children was substantial in recent years. The proportion of moderately malnourished children in the state declined from 25 per cent in 1992 to 14 per cent in 1997, and of severely malnourished from 2.0 to 0.6 per cent over the same period. The variation in achievement among the districts was, however, wide. The proportion of severely malnourished in 1997 was as much as 1.5 per cent in Nagapattinam as against 0.1 per cent in Thiruvallur and Nilgiris (GOT 1998: 482).

Public Distribution System

The PDS with the present form of family cards was started in Tamil Nadu in 1964, but it was issued to all families only in 1975. The distribution of rice under it increased greatly over the years. The average off-take per month stood at 220 thousand tonnes in 1997, rising from 102.8 thousand tonnes in 1990, 92.1 thousand in 1985 and only 7.75 thousand tonnes in 1978. The growth was high in recent years because of the widening of difference between the PDS issue price and the open market price. The issue price increased from the average of Rs. 0.84 a kg during 1980-82 (three years) to Rs. 2.44 during 1988-90 and then to Rs. 6.62 during 1995-97.

The government had to procure the required paddy through direct purchase centres, and the procurement price had to be raised substantially in recent years. The issue price charged to PDS, however, could not be raised much. It prevailed at around Rs. 2 to Rs. 3.50 per kg during 1990 to 1995 (GOT 1997: 152). The subsidy from the state government, therefore, increased rapidly in recent years. It rose to Rs. 1,000 crores in 1996-97 from Rs. 332.24 crores in 1991-92, Rs. 117.61 crores in 1987-88 and only Rs. 1.81 crores in 1980-81 (GOT 1998: 549-50).

There are 21,985 fair price shops in the state for 137.42 lakh family card holders. The rural areas account for 77 per cent of the total number of fair price shops. The amount of rice distributed to a cardholder per month is at the rate of 4 kg per adult and 2 kg per child, subject to a maximum of 12 kg. The latter has been raised to 20 kg since January 1996. The government also had a scheme for supplying Rice and Wheat at specially subsidised rate since January 1992, for the people under various projects like ITDP, Hill Area Development Programme and DPAP. There were 11,48,188 card holders under it in 1993 and the amount of Rice distributed stood at 7,490 million tonnes. This scheme has now been replaced by the revamped PDS of the Central Government.

Tamil Nadu's relative position among the states had not been bad. During 1973 to 1989, the per capita PDS distribution of foodgrains here averaged 24.38 kg, which was the fifth largest -- after Kerala, Jammu & Kashmir, West Bengal and Assam. If only the last five years, 1985 to 1989, are considered, the average comes to 35 kg, which is exceeded by only Kerala and J&K (Geetha and Suryanarayana 1993). In recent years also the situation is more or less the same. In 1993-94, the per capita distribution in Tamil Nadu stood at 19 kg, which was exceeded by two of the major states – Kerala and Andhra (Mooij 1999).

As regards the rural sector's share in PDS, Tamil Nadu's position appears worse. In the total PDS purchase of Rice during July 1986 – June 1987, rural areas accounted for 70.09 per cent – that is, less than their share of population; in neighbouring Andhra it was 81 per cent and the all-India average at 71.01 (NSSO 1990). The position of the poor in availing the PDS, however, improved significantly over the years. In 1988, as may be seen from Table 6.4, the per capita PDS foodgrains for the poor stood at 67 kg, which was lower than that in only three of the states, and it was much better than what existed in the earlier years.

Although comparable data for recent years are not available, the measures taken recently must have improved the position of the poor further. Following the example of Andhra Pradesh, the Tamil Nadu government also distributed cards in two colours. To meet the needs of far-flung hamlets part-time fair price shops were opened. There are also mobile shops to serve the people in the hilly areas. The functioning of PDS is now closely monitored by reviewing its operation in taluk and village levels. There are also flying squads for carrying out surprise inspections. After the introduction of targeting, total of foodgrains allotment to Tamil Nadu stood at 10.10 lakh tonnes in 1996-97, of which 5.4 lakh tonnes were for the families below the poverty line. These levels were exceeded by six and five of the major states, respectively. In the all India total of allotments Tamil Nadu's share was 6.1 per cent, declining from 7.4 per cent in the preceding year, that is, prior to targeting. The relative share of BPL families in total allotment was 53.5 per cent in Tamil Nadu in 1996-97 as against 42.7 per cent at the national level (Mooij 1999).

The government's failure in implementing some of the poverty alleviation measures are monumental. Land ceiling and distribution of surplus land -- as discussed in Chapter 8 – is one of them. Recently, the Tamil Nadu Agricultural Labourers Association has urged the government to take up land reforms in a big way and acquire *benami* lands for distribution among farm labourers. They have demanded immediate handing over of all excess lands which have not been handed over to the beneficiaries. The association claimed that about 3,07,251 hectares of cultivable government lands were currently lying fallow (*The Hindu* 1999). Many instances of such callousness of the government toward poverty alleviation can be cited.

IV

The Economy of Karnataka

11

Resource Mobilisation and Deployment

The budgetary resource position of Karnataka has worsened considerably over the years. Although there has been fluctuations from year to year, a deterioration in the situation is very much evident, particularly in the last few years. It may be seen from the Table below that till the end of seventies, Karnataka's overall budgetary position was not a matter of concern. The overall deficit rose to an average of Rs. 80 crores during 1985-88 from a surplus of Rs. 8.00 crores during 1975-78. In the nineties, the position deteriorated sharply, touching a deficit of as much as Rs. 373 crores in 1992-93. Of greater concern is, however, the extent of revenue deficit. In 1996-97, it touched Rs. 579 crores and the average for 1994-97 came to Rs. 271 crores, as against a surplus of Rs. 69 crores during 1975-78.

Below we give a brief look into how the resources were mobilised in order to find out what was the scope for larger mobilisation. This is followed by an analysis of the pattern of expenditure.

Resource Mobilisation

The growth in budgetary receipts of Karnataka was relatively low. Between 1965-68 and 1994-97, the aggregate of receipts registered an increase of only 50 times, from the annual average of Rs. 207 crores to Rs. 10,442 crores, as against 60 times for all states together. Consequently, its relative share in the all-states' total declined from 6.04 per cent to 5.11. The per capita receipts here averaged Rs. 2,161 during 1994-97 as against Rs. 2,255 for all-states.[1] The low level of aggregate receipts is, however, to a large extent due to the relatively small amount of central transfers, as will be evident from the analysis below.

Table 11.1

Trend in Budgetary Position of Karnataka

(Rs. in crores)

Year/ Period	Receipts			Expenditure			Rev. defic/ surpl.	Overall def./ surpl.
	Revenue	Capital	Total	Revenue	Capital	Total		
1965-68 (a.a.)	133 (64.6)[a]	73	207	130 (60.2)[b]	86	216	3	-9
1975-78 (a.a.)	557 (75.9)	177	734	488 (67.2)	238	726	69	8
1985-88 (a.a.)	2313 (74.7)	783	3096	2306 (72.6)	870	3176	7	-80
1988-89	2964 (78.1)	833	3797	3002 (79.5)	776	3778	-38	19
1989-90	3336 (74.9)	1116	4452	3483 (79.1)	918	4401	-147	51
1990-91	4084 (77.8)	1166	5250	4112 (78.0)	1162	5274	-28	-24
1991-92	4775 (76.5)	1466	6241	4954 (79.3)	1294	6248	-179	-7
1992-93	5422 (80.6)	1305	6727	5592 (78.8)	1508	7100	-170	-373
1993-94	6325 (76.9)	1896	8221	6208 (76.7)	1881	8089	117	132
1994-95	6968 (77.1)	2067	9035	7265 (82.0)	1595	8859	-297	176
1995-96	8543 (83.2)	1722	10265	8481 (81.5)	1925	10406	62	-141
1996-97	9622 (80.0)	2404	12026	10201 (85.2)	1779	11980	-579	46
1994-97 (a.a.)	8378 (80.2)	2064	10442	8649 (83.0)	1766	10415	-271	27

Source: As in Table 7.1.

Notes a: as percentage to total receipts.
b: as percentage to total expenditure.

Revenue Receipts

In the total receipts, the share of revenue receipts increased from 64.5 per cent during 1965-68 to 77.5 during 1975-78 and 80.2 during 1994-97. These proportions were better than the average for all states; in fact, in the last period it was highest among all the states. The growth in revenue receipts was, however, relatively low here. Over the entire period, it increased 62 times as against 64 times for all states together.

The low level of growth in revenue receipts was, however, largely due to the low level of central transfers. The aggregate of central transfers to the revenue account of Karnataka increased by only 46 times over the period of three-and-half decades, 1965-68 to 1994-97, as against 69 times for all states. The per capita transfer to Karnataka in the latest period was only 77.6 per cent of all-states' average as against 113.3 per cent in 1965-68. At Rs. 440 in 1994-97, it was less than in nine of the major states, including all the southern states. The share of state's total revenue from the central transfer declined to 25.4 per cent in 1994-97 from 34.7 in 1965-68. The latest proportion is less than in ten of the major states (Table 3.4).

Tax Revenue

The tax revenue in Karnataka had a relatively rapid growth. Between 1965-68 and 1994-97, the annual collection here recorded a 90-fold rise as against 72 times for all states together; only one state, Haryana, could exceed its rate of growth (Table 3.2). Tax revenue as percentage to the state's NSDP stood at 10.2 in Karnataka during 1987-90 as against the average of 7.9 for all the major states (GOT 1997: 217). In the state's total revenue, the relative share of tax revenue rose to 78.1 per cent during 1994-97 from 71.5 in 1985-88 and 58.6 during 1975-78 (Table 11.2).

Table 11.2

Trend in Tax and Non-Tax Revenue of Karnataka

(Rs. in crores)

Year/Period	*Tax Revenue*		*Non-Tax Revenue*	
	Total	*OTR*	*Total*	*ONTR*
1965-68 (a.a.)	72.4 (54.4)[a]	54.1 (74.7)[b]	61.0 (45.6)[a]	33.1 (54.3)[c]
1975-78 (a.a.)	358.1 (58.6)	266.1 (74.3)	198.9 (41.4)	152.7 (76.8)
1985-88 (a.a.)	1635.7 (71.5)	1232.1 (75.3)	649.0 (28.5)	400.5 (61.7)
1988-89	2197.4 (74.1)	1698.8 (77.3)	766.1 (25.9)	445.4 (58.1)
1989-90	2565.1 (76.9)	1932.2 (75.3)	771.3 (23.1)	502.3 (65.1)
1990-91	2992.5 (76.9)	2332.1 (77.9)	899.7 (23.1)	511.1 (56.8),
1991-92	3682.3 (77.1)	2900.2 (78.8)	1093.2 (22.9)	621.3 (56.8)
1992-93	4029.8 (74.3)	3097.8 (76.9)	1391.9 (25.7)	802.5 (57.7)
1993-94	4829.7 (76.4)	3812.3 (78.9)	1494.9 (23.6)	733.6 (49.1)
1994-95	5425.2 (77.9)	4289.3 (79.1)	1543.1 (22.1)	847.7 (54.9)
1995-96	6718.6 (78.6)	5273.9 (78.5)	1824.8 (21.4)	1235.4 (67.7)
1996-97	7497.6 (77.9)	5767.8 (76.9)	2124.5 (22.1)	1342.3 (63.2)
1994-97 (a.a.)	6547.1 (78.1)	5110.3 (78.1)	1830.8 (21.9)	1141.8 (62.4)

Source: As in Table 7.1.

Notes: a: percentage to total revenue receipts.
b: percentage to total tax revenue.
c: percentage to total NTR.

The pattern of growth in tax revenue is presented in Table 11.2. In the state's total tax revenue, the relative share of own tax revenue (OTR) increased from around 75 per cent till late eighties to 78 per cent during 1994-97, with a growth in collection by 19 times over the last two decades. In relation to the position of other states, this was a good performance. For all states, the relative share of OTR declined from 73 per cent in 1965-68 to 68 per cent in 1994-97. In the latest period, there were five states with higher contribution from OTR. In tax efforts also the position was similar. Per capita tax here came to Rs. 1,079 during 1994-97, which was exceeded by six of the major states (Table 3.2).

The scope for further increases in tax revenue was not negligible, as evident from the growth and relative contribution of some of the taxes. The OTR collection came overwhelmingly from one group of taxes. As evident from Table 11.3, taxes on commodities and services provided 87.5 per cent of the total during 1994-97, declining from 91 per cent during 1988-91. In this group again, sales tax alone contributed as much as 67 per cent of the total, rising from 56 during 1975-78.

Table 11.3

Trend in the Structure of Own Tax Revenue in Karnataka

(Rs. in crores)

Items	*1975-78 (a.a.)*	*1988-91 (a.a.)*	*1994-97 (a.a.)*
1. Taxes on income	7.5 (2.8)	38.1 (1.9)	141.2 (2.8)
(i) Taxes on profession, etc.	3.9a (52.0)b	26.9 (70.6)	105.9 (75.0)
2. Taxes on property and capital transactions	17.1 (6.4)	147.7 (7.3)	497.0 (9.7)
(i) Land revenue	5.2 (30.4)	16.5 (11.2)	31.5 (6.3)
(ii) Stamps and regist. fees	11.9 (69.6)	131.2 (88.8)	465.5 (93.7)
3. Taxes on commodit. and serv.	241.5 (90.8)	1842.7 (90.8)	4472.1 (87.5)
(i) Sales tax	134.6 (55.7)	1147.5 (62.3)	2990.1 (66.8)
a. State sales tax	107.8 (44.6)	947.3 (51.4)	2694.9 (60.3)
(ii) State excise	53.4 (22.1)	351.0 (19.0)	792.5 (17.7)
(iii) Taxes on vehicles	23.1 (9.6)	168.7 (9.2)	357.6 (8.0)
(iv) Taxes on goods and passeng.	3.8 (1.6)	55.8 (3.0)	161.6 (3.6)
(v) Taxes and duties on electricity	7.4 (3.1)	56.1 (3.0)	79.6 (1.8)
(vi) Entertainment tax	14.2 (5.9)	39.6 (2.1)	42.1 (0.9)
Total OTR	266.1 (100.0)	2028.6 (100.0)	5110.3 (100.0)

Source: As in Table 11.1.

Notes: a: average for 1976-78.
b: figures in parentheses under the sub-groups refer to percentages in relation to the respective group total.

The state excise contributed 17.7 per cent of the collection from commodity taxes during 1994-97 as against 22.1 during 1975-78. The growth in taxes here was 14.8 times over the period as against 18.5 times in the aggregate of commodity taxes. The relative contribution of taxes on vehicles also declined in this period, from 9.6 per cent to 8.0. Among other taxes, the share of duties on electricity declined from 3.1 per cent to 1.8, and of entertainment tax from 5.9 to 0.9. The only tax to show an appreciable growth was the tax on goods and passengers; with a 41-fold rise in collection over the period, its relative share rose to 3.6 per cent from 1.6.

Of the remaining two groups, collection from taxes on property and capital transactions showed an appreciable growth over the years. With a 29-fold rise between 1975-78 and 1994-97, its relative share in total OTR rose to 9.7 per cent from 6.4. This rate of growth, however, did not exhaust its potential. The rise in land revenue collection in this period was only six times, from Rs. 5.20 crores to Rs. 31.5 crores. In the total collection under the group, its relative share was down to 6.3 per cent from 30.5. The other broad group, taxes on income, had a 19-fold rise in collection, and its relative share stood at only 2.8 per cent during 1994-97, the same as that in 1975-78; three-fourths of the collection here came from taxes on profession, trades etc.

The remaining tax revenue of the government came from central transfers, on the basis of recommendations by the Finance Commissions. The total of tax transfer to Karnataka increased from the annual average of Rs. 18.3 crores during 1965-68 to Rs. 92.0 crores during 1975-78 and Rs. 1,436.8 crores during 1994-97, that is, a growth of 79 times over the entire period. The tax transfer to all states, on the other hand, increased by 84 times in this period.

Major portion of the tax transfer came from union excise duties. It contributed an average of 56.7 per cent during 1965-68, 59.7 per cent in 1975-78 and 59.5 in 1994-97. The amount transferred increased 82 times over the entire period, from Rs. 10.4 crores to Rs. 855.1 crores. Income tax contributed the balance in the latest period whereas earlier there was some contribution from estate duty also.

While there is not much that can be done by the state to raise its share of tax transfer from the Centre, in its OTR, as noted above, there is ample scope for improvement. Even the amount of tax arrear is substantial. At the end of 1991 it stood at Rs. 415.3 crores (RBIFA, 1992).

Non-Tax Revenue

The growth in NTR was at a much slower rate. Between 1965-68 and 1994-97, it had only a 30-fold rise, from Rs. 61 crores to Rs. 1,831 crores. Consequently, its relative share in total revenue declined from 45.6 per cent to 21.9 per cent over the period (Table 11.2). This is a very gloomy performance in relation to most other states. The growth in NTR for all states together was 52 times in this period, and its share in their total revenue averaged 40 per cent in the latest period.

In the NTR, a large portion came from grants by the Centre, and the state's own NTR fluctuated rather widely. The contribution of ONTR rose to the average of 76.8 per cent during 1975-78 from 54.3 during 1965-68, but in the following years it could never reach the earlier peak; the average for 1994-97 came to 62.4 per cent. Among the states, however, this is a good performance. There were only four major states with higher contribution from ONTR in the latest period (Table 3.2).

As regards grants-in-aid, the receipts by Karnataka registered a 25-fold rise between 1965-68 and 1994-97 – from Rs. 28 crores to Rs. 689 crores -- as against 54 times in the transfer to all states. The relative share of grants in total transfer here declined sharply from around 60 per cent in 1965-68 to 32 per cent in 1994-97. All the major states, except two, had higher proportion of grants in the latest period (Table 3.4).

Despite the high proportion of ONTR, there was ample scope for further growth in it. This is confirmed by a look at the trend in its components, presented in Table 11.4. Group-wise, the relative share of economic services declined from 44.5 per cent of the total in 1975-78 to 30.9 in 1994-97. For general services and dividend and profit also the relative share declined. The latter's contribution was down to only 0.4 per cent from 1.2 over the period. On the other hand, interest receipts which was already contributing a large share, improved its position further. During 1988-91, it provided 63 per cent of the total, rising from 34 per cent in 1975-78; in the last three years its share stood at 52 per cent. Social services also recorded some increase in its share.

Within economic services, forestry and wild-life was the most important item. But its share declined from 19.1 per cent of the total under ONTR during 1975-78 to 9.2 during 1994-97. The amount collected had a growth of only 3.6 times over the period. The next important item, industries, also recorded declines. Its share stood at only 4.3 per cent during 1988-91 as against three times this level in 1975-78; in recent years, however, there has been a considerable recovery. The receipts from power was down to only 2.9 per cent during 1994-97 from 6.1 in 1988-91. All the other items also recorded declines.

Table 11.4

Trend in Different Components of ONTR in Karnataka

(Rs. in crores)

Items	*1975-78 (a.a.)*	*1988-91 (a.a.)*	*1994-97 (a.a.)*
Interest receipts	52.7 (34.5)	307.9 (63.3)	591.0 (51.8)
Dividend and profits	1.9 (1.2)	2.4 (0.5)	5.0 (0.4)
General services	20.3 (13.3)	49.5 (10.2)	106.8 (9.4)
Social services	9.8 (6.4)	32.8 (6.7)	86.3 (7.6)
Economic services	67.9 (44.5)	175.9 (36.2)	352.8 (30.9)
Forestry and wild-life	29.1 (19.1)	49.5 (10.2)	104.8 (9.2)
Irrigation	4.8 (3.2)	17.9 (3.7)	17.0 (1.5)
Power	1.1 (0.7)	29.8 (6.1)	32.7 (2.9)
Village and SSI	-	20.1 (4.1)	26.8 (2.3)
Industries	19.3[a] (12.6)	20.9[a] (4.3)	98.7 (8.6)
Cooperation	1.1 (0.7)	6.8 (1.4)	14.3 (1.3)
Total (including others)	152.7 (100.0)	486.3 (100.0)	1141.8 (100.0)

Source: As in Table 11.3.

Note: a: including road tolls.

That the potential in many areas remains unexploited is evident form the sudden growth in collection from tourism. From a negligible annual average of Rs. 9 lakhs during 1988-91 it rose to Rs. 5.02 crores during 1994-97.

As regards dividend and profits, the collection here increased only 2.6 times, from Rs. 1.9 crores to Rs. 5.0 crores, over the period of two decades. The total of investment in state public sector undertakings, however, rose to as much as Rs. 11,667 crores in 1995-96. There are a number of enterprises incurring huge losses. The loss by KSRTC rose to Rs. 4,800 crores in 1995-96 (GKT 1997). The commercial loss of Karnataka Electricity Board totalled Rs. 1,409 crores in the last four years (1994-95 to 1997-98) (CMIE 1999d). With proper management of these concerns, the contributions could be significantly raised.

In social services also there was much scope for increasing the collection. The receipts from education, sports etc., rose to Rs. 18.5 crore in 1992-93 from Rs. 10.4 crores in the preceding year, but in the following years it declined and touched the low of Rs. 14.7 crores in 1996-97. In medical and public health etc., the collection reached Rs. 22.7 crores in 1993-94 from around Rs. 11 crores in the preceding two years, but in the last two years it declined.

Capital Receipts

The growth of capital receipts in Karnataka was relatively low. Between 1965-68 and 1994-97, there was only a 28-fold rise – from Rs. 73 crores to Rs. 2,064 crores – as against 38 times in case of all states together. The relative share of capital receipts in the state's aggregate of receipts declined from 36 per cent in 1965-68 to 20 per cent in 1994-97. All the major states, except Bihar, had higher proportion of capital receipts in the latest period.

Table 11.5

Trend in Composition of Capital Receipts in Karnataka

(Rs. in crores)

Items	*1975-78 (a.a.)*	*1988-91 (a.a.)*	*1994-97 (a.a.)*
Total Receipts	176.9 (100.0)	1038.3 (100.0)	2064.4 (100.0)
I. Internal debt	31.1 (17.5)	152.5 (14.7)	284.7 (13.8)
(a) Market loans	17.9	136.5	219.4
II. Loans from the Centre	84.1 (47.6)	468.5 (45.1)	1031.4 (50.0)
(a) State plan scheme	47.1	178.0	444.5
(b) Non-plan	20.5	283.1	554.8
III. Recovery of loans	22.1 (12.5)	242.1 (23.3)	177.7 (8.6)
(a) Power projects	1.0	198.1	128.7
IV. Small savings, P.F. etc.	9.1 (5.1)	117.3 (11.3)	260.0 (12.6)
V. Reserve funds	8.6 (4.9)	29.6 (2.9)	123.0 (6.0)

Source: As in the preceding table.

As regards the composition of capital receipts, the highest contributor had always been loans and advances from the Centre. Its share stood at the average of 50 per cent during 1994-97, rising from 45.1 in 1988-91 and 47.6 in 1975-78. This was followed by internal debt, whose share declined from 17.5 per cent in 1975-78 to 13.8 in 1994-97. The next important item was generally the recovery of loans. Its relative share fell sharply to 8.6 per cent in 1994-97 from 23.3 in 1988-91. Of the remaining two groups, as may be seen from Table 11.5, small savings has recorded a rapid rise. With a 29-fold rise in collection, its relative share rose to 12.6 per cent in 1994-97 from only 5.1 in 1975-78.

Looking to some of the inner items, in loans from the Centre, non-plan category generally accounted for the highest amount in recent years. Its share was as much as 60 per cent during 1988-91 and at 54 per cent during 1994-97 as against 24 per cent in 1975-78. The single most important item here was small savings, contributing almost the entire amount in recent years as against 70 per cent during 1975-78. The next important item under central loans was the state plan scheme. Its contribution stood at 43 per cent in 1994-97 and as much as 56 per cent during 1975-78. In internal debt, the share of market loans has risen noticeably over the years. In 1988-91, it contributed 89 per cent, rising from 58 in 1975-78.

A glaring shortcoming of capital receipts is its wide fluctuations from year to year. To give a few examples from recent years: Non-plan loans went up to as much as Rs. 748 crores in 1994-95 from only Rs. 237 crores in the preceding year, but in the following year it declined again to Rs. 435 crores. The recovery of loans and advances dropped to only Rs. 79.8 crores in 1992-93 from Rs. 387 crores in the preceding year. Such wide fluctuations hampered proper planning of fund deployment.

Resource Deployment

As the resource mobilisation was low, naturally the growth of expenditure in Karnataka was relatively low. The total expenditure here recorded a 48-fold rise over the three decades since 1965-68 as against 52 times for all states together. The per capita expenditure in Karnataka increased from Rs. 81 during 1965-68 to Rs. 2,168 in 1994-97, that is, a growth of 27 times; for all states it was 28 times, from Rs. 70 to Rs. 1,972. In the latest period, Karnataka's per capita was lower than that in six of the major states, as may be seen from Table 3.6.

In the total expenditure, the proportion of revenue expenditure increased from 60.2 per cent in 1965-68 to 67.2 in 1975-78 and then to 83.0 in 1994-97. In the latest period, there were as many as eight states with a lower proportion of revenue expenditure. The growth in expenditure over the entire period was 66.5 times, marginally less than the average for all states. Below we give a brief look into the trend in composition of revenue and capital expenditure in the state.

Revenue Expenditure

In the total of revenue expenditure, as evident from Table 11.6, development expenditure has shown a clear decline in relative term. It stood at the annual average of 67 per cent during 1994-97 as against 70 per cent in 1975-78; earlier, it stood at 73 per cent during 1957-60. Even after the decline however, the proportion is much higher than the all-state's average. The growth in development expenditure in the last two decades was 16.9 times as against 17.7 times in the aggregate of revenue expenditure.

Table 11.6

Trend in Composition of Revenue and Capital Expenditure in Karnataka

(Rs. in crores)

Items	*1975-78 (a.a.)*	*1985-88 (a.a.)*	*1994-97 (a.a.)*
Revenue Expenditure	488.3 (100.0)	2306.5 (100.0)	8648.9 (100.0)
I. Development expenditure	343.1 (70.3)	1590.0 (69.0)	5804.5 (67.1)
(a) Social services	182.5 (53.2)[a]	960.1 (59.8)	3234.9 (55.7)
(i) Education etc.	105.9 (30.9)	449.9 (28.3)	1693.6 (29.2)
(ii) Medical and public health[b]	47.0 (13.7)	222.2 (14.0)	654.8 (11.3)
(iii) Social security and welfare	17.7 (5.2)	94.6 (5.9)	200.0 (3.4)
(iv) Nutrition	-	48.9 (3.1)	56.9 (1.0)
(b) Economic services	160.6 (46.8)	639.9 (40.2)	2569.6 (44.3)
(i) Agriculture and allied	49.3[c] (14.4)	183.8 (11.6)	776.6 (13.4)
(ii) Rural development	-	138.0 (8.7)	370.9 (6.4)
(iii) Irrigation and flood	28.5 (8.3)	161.4 (10.2)	431.8 (7.4)
(iv) VSI	5.6 (1.6)	47.2 (3.0)	167.5 (2.9)
(v) Transport and communication	19.8 (5.8)	57.7 (3.6)	197.1 (3.4)
II. Non-development expenditure	136.8 (28.0)	657.6 (28.5)	2692.5 (31.1)
(i) Interest payment	37.9 (27.7)	284.1 (43.2)	1042.3 (38.7)
(ii) Administrative services	38.4 (28.1)	162.2 (24.7)	625.7 (23.2)
(a) Police	20.4 (14.9)	89.6 (13.6)	343.1 (12.7)
(iii) Pension etc.	23.5 (17.2)	131.5 (20.0)	581.8 (21.6)
Capital Disbursement	237.6 (100.0)	869.6 (100.0)	1766.4 (100.0)
I. Total capital outlay	93.4 (39.3)	301.6 (34.7)	1176.4 (66.6)
Development expenditure	92.2 (98.7)	291.9 (96.8)	1149.4 (97.7)
(a) Social services	5.6 (6.1)	26.3 (9.0)	67.1 (5.8)
(b) Economic services	86.6 (93.9)	265.6 (91.0)	1082.2 (94.2)
(i) Agriculture and allied	12.5 (13.6)	7.7 (2.6)	18.2 (1.6)
(ii) Irrigation and flood	52.1 (56.5)	193.1 (66.2)	818.7 (71.2)
(iii) Transport and communication	7.5 (8.1)	35.4 (12.1)	124.2 (10.8)
II. Repayment of loans to the Centre	36.1 (15.2)	184.8 (21.3)	194.6 (11.0)
III. Discharge of internal debt	15.2 (6.4)	25.4 (2.9)	27.2 (1.5)
IV. Loans by state govt.	84.5 (35.6)	357.7 (41.1)	368.3 (20.9)
(a) Development purposes	77.8 (92.1)	343.9 (96.1)	360.3 (97.8)

Source: As in Table 11.3.

Notes: a: figures in parentheses are percentages in relation to either revenue/capital expenditure or the group total.

b: including water supply and sanitation.

c: including minor irrigation.

In the development expenditure, growth in some of the items was very low. Although social services as a whole registered a rise of 17.7 times over the period and continued to account for the major share of development expenditure, the spendings on social security and welfare in it increased only 11 times, and the relative share consequently declined from 5.2 per cent to 3.4. On nutrition, the expenditure on which started only in early eighties, the relative share declined from 3.1 per cent in 1985-88 to 1.0 in 1994-97. The growth in expenditure on medical and public health was also low. Its relative share declined from 13.7 per cent in 1975-78 to 11.3 in 1994-97. Education etc., continued to account for more than half of the total expenditure under social services, except during 1985-88. Its share in total development expenditure stood at 29.2 per cent during 1994-97.

In economic services – whose relative share in development expenditure declined from 47 per cent in 1975-78 to 44 in 1994-97 – agriculture and allied sectors continued to receive the highest amount. Its relative share, however, declined and stood at 13 per cent of total development expenditure in 1994-97. Irrigation and flood control was the next important item, and its share also declined in recent years, as may be seen from Table 11.6. The lowest growth in expenditure was recorded by transport and communication, only ten times over the period of two decades, and its relative share declined from 5.8 per cent in 1975-78 to 3.4 in 1994-97. The highest growth was in case of VSI, as much as 30 times over the period, but even then its relative share stood at only 2.9 per cent during 1994-97. There was a sudden jump in expenditure on energy. The annual average even during 1991-94 was only Rs. 136 crores, but in the following three years it rose to Rs. 488.5 crores, constituting 8.4 per cent of the development expenditure.

As regards non-development expenditure, interest payments became a great burden over the years. With a growth of 27.5 times between 1975-78 and 1994-97, its relative share rose to 38.7 per cent from 27.7; in fact, during 1985-88 it had touched 43.2 per cent. Even in the aggregate of revenue expenditure its share stood at 12 per cent in the latest period. Another item with a rapid growth was pension payment. It recorded a 25-fold rise over the period, and the relative share rose to 21.6 per cent in 1994-97. In case of administrative services, although the growth in expenditure was relatively low, it still constituted nearly a quarter of the total of non-development expenditure. More than half of the spendings here was on police.

Capital Expenditure

In capital disbursement, capital outlay has shown a rapid growth in recent years. Over the last two decades, while capital disbursements as a whole recorded a 7.4-fold rise, for capital outlay it was 12.6 times. The increases were, however, mainly in the last few years, and the relative share rose to 67 per cent in 1994-97 from 35 per cent in 1985-88. The next important item was loans by the state government, with a share of as much as 41 per cent of total during 1985-88 and 21 per cent in 1994-97. The relative share of repayment of loans to the Centre also declined noticeably in this period, from 21 per cent to 11 per cent of total disbursement. The payment on discharge of internal debt had a sharper fall, as may be seen from Table 11.6.

In capital outlay, development expenditure naturally accounted for almost the entire amount. And in development expenditure again, it was economic services that received more than 90 per cent of the total. Within economic services, irrigation and flood control accounted for the lion's share, as much as 71 per cent during 1994-97, rising from 56 per cent in 1975-78. This was followed by transport and communication with 11 per cent in the latest period, declining from 12 in 1985-88.

The loans by state government were for development purposes to the extent of more than 90 per cent. In the development loans, economic services accounted for the major share – in 1994-97, it was 67 per cent of the total. Here again, power projects accounted for the lion's share in recent years.

Plan Expenditure

The growth of plan expenditure in Karnataka was appreciable. In the capital account, which was the main source, the plan expenditure increased from Rs. 117.4 crores in 1975-76 to Rs. 1,437.7 crores in 1995-96, that is, a growth of 12 times as against 8.8 times in the aggregate of capital disbursement. The relative share of plan expenditure increased from 53.9 per cent to 74.7 over the period. In the revenue account, the percentage of plan expenditure increased from 12.9 to 23.8 in this period, the amount of expenditure rising from Rs. 55 crores to Rs. 2,022 crores, that is, 36 times. Below we give a brief look into the pattern of growth in plan expenditure on a five-yearly basis.

The plan expenditure of Karnataka had a rapid growth. In current prices, between the Third Plan and the Eighth Plan, there was a rise of 56.4 times, from Rs. 264 crores to Rs. 14,894 crores. The rate of growth from plan to plan, however, varied widely, as may be seen from Table 11.7. While the Eighth Plan was nearly four times the size

Table 11.7

Sectoral Pattern of Growth in Plan Expenditure in Karnataka

(Rs. in crores)

Sectors	*Third Plan*	*Sixth Plan*	*Seventh Plan*	*Eighth Plan*	*Ninth Plan*[a]
	(1961-66)	*(1980-85)*	*(1985-90)*	*(1992-97)*	*(1997-2002)*
Agricultural and allied	66.7 (25.3)	244.3 (10.8)	353.7 (8.7)	937.8 (6.3)	1114 (4.8)
Rural development	-	127.2 (5.6)	374.7 (9.2)	843.1 (5.7)	1174 (5.0)
Irrigation and flood	30.9 (11.7)	440.5 (19.4)	776.7 (19.1)	3300.9 (22.2)	6170 (26.4)
Power[b]	69.3 (26.2)	603.2 (26.6)	828.9 (20.4)	3031.8 (20.4)	3745 (16.0)
Industry and minerals	15.5 (5.9)	162.7 (7.2)	340.6 (8.4)	809.0 (5.4)	1026 (4.4)
Village and small-scale Ind.	4.1 (1.6)	74.0 (3.3)	146.0 (3.6)	304.6 (2.0)	565 (2.4)
Transport and communication	22.5 (8.5)	145.2 (6.4)	219.6 (5.4)	866.2 (5.8)	1780 (7.6)
Education, sports etc.	16.3 (6.2)	57.6 (2.5)	155.9 (3.8)	1224.1 (8.2)	1713 (7.3)
Health and water supply	16.9 (6.4)	197.7[c] (8.7)	251.6 (6.2)	1277.8 (8.6)	2450 (10.5)
Welfare of SC, ST and OBC	3.0 (1.1)	42.0 (1.9)	75.6 (1.9)	752.1 (5.0)	800 (3.4)
Social welfare and nutrition	0.2 (neg)	29.6 (1.3)	236.2 (5.8)	229.3 (1.5)	460 (2.0)
Grand total	264.1 (100.0)	2265.0 (100.0)	4056.4 (100.0)	14894.1 (100.0)	23400 (100.0)

Source: GOM n.d., GKT 1982, 1991, 1998.

Notes: a: approved outlay.
b: energy since Seventh Plan.
c: including sanitation and sewerage.

of the Seventh Plan, the succeeding Ninth Plan was proposed to have an outlay only 57 per cent higher. Despite the overall rapid growth, per capita plan expenditure in Karnataka remained very low. During the Seventh Plan it was Rs. 928 as against the all-India average at Rs. 1,134, and in the Eighth Plan Rs. 3,144 and Rs. 4,832, respectively.

As regards the sectoral distribution of expenditure, the share of agriculture and allied services has declined drastically in the recent plans, from as much as a quarter of the total during the Third Plan to only around 5 per cent in the Ninth Plan. The allocation to rural development also declined, from 9 per cent in the Seventh Plan to 5 per cent in the Ninth Plan. Irrigation and flood control, however, continued to have a high share. It has been provided 26 per cent of the total in the latest plan, rising from 19 in the Sixth and Seventh Plans and 12 per cent in the Third Plan. Similar is the position of power. It received the highest allocation in three out of the five plans noted here. The share of transport and communication was, however, relatively low, varying between the highest of 8.5 per cent in the Third Plan and the lowest at 5.4 in the Seventh Plan. The allocation to industry was also not much, and it declined continuously in the recent plans. Within it, the VSI was the most neglected. In the Eighth Plan, Rs. 603 crores was approved for it but only half the amount could be utilised. The relative share in the aggregate of plan expenditure was down to 2.0 per cent from 3.6 in the preceding plan. In the social sector, as may be seen from Table 11.7, health and water supply always received the highest priority. The allocation to education etc., increased substantially only in the Eighth and Ninth Plans.

From the above analysis of Karnataka's budgets, it is apparent that there was ample scope for reducing and better targeting of expenditure. Some of the items that need attention are payments on salaries and wages, subsidies and transfer payments and productivity of investment in public enterprises. Salaries and wages account for a major portion of the expenditure in most departments and institutions, and it had a rapid rise over the years. The total emoluments of state public sector employees in Karnataka increased from Rs. 140.8 crores in 1981-82 to Rs. 1,017.9 crores in 1994-95, that is, 7.2 times, with the number of employees rising from 1.36 lakhs to 1.62 lakhs (GKT 1997: A-78). Was this level of rise justified from the angle of productivity of the employees, or from the angle of the state's ability to pay?

As regards subsidies and transfer payments, it largely benefits the people from non-target groups. Proper targeting will help reducing the expenditure and/or providing better services to the target groups. There is negligible user charges even for services used mainly by the better-off sections of population. Total of subsidy payments increased from Rs. 308.8 crores in 1977-78 to Rs. 1,725.6 crores in 1987-88. The recovery from social and economic services in relation to the cost declined from 29.0 per cent to 18.7 per cent in this period (Rao 1992).

Devolution to Districts

With regard to devolution of authority to the district level, Karnataka's performance is probably better than in most other states. The two-tier structure of planning was introduced here in 1978-79, and after the passing of the Zilla Parishads etc. Act, 1983 – which came into force in April 1987 – a wide range of the state's functions were transferred to the Zilla Parishads (ZPs) and Mandal Panchayats (MPs). The number of schemes transferred to the former was 257 and to the latter 89.

The ZPs did not have powers of taxation, and the finance for performing the functions came mainly from the consolidated fund of the state and grants and loans etc. A per capita grant of Rs. 7.50 to the MPs and R. 2.50 to the ZPs were made available. The MPs were given some powers of collecting taxes and fees also.

In recent years further changes have taken place in the PRIs. A new Panchayat Raj Act came into operation in May 1993, incorporating all the essential features of the 73rd Amendment of the Constitution. It provides for an elected three-tier system, as in other states. Under the Act, the finances of the Gram Panchayats (GPs) consist mainly of the following: (i) proceeds from tax on buildings, entertainment, markets, levy on water etc.; (ii) share of cess on land revenue when levied by the government; (iii) statutory grant of Rs. one lakh to each GP every year; (iv) allocation under JRY at the rate of Rs. 1.5 to Rs. 2.5 lakhs per annum; and (v) grants from the Government of India under the Finance Commission award.

The Taluk Panchayats (TPs) have no power to raise resources through taxation. An additional stamp duty at the rate of 3 per cent on the value of sale, mortgage etc., of immovable properties can be collected by the state and apportioned among the TPs in proportion to their population. A few TPs derive income from immovable assets like buildings. The ZPs, as earlier, have no power to levy tax and virtually all their resources are received from the state and Central Government as grants for implementing various programmes. The other sources are income from immovable assets, if any, and the allocation under the Finance Commission's award. The local bodies are operating under the new Act since 1995-96.

The State Government has been making allocation every year to the PRIs under both plan and non-plan accounts. But the amount provided was very low until recent years. The total of allocation increased from Rs. 916.6 crores in 1987-88 to Rs. 3,440.7 crores in 1997-98, that is, a growth of around four times. The share of non-plan outlay varied between the maximum of 61.0 per cent in 1989-90 and the minimum at 55.5 in 1994-95 (GKT 1997a). The plan allocation for district sector increased from Rs. 365 crores in 1987-88 to Rs. 1,420 crores in 1997-98. In the aggregate of district plan outlay, the share of district sector averaged 23.6 per cent during 1994-97. The central share in total district plan outlay was 18.7 per cent, and in the district sector 43.6 per cent in this period (GKT 1998a).

In the inter-district allocation, the backward districts did not always get fair treatment. During the Seventh Plan, the per capita district plan outlay was as much as Rs. 1,234 in Kodagu and Rs. 628 in Chickmagalur as against the state average at Rs. 395. In recent years, the disparity appears to have narrowed. In 1996-97, the per capita allocation varied between the highest of Rs. 472.19 in Kodagu and the lowest at Rs. 240.74 in Dharwad, with the all-districts average at Rs. 283.00 (GKT 1997, 1985).

All these are significant improvements over what existed even in early eighties. During 1979-82, the annual income per village panchayat stood at the highest of Rs. 11,522 in Dakshin Kannada and less than Rs. 7,000 in at least eight districts. The expenditure per panchayat was at the highest Rs. 8,898 in the same Dakshin Kannada and on the other side, at least three districts had less than Rs. 4,000 in the same period (GKT 1982a: II).

The centralised pattern of planning and development of the last five decades has not brought any significant change in the rural scenario. There is, therefore, need for an accelerated pace in devolution of power to the PRIs. Let the local people themselves decide the nature and pace of their development to a larger extent now.

Note

1. The population figures used are respectively of 1987 and 1994.

12

Agricultural Transformation

Karnataka's economy is heavily dependent on agriculture. Even during 1992-97, the real output from agriculture contributed 34.0 per cent of the SDP as against the all-India average at 28.8 per cent. Sixty-nine per cent of the state's population are engaged in agriculture and allied activities (RBI 1996: I, 1999: I; GKT 1997b: I: 65). The growth and diversification of this sector are, therefore, of critical importance to the well-being of the state's population. This chapter looks into the pattern of growth achieved in agriculture and the allied sectors since independence. The analysis follows the same pattern as in case of Chapter 8.

I
Agriculture

The growth of agricultural production in Karnataka was significantly better than in most other states. The average value of output increased from Rs. 520.2 crores during 1962-65 to Rs. 705.8 crores during 1980-83, that is, by 35.7 per cent as against 32.9 for all-India (at constant prices). The average value productivity per hectare here increased from Rs. 597.74 to Rs. 924.20 over the same period, that is, by 54.6 per cent; for all-India, although the growth was much less, by only 43.1 per cent, the productivity was significantly higher -- being Rs. 743.27 and Rs. 1,063.82 in the two periods, respectively. In recent years also the pattern was similar, although data on the same basis are not available. During 1990-91 to 1996-97, the SDP from agriculture had a compound annual growth of 5.0 per cent in Karnataka as against the average of 2.4 per cent for all-India (at constant prices) (RBI 1998: I,1999: I).

Foodgrains

Among the crops, the performance in foodgrains was disappointing, particularly in recent years. Between 1955-56 and 1975-76, the foodgrains output recorded an increase of 85.2 per cent, from 38.0 lakh tonnes to 70.4 lakh tonnes, but in the following two decades, ending in 1995-96, the growth was only 23.9 per cent -- to 87.2 lakh tonnes. As there was a considerable fluctuation in production from year to year, we have presented in Table 12.1 the three-yearly averages of production, yield rate and area under the crops in three time points.

The total production of foodgrains annually averaged 55.4 lakh tonnes during 1970-73 and rose to 86.7 lakh tonnes in 1994-97, that is, a growth of 56.5 per cent in two-and-half decades. The increases, however, occurred mainly in the last one-and-half decades; in the first decade, there was only a 15 per cent rise in production. The yield rate of foodgrains had recorded a rise of only 50 per cent over the entire period, from 817 kg to 1,227 kg per hectare. The growth in area was a negligible 4 per cent. In relation to the position in early sixties, all these are significant achievements; the yield rate in 1960-63 was only 536 kg per hectare.

The relative position of Karnataka among the major states was, however, very disappointing. Per capita production of foodgrains in Karnataka stood at the annual average of only 179.7 kg during 1993-96 as against the all-India average at 207.7 kg. The yield rate was also exceeded by as many as eight states, as may be seen from Table 4.1.

Among foodgrains, the most important crop in Karnataka in terms of area is jowar, even after a sharp fall over the years. The area under it stood at 29.7 lakh hectares in 1960-61, but this level could never be reached in the following years, and the average for 1994-97 came to 20.4 lakh hectares. The growth in production over the last two-and-half decades was a negligible 6.9 per cent. The yield per hectare recorded a rise of only 21.3 per cent in this period, from 717 kg to 870 kg (Table 12.1).

Rice is the next important crop, and the area under it showed a rising trend. The production here increased by 61 per cent between 1970-73 and 1994-97, consequent on a 36 per cent rise in yield rate and 19 per cent in area. The yield per hectare here was nearly three times that in jowar in the latest period. In ragi, production increased at a faster rate, by 73 per cent over the same period. It was primarily a product of yield improvement as the growth in area was nominal. The highest increase in acreage was recorded by maize -- more than a fourfold rise between 1970-73 and 1994-97, from 0.88 lakh hectares to 3.82

Table 12.1

Trend in Area, Production and Yield of Major Crops in Karnataka

Crops	1970-73 (a.a.)			1980-83 (a.a.)			1994-97 (a.a.)		
	A	P	Y	A	P	Y	A	P	Y
Foodgrains	6787	5544	817	7163	6403	893	7060	8674	1227
Jowar	2269	1656	717	2005	1553	777	2045	1770	870
Rice	1097	1933	1760	1126	2224	1977	1302	3113	2390
Ragi	958	864	900	1080	1156	1063	988	1498	1513
Bajra	433	173	384	571	230	397	370	219	575
Maize	88	313	3536	153	379	370	219	575	
Wheat	317	130	403	327	192	587	237	169	717
Arhar	271	127	453	360	155	430	390	180	455
Gram	148	48	317	142	63	443	360	172	473
Non-Foodgrains									
Groundnut	847	597	697	823	548	660	1214	1069	883
Sesamum	71	20	280	116	33	287	110	46	420
Coconut	133	676	5268	177	919	5203	270	1436	5323
Sunflower	16	3	190	111	49	457	909	373	410
Safflower	141	22	157	163	86	527	202	117	587
Linseed	50	11	200	61	13	217	26	6.8	257
Nigerseed	23	4.5	193	56	9.8	180	42	7.1	173
Sugarcane	103	8572	83600	173	13874	80337	304	26621	87123
Cotton	987	452	77	976	537	90	659	868	223
Coffee	-	-	-	106	92	867	137	129	947
Tobacco	40	19	487	51	34	663	63	51	800
Chillies	102	30	297	155	48	310	182	110	603
Cardamom	24	1.4	57	28	1.7	60	22	1.3	58
Arecanut	-	-	-	55	80	1400	80	116	1456
Potato	9.0	50	5480	14	101	7020	30	340	11397
Onions	17	97	5763	37	233	6363	79	477	6042
Banana	17	97	5763	18	97	5277	22	650	28979

Source: CMIE 1998.

Notes: A: Area in '000 ha; P: Production in '000 tonnes; and Y: Yield in kg/ha.
a: production in million nuts, and yield in nuts/ha.
b: yield in tonnes/ha.
c: Production in '000 bales of 180 kg each.

lakh hectares. The growth in production was slightly less than four times, and this was exclusively due to the rise in acreage; the yield rate showed a noticeable decline.

For all cereals, on decade basis, the performance in the eighties was very depressing. The production increased at the compound annual rate of 1.4 per cent during 1960-70 and at 2.4 during 1970-80 but during 1980-90 it was a negligible 0.3. The growth in yield rate in these periods were 1.7, 2.8 and (--)0.5 per cent respectively. The acreage declined at the rate of 0.2 per cent in the first period and 0.5 per cent in the second, and then showed an increase at the rate of 0.1 per cent (GKT 1992).

In pulses, arhar and gram were important, and in both of them there were increases in acreage. The area under arhar increased mainly in the first decade, and over the entire period of two-and-half decades there was a growth of 44 per cent. The yield rate here showed a decline, and therefore, the growth in production was not much. The performance in gram was much better. The acreage here increased by 143 per cent and the yield rate by 49 per cent over the entire period; the growth in production was 258 per cent. The production of pulses as a whole increased from the annual average of 5.81 lakh tonnes during 1985-88 to 6.49 lakh tonnes during 1993-96, that is, a mere 17.2 per cent rise. The area under pulses showed a marginal decline in this period, from 16.72 lakh hectares to 16.07 lakh hectares, and the yield rate an increase from 347 kg to 404 kg (GKT 1997).

Non-Foodgrains

Among non-foodgrains, the most important crops in terms of area are cotton, groundnut, safflower, coconut, sugarcane and chillies. The production of groundnut registered an increase of 79 per cent between 1970-73 and 1994-97, and this was a product of 43 per cent growth in acreage and 27 per cent in yield rate. This growth, however, took place entirely in the last one-and-half decades. In the all-India total production of groundnut, Karnataka's share increased from 10.9 per cent during 1970-73 to 13.0 in 1994-97. The next important oilseed is coconut, and its production recorded a rise of 112 per cent in this period. This was, however, almost entirely a product of acreage increase. The production of safflower had a much more rapid growth. There was a five-fold rise over the entire period and this was largely a product of the growth in yield rate. The acreage increased only 43 per cent as against a nearly four-fold rise in yield. The highest growth was, however, in sunflower. Production rose to 3.73 lakh tonnes in 1994-97 from a mere 3 thousand tonnes in 1970-73. This was mainly due to the growth in acreage; the yield rate was only a little more than doubled over the period. Among other oilseeds, production of sesamum was a little more than doubled, with an increase in acreage of 55 per cent and in yield rate 50 per cent. Oilseeds as a whole performed badly. The production increased from the annual average of 12.43 lakh tonnes during 1985-88 to 17.15 lakh tonnes during 1993-96, that is, a growth of 38 per cent. The increase in yield rate was only 12 per cent in this period, from 551 kg to 618 kg, and in area from 22.57 lakh hectares to 27.73 lakh hectares, that is, 22.9 per cent (GKT 1997).

In non-oilseed, the most important crop was cotton. In fact, till early eighties it accounted for the largest acreage under non-foodgrains. In recent years, there has been a sharp fall in area under it, to 6.59 lakh hectares during 1994-97 from 9.76 hectares in 1980-83. The growth in production was, however, substantial due to an impressive performance in yield rate. Production increased by 92 per cent over the period of two-and-half decades, with the yield recording a growth of 190 per cent. The next important crop, sugarcane, had a much better performance. The production increased by 211 per cent over the period, with the acreage under it getting nearly trebled; the yield rate had a nominal rise. Among other crops, chillies accounted for a relatively large acreage, and the performance was quite impressive. Production increased nearly four-fold over the period, with the yield getting doubled and the area rising by 78 per cent. Tobacco and coffee also had a significant growth in production, as may be seen from Table 12.1.

In vegetables and fruits, potato, banana, mango and onion were important. Production of potato, which had a low base, registered a seven-fold rise between 1970-73 and 1994-97, from 0.50 lakh tonnes to 3.40 lakh tonnes. The area increased more than three times and the productivity was a little more than doubled. Onions also had a noticeable growth. Production increased nearly five times with a similar growth in acreage. In fruits, banana recorded almost a seven-fold rise in production in this period with the yield rate rising by five times. Mango also had a noticeable growth in recent years. During 1990-91 to 1995-96, production increased by 48 per cent, from 6.72 lakh tonnes to 9.94 lakh tonnes. This was solely a product of acreage rise. The highest growth among the major fruits was by papaya. In the last six years, production increased by 157 per cent – from 1.85 lakh tonnes to 4.76 lakh tonnes. This was mainly due to growth in yield.

A new development in Karnataka's agriculture that needs a mention is the growth of agribusiness. This is particularly noticeable in floriculture. The countryside around Bangalore is having a rapid growth of 'polyhouses', that is, enclosures covered by polythene sheets to facilitate moisture retention and climate control. The polyhouses are growing a variety of flowers that are in great demand both locally and internationally. These are quite costly ventures and beyond the reach of even a middle-level farmer. The polyhouses assure themselves of adequate water by digging bore-wells, sometimes to depths of more than 600 feet, and use captive power generators to overcome the problem of load-shedding. The large polyhouses use even computerised technology for climate control. It has been estimated by the IDBI that for a hectare of roses the optimal investment required is Rs. 20-25 million, and at the minimum around Rs. 10 million per acre for any such farm (quoted in Panini 1999).

District-wise Disparity

The growth of agriculture in Karnataka varied widely from district to district. We look into the situation on productivity of some of the major crops. In Jowar, which is grown mainly in the districts of Bijapur, Raichur, Gulbarga, Dharwad, Belgaum, Bellary, Bidar, Mysore and Chitradurga, the yield rate during 1990-93 varied between the highest of 1,636 kg/ha in Shimoga – with a very low acreage under the crop – and the lowest at 494 kg in Bijapur, the district with the highest acreage. Between 1981-84 and 1990-93, production of jowar had increased in only seven of the districts, the rest recording declines (CMIE 1996b).

In rice, which is grown more widely, the highest yield during 1990-93 was in Mysore, at 2,992 kg/ha, and the lowest in Bidar, at 708 kg. There were eight districts with less than the state's average of 2,211 kg. Five of them – Bidar, Gulbarga, Dakshin Kannada, Uttar Kannada and Dharwad – had recorded declines in yield between 1981-84 and 1990-93. The area under rice during 1990-93 was highest in Dakshin Kannada, followed by Shimoga. In the former the area increased by 82 per cent over 1980-83, despite the decline in yield rate, whereas in the latter the area declined even with growth in productivity.

Among other crops, the yield rate in cotton during 1988-91 varied between the highest of 368 kg/ha in Kodagu, a small producer, and the lowest at 105 kg in Gulbarga, against the state average of 170 kg. Between 1981-84 and 1988-91, the yield rate in the state as a whole was doubled, but in three districts – Mysore, Hassan and Chickmagalur – there were declines. In coconut also, the variation in yield was high.

During 1988-91, it ranged between the highest of 174 thousand nuts per ha in Kodagu and the lowest at 1,301 in Chickmagalur, with the state average at 5,161. The largest producer, Tumkur, had the yield rate of only 3,574 nuts during 1988-91, declining from 6,871 in 1981-84.

Behind this pattern of development both natural and human factors were responsible. It may be noted here that about two-thirds of Karnataka's area are drought-prone with low and uncertain rainfall. Climate and soil conditions are quite a severe limitation on the extent to which the land can be utilised. But these are not totally insurmountable; with proper human efforts, the productivity of land could be considerably raised. There was also probably some scope for increasing the availability of land through reduction in other uses. Below, first we give a brief look into the pattern of land use in Karnataka, and then analyse the efforts at raising the productivity of land.

Land Use

The total reporting area of Karnataka is 190 lakh hectares, which is sixth largest among all the states, and next to Andhra Pradesh among the southern states (Table 4.4). The proportion of land under cultivation is relatively better here. In 1992-93, it stood at 73.3 per cent, rising from 65.2 per cent in 1970-71. The all-India average in these years were, respectively, 64.2 per cent and 58.5 per cent. The per capita land under cultivation stood at 0.31 hectare in 1992-93 as against the all-India average at 0.23 hectare. Only two states, Madhya Pradesh and Gujarat, had higher levels than Karnataka's.

The proportion of area under non-agricultural use was relatively low here, being at 5.0 per cent in 1970-71 and 6.3 per cent in 1992-93 as against the all-India average at 5.4 per cent and 7.2 per cent, respectively. The area under forest was, however, relatively low. In 1995-96, it stood at only 16.1 per cent as against the all-India average at 22.6 per cent. The culturable waste is also very low. Presently, it is only 2.3 per cent of the total reporting area, which is less than half the all-India average. Thus, the scope for bringing new land under cultivation is very limited.

Productivity Promoting Factors

In the situation of land scarcity, the only way out is to raise the productivity of the existing land. A combination of three types of arrangement is possible here: first, to raise the cropping intensity of land; secondly, to improve the irrigation facility and make optimum application of different inputs; and third, to change crops in response to the trend in yield rate and market demand. On the first, there is considerable scope for improvement. The cropping intensity in Karnataka had been very low. The gross cropped area as percentage to the net increased from 106.4 in 1971-72 to 108.1 in 1981-82 and 114.8 in 1995-96; the all-India average in these years were 118.2, 124.6 and 131.2 respectively. The situation on the second method, that is, application of different inputs, is discussed below. The third is probably a more difficult option; the farmers have to be much more commercially motivated than at present. Motivation is, however, a critical factor behind each of the options, and it depends on a variety of factors. An important consideration is the pattern of landholding; therefore, a look into its status first.

Landholding Pattern

As in most other states, by mid-fifties, land reform measures were initiated in Karnataka. Inam Abolition Acts were passed in 1954 and 1955 and all the large *inamdari* intermediaries were abolished. The implementation was, however, very slow and could not be done through formal administrative channels; it was only the courts which applied the Act whenever the tenants claimed ownership. The *inam* lands were held mostly by the Brahmins who were absentee landlords and had some influence over the state bureaucracy.

The second phase of land reforms came after the reorganisation of the state in 1956. The Karnataka Land Reforms Act, 1961 was passed in 1962 and brought into effect from October 1965. The long delay provided a typical example of how group interests operated through political pressures. The Lingayat and Vokkaliga communities, who mainly controlled the land, together accounted for 61 per cent of the legislators in 1962 and 67 per cent in 1967. Their combines share in households operating 10 acres and above was 89.5 per cent in 1961 (Thimmaiah and Aziz 1984: 27, 30).

Given this position of the landed community, the provisions of the Act could not be framed in a way as to make available any substantial amount of land for redistribution. First, they managed to get a high ceiling on landholdings – as much as 27 standard acres per family of five members. Then differential ceilings on the basis of soil fertility, irrigation facilities and land use pattern gave them undue advantages. In terms of dry land, 27 standard acres were declared as equivalent to 216 acres. There was also provision for extra acreage for each individual member beyond five, and it could go up to the maximum of 432 acres of dry land. Attempts were also made to take full advantage of the exemptions allowed for widows and physically handicapped, as also the provision to treat each adult son as an independent unit.

The Act of 1961 was amended in 1973, following the Planning Commission's guidelines for stringent land reforms. The land ceiling was drastically reduced to just 10 standard acres. Further, dairy farming, poultry farming and the breeding of livestock which were earlier not considered as agriculture now came to be included in agricultural lands. And then, each additional member of a family was now allowed only two additional units upto a maximum of 20 units in the aggregate.

There were, however, certain other changes that greatly nullified the reduction in ceiling. A unit was defined in such a way that privately irrigated land was put in an advantageous position. A farm with the best quality of land and fully irrigated through private sources now faced a ceiling of 25 acres, and this was not much of a reduction from the earlier ceiling. Another major benefit for the large holders was the redefinition of the family. Presently, an adult son could claim to be a separate family even in a joint family.

On tenancy reforms, there was not much of a resistance and the regulations of 1961 itself provided for stiff provisions. The crop share was fixed at a fourth of the gross produce in case of the irrigated lands and a fifth in case of other lands, and the tenures were regulated. However, there were many exemptions from the tenancy legislation, and large number of holdings were held in the names of widows, disabled members of a family and soldiers and seamen. The right to resumption of tenanted land was also liberal. The number of evictions under the pretext of self-cultivation increased greatly.

The amendment in 1973 improved the situation remarkably. The exemptions and the right to resumption of tenanted land were abolished for all but soldiers and seamen. The Act granted tenants the right to purchase the tenanted land at a pre-determined fixed price which was less than the market price. The State Land Development Bank was to grant loans to poor tenants at low interest for this purpose. As on January 1999, there were 6.05 lakh tenants in Karnataka with ownership conferred or rights protected having an area of 26.32 lakh acres (GOI 1999).

An important feature of the 1973 Act was the provision for setting up of land tribunals. There was to be a minimum of one tribunal for each taluka. All powers of deciding whether a person was a tenant, identifying surplus land and distributing it, among other powers, were vested with the tribunal. Its verdict could be questioned only in the High Court. The operation of the tribunals was, however, far from satisfactory. Although it was supposed to be a people's court, virtually it became a legal court demanding the parties to produce documentary evidence. The landlords, well trained in the act of litigation, were always one-up over uniformed tenants.

The achievement on redistribution of surplus land was very dismal. According to a study by Narendra Pani (1984), in as many as six districts not a single acre of land was redistributed until October 1980. In 13 of the 19 districts in the state, the surplus land distributed was well below 20 per cent. In 1981, out of the total of 2,79,209 acres declared surplus, only 1,12,761 acres -- that is, 40.5 per cent -- could be taken possession. The land distributed totalled 63,373 acres to 13,120 beneficiaries. As regards the latest situation, till September 1998, out of the total land declared surplus at 2,67,758 acres only 1,18,441 could be distributed to 32,047 beneficiaries; the per capita benefit came to 3.70 acres here as against the all-India average at 0.96 acre (Deb 1986: 32; GOI 1999). Part of the reason behind the low surplus is the success in tenancy reform. After the land had been granted to the tenants, surplus land could not be of high order.

This level of redistribution could not reduce the concentration in landownership much. For the top 10 per cent of rural households the proportion of total land owned declined from 54.9 per cent in 1953-54 to 47.2 in 1961-62 but in the following years it increased to 50.4 per cent in 1982. For the top 20 per cent also the trend was similar. In case of bottom 40 per cent, the share of land increased till 1971-72 – from 0.44 in 1953-54 to 1.60 per cent – but in the following years it declined -- to 0.92 per cent in 1982. The bottom 40 per cent in Karnataka was poorer in relation to the all-India average; in the latter, their share of land was 1.20 per cent in 1982. Percentage of households owning no land was also higher in Karnataka, being at 13.7 per cent as against the all-India average at 11.3 (Sharma 1994).

In operational holdings also the land concentration did not decline much. The proportion of marginal holdings in total number increased from 28.8 per cent in 1970-71 to 49.7 in 1991-92, but their share in total area of land increased by only 4.5 percentage points – from 5.1 per cent to 9.6. The proportion of marginal holdings in Karnataka is, however, much less than that in all-India, and lowest among the southern states, as may be seen from Table 4.5.

Small and semi-medium holdings in Karnataka appear to have gained more from the land reforms. Their share in total number declined but in area it increased. The proportion of small holdings decreased from 22.8 per cent in 1970-71 to 20.3 per cent in 1991-92 and the share in area increased from 10.7 per cent to 15.4 per cent in the same period. For the semi-medium holdings, the share in number declined from 25.4 to 18.0 per cent, and in area it increased from 23.0 to 25.2 per cent. The proportion of small and medium holdings in Karnataka was higher than in all-India.

The large holdings continue to account for a large share of the area. With only 2.3 per cent of the total number of holdings in 1991-92, they accounted for 19.0 per cent of the total area. In 1970-71, the proportions were 5.4 per cent and 26.9 per cent respectively. At the all-India level, the proportion of large holdings was always less than in Karnataka.

The average size of holding in Karnataka declined from 2.41 ha in 1985-86 to 1.85 in 1991-92. For all other southern states, as well as at the national level, it was significantly lower in 1991-92. Despite this, however, number of sub-marginal holdings was not small in Karnataka. Holdings with 0.50 hectare or less constituted 32.7 per cent of the total, and those with 0.20 hectare or less 21.2 per cent (NSSO 1997). Recent studies have shown that small farmers are not economically efficient due to their inability to command the required resources. Therefore, some way needs to be found out for better utilisation of the sub-marginal plots.

As regards the extent of tenancy, its incidence in Karnataka appears to be relatively low. According to the NSSO, the percentage of tenant holdings here declined from 10.7 in 1981-82 to 8.0 in 1991-92; at the all-India level, it declined from 15.2 to 11.0 per cent. Most of the major states had higher proportion of tenant holdings. The percentage share of leased-in area in Karnataka increased from 6.0 to 7.4 in this period as against from 7.2 to 8.3 at the national level (Sharma 1994).

On terms of lease, there has been a radical change in the last decade. In 1991-92, fixed money system accounted for 20.4 per cent of the total area leased in as against only 0.36 per cent in 1981-82. The proportion under fixed produce also increased from 4.7 per cent to 14.7 in this period. The share of produce system remained at almost the same level, around 29 per cent of the total. Thus, these three systems together accounted for 64 per cent of the total leased-in area in Karnataka in 1991-92 as against only 34 per cent in 1981-82. A variety of other systems accounted for the rest.

Irrigation Facilities

Provision of irrigation facility is of critical importance for agricultural growth everywhere. But this is particularly so in case of Karnataka where rainfall is scanty in as many as 14 districts, out of 20. Against the state average of 1,139 mms normally, these districts have between 600 and 900 mms. The potential for developing irrigation facility is also not negligible. There are as many as 18 major rivers in the state, with Krishna having a length of 483 km, Tungabhadra 381 km, Cauvery 320 km, Malaprabha 304 km, Vedavati 293 km and Bhima 290 km. The Krishna system has utilisable water resources of 26,800 m.cum., the Cauvery 12,000 and the west flowing rivers 22,000 (GKT 1996, 1982a: I).

The performance in provision of irrigation facility has been, however, very poor. The total of area under irrigation increased from 7.49 lakh hectares at the end of 1955-56 to 10.22 lakh hectares in 1966-67 and 23.25 lakh hectares in 1994-95, that is, only a trebling over the period of four decades. The net irrigated area as percentage to the state's cropped area increased from 7.3 in 1961-62 to 15.3 in 1975-76 and 22.1 in 1995-96. These were much below the all-India average, as may be seen from Table 4.6. The proportion of area under foodgrains irrigated constituted only 27.9 per cent in 1992-93, rising from 14.3 per cent in 1970-73 and 10.8 per cent in 1960-63. The all-India average stood at 49.6 per cent in 1992-93, and all the other southern states also had higher levels. Among the crops, while rice had 61 per cent of its cropped area irrigated in 1986-87, for coarse cereals it was only 8 per cent and for pulses 4 per cent. In non-foodgrains, sugarcane had 99 per cent of the cropped area irrigated as against only 20 per cent in groundnut and 18 per cent in cotton.

Among the states, Karnataka's relative position in the potential itself was, however, low. In major and medium irrigation, the ultimate potential is only 25 lakh hectares, which is lower than that in nine of the major states. The utilisation of even this potential was not high. Till 1991-92, only 15 lakh hectares – that is, 60 per cent of the potential – could be created. There were as many as seven states with a higher level of creation (Table 4.6). The Eighth Plan had a target of creating 6.50 lakh hectares but only 2.34 lakh hectares could be created. The utilisation of created potential was still worse. Against the target of 5.20 lakh hectares in this plan, only 1.87 lakh hectares could be achieved (GKT 1998: I: 175).

In minor irrigation also Karnataka's position was unsatisfactory. The potential was naturally low due to the hard rocks of Karnataka being not sufficiently porous. The ultimate potential in minor irrigation is only 21 lakh hectares, which is lower than that in most of the major states. The potential created by March 1997 was to the extent of 17 lakh hectares, that is, 81 per cent; this is way behind the all-India average, being 88 per cent of the potential even in 1991 (Table 4.6).

In minor irrigation, surface water accounted for the major portion in Karnataka. In the total of area irrigated by all sources, tanks alone accounted for 31.3 per cent in 1966-67. In recent years, however, its share has declined drastically – to only 10.7 per cent in 1994-95. The wells have gained significantly over the years. Its share rose to 35.0 per cent from 17.4 per cent in the same period (GKT 1972, 1997).

District-wise disparity in the provision of irrigation facility continued to be very wide, as may be seen from Table 12.2. In 1966-67, that is, two decades after independence, less than 10 per cent of the net sown area was irrigated in seven of the districts, in Gulbarga it was as low as 1.3 per cent. On the other hand, Shimoga had as much as 48 per cent, Dakshin Kannada 35 per cent and Mandya 32 per cent. After another nearly three decades, in 1994-95, also the disparity was not much reduced. Many of the districts with high irrigation facility improved their position further, while there were still three districts with less than 10 per cent of the net sown area irrigated.

A large number of districts had to depend on costlier sources of irrigation. Bidar was entirely dependent on wells in 1994-95. The reliance on tanks – whose maintenance was generally very poor – was to the extent of 42 per cent in Uttar Kannada and 38 per cent in Shimoga and Hassan. Borewells, which could be afforded mainly by the richer farmers, accounted for 65 per cent of the total irrigated area in Bangalore (R), 62 per cent in Bangalore and 54 per cent in Kolar as against the state average of 15.4 per cent.

The public investment in irrigation increased significantly only in the recent plans. In the Second Plan, Rs. 27.10 crores was spent on it, constituting 19.3 per cent of the aggregate plan outlay. But, in the Third Plan, with Rs. 30.86 crores, the relative share declined to 11.7 per cent. Moreover, minor irrigation which is much more cost affective did not get its due share of attention. In the total outlay for irrigation, it share declined from 15.8 per cent in the Seventh Plan to 9.1 per cent during 1990-95 (GKT 1997: A-24).

While huge investments were made in large and medium projects adequate attention was not given to utilisation of the facility created. Command Area Development Authorities were created for ensuring effective utilisation of the waters, but their activities remained far from satisfactory. During the Eighth Plan, the target for coverage by field channels was 4.20 lakh hectares but the achievement came to only around 1.30 lakh hectares. Similarly, on land levelling, against the target of 2.98 lakh hectares only 1.08 lakh hectares could be covered.

In minor irrigation also there were some difficult problems. Even when the funds allotted were completely spent, or even over-spent, physical targets often remained unachieved. For example, on surface water, the Eighth Plan had approved an outlay of Rs. 271.40 crores but the actual expenditure came to Rs. 302.67 crores. On the physical side, the targets were only half achieved – 27.54 thousand hectares against 53 thousand hectares.

In groundwater, the problems are of a different nature. Overexploitation has become quite severe in some of the areas. Recently 22 taluks have been declared as grey and 21 dark (GKT 1998). Steep rise in groundwater exploitation has disturbed the balance between groundwater recharge and extraction and resulted in decline of water levels in many areas. The utilisation of groundwater potential had reached 70 per cent in Kolar by 1980, 60 per cent in Tumkur and 51 per cent in Bangalore (GKT 1982a: I).

There is a strong link between pumpset energisation and borewell construction because borewells cannot be operated efficiently without electric connection. The government adopted the policy of supplying power at a low and flat tariff since February 1981. As the borewells can be operated continuously, the flat tariff was a strong incentive for incessant pumping and cultivation of water-intensive crops. In the absence of metered power supply farmers used the water indifferently, least caring for conveyance, distribution and application efficiencies. Appropriate pricing of electricity was needed to discourage liberal withdrawal of groundwater, but the government instead took the decision to give free power to agricultural pumpsets upto 10 HP since June 1992. This has further encouraged construction of borewells.

Provision of Inputs

In the provision of different inputs also Karnataka's position was not satisfactory. The area under HYV was relatively low here. In the state's total of gross cropped area it covered only 32.9 per cent during 1994-97 as against the all-India average at 39.2 per cent; as many as seven of the major states had better position than Karnataka's (Table 4.7). This is the situation despite a higher growth in area under HYV here than at the national level. Between 1987-90 and 1994-97, the former registered a rise of 97.6 per cent as against 25.3 per cent in the latter.

District-wise, there was wide variation in the proportion of area covered. While Bangalore had 56.1 per cent of the total sown area under HYV in 1994-95 and Shimoga 54.1 per cent, for three districts, viz., Bidar, Bijapur and Dharwad, it was less than 15 per cent (Table 12.2).

Table 12.2

District-wise Disparity in Provision of Irrigation Facility, Use of Inputs and Bank Credit in Karnataka

Districts	*Net irrigated area as % to net sown area*		*HVY area as % to total sown area: 1994-95*	*Fertiliser consumption per ha (kg) 1994-95*	*Loans per ha (Rs.) as on 31.3.94*	
	1966-67	*1994-95*			*From PACS*	*From PLDBs*
Bangalore	—	18.0	56.1	215.4	431	450
Bangalore (R)	13.2	19.3	44.7	78.6	336	212
Chitradurga	12.7	20.0	33.1	8.4	124	191
Kolar	17.0	20.3	32.4	8.8	197	173
Shimoga	48.3	48.5	54.1	10.6	248	183
Tumkur	10.9	13.0	28.6	4.7	190	261
Belgaum	6.9	31.7	20.8	60.7	378	86
Bijapur	3.2	23.4	12.0	29.5	136	68
Dharwad	5.4	19.2	14.0	48.7	231	56
Uttar Kannada	13.6	22.2	42.5	41.4	1157	354
Bellary	7.6	32.6	37.5	119.6	312	76
Bidar	3.4	7.6	11.8	19.8	442	71
Gulbarga	1.3	9.6	27.3	18.7	85	51
Raichur	12.1	25.4	30.5	102.3	28	110
Chikmagalur	21.9	10.6	32.5	90.5	227	172
Dakshin Kannada	35.1	45.0	35.5	62.9	3191	198
Hassan	19.0	20.4	47.0	94.4	31	131
Kodagu	7.4	2.2	20.0	146.5	1462	77
Mandya	31.8	46.1	42.1	164.7	122	107
Mysore	13.5	25.7	40.4	88.7	96	144
State	10.2	22.3	28.1	68.5	286	118

Source: GKT 1972, 1996.

There were a number of reasons behind the low adoption of HYV seeds. Often there was the problem of inadequate production. During the Eighth Plan, production of cereal seeds was only 97 thousand tonnes and of pulses 17 thousand tonnes. The targets for distribution in this period was 110 thousand tonnes of cereals and for pulses 33 thousand tonnes, but the achievements came to 93 thousand tonnes and 20 thousand tonnes, respectively (1997b: I: 65,67). The infrastructural facilities also continued to be very inadequate. For the entire state, there were only two seed testing laboratories, at Hebbal and Dharwad, for promoting quality control. The low adoption was also due to the fact that local improved varieties had an edge over the HYVs in terms of suitability to agro-climatic conditions, lesser fluctuations in yield and prices and lower costs.

In the consumption of fertilisers also Karnataka's position was relatively poor. The per hectare consumption here stood at the average of 79.0 kg during 1995-98, which was lower than the levels in seven of the major states (Table 4.7). The growth in consumption between 1975-76 and 1997-98 was 4.5 times in case of Karnataka, from 20.2 to 90.1 kg, as against 5.1 times for all-India, from 17.1 to 87.5 kg. In the pre-green revolution period, Karnataka's relative position was significantly better. As may be seen from Table 4.7, in 1966-67, its per hectare consumption stood at 21.5 kg, which was exceeded by only one of the major states. As regards the use of alternative or complementary types of nutrients, very little progress has been made. The government has schemes for popularising bio-fertilizers and for producing compost and green manure but the funds allocated for them are negligible.

The district-wise variation in consumption of chemical fertilisers was very wide, as evident from Table 12.2. In 1994-95, while Bangalore had as much as 215 kg/ha and Mandya 165 kg/ha, there were six districts with less than 20 kg/ha. Behind the low consumption many factors worked, but inadequate efforts from the side of government was an important reason.

In plant protection measures, Karnataka was significantly behind a number of major states. In 1994-95, in the all-India total consumption of pesticides, Karnataka's share was only 5.4 per cent as against Andhra's 16.1 and Tamil Nadu's 11.8 per cent; there were eight states with higher shares than Karnataka's (CMIE 1996b). The increase in consumption over the years was nominal. Between 1981-82 and 1995-96, it fluctuated between the highest of 4,486 tonnes in 1987-88 and the lowest at 3,190 tonnes in 1981-82. During the Eighth Plan, the consumption annually averaged 3,859 tonnes. The area covered by plant protection stood at the average 59.60 lakh hectares during the

Eighth Plan, constituting nearly half of the total sown area. Integrated pest management has not received any attention worth the name, and therefore, use of complementary or alternative methods of plant protection has not made any noticeable progress.

In mechanisation of agriculture Karnataka is lagging behind a number of states. Even in use of pumpsets, although we have noted above the overexploitation of groundwater, Karnataka's position was exceeded by five of the major states in 1993-94 (Table 4.7). Between 1968-69 and 1995-96, total number of pumpsets/tubewells energised here increased from 0.92 lakh to 10.15 lakh, that is, 11 times. The growth in the pre-green revolution period appears to be faster. Between 1956 and 1967, there was a seven-fold rise in number of pumpsets, from 7.9 thousand to 54.6 thousand. As regards use of tractors, in 1990-91 the state accounted for only 3.4 per cent of the total number in the country as against the highest of 23.4 per cent in Punjab. Among the southern states, however, it had the largest number. Number of tractors and power tillers totalled 48,761 in 1990, rising from 14,000 in 1977 and only 1,000 in 1961. An overall indicator of the extent of mechanisation in agriculture is the level of electricity consumption, and here Karnataka's position is not bad. Per capita consumption in agriculture stood at 130.38 kwh in 1993-94, which was exceeded by only four of the states, viz., Punjab, Haryana, Gujarat and Andhra Pradesh.

Provision of Bank Credit

Cooperative Credit Institutions

For short and medium term credit, as in other states, there is a three-tier structure in cooperative credit. At village level, presently there are 4,350 primary credit societies (PACS), and at district level 19 central cooperative banks. For long-term credit, there are 177 primary cooperative agricultural and rural development banks at taluk level, in addition to the apex institution. The NABARD provides refinance facility to both the apex institutions.

The credit flow from cooperatives cannot be considered appreciable. Although the total of credit had a little more than five-fold rise between 1982-83 and 1995-96, from Rs. 120.7 crores to Rs. 642.3 crores, it was accompanied by wide fluctuations. The annual flow reached Rs. 327 crores in 1988-89, from only Rs. 156 crores in the preceding year, but declined again to as low as Rs. 122 crores in 1990-91. In the total credit, the share of short-term was at the highest 81 per cent in 1985-86 and at the lowest 42 per cent in 1991-92. In case of long-term credit, the proportion varied between the highest of 56 per cent in 1991-92 and the lowest at 13 per cent in 1985-86. In the last three years, 1993-96, the total credit averaged Rs. 484 crores annually, and the share of short-term credit in it was 67.2 per cent and of long term 28.2 per cent (GKT 1997: A-73).

In the pre-green revolution period, as the base was low, the growth in credit was substantial in response to the measures taken. Loans advanced by primary societies rose to Rs. 154.7 crores in 1966-67 from Rs. 52.9 crores in 1960-61 and only Rs. 12.8 crores in 1956-57. Number of societies increased from 12,509 to 19,335 over the decade, and membership from 17.57 lakhs to 38.17 lakhs (GKT 1972: 347).

The performance of cooperative credit on recovery of loans was very depressing. In case of short term loans, recovery as percentage to demand varied between the highest of 80.7 in 1994-95 and the lowest at 18.6 in 1989-90; on medium-term credit, the variation was between 4.8 in 1990-91 and 60.1 in 1994-95; and in long-term, between 24.0 in 1989-90 and 65.1 in 1987-88 (GKT 1997).

A comparison with the situation in other states presents Karnataka in a very poor light. In 1992-93, loans issued per hectare from the PACS stood at only Rs. 213, which was much lower than the all-India average; there were seven states providing a larger credit than Karnataka. The growth in credit here was only 131 per cent between 1981-82 and 1992-93 as against 243 per cent for all-India. The credit outstanding stood at Rs. 394 crores at the end of March 1993 and constituted 3.8 per cent of all-India total (Table 4.8). In the last three years, however, there has been some significant improvement. At the end of March 1996, the outstanding credit rose to Rs. 508.12 crores, constituting 4.5 per cent of all-India total (RBI 1999: II).

The beneficiaries from cooperative credit were mainly large farmers. The share of those owning land upto 2 hectares was only 22.3 per cent in the credit outstanding at the end of March 1996, and for tenant cultivators, agricultural labourers and others at 8.8 per cent. At the national level, the proportions were 29.6 per cent and 6.1 per cent respectively.

As in other areas, here also the district-wise disparity was wide. As evident from Table 12.2, per hectare loans from PACS at the end of March 1994 was less than Rs. 100 in four districts – Raichur, Hassan, Gulbarga and Mysore – as against the highest of Rs. 3,191 in Dakshin Kannada and the state average at Rs. 286. In case of PLDBs, however, the variation was much less, between Rs. 51 in Gulbarga and Rs. 450 in Bangalore.

Commercial Banks

The role of commercial banks in providing agricultural credit was also not satisfactory. Agricultural advances outstanding in Karnataka as a proportion to all-India total declined from 10.5 per cent in 1971 to 8.6 in 1996, as the growth in amount was 57 times here as against 70 times in all-India. There were four states with higher shares in 1996. Agricultural advances as percentage to total bank advances in the state was 15.4. Although this was higher than the all-India average, there were eight major states providing higher proportions to agriculture, as evident from Table 4.8.

Short-term loans per hectare came to only Rs. 426 in Karnataka in 1996-97 as against the highest of Rs. 1,909 in Kerala. The remaining two southern states also provided a much larger amount. More disconcerting is, however, that the marginal farmers were neglected to a larger extent here. The share of those owning land upto 2.5 acres was only 17.2 per cent of the total amount in 1996-97 and in number of accounts 29.4 per cent. In the all-India average, these were respectively, 30.4 and 40.8. The marginal farmers' share in Karnataka seems to be declining over the years. In 1979-80, they accounted for 20.8 per cent of the total amount and 43.3 in number of accounts (RBI 1983: II, 1999: II).

As regards Grameen Banks, Karnataka had 13 banks with 1,074 branches in 1996. Their combined deposits at the end of March 1996 stood at Rs. 967.4 crores, constituting 6.8 per cent of the aggregate with all RRBs in the country. The C-D ratio of RRBs in Karnataka stood at 92 per cent as against the all-India average at 53 per cent.

The agricultural advances of RRBs in Karnataka have shown a relative decline. In 1990, it constituted 64.5 per cent of the aggregate of advances outstanding but on March-end 1996 it was down to 55.1. Even after the fall, however, Karnataka's was the second largest proportion among the major states, next only to Gujarat. The per hectare agricultural advances here came to Rs. 396 in 1996, which is more than double the average for all-India and could be exceeded by only two states – Kerala and Andhra (Table 4.8).

The performance of RRBs varied widely across banks. For example, the amount of crop loans outstanding at the end of September 1989 was at the highest Rs. 38.08 crores in Malaprabha as against only Rs. 28 lakhs in Varada and Rs. 47 lakhs in Netravati. The term loans outstanding to agriculture on the same date was less than Rs. 2 crores in six banks as against the highest of Rs. 17.85 crores in Malaprabha.

Other Factors

Among other production promoting factors, we may give a brief look into the situation on crop insurance and certain aspects of marketing. The Comprehensive Crop Insurance Scheme was introduced in Karnataka as late as 1985, despite the fact that a large part of the state is prone to frequent natural calamities. The scheme, however, did not prove very attractive to the farmers. Even in recent years its coverage was relatively low, particularly in relation to Andhra Pradesh. During 1993-96, the total number of farmers covered was 7.61 lakh, and annually increased from 1.94 lakh in 1993-94 to 3.39 lakh in 1995-96. The area covered totalled 12.89 lakh hectares and increased from 3.25 lakh hectares to 5.60 lakh hectares. The sum insured stood at Rs. 13881.93 lakhs in 1995-96, rising from Rs. 6,802.18 lakhs in 1993-94. The claims paid in 1993-94 constituted 4.02 per cent of the sum insured and in 1994-95 at 1.17 per cent, to 0.194 lakh and 0.135 lakh farmers, respectively (GKT 1997: 27).

As regards marketing, on the organisational side, number of cooperative marketing societies are relatively few and spatially not well spread-out. At the end of March 1994, there were 647 societies in the state, and 74 per cent of them were concentrated in seven districts, viz., Raichur, Dharwad, Mysore, Tumkur, Bijapur, Chitradurga and Bellary (GKT 1996: 50).

The availability of regulated markets in Karnataka appears to be better than at the national level. Total number of regulated markets here, including sub-markets, stood at 466 in 1996-97, rising from 411 in 1990-91. The number of main markets in the latest year was 135. On the average there is one for 27 thousand hectares of gross sown area. Karnataka's share in all-India total number of regulated markets is 6.68 per cent (Thippaiah and Deshpande 1998). As regards the value of turnover in regulated markets, the annual average came to Rs. 289,314.8 lakhs during 1989-90 to 1993-94, with contribution from foodgrains at 21.49 per cent, fibres 19.04 per cent, oilseeds 14.40 per cent and pulses 8.61 per cent. Among other commodities, arecanut contributed 12.50 per cent and jaggery 5.17 per cent.

The prices of agricultural commodities in Karnataka had an appreciable rise over the years. The index number of wholesale prices stood at 369 in 1995-96, with the base year 1981-82=100. At all-India level, for primary articles it stood at 323. Commodity group-wise information on this basis is not available; we may look at the situation on a particular time-point only, as an example. In October 1996, the index number for condiments and spices in Karnataka stood at 500, of pulses 479 and cereals 373 as against 392 for all commodities. On the low side were sugar and gur at 251 and oilseeds 297.

The gap between wholesale price and support price was often very wide in some of the commodities. In tur, for example, during 1988-89 to 1996-97 the support price varied between 40.4 per cent to 64.9 per cent of the wholesale prices and averaged 53 per cent. Over the entire period, while the wholesale price increased by 167.5 per cent, for support price it was only 133.3 per cent. For paddy, on the other hand, the support price was on the average 78 per cent of the wholesale price and in case of groundnut 74 per cent. The differentials presumably followed from the policy on land utilisation and priorities of agricultural production.

II
Allied Activities

Animal Husbandry

The growth in number of livestock over the years has not been significant in Karnataka. It was estimated at 47.36 million in 1992, rising from 31.77 million in 1977 and 20.49 million in 1966, that is, a growth of 131 per cent over the entire period of 26 years. In the total number, poultry accounted for 34 per cent in 1992, followed by cattle 28 per cent. In 1977, their shares were, respectively, 31 per cent and 32 per cent (GKT 1998: 104, 1982a: I: 703-04,1972). Among other animals, goats, sheep and buffaloes were important. From the angle of productivity, cattle, buffaloes and poultry were important. Below we give a brief look into the pattern of their growth over the years.

Cattle and Buffalo Development

So far as the growth in number is concerned, cattle and buffalo presented a very depressing picture. Number of cattle declined from 96.86 lakhs in 1966 to 71.48 lakhs in 1972, and then increased to 101.74 lakhs in 1987 and 131.7 lakhs in 1992, that is, over the entire period a growth of only 36 per cent. The relative position of Karnataka among the states was also not good. Between 1972 and 1987, the number of cattle at the national level increased by 56 per cent as against 42 per cent here. There were six major states with a much higher growth than Karnataka's, as may be seen from Table 4.9.

In the total number of cattle, the proportion of females – more important from the angle of milk production – increased from 46.8 per cent in 1972 to 54.2 in 1987. This was a favourable position in relation to all-India; in the latter, the proportion of females was 49.5 per cent in 1987. The sex ratio for adult cattle in Karnataka increased from 0.98 to 1.87 over the period as against 0.76 to 0.98 at the national level.

The proportion of cross-bred in cattle was also relatively better here. In 1987, with the total number at 7.19 lakhs, it constituted 7.1 per cent as against 5.7 per cent at the national level. The proportion of females in cross-bred was as much as 82.9 per cent in Karnataka as against 65.4 in all-India. There were only two states with higher proportion of females. Karnataka's share in all-India total number of cross-bred was 6.3 per cent in 1987, and in females 8.0 per cent (Table 4.9).

In buffaloes, which are kept mainly for milk production, the number increased at a faster rate. According to the 1966 census, Karnataka had 29.46 lakh buffaloes, and the estimate for 1992 was 42.5 lakh, which means a 44 per cent rise over the 26-year period. Comparison with the all-India situation is possible only for a 15-year period, and here Karnataka's growth appears relatively low. Between 1972 and 1987, the number of buffaloes here increased by 95 per cent, from 20.69 lakh to 40.35, as against 107 per cent at the national level. In number of females also the situation was similar, the growth over the period being, respectively, 94 per cent and 110 per cent. The proportion of females in the total number here had a marginal decline, from 85.3 per cent in 1972 to 84.7 in 1987. It, however, continued to be significantly higher than the all-India average situation. In 1987, there were only three states with higher proportion of females than in Karnataka.

The favourable female ratio in both cattle and buffalo was reflected in the growth of milk production. Between 1971-72 and 1995-96, milk production here had a four-fold rise, from 7.6 lakh tonnes to 31.8 lakh tonnes. This was much better than the all-India growth. In terms of per capital production, however, the situation was quite depressing. Karnataka had only 65 kg in 1994-95, which was exceeded by as many as eight of the major states (Table 4.10).

The productivity of Karnataka's cattle and buffalo was relatively low. The yield per day of an indigenous cattle averaged only 1.61 kg during 1985-88 as against around 3 kg in Kerala and Tamil Nadu. In cross-bred, the yield rate in Karnataka was 5.253 kg in 1987-88 as against 7.943 kg in Gujarat and 6.456 kg in Punjab. In buffalo, the yield averaged 2.250 kg during 1985-88 as against more than 3 kg in Tamil Nadu and Kerala.

Inadequate availability of fodder and lack of proper veterinary services were the two important factors behind the low yield. The area under production of fodder stood at only 1,120 hectares in 1995-96 and the production at 186 lakh tonnes. Intensive fodder cultivation in livestock farms was taken up only in recent years. Training facilities in fodder development continued to be very meagre. As regards veterinary facilities, apparently there has been a rapid growth over the years. Number of veterinary institutions increased from 234 at the end of First Plan to 876 at the end of the Fourth Plan and 3,437 in 1995-96. Number of hospitals in them increased from 36 in 1973-74 to 244 in 1995-96, of taluk-level dispensaries from 253 to 700 and primary centres from 587 to 1,920; there are also presently 173 mobile clinics. Number of artificial insemination centres stood at 400 in 1995-96. All these were however, far from adequate, particularly from the angle of quality of services. The targets on vaccination often remained unachieved, and the success rate in artificial insemination was low even under the frozen semen technique.

District-wise, the facilities and growth of bovine population were highly concentrated in a few of them. At the end of March 1980, out of the total number of 1,846 veterinary institutions in the state, Bangalore division (comprised of four districts) alone accounted for one-third, and another quarter by Mysore, Dharwad and Belgaum together. The growth of bovine population also followed the same pattern. In 1977, four districts, namely, Dharwad, Belgaum, Mysore and Shimoga, together accounted for 36 per cent of the total. The buffalo population in it was more heavily concentrated. Six districts, viz., Belgaum, Dharwad, Bijapur, Chitradurga, Dakshin Kannada and Tumkur, accounted for half of the total. This level of concentration could be only partly explained by the climatic conditions.

Poultry Development

Over the years a variety of measures were taken for developing the poultry sector in Karnataka. The Applied Nutrition Programme was launched in 1963-64 with the objective of developing a comprehensive programme of education and training in modern poultry farming and to improve the local diet through production and use of eggs. The development of poultry among the weaker sections was taken up in late seventies. The programme was utilised particularly for rehabilitation of the tribal population in Mysore, Kodagu, Dakshin Kannada and Chikmagalur districts.

The infrastructural situation has improved considerably in recent years. Presently, there are 31 poultry farms under the technical control of the government, comprised of one state poultry breeding and training centre, three regional centres, eight district poultry rearing and training centres, 13 poultry rearing centres, five intensive poultry production and egg marketing centres and one poultry and livestock quality control cell. In 1995-96, 5,922 persons were trained in poultry rearing and 1.37 lakh chicks were produced.

The growth in number of poultry was, however, not anything appreciable. It increased from 76.68 lakh in 1956 to 88.41 lakh in 1961 but in 1966 it stood at only 82.77 lakh. In the following years it rose again to reach 101.63 lakh in 1972, but in 1977 it was down to 96.96. The latest estimate places the number of poultry at 161.6 lakh in 1992. Ignoring fluctuations, the increase over the entire period of 36 years was thus only 111 per cent. Moreover, the growth was heavily concentrated in a few districts. Data for recent years are not available, but in 1977 four districts -- Bangalore, Dakshin Kannada, Kolar and Mandya -- together accounted for 38.5 per cent of the total, for the first two 22.2 per cent. Another 36 per cent came from Mysore, Tumkur, Belgaum, Hassan, Shimoga and Bijapur combined (GKT 1982a).

In the production of eggs, Karnataka's position was low. In 1993-94, it stood at only 1,445 million in number, constituting 5.9 per cent of all-India total. In 1995-96, however, the production reached 1,558 million. The per capita production here was only 31 in 1993-94 as against the highest of 109 in Punjab. Among the southern states, it had the lowest level of production (Table 4.10).

Fishery Development

Karnataka is endowed with rich aquatic resources. For marine fishery, it has 27,000 sq km of rich continental shelf on the 300 km coastline. For inland fisheries, there are 6.31 lakh hectares of water areas, comprised of 4.15 lakh hectares of tanks and ponds and 2.16 lakh hectares of reservoirs. In addition, the state has 6,000 kms of rivers and 8,000 hectares of brackish water area (GKT 1998: 122).

The utilisation of all these resources is, however, far from satisfactory. Marine fish production increased by only 58.8 per cent between 1976-79 and 1993-96, from the annual average of 118.8 thousand tonnes to 188.6 thousand tonnes. In-between, again, there was a continuous decline in production during 1989-95. In the total production of fish, the share of marine catches varied between the highest of 82.6 per cent in 1985-86 and the lowest at 70.0 per cent in 1993-94 in the last one-and-half decade.

In inland fish production, the situation was worse, with wider fluctuations from year to year. Production reached 47.9 thousand tonnes in 1981-82, from 20 thousand tonnes in 1957-58, but in the years till 1987-88 it remained at much lower levels. In the following years till 1995-96 again, it fluctuated between the highest of 87.4 thousand tonnes in the last year and the lowest at 24.6 thousand tonnes in 1993-94. On the basis of three-yearly average, the inland catches increased by only 36.6 per cent between 1981-84 and 1993-96, from 44.5 thousand tonnes to 60.8 thousand tonnes.

A comparison with the situation in other states places Karnataka in a very low position. Between 1984-87 and 1991-94, total of fish production here increased by only 15.8 per cent as against 53.2 per cent at the national level. Karnataka's share in all-India production declined from 7.4 per cent to 5.6 per cent over the period. This is a very poor performance in relation to the neighbouring states. Kerala accounted for as much as 13 per cent of the all-India total production during 1991-94 (Table 4.11). The annual growth in fish production was at the rate of 14.7 per cent in Andhra during 1991-97 and in Kerala 10.9 per cent as against Karnataka's only 6.6 per cent (RBI 1999: I).

Export of fish from Karnataka showed a noticeable growth only in recent years. The quantum of export reached 3,508 tonnes in 1982-83 but in the following years it remained at much lower levels. During 1994-96, however, the annual average rose to 8,128 tonnes. The value of export averaged Rs. 14.48 crores during 1982-85 and rose to Rs. 105.97 crores in 1994-96 at current prices.

The low growth in fish production was due to a number of reasons. In marine fishery, inadequate mechanisation and lack of infrastructure were the main reasons. Till the end of seventies, mechanised fishing was confined to trawling for demersal fishes while the pelagic fishes were landed almost entirely by traditional fishing gear. For the first time in 1975-76, purse seining for mackerel and sardines was introduced on a commercial scale. The traditional and the most common fishing craft in use was the dug-out canoe with length varying between 4 and 11 metres. There were about 8,000 canoes on the Karnataka coast in 1979 (1982: I: 745). The fishing was largely confined to inshore areas, and this led to overexploitation and decline in catches.

In recent years, however, mechanisation has made a significant progress. There are presently 327 purse seines, 2,471 shrimp trawlers, 1,639 gillnetters and 11,500 traditional boats operating in Karnataka coast; deep sea vessels numbered 22 in 1997 (GKT 1998: 122). The berthing and landing facilities are still far from adequate for proper exploitation of the resources. Presently, there are only five minor fishing harbours and 24 fish landing centres. The freezing and processing facilities are also inadequate.

In inland fishery, the utilisation of water area is at a very low level. At the end of seventies, no more than a quarter of the total area was under fish culture, and even now probably it will not be more than half. Fish production is largely confined to a few districts. In 1981-82, in the total production at around 48 thousand tonnes, seven districts, viz., Bangalore, Mysore, Bellary, Tumkur, Raichur, Hassan and Chitradurga, together contributed 68 per cent, for the first three 38 per cent. In 1990-91, the share of these seven districts declined to 66 per cent, but for the first three it rose to 43 per cent. On the other hand, there were six districts, viz., Uttar Kannada, Dakshin Kannada, Kodagu, Bijapur, Chikmagalur and Bidar, contributing only 5 per cent of the total. In none of them there was any perceptible growth in production over the years. Their share of total water bodies in the state was 16.3 per cent – 65 thousand hectares out of 399 thousand hectares (GKT 1994: Table 4.41).

An important reason behind the low growth in inland fishery is inadequate availability of fish seed for intensive stocking and culture. The requirement of fish seeds (fry and fingerling together) at the end of seventies was estimated at 40 crores per annum but the production stood at only 10 crores. In recent years seed production has risen significantly but still there are scarcities in terms of individual species. Presently, 58 fish seed production and rearing farms are producing about 7 crores of fry annually (GKT 1997b: I: 124).

Intensive fish culture did not receive any attention worth the name until recent years. Only in the Eighth Plan some important measures were taken in this direction. Integrated Reservoir Fisheries Development Project is now operating in three districts – Mysore, Mandya and Hassan. Some measures have also been taken to augment the productive capacity of fish ponds. There are 12 Fish Farmers' Development Agencies to look after the intensive fish culture programme. Utilisation of brackish water on a scientific basis has also been given some attention in recent years.

The facilities for preservation and processing of fish continued to be very inadequate. At the end of Fifth Plan, total capacity of ice plants per day stood at only 781 tonnes, of cold storage 796 tonnes, freezing capacity at 117.5 tonnes per day and 2,361 tonnes of frozen storage. There were four units for fish meal production and 12 canning plants. Presently, ice plants capacity per day is 1,938 tonnes and cold storage capacity at 2,426 tonnes, that is, a growth of 148 per cent and 205 per cent, respectively, over 1979-80. The proportion of total catch marketed declined to 48 per cent in 1991-92 from 58 per cent in 1987-88, and that frozen rose to 7.3 per cent from 4.9 per cent. The proportion cured increased from 18 per cent to 24 per cent in this period and that used for manure from 9.2 per cent to 11.6 per cent (GKT 1994).

The cooperativisation or unionisation of fishermen did not grow to the desired extent. At the end of 1989, out of the total active fishermen population of 1.42 lakh only 0.75 lakh were members of societies. In some of the districts the membership was very low. In Bangalore (R), only 18 per cent of total fishermen were members of societies, and in Tumkur 19 per cent. There were a total of 275 societies in 1989, and 48 per cent of them were in four districts, namely, Dakshin Kannada, Uttar Kannada, Dharwad and Mysore; their share in fishermen population was 62 per cent (GKT 1994).

Forestry

Karnataka has the lowest proportion of area under forest among the southern states. At 16.1 per cent of its geographical area in 1995-96, it was much behind the national average also (Table 4.4). Between 1956 and 1981, around 2.23 lakh hectares of forest land were lost for different purposes. Thirty per cent of it went to extension of cultivation, 19 per cent to mining, 18 per cent to hydroelectric projects, 16 per cent by direct submersion and 12 per cent for rehabilitation of the displaced (GKT 1982a: I: 130).

The denudation of forest areas also continued unabated. Denuded forest area in Uttar Kannada increased from 11.6 per cent of total geographical area in 1960 to 30.5 per cent in 1980, and in Shimoga from 6.9 to 22.6 per cent. Even in the reserved forest area, the proportion of denuded area in Uttar Kannada increased from 2.9 to 18.7 per cent and in Shimoga from 10.8 to 41.4 per cent over the same period. The latest position is that although 20.3 per cent of the land area (38,724 sq kms out of 190,494) is legally classified as forest, only 11 per cent is well wooded and the remaining degraded (quoted in Nadkarni et al 1989: 53).

The denudation of unreserved forests has adversely affected the local needs. While the requirement of firewood increased sharply due to population growth, the area available to satisfy the need declined rapidly. The easy approach to meet the problem was to liberalise the access to both reserved and unreserved forests, in practice if not officially. Villagers were officially allowed to remove only headloads of dead firewood from reserved forest but actually it went beyond this. It has been estimated that the annual increment available for removal in Karnataka was about 4.32 million cubic metres in early eighties but the removal on headloads alone was of the order of 10 million (Shyam Sunder and Reddy 1986: 15).

The commercial return from forest has declined sharply over the years. Total of timber extracted declined from 333.5 thousand cms in 1980-81 to 124.5 thousand cms in 1988-89. Sawn timber sold was down to 2,617 thousand cms from 10,805 thousand cms, and of timber in round pole from 104.2 thousand cms to 38.7 thousand cms. Plywood sales declined to only 8,200 thousand cms from 130.7 thousand cms and of match wood from 15.7 thousand cms to 1,252 thousand cms over the same period. Most of the minor forest produce also recorded declines (GKT 1994: Table 1.11).

The revenue of forest department increased at a much slower pace than the growth in expenditure, so much so that in recent years the latter has exceeded the former. Between 1965-66 and 1980-81, the revenue increased by 4.6 times, from Rs. 10.1 crores to Rs. 46 crores, and the expenditure by five times, from Rs. 5.1 crores to Rs. 25.7 crores. But in the following period of 16 years the growth in expenditure was 6.3 times, the amount in 1995-96 being Rs. 160.6 crores, as against only 2.3 times in revenue, at Rs. 105.8 crores (GKT 1982a: 165,1997).

The government's efforts at preserving the forest, not to speak of developing it, was very inadequate for the task at hand. The growth in plan expenditure on forest was very small until the recent years. The Third Plan had provided only Rs. 4.46 crores and the following two plans together Rs. 13.69 crores. It was only since the Sixth Plan the allocation to forestry increased noticeably. Starting with Rs. 30.7 crores in the Sixth Plan, it rose to Rs. 206.8 crores in the Eighth Plan.

In the three decades of planned development efforts, ending in

1980-81, plantations to the extent of only 537,016 hectares and roadside plantations of 623 kms could be raised under different programmes. Under social forestry, 27,331 hectares were covered during 1983-84 to 1987-88 but in the following five years it totalled only 14.62 thousand hectares. The state government had transferred 772.7 thousand hectares of vacant waste land to the Forest Department by January 1989 but only 67 thousand of it could be developed by mid-1993. In the Eight Plan, the target on social forestry was to cover 38,970 hectares but only 16,141 ha could be covered. Similarly, on soil conservation through afforestation the target and achievement were respectively, 12,850 hectares and 5,428 hectares (GKT 1994,1998: I).

There was wide variation in performance from year to year. In the last 11 years, 1985-86 to 1995-96, number of trees planted under afforestation varied between the highest of 3152 lakhs in 1987-88 and the lowest at 374 lakhs in 1992-93. Additional area brought under forestry was at the highest 79.1 thousand hectares in 1986-87 and at the lowest 29.6 thousand hectares in 1990-91. The implementation of programmes was very slow in some of the districts. For example, under the social forestry programme, the area covered during 1983-88 was only 120 hectares in Bangalore and 176 hectares in Kodagu as against the highest of 3,167 hectares in Tumkur and more than 2,000 hectares in five districts (GKT 1997).

As the measures taken proved very inadequate, in recent years the government was compelled to introduce some innovations in forest management. As in case of other states, Karnataka government has also introduced participatory forest management. The Village Forest Committee scheme is being implemented since 1994. Till March 1997, 415 VFCs have been set up. The Western Ghats Forestry Project is being implemented with assistance from the United Kingdom for protecting and developing forest through participation of local people (GKT 1997). Steps are also being taken under the Conservation of Forests and Natural Eco-System Act to protect the forests. Encroachment on forest land and other unauthorised activities are likely to be greatly curbed now as the state has been armed with extensive punitive powers against the offenders.

However, the allocation of finance on forestry in the Ninth Plan (1997-2002) does not appear adequate, given the task at hand; only Rs. 350 crores, constituting 1.5 per cent of the grand total of plan outlay, have been provided. The magnitude of task involved may be gauged from the fact that even to bring the forest area to 20 per cent of the total, 601,600 hectares have to be afforested (GKT 1998: I).

13

Industrial Growth and Structural Change

In the industrial development of the country, Karnataka is a 'pioneer' state. Here some factories were set up as early as the last century, under what was called the indirect rule. Later in the beginning of this century, the old kingdom of Mysore took the lead in encouraging the growth of industry. It was the first state to invest in power generation: electric power became available in 1902 with the commissioning of the Sivasamudram hydroelectric project. The power generated was supplied to the Kolar Gold Fields, and the state set up a number of other manufacturing units. At the time of independence, therefore, Karnataka was one of the industrially advanced states in the country.

The object of this chapter is to look into the pattern of industrial growth in the post-independence era. The analysis follows the same pattern as in the preceding chapters on industry.

The industrial growth of Karnataka in the post-independence period, particularly in recent years, has not been satisfactory. With the base of 1980-81 = 100, the general index of industrial production stood at 341.41 in 1994-95, and for manufacturing at 346.22. During 1991-92 to 1996-97, Karnataka had a compound annual growth of only 5.3 per cent in manufacturing as against the all-India average of 9.0 per cent. The share of manufacturing in SDP averaged 17.2 per cent here during 1994-97 as against 21.3 per cent in all-India (GKT 1997: 44; RBI 1998: I,1999: I). In the provision of employment also the relative position was poor. The contribution of secondary sector as a whole in total employment declined from 12.15 per cent in 1981 to 10.71 in 1991. There were six states in the latest year with higher shares of employment provided by this sector (GOI 1983, 1993). Below we give a brief look into the growth of different sectors.

Factory Sector

The performance of the factory sector in Karnataka was quite impressive. Over a period of three-and-half decades, between 1960 and 1994-95, the value of output here recorded a growth of 267 times, from Rs. 92 crores to Rs. 24,498 crores, as against only 148 times for all-India. Its relative share in all-India total rose to 4.7 per cent from 2.6. However, in the latest year there were six states with higher shares than Karnataka's (Table 5.1).

The position of net value added was quite depressing. It increased by only 224 times over the period, and consequently, in relation to output the ratio declined from 0.29 in 1960 to 0.24 in 1994-95. Nevertheless, this was the highest ratio among the major states. The per capita value added increased 19.8 times between 1970-71 and 1994-95, from Rs. 62 to Rs. 1,229, as against 20.8 times for all-India, from Rs. 57 to Rs. 1,185.

The growth in employment over the years was insignificant. It increased only four times, from 1.10 lakh in 1960 to 4.67 lakh in 1994-95. This was, however, higher than the all-India growth, the latter being only three times. The productivity of employees here also had a higher growth. The output per employee increased from Rs. 8 thousand in 1960 to Rs. 45 thousand in 1977-78 and Rs. 524 thousand in 1994-95, that is, a rise of 65 times over the entire period; for all-India, the growth in this period was only 47 times, from Rs. 12 thousand to Rs. 569 thousand (Table 5.1). Moreover, this was achieved with a lower rate of increase in fixed capital per employee. The fixed capital per employee here increased 54 times over the entire period, from Rs. 4 thousand in 1960 to Rs. 216 thousand in 1994-95, as against 69 times at the national level, from Rs. 4.4 thousand to Rs. 305 thousand.

The capital-output ratio in Karnataka showed a decline in recent years. It stood at 0.41 in 1994-95 as against 0.52 in 1977-78 and 0.48 in 1960. In relation to the all-India average, while it was higher in the earlier years, in the latest year it was significantly lower. The fixed capital to net value added also had a similar trend. At 1.71 in 1994-95, it was the lowest among all the major states. Karnataka's relative share in all-India total of the factory sector's fixed capital stood at only 3.6 per cent in 1994-95, declining from 4.3 per cent in 1977-78 (Table 5.1).

Structural Change

In terms of output value, as may be seen from Table 13.1, the major industries in the factory sector of Karnataka are machinery and equipment, food products, electricity, metal and alloys, basic chemicals, non-metallic mineral products, cotton textiles, transport equipment,

Table 13.1

Industrial Structure of Karnataka (Factory Sector)

Industry	*%share of total (1994-95)*			*Fixed capital per employee (Rs. '000)*			*Output per employee (Rs.'000)*			*Net value added to output*	
	Output value	*Employ-ment*	*Fixed capital*	*1989-90*	*1994-95*	*%rise*	*1989-90*	*1994-95*	*%rise*	*1989-90*	*1994-95*
Electricity	11.1 (7.3)	8.0	13.6	284	134	(-)52.8	219	728	232.4	0.22	0.36
Machinery and equipment	24.4 (21.6)	18.1	16.8	91	200	119.8	280	709	153.2	0.26	0.26
Non-met.mineral prod.	5.0 (5.2)	6.0	12.2	160	440	175.0	202	439	117.3	0.31	0.23
Food products	14.2 (17.7)	11.4	5.3	45	101	124.4	295	653	121.4	0.12	0.15
Basic chemicals	6.5 (6.1)	3.6	4.0	105	238	126.7	348	936	169.0	0.25	0.35
Metal and alloys	7.9 (10.3)	4.6	7.3	76	338	344.7	480	898	87.1	0.18	0.15
Cotton textiles	4.8 (4.4)	6.6	2.2	31	73	135.5	104	379	264.4	0.20	0.30
Transport equipment	4.7 (5.1)	5.5	3.2	124	124	nil	224	450	100.9	0.28	0.14
Paper and its products	4.4 (5.6)	3.9	2.7	176	150	(-)14.8	266	585	119.9	0.18	0.35
Beverages and tobacco	2.7 (3.7)	3.1	2.8	96	195	103.1	307	469	52.8	0.34	0.13
Textile products	3.6 (1.8)	13.7	3.3	10	53	430.0	89	139	56.2	0.21	0.26
Rubber, plastic etc.	3.1 (3.1)	2.7	2.3	104	184	76.9	365	603	65.2	0.10	0.04
Metal products	2.5 (2.2)	3.1	2.0	52	338	550.0	210	898	327.6	0.21	0.25
Wool, silk etc.	1.5 (1.0)	1.9	0.9	104	101	(-)2.9	147	419	185.0	0.23	0.28
Leather and its products	1.1 (1.1)	1.7	0.5	34	64	88.2	343	344	0.3	0.14	0.18
Total (incl.others)	100.0	100.0	100.0	96	216	125.0	240	524	118.3	0.22	0.24

Source: CMIE 1997b; GOI 1997.

Note: figures in parentheses relate to 1989-90.

paper and its products, textile products and rubber, plastic etc. These eleven industries together accounted for 90 per cent of the total output in 1994-95, with the share of first three at half of the total. Below we give a brief look into how these industries progressed in the last six years, that is, under the new policy of economic liberalisation.

The most important industry in Karnataka, machinery and equipment, raised its share of total output further in the last six years, from 21.6 per cent in 1989-90 to 24.4 per cent in 1994-95. Its share of fixed capital, however, declined from 17.7 to 16.8 per cent in this period. In employment also there was a nominal decline, from 18.5 to 18.1 per cent, although it continued to be the largest provider of employment. The productivity of employees had a 153 per cent rise over the period, with the fixed capital per employee rising by 120 per cent. The level of output per employee here continued to be higher than the all-industry average and in case of fixed capital lower. The net value added in relation to the gross remained static at 0.26 in this period (Table 13.1).

Food products, the next important industry in Karnataka in terms of output value, showed a depressing performance in this period. Its share of output value declined from 17.7 per cent in 1989-90 to 14.2 per cent in 1994-95. In employment also, its share decreased, from 14.4 per cent to 11.4 per cent. The output per employee here recorded an increase of only 121 per cent with the fixed capital rising by 124 per cent. The ratio of net value added to output registered a small rise but it continued to be much below the all industries' average.

The electricity industry, which accounted for the largest share of fixed capital until recently, has undergone some significant changes. Its share of output value increased from 7.3 per cent in 1989-90 to 11.1 per cent in 1994-95, whereas in fixed capital it was down to 13.6 per cent from 23.8 per cent. The fixed capital per employee was less than halved over the period down to Rs. 1.34 lakh from Rs. 2.84 lakh, but the output per employee had a 232 per cent rise in this period, from Rs. 2.19 lakh to Rs. 7.28 lakh. The net value added to output also registered a significant rise.

The metal and alloys industry is also going through a significant change. The amount of fixed capital here recorded a noticeable rise over the period but the growth in output was very low. Its share of total fixed capital in the factory sector increased from 4.1 to 7.3 per cent, but in value of output there was a decline from 10.3 to 7.9 per cent. The fixed capital per employee was more than quadrupled but in output per employee it could not be doubled even. The net value added to output which was already very low recorded a further decline. In the provision of employment also its share decreased from 5.2 to 4.6 per cent.

Among the industries with high share of fixed capital, non-metallic mineral products is an important one. But its performance in recent years has been quite depressing. Its share of fixed capital increased from 10.3 per cent in 1989-90 to 12.2 per cent in 1994-95 but in output there was a marginal decline from 5.2 per cent to 5.0 per cent. The output per employee here had a growth of only 117 per cent with the fixed capital rising by 175 per cent. The net value added to output also recorded a noticeable decline (Table 13.1).

In the provision of employment, textile products became an important industry in recent years. Its share of total employment in the factory sector stood at 13.7 per cent in 1994-95, rising from only 4.7 per cent in 1989-90. Its share of output value was also doubled, rising from 1.8 to 3.6 per cent. This was, however, accompanied by a sharp rise in fixed capital, from only 0.5 per cent of the total to 3.3. Fixed capital per employee had a more than five-fold rise over the period but the growth in output was by only 56 per cent.

Cotton textile is another important industry in the provision of employment. Its share in total employment has, however, declined from 10.2 to 6.6 per cent in this period. The output per employee here recorded a 264 per cent rise with fixed capital per employee rising by only 135 per cent. The net value added to output also registered a substantial rise.

The worst performance was probably in paper and its products. Its relative share in the factory sector's total declined in all the variables. In fixed capital, the share was down to 2.7 from 9.3 per cent, in employment from 5.0 to 3.9 per cent and in output from 5.6 to 4.4 per cent. The only appreciable thing was a near doubling of the net value added to output. Beverages and tobacco also did not perform well. The fixed capital per employee was more than doubled here but the output per employee had only a 53 per cent rise. The net value added to output was reduced drastically in this period. The transport equipment was another industry with depressing performance. There was an absolute decline in value of fixed capital, and the net value added to output was halved over the years. The share of output also declined from 5.1 per cent to 4.7 per cent.

As regards the spatial distribution of industries, most of the factories were concentrated in a few districts. In 1994-95, Bangalore alone accounted for 46.5 per cent of the total number, 3,608 out of 7,765. Three more districts – Dharwad, Dakshin Kannada and Mysore – together contributed another 20 per cent. In the total number of employees, the share of these four districts was 69 per cent. On the other hand, six districts – Kodagu, Chikmagalur, Mandya, Bidar, Uttar Kannada and Hassan -- had a combined share of only 4.5 per cent in total number of factories and 5.0 per cent in total employment (total 13.3).

The annual growth rate of the factory sector varied widely from district to district. Between 1960 and 1981, employment increased at the rate of 3.01 per cent in Shimoga and 3.83 in Chitradurga, as against the state average of 5.72 per cent. Bangalore with heavy concentration of factories, on the other hand, had an annual growth of 6.27 per cent. In some of the districts, the base was so low that even a high growth could not bring any noticeable change in the employment share. For example, Bidar had an annual growth of 17.14 per cent in this period but the total employment here even in 1994-95 stood at only 4,500 (Table 13.3).

Small-Scale Industries

Modern SSIs

According to the first census survey, in 1972, Karnataka had only 5,618 working units with an investment in fixed assets of Rs. 43.79 crores. In the all-India total, both constituted a little more than 4 per cent. The value of output totalled Rs. 79.77 crores and employment at 64.4 thousand, constituting respectively, 3.06 and 3.90 per cent of all-India total. These proportions are quite low in relation to the size of the state, or the performance in the neighbouring states. In the state's total value-added from all manufacturing industries, the SSIs contributed only 14 per cent and in total employment 6 per cent.

In the following years, it appears the growth was faster. Number of working units in this sector rose to 40,500 in 1987-88 and then to 55,893 in 1996-97 (GOI 1992;GKT 1998: I), from only 7,062 in 1972-73, that is, an eight-fold rise over the entire period. Between 1972-73 and 1987-88, the value of plant and machinery in the sector had grown 4.8 times, from Rs. 23.94 crores to Rs. 115.82 crores, of output 11 times, from Rs. 79.8 crores to Rs. 893.4 crores, and net value added 10 times, from Rs. 28.8 crores to Rs. 294.3 crores. The growth in employment was, however, much less -- only 3.8 times, from 0.643 lakh to 2.440 lakh. For the latest year, data on all the variables are not available but the amount of investment stood at Rs. 1,167.56 crores and the employment at 3.11 lakh (GKT 1998: I: 236).

The position of the technical coefficients improved significantly, except for net value added to output. The output per employee had a growth of 195 per cent, from Rs. 12,411 in 1972 to 36,609 in 1987, with fixed capital per employee rising by only 27 per cent, from Rs.

3,723 to Rs. 4,746. The capital output ratio declined to 0.13 from 0.30 over the period. Only the net value added to output recorded a decline from 0.36 to 0.32 in this period.

Table 13.2

Structural Changes in the Modern SSI of Karnataka

Industry	*Value of Output (Rs. in Lakhs)*		
	1972	*1987*	*CAGR*
Food products	1053 (13.2)	71570 (28.3)	26.8
Beverages and tobacco	13 (0.2)	6094 (2.4)	39.4
Textile products	186 (2.3)	6588 (2.6)	19.2
Wood and its products	414 (5.2)	12817 (5.1)	15.1
Paper and products	376 (4.7)	28960 (11.5)	22.8
Leather and its products	79 (1.0)	3800 (1.5)	19.0
Rubber, plastic, etc.	625 (7.8)	13819 (5.5)	12.4
Chemicals and its products	1358 (17.0)	18582 (7.3)	9.8
Non-metallic mineral products	558 (7.0)	8083 (3.2)	9.1
Basic metals	462 (5.8)	14317 (5.7)	13.7
Metal products	1134 (14.2)	31299 (12.4)	14.4
Machinery	598 (7.5)	12274 (4.9)	12.3
Electrical machinery	662 (8.3)	13247 (5.2)	14.1
Transport equipment	250 (3.1)	4279 (1.7)	11.1
Total (including others)	7977 (100.0)	252689 (100.0)	17.5

Source: GOI 1976, 1992.

Note: CAGR: Compound annual growth rate.

As regards the industry-wise structural change, there has not been much diversification over the years. As evident from Table 13.2, in 1972 three industries – chemicals, metal products and food products – together accounted for 44 per cent of total value of output. Another 31 per cent came from machinery including electrical, rubber, plastic etc., and non-metallic mineral products. In 1987, the share of first three industries increased further to 48 per cent and for the following three it declined to 19 per cent. The highest growth in value of output over the period was in beverages and tobacco, a compound annual growth of 39.4 per cent, followed by food products 26.8 per cent and paper and its products 22.8 per cent. The data for recent years are not available, but as in case of the factory sector, some significant changes must have taken place.

Table 13.3
District-wise Industrial Situation in Karnataka

Districts	*Factory sector*		*SSI Units (1987-88)*		
	CAGR in employment 1960-81	*No. of employees (in '000) 1994-95*	*Total no.*	*Production*	
				%to total	*value per unit (Rs.'000)*
Bangalore (U)	6.27	4053	6051 (-)[b]	47.1	1965
Bangalore (R)	-	192	697 (100.0)	0.5	189
Belgaum	8.59	450	2755 (36.4)	3.2	296
Bellary	6.91	187	2027 (30.8)	2.4	305
Bijapur	11.65	126	1712 (51.1)	1.3	196
Bidar	17.14	45	972 (47.2)	1.2	314
Chikmagalur	11.99	40	1002 (44.7)	0.8	191
Chitradurga	3.83	232	2139 (32.0)	3.5	414
Kodagu	14.25	23	305 (61.3)	0.3	241
Dharwad	7.84	616	4814 (49.9)	7.2	376
Gulbarga	4.75	224	1419 (35.2)	0.9	160
Hassan	5.33	70	1164 (33.8)	4.3	943
Uttar Kannada	5.89	131	895 (64.5)	0.8	260
Dakshin Kannada	-0.34	438	3867 (53.4)	13.1	856
Mandya	6.71	102	955 (57.6)	1.1	204
Kolar[a]	-	174	1315 (32.2)	0.9	241
Mysore	4.01	568	2211 (32.1)	3.1	353
Raichur	10.40	144	1594 (46.7)	2.2	352
Shimoga	3.01	258	2928 (48.7)	3.6	314
Tumkur[a]	-	107	1803 (46.2)	2.4	339
Total	5.72	8180	40525 (38.3)	100.0	624

Source: GOI 1992; Vyasulu 1995; GKT 1996.
Notes: a: for factory sector, these two districts are included in Kodagu.
b: percentage in rural areas.

The growth of SSIs was not well spread-out among the districts, or to the rural areas. As evident from Table 13.3, in the total value of output from the sector in 1987-88, two districts, namely, Bangalore (Urban) and Dakshin Kannada, together contributed as much as 60 per cent. Another six districts, viz., Dharwad, Hassan, Shimoga,

Chitradurga, Belgaum and Mysore, together provided a quarter. Value of production per unit ranged between the highest of Rs. 19.65 lakh in Bangalore (U) and the lowest at Rs. 1.60 lakh in Gulbarga. The share of rural areas in total number of units was very low in many of the districts, and in the state as a whole it was 38.3 per cent.

The capacity utilisation by the units was generally poor. There was only five districts with above 60 per cent utilisation, and seven had below 50 per cent. The proportion of closed units in the total varied between the minimum of 17.3 per cent in Bidar and the maximum at 38.7 in Mandya, with the state as a whole at 26.3 per cent. Among the reasons behind closure, the most common was found to be financial problem, 33 per cent of the total number, followed by marketing problem 16 per cent (Vyasulu 1995).

Khadi and Village Industries

The performance of KVI in Karnataka was not at all satisfactory. The value of production here registered a rise of only 321 per cent between 1982-83 and 1993-94, from Rs. 50 crores to Rs. 161 crores. This was much behind the all-India growth, as may be seen from Table 5.4, and consequently its relative share in the latter declined from 6.6 to 5.0 per cent. All the neighbouring states had a faster growth than Karnataka's. In employment too the growth was low. Over the 12-year period, there was only a 47 per cent rise, from 1.7 lakh to 1.72 lakh persons, as against 55 per cent at the national level. The productivity of the employees was, however, much better here than the all-India average. At Rs. 9,337 per employee in 1993-94, it was 55 per cent higher than the national average. In 1982-83, the situation was still better.

As regards the composition of production, in 1993-94, khadi provided 10.7 per cent of the total, valued at Rs. 17.18 crores, and the balance by village industries. In khadi, cotton accounted for the lion's share of 62.3 per cent, followed by woollen 23.8 per cent and the balance by silk. In village industries, in the total value of Rs. 143.4 crores, seven items -- ghani oil, PCPI, biogas, cottage leather, cane gur and khandsari, carpentry and blacksmithy and cottage pottery -- together contributed as much as 87 per cent. The share of ghani oil alone was 29.7 per cent, followed by PCPI 15.0 per cent and biogas 10.2 per cent. In ghani oil, Karnataka accounted for 13.1 per cent of all-India total production this year.

In the provision of employment, khadi's contribution was more than double its share in production, being 23.3 per cent of the total. In village industries, relatively high employment was provided by cottage leather, bee-keeping, cottage pottery and carpentry and blacksmithy. Their combined share in 1993-94 was 52.3 per cent, which is more than double their share in production. The most labour-intensive activity was bee-keeping, with only 0.9 per cent of total production; its share in employment was 14.4 per cent.

That the potential for growth in KVI is immense is evident from a look at the production situation in neighbouring Tamil Nadu. In khadi, Karnataka's production in 1993-94 was only a quarter of the total in Tamil Nadu. In silk khadi, the latter's production was eleven times that of the former. Among village industries, in cottage match Tamil Nadu's production was six times that of Karnataka's, in bee-keeping four times, in polyvastra around six times and in cottage soap around 13 times.

Household Enterprises

The household enterprises, as noted in the relevant preceding chapters, include those working on own account and also those employing not more than five hired workers, designated respectively, as OAMEs and NDMEs. This sector is very large in every state, at least in terms of employment. In Karnataka, total number of such enterprises was estimated at 924,973 in 1989-90, that is, nearly 20 times the number in modern SSI. In the all-India total number of such enterprises Karnataka's share was 5.3 per cent. These enterprises are located mostly in rural areas. In Karnataka rural areas share was 73 per cent of the total.

The rural enterprises were generally smaller than the urban ones. The OAMEs accounted for 96 per cent of the total here as against 83 per cent in urban areas. The value of output per enterprise averaged only Rs. 6,132 in rural areas whereas in urban areas it was as much as Rs. 22,899. The range was wider in the former than in the latter. The highest output per enterprise was as much as 56 times the lowest in rural areas, being Rs. 31,991 in paper products and only Rs. 570 in electrical machinery, appliances etc. In urban areas, it was between Rs. 96,091 in agro-processing and Rs. 4,775 in beverages and tobacco, that is, only 20 times.

In terms of provision of employment, the important industries in rural areas are beverages and tobacco, wood and wood products, food products, repair services, non-metallic mineral products, wool, silk and synthetic textiles, leather etc., textile products and cotton textiles. However, the first two alone accounted for 63 per cent of the total, with the share of beverages etc., at 45 per cent. Another fifth came from the following four industries. In urban areas, the concentration was much less. Here, six industries -- beverages, repair services, basic chemicals, wood and wood products, cotton textiles and textile products -- together accounted for 64 per cent of total employment, with the first two contributing 32 per cent.

With regard to value addition by household enterprises, there was a significant difference between the rural and urban areas. The gross value added as percentage to total output per enterprise averaged 72 in the former as against only 49 in the latter. The variation among industries in the rural areas was between 99 per cent in beverages etc., and 34 in agro-processing, and in urban areas between 91 in beverages etc., and 21 in textile products. In the method of marketing also the rural and urban areas differed widely. In the total output, the proportion of work done for other enterprises averaged 61 per cent in rural areas, with 90 per cent in case of eight industries. In urban areas, the average for all industries came to only 37 per cent.

Karnataka's relative position among the states with regard to household enterprises is quite depressing. As may be seen from Table 5.5, in rural areas, the value of fixed assets per enterprise was only Rs. 4,089 in Karnataka as against Rs. 6,338 at the national level; Karnataka's was the lowest among southern states also. With regard to value of working capital per enterprise, the situation was still worse. In Karnataka it was only Rs. 140 as against Rs. 523 for all-India. In urban areas, the situation was only slightly better. The value of fixed assets per enterprise stood at Rs. 13,441 here as against Rs. 18,690 at the national level. Among the southers states, however, the level was exceeded by Kerala only.

On the health of industrial units in Karnataka, as in other states, no comprehensive data are available. The situation is particularly depressing for the household enterprises; there is virtually no monitoring at all of their sickness or death. Only some data are available on the large-scale sector and stronger among the SSI units.

In the large-scale sector, Karnataka's position appears to have worsened over the years. Number of sick units here, as may be seen from Table 5.6, increased from 20 in June 1982 to 82 in March 1990 and then to 144 in March 1996. Karnataka's relative share in all-India total number of sick units rose to 5.8 per cent in 1996 from 4.6 per cent in 1982. The growth in outstanding bank credit with them was, however, relatively low. It increased by three-and-half times over the period, from Rs. 141 crores to Rs. 493 crores, as against 5.1 times at all-India level. The proportion in the latter declined from 8.2 per cent to 5.6.

The situation of SSI units has improved significantly in recent years. Between 1985 and 1994, number of sick units increased by 165 per cent, but in March 1997 it was reduced by more than half. Karnataka's share in all-India total number rose to 5.9 per cent from 4.8 per cent and then declined to 3.0 per cent. Among the southern states, it had the smallest number of sick units in 1997. The outstanding bank credit also moved in a similar way. It increased by 162 per cent between 1985 and 1994 and then registered a nominal decline. Karnataka's relative share in all-India total of bank credit with the SSI declined from 7.3 per cent in 1985 to 5.6 in 1997 (Table 5.6).

The industrial situation of a state depends on a variety of factors, as noted in the preceding chapters. Below we give a brief look into the position of only two of them: provision of bank credit, both short and long, and the infrastructural situation.

Provision of Bank Finance

So far as working capital is concerned, large-scale industries generally do not suffer from any scarcity in meeting their genuine needs. The problem was actually with the small and tiny sectors, particularly the latter. To look into the situation in recent years, between 1988-89 and 1994-95, the outstanding bank credit to industry from the SCBs registered a 130 per cent rise – from Rs. 2,460 crores to Rs. 5,662 crores – as against 113 per cent in the aggregate of bank credit to Karnataka. The relative share of industrial credit rose to 44.1 per cent from 40.8. An overwhelming proportion of this credit, however, went to the large and medium industries. The share of SSI, including artisan and village industries, was only 20.6 per cent in 1994-95, declining from 32.7 in 1988-89. The growth in credit to them was by only 45 per cent, from Rs. 805.3 crores to Rs. 1,168.9 crores. The provision to artisan and village industries was very small. The amount outstanding against them in this period fluctuated between the highest of Rs. 54.4 crores in 1990-91 and the lowest at Rs. 42.7 crores in 1992-93 (CMIE 1998b).

The relative position of Karnataka among the states in providing credit to SSIs was also not good. As may be seen from Table 5.7, in the aggregate of credit to SSIs its share showed a declining tendency in recent years – down to 6.0 per cent in 1995 from 6.5 in 1983. In the number of units assisted, the fall was from 6.8 per cent to 4.4 in this period. The neighbouring states of Maharashtra and Tamil Nadu, which already had high shares, on the other hand, raised them further.

In the provision of term loans to industries, Karnataka's position was quite good. Per capital cumulative assistance by all financial institutions till March 1997 stood at Rs. 3,189 in Karnataka as against the all-India average of Rs. 2,587. However, in neighbouring Maharashtra and Tamil Nadu it was at higher levels. In recent years also the trend was similar. The average for 1992-97 came to Rs. 429 here as against Rs. 347 for all-India (Table 5.8).

Major portion of this assistance had been provided by all-India financial institutions. Their share in the cumulative total till March 1997 was as much as 89 per cent; the balance came from the SFC and SIDC. The per capita assistance from the SFC till March 1997 was only Rs. 659, and from the SIDC Rs. 229. However, in relation to the performance in other states, these were excellent achievements. The all-India average of per capital assistance from SFCs in this period was only Rs. 223 and in case of SIDCs Rs. 103. The KSFC's assistance was the highest among all the states.

As regards assistance to the SSI, the SIDBI, which came into existence only in 1990, provided a per capita cumulative assistance of Rs. 372 till March 1997 as against the all-India average at Rs. 197; Karnataka was second only to Gujarat. The KSFC's level of assistance was also substantial. It provided a cumulative total of Rs. 1,365.5 crores till March 1994, constituting 11.5 per cent of all-India total. There were only two states, Maharashtra and Gujarat, providing a higher amount to SSIs. However, in the aggregate of assistance provided by the KSFC, the share of SSI was only 67.5 per cent, which is lower than the average for all SFCs, being 70.5 per cent (Table 5.8).

Infrastructural Situation

The position of infrastructure in Karnataka had been relatively weak. An infrastructure development index prepared for 1992-94 by using 13 indicators placed Karnataka in ninth position. The value for it was 96.5 (taking all-India=100) as against the highest of 191.5 in Punjab. All the neighbouring states, except Andhra, had higher values (Table 1.1). Among the districts there were wide gulfs in availability of infrastructure. An index prepared for 1991 by using ten infrastructural items gave Bangalore 33,140 as against less than 3,000 in 11 districts, with Bidar having only 1,306 and Kodagu 1,748. In 1976, Bangalore scored 44,812 and ten districts had less than 3,000 with the lowest at

1,000 in Bidar (Prahladachar 1996). Thus, there has been an insignificant reduction in disparity over the years.

These indices are based on a number of items some of which do not have any direct relevance to industrial growth. Therefore, we give a brief look below into two of the critical items, availability of power and of transport.

On the availability of power Karnataka's position has not been satisfactory. The electricity generation fell far short of the requirement in recent years. In 1995-96, the shortfall in generation as compared to unrestricted demand stood at 28.6 per cent and rose to as much as 47.8 per cent in 1996-97. After import from neighbouring states and the contribution of central stations, the state was left with an annual deficit of 4,924 million units in 1996-97 (GKT 1998: I: 201). Power consumption rose to 15,984 million units in 1995-96 from 6,032 million units in 1981-82 and 2,947 million units in 1970-71, that is, a 5.4-fold rise over the 26-year period. The electricity generation in this period had a growth of only 3.2 times -- from 4,883 million units in 1970-71 to 15,534 million units in 1995-96. Import of electricity rose to 4,820 million units from only 846 million units in 1983-84 and 2 million units in 1970-71.

Karnataka's power generation mix is about 75 per cent hydel and only 25 per cent thermal. The power sector therefore, relies largely on good monsoons. However, the potential even in the former is still largely unexploited. Karnataka is endowed with a hydropower potential of about 7,800 MWs, of which only about 2,500 MWs has been harnessed. The cumulative total of installed capacity from all sources is presently 3,510 MWs, which is half the level in Tamil Nadu. The Eighth Plan had a target of creating 1,140 MWs of additional capacity but only 379 could be created (GKT 1997: A-28, 1998: 201).

The power consumption by industries had a slow growth in recent years. It increased from 5,055 million kwh in 1988-89 to 6,499 mkwh in 1995-96, that is, by 28.6 per cent, as against 34.2 per cent in overall consumption. The relative share of industry consequently declined from 41.5 per cent to 39.8. The average tariff rate for industries came to 273.81 paise/kwh in 1995-96 as against the average for all consumption at 114.36 paise (GKT 1997: Table 4.7). The industrial power consumption varied widely among the districts. While for the state as a whole the per capita consumption came to 90 kwh in 1993-94, in Bidar it was only 16 kwh and in Raichur 35 kwh.

As regards transport facility, availability of roads in Karnataka is not totally disappointing. In 1995-96, it had 744 km of road length per thousand sq km of area as against the national average at 731 km. There were, however, eight major states -- including two from South India -- with higher road length. The proportion of unsurfaced roads in Karnataka was relatively low. It stood at only 31.67 per cent in 1995-96 as against 44.50 at the national level. Among the southern states it has the lowest proportion of unsurfaced roads (CMIE 1998a). On the availability of vehicles, however, Karnataka's position is not good. In 1996-97, vehicle density per sq km was only 13.26 here, which was lower than the levels in seven of the major states, including two southern states -- Tamil Nadu and Kerala (CMIE 1999e). As regards railways, the situation here is quite depressing. Route length per thousand sq km stood at only 16.29 km in 1994-95, and this was the lowest among the southern states (CMIE 1997b).

That the industrial climate and infrastructural situation in Karnataka are less attractive is evident from some other data also. Number of companies at work in Karnataka at the end of February 1998 stood at only 21,146 with the paid-up capital at Rs. 8,5674 crores, constituting 4.26 per cent of all-India total. Th per capita paid-up capital (on the basis of population estimate for 1997) came to only Rs. 689.58 in Karnataka as against the all-India average at Rs. 2,104.69 and Maharashtra's Rs. 4,341.12. The situation appears to have improved somewhat in recent years. Number of joint stock companies registered annually in Karnataka averaged 2,003 during 1993-96 as against only 733 during 1985-88 (GKT 1997). Presumably, this is a product of the new liberalised policy.

The central investment in public sector undertakings was also low in Karnataka. The investment in gross block increased from Rs. 845 crores in 1980-81 to Rs. 4,260 crores in 1993-94, that is, a growth of only five times as against nine times in all-India total from Rs. 21,182 crores to Rs. 198,912 crores. Karnataka's share in the latter declined from 4.0 per cent to 2.1 in this period. The position of the neighbouring states was incomparably better. Investment in Maharashtra increased 21 times in this period and in Andhra Pradesh 16 times. Their share in all-India total rose to 19.8 per cent and 8.1, respectively, in 1993-94 from 8.6 and 4.7 in 1980-81. The growth of employment in central PSUs was negative in case of Karnataka – declining from 1.17 lakh persons to 1.03 lakh over the period – as against a 43 per cent rise in Maharashtra and 36 in Andhra (CMIE 1996c). The assurance of bringing regional balance in development was apparently only a lip-service.

14

Towards Poverty Alleviation

We have noted in Chapter 2 that the poverty situation in Karnataka was very grim at least till the end of seventies, and in the following years also the improvement here was less satisfactory than in a number of states. The percentage of rural population below the poverty-line was 55 in 1973-74, which was higher than in six of the major states. After two decades, in 1993-94, although it declined to 30 per cent the relative position remained the same. The proportion of rural households with monthly per capita expenditure of less than Rs. 300 was as much as 72 per cent in 1993-94 (NSSO 1998b). The object of this chapter is to look into how some of the special programmes launched for the weaker sections were implemented in Karnataka.

Wage Employment Programmes

Programmes for wage employment were particularly important in Karnataka as the state had a large proportion of agricultural labourers. In the total of main workers in rural Karnataka, agricultural labourers constituted 32.4 per cent in 1981 and increased to 35.9 in 1991; the all-India averages in these years were respectively, 30.1 and 32.3 per cent (GOI 1993). The wage employment programmes, however, did not get any importance in the state until recent years.

The first scheme to be launched was the crash scheme for rural employment in 1971, that is, two decades after economic planning started. It created a total of 137.48 lakh mandays during 1971-72 to 1973-74, that is, an annual average of 45.83 lakh mandays, with a total expenditure of Rs. 603.48 lakhs. In the all-India total of employment created under the scheme, Karnataka's share came to 4.35 per cent. Among the activities undertaken, construction of roads accounted for as much as 73.4 per cent of total expenditure, followed by minor irrigation 14.8 per cent (GOI 1979).

In the following years until 1980, there was no national employment programme in operation in Karnataka. The NREP was launched in September 1980, and in 1983 came the RLEGP for providing some guaranteed employment.

The expenditure under NREP totalled Rs. 113.61 crores during 1980-85 and Rs. 150.77 crores in the following four years. Under RLEGP Rs. 136.11 crores were spent during 1983-89 (GKT 1991a). The unemployment situation, however, continued to be worse than in most other states. According to the NSS, the person rate of unemployment in Karnataka stood at 29.06 in 1983, which was higher than the level in 12 of the major states (NSSO 1987). In 1989, as observed in the preceding chapters, the JRY was launched and to it the NREP and RLEGP were merged. Below we give a brief look into the operation of JRY in Karnataka.

The Jawahar Rozgar Yojana

Under the scheme, since inception to March-end 1997, 3411 lmd of employment were generated in Karnataka, incurring an expenditure of Rs. 1,156.26 crores. The community assets created were of various types. Till the end of March 1996, a total of 46,498 ha was covered by social forestry, with trees planted numbering 1,551 lakh. Soil conservation work was done on 30,933 ha, land development works 15,193 ha and flood protection works on 2,039 ha. Buildings and house construction constituted a very large proportion of the works. Total number constructed under the scheme, including the IAY, came to 172,240 till the end of March 1996. In the total, IAY contributed 49.0 per cent. Among other works, construction of rural roads totalled 81,601 kms, of village tanks 3,013 number, drinking water wells, ponds etc., 28,246 and sanitary latrines 15,907. The year-wise break-up of the progress in JRY is presented in Table 14.1.

The growth in expenditure varied widely from year to year. Whereas in 1993-94 there was a 40 per cent rise over the preceding year, in the following year it was down to a rise of only 5 per cent; earlier, 1990-91 had recorded a negative growth. Moreover, there was no clear relation between the amount spent and number of mandays created. In two of the years, increase in expenditure was accompanied by a large decline in employment. The cost per manday created had a steep rise suddenly in 1994-95 over the preceding year.

In the nature of activities chosen also no definite priorities seem to have been followed. Almost in every item there was wide fluctuation

Table 14.1

Progress of JRY in Karnataka: Expenditure, Employment and Asset Creation

Year	Amount utilised (Rs. lakhs)	Employment generated ('000 nos.)	Cost per manday (Rs.)	Community Assets		Created			
				Social forestry no.of trees ('000)	Soil conservation (ha)	Wells and Ponds (nos.)	Rural roads (kms.)	School bldgs. (nos.)	Construction of houses (nos.)
1989-90	10943 (-)[a]	40758 (-)[a]	26.85	41017	3795	885 (567)[b]	23134	3915	13284 (6321)[c]
1990-91	10892 (-0.47)	48657 (19.4)	22.39	12748	1266	1093 (612)	9370	2881	11324 (5214)
1991-92	11083 (1.75)	40164 (-17.45)	27.59	48314	15075	2600 (2028)	11730	3038	9845 (5216)
1992-93	12534 (13.09)	41792 (4.05)	29.99	1518	4001	5403 (3803)	9615	2911	11731 (5118)
1993-94	17571 (40.19)	58864 (40.85)	29.85	27273	3663	4814 (4081)	9511	3780	17436 (10496)
1994-95	18502 (5.30)	39713 (-32.53)	46.59	17519	2810	8234 (6001)	8023	1880	18701 (13911)
1995-96	21987 (18.84)	46074 (16.02)	47.72	6714	323	5217 (4572)	10218	2614	44835 (38132)

Source: GKT 1997.

Notes: a: figures in parentheses here are percentage increase/decrease over the preceding year.
b: construction of wells under MWS.
c: construction under IAY.

from year to year. Number of trees planted under social forestry varied between the highest of 483 lakhs in 1991-92 and the lowest at 15 lakhs in 1992-93. The soil conservation work covered 15,075 ha in 1991-92 but in the following years it declined drastically and in the last year stood at only 323 ha.

The district-wise performance in JRY varied widely. The allocation of fund itself was not always linked to the urgency of need. For example, in 1996-97, Dharwad received as much as 9.56 per cent of the total but Belgaum with the same population size got only 3.83 per cent. Similarly, Kodagu received 2.20 per cent and Mandya only 1.99 per cent although the latter's population was more than three times the former's. The cost per manday created differed widely from district to district. In 1996-97, at the highest it was Rs. 70.84 in Mandya and at the lowest Rs. 39.26 in Hassan.

In the employment generated, the share of SC/ST often fell short of the norm in many districts. For example, in 1996-97, there were four districts, namely, Bangalore (R), Bellary, Dakshin Kannada and Uttar Kannada, each having less than 30 per cent of total for them, in the first one only 11.7 per cent. For landless labourers, the deprivation was more severe. In the total employment created their share was less than 20 per cent in seven districts, namely, Bangalore (R), Dakshin Kannada, Tumkur, Kodagu, Kolar, Belgaum and Hassan; in the first three it was less than 10 per cent.

The relative position of Karnataka among the states was also not satisfactory. In the all-India total of fund spent on this programme during 1989-95, Karnataka's share was only 4.7 per cent, that is, less than its population share. In the total employment generated, the share of SC/ST in Karnataka was 40.1 per cent as against the all-India average at 55.6. The proportion for landless here was only 38.6 per cent as against 45.5 in all-India (Table 6.1).

In the implementation of JRY there was large-scale violation of the guidelines in Karnataka. The first concurrent evaluation (1992) had found the following major deficiencies (Neelakantan 1994):

(i) The wage/non-wage ratio in Karnataka this year was 52: 48 as against the laid down norm of 60: 40. This was a serious violation given the fact that the programme is primarily for employment creation. However, Karnataka's is not an isolated case; even the all-India average came to 53:47. The wage rates paid were also in violation of the norm. The requirement was to pay the local off-season rates but the payments made were much lower. The off-season rates for male unskilled and skilled workers were, respectively, Rs. 23.63 and Rs. 50.48 but the rates paid were Rs. 16.03 and Rs. 32.01. The stipulation that man and woman be paid equal wages was also violated, as in most other states.

(ii) The quality of assets created was found to be inferior to a larger extent in Karnataka. The proportion of satisfactory assets was 66.75 per cent here as against 73.80 at the national level. Incomplete assets constituted 23.76 per cent and 15.71 per cent, respectively.

(iii) The extent of additional employment created was relatively low here. A JRY worker could get only 2.59 persondays of work under JRY in a month as against 3.81 at the all-India level. For other members of the family it was, respectively, 0.87 and 1.34 persondays. Moreover, non-poor benefiting from the scheme was very high here. Those with income level of above Rs. 6,400 – that is, the poverty-line income -- constituted 56.16 per cent of total workers.

(iv) The involvement of contractors in execution of works, which was prohibited, was found to be very high in Karnataka. It was to the extent of 19.25 per cent of works as against 4.25 per cent at the national level. Further, the requirement of properly maintaining the muster rolls was violated to a large extent. It was not even available in 8.08 per cent of cases, not to speak of maintaining properly.

(v) The guidelines required discussion of the Annual Action Plan at Gram Sabha meetings but its observance was generally an exception here. In only 14 per cent of cases it was observed as against 60.7 per cent at the national level.

All these deficiencies were probably corrected somewhat in the following years. But the more disturbing aspect presently is that the scheme is being drastically reduced in size. In 1998-99, total fund available for the JRY was only Rs. 95.41 crores and the target for employment fixed at 188.8 lmd (GOI 1999). These constitute, respectively, 43.3 and 41.0 per cent of what were achieved in 1995-96. This is of course, party due to the fact that the intensive JRY has now been taken out of it and included in the EAS.

Employment Assurance Scheme

Under the EAS, launched in October 1993, no financial or physical targets are fixed; expenditure is incurred according to the requirements of the taluks. Block-wise list of projects are required to be prepared in December every year. Fifty per cent of the expenditure here is stipulated to be spent on watershed development. The area coverage of the scheme has increased significantly over the years. In 1993-94, it operated in only 94 taluks of Karnataka but presently it is 162.

Since the inception of the scheme to March-end 1997, 797.48 lakh mandays of employment were created in Karnataka by spending Rs. 351.54 crores. The annual expenditure increased from Rs. 6.78 crores (for six months) in 1993-94 to Rs. 80.24 crores the following year and Rs. 143.07 crores in 1996-97. Although the number of taluks under the scheme has increased, the expenditure has recorded an absolute fall in the recent years. In 1998-99 only Rs. 134.92 crores was made available, constituting 4.8 per cent of the fund available at the national level; the shares of Andhra and Tamil Nadu were around 9 per cent each (GOI 1999; GKT 1997c).

The expenditure incurred was always less than what was available. In 1993-94, the amount utilised was only 19.2 per cent of that available and in 1994-95 it increased to 72.7 per cent. This was the situation despite the fact that all those who were registered could not be provided with employment. The number registered in 1994-95 stood at 21.26 lakhs but only 14.31 lakhs could get employment; and that too for only 12.4 mandays each as the total employment generated this year was 177.45 lakh mandays. Karnataka's was, however, not an exceptional situation. Even at the national level, the fund utilised was always less than what was available. In 1993-94 and 1994-95, the utilisations were to the extent of 33.5 and 69.6 per cent, respectively (GOI 1996c).

In the employment created, the weaker sections did not always get their due share. In 1994-95, for example, the share of SC/ST in total employment was only 35.2 per cent in Karnataka as against 58.6 per cent at the national level; for women, these were respectively, 22.0 and 30.9 per cent; in case of landless however, the proportions were 43.8 and 23.3 per cent.

As regards assets creation, in the total expenditure till March 1996, roads alone accounted for 32.0 per cent, followed by soil conservation including social forestry and silvipasture 29.6 per cent and minor irrigation and building construction together 37.7 per cent, distributed almost equally. In the total number of completed works at 40,796, however, the share of soil conservation etc., was 55.3 per cent, of roads 15.5 and buildings 14.8 (GKT 1997c).

District-wise, the nature of performance varied widely. In 1996-97, for example, out of 314.18 lakh mandays created, seven districts – Kolar, Bijapur, Dharwad, Chitradurga, Belgaum, Tumkur and Mysore

– together contributed 55 per cent. The utilisation of available fund was very low in some of the districts. In Mandya it was only 2 per cent and in Uttar Kannada 33 per cent as against the state average of 74 per cent this year. Among the beneficiaries from employment, the share of SC/ST varied between 53 per cent in Mysore and the lowest of 7 per cent in Kodagu, with the average for all districts at 37. The representation of women varied between 40 per cent in Bellary and only 3 per cent in Kodagu, with the state as a whole at 29. For landless workers, the proportion was as much as 75 per cent in Bidar but six districts had less than 10 per cent, with the state average at 42 (GKT 1997c).

The employment schemes in operation could not bring any noticeable improvement in the situation. Participation in public works per thousand households increased from 32 in 1987-88 to 39 in 1993-94. These were much behind the all-India averages, being 64 and 59, respectively (NSSO 1998a). The concurrent evaluation of JRY in 1992 had found that a JRY worker in Karnataka could get a total of 20.4 mandays of employment in a month, including 17.81 under other programmes. The impact on wage rates also appears to be negligible. According to a study by Jeemol Unni, the real agricultural wage rate (at 1960-61 prices) for adult males in Karnataka was the lowest among the southern states. It stood at the average of Rs. 2.2 during 1993-95 as against Rs. 3.4 in Kerala, Rs. 2.8 in Andhra and Rs. 2.4 in Tamil Nadu (Unni 1997).

Self-Employment Programmes

As we have noted in Chapter 6, the first discernible measure for creating self-employment opportunities in rural areas came only in 1971, with the launching of the Small Farmers' Development Agency. However, it was not particularly focused on the population below the poverty-line. The programme specifically targeted towards the weaker sections came only in 1980, designated as the Integrated Rural Development Programme. The procedure for its implementation has been described in Chapter 6; here we only look into how the programme was implemented in Karnataka.

IRDP

Since the inception to March-end 1997, the programme assisted 22.46 lakh families by providing subsidy totalling Rs. 403.91 crores and bank credit to the extent of Rs. 847.52 crores. On annual basis, the investment (subsidy plus credit) increased from Rs. 29.3 crores in 1980-81 to Rs. 71.9 crores in 1990-91 and Rs. 148.5 crores in 1996-97, that is a growth of five times over the entire period. It was, however, not a steady growth, as may be seen from Table 14.2. The number of beneficiaries rose to the maximum of 2.02 lakhs in 1983-84 and at the minimum 0.87 lakh in 1981-82. Per capita investment increased from Rs. 2,690 in 1980-81 to Rs. 12,703 in 1996-97, that is, a growth of 4.7 times. The proportion of subsidy in investment showed a rising tendency. It averaged 24.5 per cent during 1980-83 and rose to 33.1 during 1994-97. Among the beneficiaries, the proportion of SC/ST could never reach the stipulated norm.

Table 14.2

Trend in Assistance Under IRDP in Karnataka

Year	*Total investment (Rs. lakhs)*	*Subsidy (Rs. lakhs)*	*Per capita investment (Rs.)*	*No. of beneficiaries (in '000)*
1980-81	2929	642 (21.9)[a]	2690	108.9 (16.3)[b]
1981-82	3140	801 (25.5)	3591	87.4 (-)
1982-83	5591	1462 (26.2)	3126	178.8 (-)
1983-84	5528	1676 (30.3)	2734	202.2 (-)
1984-85	6130	1869 (30.5)	3356	182.6 (26.9)
1985-86	5363	1638 (30.6)	3604	148.8 (24.6)
1986-87	6008	1817 (30.2)	4135	145.3 (27.4)
1987-88	7487	2234 (29.8)	4675	160.1 (25.6)
1988-89	7918	2346 (29.6)	5070	156.2 (9.6)
1989-90	7410	2244 (30.3)	5283	140.3 (28.8)
1990-91	7194	2410 (33.5)	5754	125.0 (36.4)
1991-92	6409	2191 (34.2)	5889	108.8 (40.7)
1992-93	6468	2193 (33.9)	6228	103.9 (38.4)
1993-94	9202	3187 (34.6)	6926	132.4 (37.8)
1994-95	10150	3429 (33.8)	8067	125.8 (38.5)
1995-96	12457	4258 (34.2)	10408	119.7 (37.7)
1996-97	14849	4645 (21.3)	12703	116.9 (36.1)

Source: GKT 1997c.

Notes: a: as percentage to total investment.
b: percentage of SC/ST.

The relative position of Karnataka among the major states does not appear satisfactory. In 1997-98, to look at the latest position, the total of fund utilised here constituted only 4.9 per cent of all-India total as against 8.4 per cent in Tamil Nadu and 5.4 per cent in a small state like Orissa. In the all-India total number of beneficiaries, its share was 5.5 per cent as against 10.6 in case of Tamil Nadu. The proportion of SC/ST beneficiaries in the state's total was only 39.7 per cent this year as compared to 46.4 at the national level. Earlier, the situation was still worse. In 1990-91, the state's share in all-India total of fund utilised was only 3.8 per cent and in number of beneficiaries 4.3 per cent. The coverage of SC/ST was only 36.4 per cent as against 48.7 at the national level. The per capita investment here continued to be relatively low. In 1997-98 it stood at Rs. 15,516 as against the all-India average of Rs. 18,200 (Table 6.2).

District-wise, there was considerable variation in performance. To look at the situation in 1996-97: In as many as 12 districts, the district's share of total spending under IRDP was less than its share in total rural population. Belgaum had the highest share of 10.60 per cent in total spending with its population share at 8.83 per cent and Chikmagalur 5.54 and 2.72 per cent, respectively. On the other hand, Bidar had 2.07 and 3.25 per cent respectively, Bellary 3.19 and 4.27, Hassan 3.58 and 4.17 and Tumkur 4.95 and 6.19 per cent (GKT 1997c). Per capita investment varied between the highest of R. 16,584 in Raichur and the lowest at Rs. 8,917 in Mandya. The credit-subsidy ratio was only 1.07 in Chitradurga as against 2.96 in Bellary. The norm for SC/ST representation could be fulfilled by only eight districts, and on women by six districts.

There were many loopholes in implementation of the programme. Wrong identification of families and supply of substandard assets were quite common. The role of after-care support or monitoring was not given any importance. As a result many of the poor beneficiaries sold off the asset soon after obtaining it. The support provided often proved to be of relief nature, rather than a step toward making the beneficiary cross the poverty-line on a sustainable basis.

The target approach and intervention by politicians added greatly to the problem of proper management of the programme.

TRYSEM and DWCRA

The TRYSEM, as seen in Chapter 6, provides training to rural youths selected from among the families identified under the IRDP. Since inception to March 1997, 1.68 lakh youths were trained in Karnataka under the programme with an expenditure of Rs. 36.60 crores. The number trained annually did not have a steady growth. Thus, while it rose to 9,706 in 1984-85 from 4,130 in 1980-81, in the following six years it remained at lower levels. The highest number trained in a single year was 18,096 in 1996-97. The number trained did not have any clear relationship with the amount spent. Thus, while the amount spent under the scheme increased from Rs. 489 lakhs in 1994-95 to Rs. 666 lakhs in the following year, the number trained declined from 17,542 to 16,602 (GKT 1997c).

As regards placement, the situation has been quite gloomy. In 1989-90, only 22.7 per cent of the total number trained could be employed, 1,469 out of 6,455. The proportion getting employed on wages was 3.8 epr cent. In recent years the situation has improved considerably. During 1995-97, 46.7 per cent of the total number trained got employed. In 1995-96, 33.8 per cent of the youths were self-employed and 15.6 per cent on wages.

The relative position of Karnataka among the states appears to have improved considerably in recent years. Its share in the all-India total number trained rose to 6.2 per cent in 1995-96 from 3.0 per cent in 1989-90. The proportion of SC/ST trained has also improved significantly. Their share in Karnataka and at the national level in 1989-90 were, respectively, 24.7 and 44.5 per cent, and in 1995-96 49.4 and 47.7 per cent. In placement also the situation was similar.

District-wise, there was extreme of variation in performance. In 1996-97, for example, in the total number trained, five districts – Belgaum, Uttar Kannada, Mysore, Gulbarga and Dharwad – together accounted for 37 per cent, with the first one alone contributing 11 per cent. The achievement, in relation to target, was to the extent of 211 per cent in case of Belgaum as against the lowest of 54 per cent in Raichur and the state average at 110 per cent. In Hassan, while the financial achievement was 238 per cent of the target, on number trained it was only 87 per cent. The norm regarding SC/ST was violated in most of the districts. In only four districts the proportion was 50 per cent or above. As regards placement of the trainees, none could be employed this year in four of the districts.

As regards the programme on women and children, Karnataka's performance has not been significant. The allocation of finance for it was very meagre until recently. During 1992-95, a total of Rs. 234 lakhs was allocated to the scheme, of which Rs. 213 lakhs could be spent. Number of groups formed in this period was 1,651 against the target of 1,866. In the last two years, 1995-97, however, there was a big jump in the expenditure on it. The total amount spent rose to Rs. 602 lakhs, that is, nearly three times that spent in the preceding three years; the allocation was of course, as much as Rs. 966 crores, that is, more than four times that in the earlier period. The target on formation of groups was 3,866 during 1995-97 but only 2,888 could be formed (GKT 1997c).

District-wise, there was wide disparity in performance. In 1996-97, the fund utilisation in relation to the target varied between the maximum of 148 per cent in Kolar and the minimum at 54 per cent in Bidar, with the state average at 72 per cent. In physical term, the variation was of incredible nature. The achievement in relation to target was 597 per cent in case of Bijapur as against the minimum of 36 per cent in Mandya. There was almost no relationship between the financial and physical achievements. The expenditure per group came to only Rs. 2,300 in Bijapur as against Rs. 87,350 in Dharwad, with the state average at Rs. 21,279. Five districts, viz., Bijapur, Belgaum, Bellary, Chitradurga and Hassan, together accounted for 46.8 per cent of the total number of groups formed, with the first one alone contributing 21.6 per cent. The share of these districts in total spending came to 32.6 per cent (calculated from GKT 1997c).

Minimum Needs Programme

Although the situation on certain basic services was far from satisfactory in Karnataka, the MNP could be launched here only in the Fifth Plan, along with that in the other states. And then also the fund allocation for it was not significant. The Sixth Plan provided for an outlay of Rs. 207.86 crores, constituting 9.2 per cent of the grand total. In the all-India total outlay under MNP, Karnataka's share came to only 4.2 per cent.

With this level of outlay, the targets set were however, very ambitious. To mention a few of them: On elementary education, 95 per cent enrolment to be achieved in the age-group 6-11 and 50 per cent for 11-14; rural water supply to cover all the remaining problem villages by 1985 excepting some difficult hilly areas; Rural roads to cover 50 per cent of the villages required to be covered; and housing assistance to be provided to all remaining households by allotting house-sites, and assistance for construction of houses to 25 per cent of the eligible households.

Out of the total fund allotted to MNP in the Sixth Plan, rural housing received the highest of 26.5 per cent, followed by rural roads 21.6, elementary education 14.4, rural health 9.6 and rural water supply 9.1 per cent. Thus, these five items together accounted for 81.2 per cent of the total (Table 14.3). This pattern of distribution was significantly different from that at the national level. In the latter, rural water supply, rural roads and elementary education together accounted for 69.7 per cent of the total (Deb 1997: 241).

Table 14.3

Trend in Outlays under the Minimum Needs Programme in Karnataka

(Rs. in lakhs)

Programmes	*Sixth Plan (1980-85)*	*Seventh Plan (1985-90)*	*Eighth Plan (1992-97)*
Rural electrification	140 (0.7)	5368 (7.1)	7493 (3.4)
Rural roads	4500 (21.6)	4944 (6.6)	12000 (5.4)
Rural housing	5500 (26.5)	8440 (11.2)	46920 (21.3)
Elementary education	3000 (14.4)	5401 (7.2)	71657 (32.5)
Adult education	500 (2.4)	2217 (2.9)	2281 (1.0)
Rural health	2003 (9.6)	7871 (10.5)	13050 (5.9)
Rural water supply	1900 (9.1)	20551 (27.3)	53110 (24.1)
Nutrition	2243 (10.8)	18361 (24.4)	5750 (2.6)
Environmental improvement of slums	1500 (7.2)	1136 (1.5)	4440 (2.0)
Rural fuelwood plantation	1230 (5.9)	899 (1.2)	1400 (0.6)
Grand total	20786 (100.0)	75232 (100.0)	220628 (100.0)

Source: GKT 1985, 1997.

In the Seventh Plan, as evident from Table 14.3, the expenditure on MNP was more than trebled, rising to Rs. 752.3 crores, and constituted 18.5 per cent of the grand total. In the sectoral outlays, the share of rural water supply and nutrition increased dramatically – for the former to 27.3 per cent of the total and for the latter to 24.4 per cent. The share of rural roads and rural housing, on the other hand, recorded sharp declines. For elementary education also, the proportion was halved, declining to 7.2 per cent. Rural fuelwood plantation, which is of critical importance for the poor people, had a drastic decline in this plan – from 5.9 per cent of the total in the Sixth Plan to only 1.2 per cent. This pattern of distribution was at variance with that for all-India. In the latter, rural water supply and elementary education together received as much as 55.7 per cent. One may question the pattern of priorities followed in Karnataka, but the basic problem is that every sector required a much higher allocation, given the magnitude of the problem.

During the Eighth Plan, the growth of outlay on MNP decelerated. There was an increase of only 193 per cent over the preceding plan, and its relative share in the total plan outlay declined to 14.8 per cent. The sectoral priorities changed again. Three areas, viz., elementary education, rural water supply and rural housing, together received as much as 78 per cent of the total outlay, for the first one alone 32.5 per cent. The most drastic decline over the preceding plan's level was in case of nutrition; even the absolute amount was down to only one-third. The relative shares of rural health, rural electrification and rural roads also declined noticeably. Adult education which never received much attention, got only one per cent in this plan, and for rural fuelwood a negligible 0.6 per cent.

Given the size of the problem, and the leakages of fund, all these expenditures were utterly inadequate for raising the level of social services to a minimum desirable level. The enrolment rate in I-IV standards reached 94.20 per cent only in 1996-97, and that too continued to be plagued by a drop-out rate of 19.68 per cent. The incentives like free textbooks, uniforms and midday meals could not stop the dropping out from schools. The midday meals covered 47.80 lakh children in 1996-97 as against the enrolment of around 55 lakh in standards I-IV. On drinking water facility, even in 1996-97, there were 4,104 villages yet to be covered and 34,893 partially covered. As regards village roads, at the end of March 1995, although the number of villages not connected by roads stood at only 151, 48.4 per cent of the total number of roads were *katcha* and non-motorable and fair-weather roads (GKT 1997, 1998).

Public Distribution System

The PDS in Karnataka does not seem to have benefited the weaker sections much, at least until recent years. Even the share of rural areas as a whole was relatively low. We may quote here the findings of a NSSO survey for the period July 1986 to June 1987 (NSSO 1990). On the most important item, rice, the rural area's share in Karnataka was found to be only 55.75 per cent of the total purchases from the PDS. This was much below the level in most other states, the all-India average in this period being 71.01 per cent. Even for foodgrains as a whole it was low. The ratio of rural to urban per capita foodgrain consumption from the PDS was found to be only 0.637 in Karnataka, and this was exceeded by as many as eight major states. On other items also the situation was no better. In edible oil, the rural area's share in total purchases was 33.36 per cent in Karnataka as against the all-India average at 58.71 per cent; in sugar, the shares were, respectively, 47.88 and 78.81 per cent; and in kerosene 45.72 and 54.58 per cent.

A look into the proportion of total purchase made from the PDS also reveals a strong urban bias. In case of rice, the proportion in rural areas was 22.22 per cent as against 25.69 in urban areas. For edible oils, these were respectively 10.57 and 27.75 per cent, in sugar 44.35 and 58.45 and, in kerosene 38.76 and 42.59 per cent. At the national level, except for sugar, the proportions in rural areas were higher.

The weaker sections were not much benefited from the PDS. In case of rice, the bottom two decile groups in rural areas made 26 per cent of their total purchases from the PDS; in edible oils, for the first decile it was 12.01 per cent and for the second 7.18 per cent; in kerosene, 43.70 and 34.33 per cent, respectively; and in sugar 46.10 and 48.86 per cent. These proportions were not higher than the average for all categories in every case.

As the above data relate to only one year, in order to get a more realistic idea, we refer to another study covering a long period (Geetha and Suryanarayana 1993). According to this study, the per capita PDS of foodgrains in Karnataka averaged 19.48 kg per annum during 1973 to 1989, and varied between 11.29 and 28.38 kg. There were six major states -- including Kerala, Tamil Nadu and Maharashtra among the neighbouring states -- with higher mean availability. In recent years also the situation has not improved much. In 1993-94, the per capita distribution of foodgrains in Karnataka stood at 18 kg and it was exceeded by four of the major states (Mooij 1999).

As regards the availability to poor population – that is, those below the poverty-line – the per capita PDS for them stood at only 24 kg per annum in 1974 and rose to 55 kg in 1977; in the following years until 1987, however, it was at much lower levels, as may be seen from Table 6.4. In relation to other major states, Karnataka's position deteriorated significantly. Even in 1987, when the highest quantity was supplied to poor, there were nine states, including the three southern states, providing larger quantities to their poor.

In recent years, the position of the poor in Karnataka must have improved considerably. There are presently 112.40 lakh cardholders in Karnataka, of which 79.7 per cent are in rural areas. Green or tricolour cards were issued to those with an annual income of less than Rs. 6,400. Green cardholders get 10 kg of foodgrains a month at subsidised rates, and they constitute 71.3 per cent of the total in rural areas. Under the revamped PDS, introduced in June 1992, Karnataka has 94 blocks in 14 districts. In these areas, 18 kg of Rice and 2 kg of wheat are given to cardholders -- 10 kg at the rate applicable to green cards and the rest at lower RPDS rates.

In November 1996, there were 19,552 fair price shops functioning in the state, 72.9 per cent of which were in rural areas. There are 13 mobile fair price shops set up in 13 integrated tribal areas. Fair price shops per lakh population is 196 in Karnataka. The government has constituted a vigilance committee for each fair price shop to supervise the distribution of essential commodities. During 1993-96, the off-take from PDS averaged 830.9 thousand tonnes of rice and 265.3 thousand tonnes of wheat (GKT 1997).

The relative position of Karnataka among the major states, however, does not appear satisfactory even now. The total allotment of foodgrains declined from 18.03 lakh tonnes in 1995-96 – that is, before targeting -- to only 9.00 lakh tonnes in 1996-97, after targeting; the relative share in all-India total allotment was down to 5.46 per cent from 7.05 per cent. The allotment for BPL families in 1996-97 constituted only 38.3 per cent of the total to Karnataka as against 42.7 per cent at the national level (Mooij 1999).

Poverty alleviation required multi-pronged attack on poverty. There was need not only of specific measures for those lying below the poverty-line, but also of determined efforts towards developing the backward areas. But the required initiative was either not coming at all, or coming too slowly. As an example of the government's lack of seriousness towards developing the backward areas, we may cite here the situation of Hyderabad-Karnataka region.

The Hyderabad-Karnataka Region

The H-K region was a part of the former Hyderabad state and historically it was backward as the government there did not have a development perspective. But after integration into the Mysore State the new government also did not take much interest in its development. The per capita income of the three districts -- Bidar, Gulbarga and Raichur – that comprised it did not show any noticeable growth over the years, as noted in Chapter 2. In relation to the state average, the most backward district, Bidar, had only 67.2 per cent in 1960-61 and stood at 71.2 per cent in 1994-95. A composite index of development prepared by the State Planning Department gave the three districts an average of 62.4 in 1960-61, taking the state average at 100, and 76.2 in 1979-80. There was no change in their ranks over the years, being always the last three (GKT 1981, 1990: 1: Table 11).

The level of development of some of the infrastructure was very poor. Net irrigated area as percentage to net sown area in the region (including Bellary district) was only 8.3 in 1976-77 and increased to 17.3 in 1991-92. Per capita consumption of power in the region was only 112 kwh in 1993-94 as against 313 kwh for the state. In agriculture, the consumption per hectare of gross cropped area was only 12 kwh as against 512 kwh in the state (Pasha 1996; Samuel 1996).

Bidar district provides a telling example of neglect by the state. Though some 82 per cent of its total land is cultivated, only 8 per cent of the cultivated area is irrigated. The two major irrigation projects, Karanja started in 1963 and Chulkinala started in 1972, are yet to be completed (Vasavi 1999). Bidar was once a home to many cottage industries, such as cotton and oil-ginning mills. But now there are few industries to draw on local raw materials or skills.

There was demand for constitution of a special development board for the region since the reorganisation of the state. But a committee for this purpose could be set up only in May 1980, and the Hyderabad-Karnataka Development Area Board set up after another more than a decade, in December 1992.

V

The Economy of Kerala

15

Resource Mobilisation and Deployment

The budgetary position of Kerala government was no better than that of most other states. Particularly distressing was the extent of deficit on revenue account. During 1994-97, it annually averaged Rs. 481.9 crores as against Rs. 126.5 crores during 1985-88. The overall situation was, however, not so bad. In the last seven years of the nineties, it had surplus in all but one, and the average for 1994-97 came to Rs. 161.9 crores. Below we give a brief look into the trend in different types of receipts and expenditure.

Resource Mobilisation

The aggregate of budgetary receipts of Kerala government increased from the annual average of Rs. 146 crores during 1965-68 to Rs. 7,103 crores in 1994-97, that is, a growth of around 49 times over the period of three decades. This is much lower than that registered by all states together, being 60 times, and consequently, its relative share in the latter declined to 3.5 per cent from 4.3 over the period. The per capita receipts in 1994-97, averaged Rs. 2,232 which was marginally lower than the all-states, average (Table 3.1).

Revenue Receipts

In the total receipts, revenue receipts, which is more important, played a relatively larger role here. Ignoring fluctuations, as evident from Table 15.1, its share rose to 76.2 per cent in 1994-97 from 70.5 in 1965-68. In the latest period, there were five states with higher contribution from revenue receipts (Table 3.1). The growth in revenue receipts was relatively low here. Over the entire period, it was by 52.5 times as against 64.1 times for all states together. Despite this, the per capita revenue receipts of Kerala during 1994-97 came to Rs. 1,700

Table 15.1

Trend in Budgetary Position of Kerala

(Rs. in crores)

Year/Period	*Receipts*			*Expenditure*			*Revenue deficit/ surplus*	*Overall deficit/ surplus*
	Revenue	*Capital*	*Total*	*Revenue*	*Capital*	*Total*		
1965-68 (a.a.)	103.5 (70.7)a	42.8	146.3	98.9 (67.6)b	47.3	146.2	4.6	0.1
1975-78 (a.a.)	389.0 (77.0)	116.4	505.4	395.5 (75.8)	126.5	522.0	-6.5	-16.6
1985-88 (a.a.)	1507.4 (71.8)	591.9	2099.3	1633.9 (76.6)	500.0	2133.9	-126.5	-34.6
1988-89	1897.1 (76.7)	577.0	2474.1	2061.0 (81.8)	459.9	2520.9	-163.9	-46.8
1989-90	2047.6 (71.5)	816.9	2864.5	2298.1 (79.5)	590.9	2889.0	-250.5	-24.5
1990-91	2503.5 (71.9)	976.9	3480.4	2824.8 (81.6)	635.9	3460.7	-321.3	19.7
1991-92	2852.1 (72.1)	1105.0	3957.1	3216.4 (80.3)	788.7	4005.1	-364.3	-48.0
1992-93	3318.7 (74.5)	1134.1	4452.8	3656.1 (83.8)	706.6	4362.8	-337.4	90.0
1993-94	3922.0 (74.9)	1315.7	5237.7	4293.4 (83.6)	844.9	5138.2	-371.4	99.5
1994-95	4666.4 (73.4)	1691.9	6358.3	5066.3 (85.0)	892.4	5958.7	-399.9	399.6
1995-96	5423.6 (77.6)	1563.3	6986.9	5826.4 (84.2)	1095.5	6921.9	-402.8	65.0
1996-97	6145.1 (77.2)	1818.3	7963.4	6788.1 (85.5)	1154.4	7942.5	-643.1	20.5
1994-97 (a.a.)	5411.7 (76.2)	1691.2	7102.9	5893.6 (84.9)	1047.4	6941.0	-481.9	161.7

Source: As in Table 7.1.

Notes: a: as percentage to total receipts.
b: as percentage to total expenditure.

which was significantly higher than the average for all states. In the total revenue, tax revenue always accounted for the major share. We analyse below the pattern of its growth over the years.

Tax Revenue

Kerala's performance in collection of tax revenue has been quite impressive. As evident from Table 15.2, the amount collected increased from the annual average of Rs. 60 crores during 1965-68 to Rs. 1,129 crores in 1985-88 and then to Rs. 4,399 crores in 1994-97, that is, a growth of 73 times over the entire period. There were only four major states recording a higher growth (Table 3.2). The relative share of tax revenue in the total rose to 81 per cent in 1994-97 from 75 in 1985-88 and 58 in 1965-68. In the latest period there were only two states with higher contribution from tax revenue. In relation to the state's NSDP, tax revenue contributed 11.2 per cent during 1984-90 as against the average of 8.0 per cent for all the major states (GOT 1997: 217).

Table 15.2

Trend in Tax and Non-Tax Revenue of Kerala

(Rs. in crores)

Year/Period	*Tax Revenue*		*Non-Tax Revenue*	
	Total	*OTR*	*Total*	*ONTR*
1965-68 (a.a.)	59.7 (57.7)[a]	45.6 (76.4)[b]	43.8 (42.3)[a]	17 9 (40.9)[c]
1975-78 (a.a.)	246.9 (63.5)	181.5 (73.5)	142.1 (36.5)	69.4 (48.8)
1985-88 (a.a.)	1129.4 (74.9)	838.1 (74.2)	378.0 (25.1)	150.4 (39.8)
1988-89	1502.3 (79.2)	1065.5 (70.9)	394.8 (20.8)	181.4 (45.9)
1989-90	1688.4 (82.5)	1232.5 (73.0)	359.2 (17.5)	174.4 (48.6)
1990-91	1859.8 (74.3)	1373.5 (73.9)	643.7 (25.7)	220.5 (34.3)
1991-92	2250.4 (78.9)	1673.9 (74.4)	601.8 (21.1)	323.2 (39.1)
1992-93	2573.9 (77.6)	1887.0 (73.3)	744.8 (22.4)	279.4 (37.5)
1993-94	3096.0 (78.9)	2344.9 (75.7)	826.0 (21.1)	323.2 (39.1)
1994-95	3637.5 (78.0)	2799.1 (77.0)	1028.9 (22.0)	396.3 (38.5)
1995-96	4419.6 (81.5)	3382.7 (76.5)	1003.9 (18.5)	535.5 (53.3)
1996-97	5141.1 (83.7)	3898.5 (75.8)	1003.9 (16.3)	513.8 (51.2)
1994-97 (a.a.)	4399.4 (81.3)	3360.1 (76.4)	1012.2 (18.7)	481.9 (47.6)

Source: As in the preceding table.

Notes: a: percentage to total revenue receipts.
b: percentage to total tax revenue.
c: percentage to total non-tax revenue.

In the tax revenue, as evident from Table 15.2, the proportion of own tax revenue did not show any consistent rise, rather it recorded declines until recent years. The contribution stood at 76.4 per cent in 1965-68, and after declines to lower levels rose again to the same level in 1994-97. The growth in collection over the entire period was 74 times, from Rs. 46 crores to Rs. 3,360 crores. Although this performance was better than the average for all states, in the latest period there were six states with higher contribution from OTR (Table 3.2). In tax efforts, that is, per capita tax collection, also Kerala's position was similar. It increased from Rs. 27.44 in 1967-68 to Rs. 1,120 during 1994-97, that is a growth of 41 times. There were only five states with higher per capita tax in the latest period.

Table 15.3

Trend in Composition of Own Tax Revenue in Kerala

(Rs. in lakhs)

Items	*1975-78 (a.a.)*	*1988-91 (a.a.)*	*1994-97 (a.a.)*
1. Taxes on income	660 (3.6)	1712 (1.4)	1847 (0.5)
2. On property and capital transactions	1856 (10.2)	12722 (10.4)	36749 (10.9)
(i) Land revenue	340 (1.9)	1254 (1.0)	2289 (0.7)
(ii) Stamps and regist.fees	1487 (8.2)	11007 (9.0)	33663 (10.0)
(iii) Urban immov. property	29 (0.2)	467 (0.4)	796 (0.2)
3. On commodities and services	15636 (86.1)	107943 (88.2)	297413 (88.5)
(i) Sales tax	10590 (58.3)	78643 (64.3)	230773 (68.7)
(a) State sales tax	9582 (52.8)	71996 (58.8)	208844 (62.2)
(ii) State excise	2958 (16.3)	17257 (14.1)	40700 (12.1)
(iii) Taxes on vehicles	1518 (8.4)	6992 (5.7)	21812 (6.5)
(iv) Taxes on electricity	421 (2.3)	4906 (4.0)	3475 (1.0)
Total	18152 (100.0)	122383 (100.0)	336009 (100.0)

Source: As in Table 15.1.

The trend in composition of OTR is presented in Table 15.3. As in other states, here also taxes on commodities and services contributed an overwhelming proportion of the total. Its share stood at 88.5 per cent during 1994-97 and 86.1 in 1975-78. In this group again, sales tax alone contributed 77.6 per cent of the total in 1994-97, rising from 67.7 in 1975-78; state sales tax provided more than 90 per cent of it. State excise was the next important item in this group, and its share declined from 18.9 per cent to 13.7 over the period. Taxes on vehicles and on electricity were the other two important items, but the collection from them had a relatively low growth. The relative share of the former declined from 9.7 to 7.3 per cent, over the period.

Of the remaining two groups, taxes on property and capital transactions had a share of around 11 per cent in 1994-97 and 10 per cent earlier. Here stamps and registration fees contributed more than 90 per cent in recent years and 80 per cent during 1975-78. The land revenue which contributed 18 per cent in 1975-78, now provided only 6 per cent with a growth in collection of 6.7 times. The urban immovable property tax had a rapid growth in collection but then also its relative share was very low – only 2.2 per cent of the group total (Table 15.3).

The taxes on income had a negligible contribution in Kerala. The collection increased from an annual average of Rs. 6.6 crores in 1975-78 to Rs. 18.5 crores in 1994-97, and its relative share in OTR declined from 3.7 per cent to a negligible 0.5. Here agricultural income tax was the only contributor in recent years. Profession tax which is there in most other states is no longer levied here, being transferred to local bodies. During 1975-78 it contributed an average of Rs. 5 lakhs.

From the above, it is apparent that there is ample scope for raising the tax collection in Kerala. There are a good number of items where the rate of growth is quite low, and in some there has been even absolute declines. To give one example, the collection from taxes on goods and passengers was an average of Rs. 1.09 crores during 1975-78 but over the years it became almost non-existent.

In the total tax revenue, transfers from the Central Government contributed a significant proportion. It was generally around a quarter, and the amount transferred increased from the average of Rs. 14.1 crores during 1965-68 to Rs. 65.3 crores in 1975-78 and Rs. 1,039 crores during 1994-97, that is, a growth of 74 times over the entire period. The tax transfer to all states together had risen by 85 times in this period, and consequently, Kerala's share in the total declined from 4.0 per cent to 3.5 per cent.

Major portion of the tax transfer came from union excise duties. During 1994-97 it accounted for 59.0 per cent, and the balance came from income-tax. Two decades earlier, in 1975-78, the shares were respectively, 58.0 and 41.3 per cent. The amount transferred under union excise duties increased from Rs. 37.9 crores to Rs. 625.2 crores, and under income tax from Rs. 26.9 crores to Rs. 405.8 crores in this period.

Non-Tax Revenue

Kerala's performance in non-tax revenue was very depressing. Its relative share in total revenue was less than halved over the years, falling from 42.3 per cent in 1965-68 to 20.1 in 1994-97. The growth in collection was only 23 times over the entire period as against 52 times for all states together. In fact, Kerala's was the lowest growth among all the major states, as may be seen from Table 3.2.

In the NTR, the share of state's own collection, as evident from Table 15.2, increased from 40.9 per cent in 1965-68 to 48.8 in 1975-78, but in the following years it remained at a much lower level and then rose to the average of 47.6 in 1994-97. The growth in collection was only 27 times over the entire period as against 50 times for all states together. The ONTR's contribution in NTR was higher than Kerala's in as many as ten states in 1994-97, including all the southern states. In order to locate the areas of weakness, below we give a brief look into the composition of Kerala's ONTR.

Group-wise, the highest contributor to ONTR had always been the economic services. Its share in the total, however, declined from 51.5 per cent in 1975-78 to only 35.5 in 1988-91 and then rose to 47.2 in 1994-97. Within economic services, as may be seen from Table 15.4, the single most important item was forestry and wildlife. Its share in the group total stood at 67.3 per cent in 1994-97, rising from 55.3 in 1988-91. Even in the aggregate of ONTR it contributed 31.8 per cent in the latest period. This is apparently quite natural, given the proportion of forest area in the state. But the question remains, how long it can be maintained in view of the need for protecting the forests.

The contribution from all other items were very low. Some of them no doubt registered a rapid growth, but even then the relative shares remained low. For example, the contribution from industries in the group total stood at only 6.2 per cent in 1994-97, even after a growth in collection of 108 times over 1975-78. Cooperation had registered a growth of 18 times over the period, but its relative share stood at only 5.6 per cent in 1994-97. Crop husbandry also provided a similar share with a growth of around 14 times. The collection from irrigation facilities was an average of only Rs. 2.89 crores in 1994-97, rising from Rs. 1.01 crores in 1975-78, although the investment here was not negligible.

The next important group was general services, with a contribution of 27.7 per cent in 1994-97, rising from 13.6 during 1975-78. State lotteries had been the single largest item here, contributing as much as

69.5 per cent of the total during 1988-91. In the neighbouring states it had a much less significant role, and the average for all states came to 34.6 per cent during 1988-91. The collection from general services is likely to decline noticeably in the near future as the court has banned lotteries recently. As regards contribution from social services, with a growth in collection of only a little more than four times over the last two decades, its relative share in total ONTR declined from 17.7 per cent to 10.7 per cent. The most important contributor here was education, sports etc., accounting for 54.2 per cent of the total during 1994-97, followed by medical services etc., 30.4 per cent.

Table 15.4

Trend in the Components of ONTR in Kerala

(Rs. in lakhs)

Items	*1975-78 (a.a.)*	*1988-91 (a.a.)*	*1994-97 (a.a.)*
Interest receipts	1095	2470	6459 (5.9)[d]
Dividends and profits	103	151	478 (4.6)
General services	944	6587	13351 (14.1)
Social services	1226	3193	5136 (4.2)
Economic services	3575	6810	22762 (6.4)
Crop husbandry	104	287	1415 (13.6)
Animal husbandry	58	284	403 (6.9)
Fisheries	53	72	109 (2.1)
Forestry and wildlife	2487	3763	15322 (6.2)
Cooperation	70	480	1280 (18.3)
Major and med. irrigation	101[a]	190	222
Minor irrigation		79	67 (2.9)
Village and SSI	13[b]	100	216 (108.0)
Industries		173[c]	1188
Tourism	-	79	408 (-)
Total ONTR	6944	19210	48188 (6.9)

Source: As in Table 15.1.

Notes: a: includes irrigation, navigation, drainage and flood control.

b: includes receipts from mines and minerals other than royalty on minerals and mineral concession fees.

c: includes non-ferrous mining and metallurgical industries and other industries.

d: figures in parentheses are growth between 1975-78 and 1994-97 in number of times.

Of the remaining two groups, interest receipts play a relatively low role here. Its contribution to total ONTR was only 13.4 per cent in 1994-97 as against 15.7 in 1975-78. In most of the other states, this item played a much bigger role. As regards dividend and profit, the picture is very gloomy in Kerala. During 1994-97, it provided an annual average of Rs. 4.78 crores, constituting a negligible 1.0 per cent of the total. There were 96 government companies operating in the state in 1995-96, rising from 85 in 1987-88. The total of capital invested in them rose to Rs. 2,230.50 crores in 1996-97 from Rs. 852.69 crores in 1987-88. But a majority of them had been incurring losses. In 1991-92, 57 of the units incurred a total loss of Rs. 86.72 crores and in 1996-97 for 41 companies it was Rs. 139.62 crores (GKL 1997). Among statutory bodies, Kerala State Electricity Board had incurred a total loss (commercial) of Rs. 690 crores in the last four years (1994-95 to 1997-98) alone (CMIE 1999d).

In the NTR, grants from the Centre generally accounted for the major portion and rose to the highest of 66 per cent in 1990-91. The amount of grants increased from the annual average of Rs. 25.8 crores in 1965-68 to Rs. 72.6 in 1975-78 and then to Rs. 530.3 crores during 1994-97, that is, a growth of 20.6 times over the entire period. This is less than half the growth in grants to all states, being 54 times over the same period. In the total transfer to Kerala, the share of grants declined from 64.5 per cent in 1965-68 to 52.6 in 1975-78 and 33.8 in 1994-97.

Looking to the aggregate of central transfer to the state, it declined from 38.8 per cent of the state's total revenue in 1965-68 to 35.5 in 1975-78 and further to 29.0 per cent during 1994-97. In the latest period, there were eight major states receiving a higher share of their respective total revenue from the Centre. The per capita transfer to Kerala increased from Rs. 21 during 1965-68 to Rs. 56 during 1975-78 and Rs. 493 in 1994-97, that is, a growth of 23 times over the entire period; for all states, the growth in this period was from Rs. 15 to Rs. 567 (Table 3.4).

Capital Receipts

The growth of capital receipts in Kerala was relatively high. Between 1965-68 and 1994-97, there was an increased of 39.5 times as against 37.8 times in the aggregate for all states. However, in the total budgetary receipts of the state its share declined from 29.3 per cent in 1965-68 to 23.8 in 1994-97, with considerable fluctuations in-between. For all states together the reliance on capital receipts had a sharper fall in this period, from 37.5 to 23.8 per cent.

As regards the composition of capital receipts, the largest proportion always came as loans and advances from the Centre, as in case of other states. However, there has been a sharp decline in it over the years – from 81.2 per cent of the total during 1965-68 to 53.8 in 1975-78 and then, after a rise to 57.1 per cent in 1985-88, to only 38.3 per cent during 1994-97. This is a relatively low dependence on the Centre as the average proportion for all states came to 51.0 per cent during 1994-97.

Within central loans also certain changes have come over the years. The relative share of state plan schemes declined from 63.1 per cent during 1975-78 to 52.4 during 1994-97 whereas that for non-plan rose to 47.0 per cent from 15.7 over the same period. Further, as the combined share of these two items has risen to as much as 99 per cent, the loans under central plan schemes and centrally sponsored schemes have become negligible. Another change is that, in the non-plan loans the share of small savings has risen noticeably in recent years. During 1994-97 it accounted for almost the entire amount as against 43.8 per cent during 1975-78.

The next important contributor in capital receipts had been generally the internal debt. Its share rose to 25.9 per cent during 1994-97 from 11.8 in 1975-78. Here market loans provided the overwhelming proportion. The growth in receipts from internal debt in this period was 32 times, from the annual average of Rs. 13.7 crores during 1975-78 to Rs. 438.1 crores during 1994-97. Small savings, PF, etc., also provided a similar proportion, rising from 13.3 per cent to 29.3 over the same period. Major portion of the contribution here came from state provident fund – 58.9 per cent in 1994-97 as against 51.6 during 1975-78.

The remaining capital receipts came mainly from recovery of loans and deposits and advances. The former contributed Rs. 40.5 crores in 1994-97 as against Rs. 15.2 crores in 1975-78, that is, a growth of only 2.7 times as compared to 14.5 times in the aggregate of capital receipts. This item could have made a much larger contribution if the repayments were made in due time. The ratio of recovery to loans outstanding fluctuated between 7.74 per cent in 1995-96 and 3.97 per cent in 1992-93, in the last six years (GKL 1998).

The gross fiscal deficit – which in effect is the total additional borrowing in a given period – of Kerala government has risen rapidly in recent years. It stood at Rs. 1,661 crores in 1996-97 as against Rs. 732

crores in 1992-93, constituting respectively, 5.83 and 4.26 per cent of SDP. In 1995-96, with 5.25 per cent, Kerala had the fourth highest ratio among 16 major states. Tamil Nadu and Karnataka had 2.18 and 2.82 per cent, respectively, in this year (GKL 1998: 130).

The growth of fiscal deficit need not be objected to, if it is used for financing productive investment. But what is happening is its increasing use for covering revenue deficit. In 1996-97, 38.7 per cent of GFD was used to cover revenue deficit, rising from 36.1 in 1994-95. The average for 16 major states, on the other hand, declined from 36.3 per cent to 26 per cent in this period. Using loans to finance revenue expenditure has wide ramifications. It adds to the interest liability which, once again, increases the revenue deficit.

The total debt outstanding of Kerala government has more than doubled in the last six years. It increased from Rs. 5,466 crores in 1991-92 to Rs. 11,671 crores in 1996-97. The debt/SDP ratio stood at over 40 per cent in Kerala during 1994-97; for the major states, the average came to 30.75 per cent in 1994-95 and 32.23 in 1995-96. The per capita debt of the state increased from Rs. 1,491 in 1991 to Rs. 3,235 in 1996. Kerala is now the third highest indebted state (GKL 1998: 131).

Resource Deployment

The growth of budgetary expenditure in Kerala was relatively low. Between 1965-68 and 1994-97, it had multiplied 47 times -- from the annual average of Rs. 146.2 crores to Rs. 6,941.0 crores -- as against 52 times for all states together. In per capita term, however, Kerala's situation was significantly better than most other states. With the annual average of Rs. 2,246 in 1994-97, its level could be exceeded by only five states. Earlier, during 1965-68, at Rs. 76, there were eight states ahead of it (Table 3.6).

In the total expenditure, the proportion of revenue expenditure had grown from 67.6 per cent during 1965-68 to 76.6 during 1985-88 and then to 84.9 during 1994-97. Most other states had a lower proportion of revenue expenditure, and the average for all states stood at 81.6 per cent in the latest period. The growth in revenue expenditure was, however, relatively low here. Below we give a brief look into the changes in composition of revenue and capital expenditures.

Revenue Expenditure

A disturbing trend in revenue expenditure is the rapid growth in non-development expenditure. Between 1975-78 and 1994-97, it had grown

Table 15.5

Trend in Composition of Revenue and Capital Expenditure in Kerala

(Rs. in crores)

Items	*1975-78 (a.a.)*	*1985-88 (a.a.)*	*1994-97 (a.a.)*	*Col. (4) as multiple of col. (2)*
(1)	*(2)*	*(3)*	*(4)*	*(5)*
Total Revenue Expenditure	395.5	1633.9	5893.6	14.9
I. Development expenditure	286.8	1107.5	3491.8	12.2
A. Social services	207.2	799.8	2361.4	11.4
Education, etc.	141.9	474.3	1467.5	10.3
Medical, etc.	42.6[a]	126.6	349.7	10.5
Social security and welfare	13.7	45.5	102.8	7.5
Nutrition	-	4.6	10.8	-
B. Economic services	79.6	307.7	1130.4	14.2
Agriculture and allied	38.3	107.3	471.1	12.3
Rural development	-	77.8	213.9	-
Irrigation and flood	4.1	33.0	113.8	27.7
Village and SSI	3.5	15.8	95.0	27.1
Transport and communication	15.1	47.0	139.6	9.2
II. Non-development expenditure	108.2	524.3	2316.2	21.4
Interest payment	33.9	172.8	949.1	28.0
Administrative service	33.1	116.9	366.1	11.1
Police	18.1	62.8	209.1	11.6
Pension	17.8	168.5	678.7	38.1
Capital Disbursements	126.5	500.0	1047.4	8.3
I. Total capital outlay	59.5	197.8	544.0	9.1
Development expenditure	58.1	189.7	520.7	9.0
A. Social services	12.2	49.4	65.5	5.4
B. Economic services	45.9	140.3	455.1	9.9
Agriculture and allied	2.4	16.3	53.8	22.4
Irrigation and flood	25.7	63.6	165.1	6.4
Transport and communication	6.9	40.6	133.1	19.3
II. Repayment of loans to the Centre	37.6	194.5	148.8	4.0
III. Discharge of internal debt	4.2	16.9	22.1	5.3
IV. Loans by State Government	25.2	90.6	332.5	13.2
Development purposes	22.3	75.4	327.4	14.7

Source: As in the earlier tables.

Note: a: including sanitation and water supply.

by 21.4 times as against 15 times in the aggregate of revenue expenditure. Consequently, its relative share in the latter rose to 39.3 per cent from 27.3 over the period. In non-development expenditure, interest payment was the main burden, and it had grown 28 times in this period. The relative share of interest payment in the total rose to 41.0 per cent in 1994-97 from 31.3 in 1975-78. Even in the aggregate of revenue expenditure it constituted 16.1 per cent in the latest period. Pension payments accounted for the next highest share, and it had the fastest growth among all the items, as may be seen from Table 15.5. Its relative share in non-development expenditure rose to 29.3 per cent from 16.5, over the period of two decades.

As regards development expenditure, it recorded a growth of only 12 times over the period, and consequently its relative share declined from 73 to 61 per cent. This is the lowest proportion among the southern states. Within development expenditure, the social services had registered a lower growth than economic services. The expenditure on the former, as evident from Table 15.5, had increased 11.4 times between 1975-78 and 1994-97 as against 14.2 times in the latter. Social services, however, still accounts for a larger share of the total. During 1994-97, its share was 67.6 per cent, declining from 72.2 per cent in 1975-78.

In social services, education etc., always accounted for the largest proportion. In 1994-97, it stood at 62.1 per cent, declining from 68.5 in 1975-78. The lowest expenditure under social services had been on nutrition. During 1994-97, it annually averaged Rs. 10.8 crores, constituting just around half of one per cent. This is really strange because the extent of malnutrition in Kerala is not low. Surveys conducted in recent years showed that 47.4 per cent of children suffered from mild form of malnutrition, 32.9 per cent from moderate malnutrition and 2 per cent from severe malnutrition (GKL 1998: 120-21).

In economic services, agriculture and allied sectors accounted for the largest share throughout the period, and stood at 41.7 per cent during 1994-97 as against 34.9 in 1985-88. Rural development, a relatively new item, accounted for 18.9 per cent in 1994-97 and transport and communication 12.3 per cent; both the items had larger share in 1985-88. The highest growth in expenditure was recorded by irrigation and flood control, followed by village and small-scale industries. But their relative share in the total was not much. With a growth of 28 times in expenditure, the former's share rose to 10.1 per cent in 1994-97 from 5.2 in 1975-78; the latter raised its share to 8.4 per cent from 4.4 over the same period.

Capital Expenditure

In capital disbursements, the proportion of capital outlay varied rather widely. It declined to 39.6 per cent of the total during 1985-88 from 47.0 in 1975-78, and then rose again to 51.9 per cent in 1994-97. For all states, the proportion averaged 53.6 per cent in the latest period. Among the neighbouring states, while Tamil Nadu had a much lower proportion of capital outlay in the latest period, for Karnataka it was much higher. Development expenditure generally constituted more than 95 per cent of the capital outlay, as in case of other states.

In the development expenditure, economic services accounted for the predominant share -- as much as 87 per cent during 1994-97, 74 per cent in 1985-88 and 79 in 1975-78. In economic services, irrigation and flood control and transport and communication were provided the major portion. However, while the share of the former declined from 56.0 per cent during 1975-78 to 36.3 in 1994-97, for the latter it increased to 29.2 from 15.0 over the same period. Agriculture and allied sector, despite a rapid growth, received only 11.8 per cent of the total in 1994-97.

Next to capital outlay, the largest outgo in recent years was on account of loans and advances. Its relative share in total capital disbursement rose to 31.7 per cent in 1994-97 from 19.9 in 1975-78, with a 13-fold rise in amount disbursed. Development purposes always accounted for the overwhelming proportion here, and within it economic services. During 1994-97, 75 per cent of the total went to economic services, Rs. 246 crores out of Rs. 327 crores.

A bigger burden, until recent years, was however, the repayment of loans to the Centre. As may be seen from Table 15.5, it constituted 38.9 per cent of total capital disbursement during 1985-88, rising from 29.7 per cent in 1975-78; during 1994-97, however, it stood at the average of 14.2 per cent. The debt outstanding with Central Government rose to Rs. 4,815 crores in 1996-97, rising from Rs. 1,382 crores in 1986.

Plan Expenditure

In the budgetary expenditure of Kerala government, plan expenditure constituted a relatively low share. In 1995-96, in the aggregate of expenditure it accounted for 24.1 per cent, with the proportion in capital account at 68.0 per cent and in revenue account at 15.8 per cent. In 1989-90, these were, 23.4, 60.9 and 13.8 per cent respectively; and further backward, in 1975-76, 19.0, 50.5 and 9.1 per cent. The growth in plan expenditure over a long period and the sectoral pattern are presented in Table 15.6.

Table 15.6

Trend in Sectoral Pattern of Plan Expenditure in Kerala

(Rs. in crores)

Sectors	*Total till Third Plan*	*Total till 31.3.1980*	*Sixth Plan (1980-85)*	*Seventh Plan (1985-90)*	*Eighth Plan (1992-97)*[c]	*Ninth Plan (1997-2002)*[c]
Agriculture and allied	36.30 (12.6)	254.93 (14.9)	350.56 (19.5)	431.05 (16.9)	660.50 (12.1)	898.50 (5.6)
Cooperation[a]	16.39 (5.7)	44.96 (2.6)	38.57 (2.1)	30.96 (1.2)	-	-
Irrigation and power	124.79 (43.3)	669.87 (39.2)	618.12 (34.3)	812.66 (31.9)	1930.00 (35.3)	3699.00 (23.0)
Power	93.36 (32.4)	423.88 (24.8)	321.80 (17.9)	419.12 (16.5)	1796.43 (32.9)	2671.00 (16.6)
Industry and minerals	20.91 (7.2)	180.19 (10.5)	166.47 (9.2)	272.61 (10.7)	810.00 (14.8)	1125.86 (7.0)
Transport and communication	22.50 (7.8)	128.06 (7.5)	118.61 (6.6)	273.58 (10.8)	433.00 (7.9)	569.00 (3.5)
Social services	65.22 (22.6)	382.80 (22.4)	479.12 (26.6)	664.15 (26.1)	1077.18 (19.7)	2863.74 (17.8)
Grand total[b]	288.42 (100.0)	1709.09 (100.0)	1801.62 (100.0)	2546.91 (100.0)	5460.00 (100.0)	16100.00 (100.0)

Source: GKL 1994, 1997a.

Notes a: for Eighth and Ninth Plans, included in agriculture and allied sector.
b: in Ninth Plan, Rs. 6,000 crores for grants-in-aid to local bodies are included.
c: outlays, not actual expenditure.

In the first 15 years of economic planning in the state, the grand total of expenditure came to Rs. 288.4 crores; and in the following 14 years, five times this amount (Rs. 1,420.7 crores) was added, the cumulative total rising to Rs. 1,709 crores in March 1980. This is a substantial growth, although in depreciated money value. In the following years, the growth was more rapid. The total for Sixth, Seventh and Eighth Plans came to Rs. 9,809 crores. The per capital plan expenditure of Kerala was, however, generally less than all-India average.

Sectorally, in the first one-and-half decade, irrigation and power deservedly got the lion's share of 43.3 per cent of the total. Despite this, however, as we shall see in the subsequent chapters, the irrigation and power situation were not comfortable. Social services got the next highest allocation of 22.6 per cent, followed by the agriculture and allied sectors 12.6 per cent. In the following 14 years, the relative share of irrigation and power declined while that of industry and minerals increased. Social services maintained its share more or less, and agriculture raised it substantially. The cumulative position till March 1980 may be seen from Table 15.6.

In the following plans also, the sectoral priorities varied considerably. However, irrigation and power continued to receive the highest allocation; the average for the four five-year plans came to 31.1 per cent. The share of irrigation in it was low, only 10.1 per cent of the total. Social services received an average of 22.5 per cent, agriculture and allied sectors 13.5, industry and minerals 10.4 and transport and communication 7.2 per cent.

A distinguishing feature of Kerala's budgetary expenditure is that a very high priority was given to expenditure on social services. In the aggregate of expenditure, its share varied between 53 per cent in 1971-72 and the lowest of 31 per cent in 1989-90; the average for 1994-97 came to 37 per cent. Naturally it was reflected in the availability of educational and health facilities. Another noticeable feature is the activation of local self-governments and transfer of resources to them. We give a brief look into this aspect below.

Local Bodies

On decentralised planning and resource mobilisation Kerala government took some important steps in recent years. In 1989-90, for the first time, village panchayats were provided with untied plan grants for utilisation according to their own priorities. Detailed guidelines were issued for the formulation of local level plan. In the Eighth Plan, the share of each district was initially fixed on the basis of average of last ten years' annual plan outlays, and subsequently a more objective set of criteria was adopted. Nearly 77 per cent of the outlays was to be earmarked for schemes to be drawn up by the village panchayats. The amount provided was, however, not much. In 1995-96 it amounted to only Rs. 30 crores, and in the next year raised to Rs. 143 crores. The urban local bodies were provided Rs. 69 crores as untied plan grants for the first time in 1996-97.

The success in decentralised planning was however, very limited. A review of utilisation of the untied funds revealed that none of the local bodies prepared any plan. The method generally followed was to divide funds equally between ward members for various works, mostly roads, selected by them. The state government nevertheless, was not discouraged by the experience; rather it was decided to increase the allocation for this purpose. From 1997-98, 35-40 per cent of the state plan outlay was to be earmarked for programmes drawn up by the local bodies (GKL 1998:148-49). The People's Campaign for Decentralised Planning was launched in August 1996 for equipping the local bodies to prepare their own five-year plans.

As regards the financial position of panchayats, due to lack of data we note here the situation in only one of the recent years. In 1993-94, the total receipts of gram panchayats (GPs), numbering 990, came to Rs. 136.18 crores, that is, an average of Rs. 13.76 lakhs per panchayat. In the aggregate of receipts, taxes contributed 60.7 per cent, non-tax revenue 11.5 per cent and grants 24.2 per cent. In the aggregate of tax receipts at Rs. 82.69 crores, own taxes contributed 53.0 per cent, followed by assigned taxes 37.9 per cent and and the balance from shared taxes (GKL 1998:145). In the OTR, tax on buildings accounted for around 50 per cent and professional tax 29 per cent. The assigned taxes were surcharge on stamp duty and basic tax. In non-tax revenue, income from properties accounted for 50-60 per cent of the total. The grants-in-aid for the local bodies included tied or specific purpose grants, in addition to the untied grants noted above. The untied portion constituted 63 per cent of the total in 1993-94. The capital receipts of GPs constituted only 3.5 per cent of the total this year.

The gram panchayats varied widely in terms of their revenue. Although recent data are not available, in 1983, according to a classification than in practice, there were 339 special grade GPs with annual revenue of over Rs. 1.75 lakh, 435 first grade GPs with Rs. 1.00 lakh to Rs. 1.75 lakh, 206 second grade with Rs. 50 thousand to one lakh and 10 GPs with revenue below Rs. 5,000 (GKL 1998: 145).

As regards expenditure, the establishment charges are a major claimant to the income of GPs. In 1993-94, it accounted for 36.7 per cent of the total expenditure of Rs. 123.37 crores. Public works, such as roads and buildings, constituted the main developmental activity, accounting for 42.4 per cent of the total. The share of streetlighting was 6.4 per cent, of education 2.6, public health 2.1 and drinking water 1.7 per cent. The low expenditure on water supply is partly due to its centralisation under Kerala Water Authority. The plan expenditure of panchayats is confined to the untied plan grants, and the schemes mandatorily implemented through them.

The urban local bodies numbered 55 and they had a combined total receipts of Rs. 111.43 crores in 1993-94. In their total receipts, capital receipts constituted 14.6 per cent. In the total of revenue receipts at Rs. 95.11 crores, the share of tax revenue was 70 per cent, own non-tax revenue 21.5 per cent and the balance grants. In the tax revenue, own taxes constituted 83.3 per cent, assigned taxes 11.7 and the balance shared taxes.

The total expenditure of municipalities and corporations came to Rs. 116.59 crores in 1993-94, of which 15.9 per cent went for establishment charges. Among developmental activities, public works constituted 32.9 per cent of total expenditure, followed by public health 21.2, drinking water 9.0 and streetlighting 6.2 per cent. The expenditure on debt servicing constituted 8.6 per cent (GKL 1998: 147).

16

Agricultural Transformation

Although agriculture is a critical sector to Kerala's economy, as in other states, its relative contribution has declined noticeably over the years. During the Eighth Plan (1992-97) it provided 30.86 per cent of the state's income as against 33.79 per cent in the Sixth Plan (1980-85) and 49.6 per cent in the Third Plan (GKL 1969, 1992, 1998). As compared to many other states Kerala is less dependent on agriculture. In 1994-97, the proportion of SDP derived from agriculture stood *at* to remain 27.6 per cent here and it was exceeded by as many as nine of the major states (RBI 1998, 1999). Among the southern states, only Tamil Nadu had less dependence on agriculture. In employment, agricultural workers constituted 56 per cent of the rural workforce in Kerala as against 79.8 per cent at the national level in 1991 (Table 2.2).

The object of this chapter is to look into the pattern of growth of agriculture and allied sectors since independence. The analysis is on the lines followed in the preceding chapters on agriculture. First, agriculture proper has been discussed, and then a brief analysis of the allied sectors.

I
Agriculture

Till early eighties agricultural growth in Kerala was one of the lowest. Between 1960-61 and 1982-83, production of all crops together increased at an annual rate of 1.71 per cent as against 2.48 per cent at the national level. However, in the sub-period of 1960-61 to 1974-75, the growth rates were, respectively, 3.22 per cent and 2.19 per cent. It was the negative growth of 0.39 per cent in the following years that brought down the rate for the entire period. The yield rate in Kerala increased at a slower rate than in all-India. During 1960-61 to 1982-83, the former had only 0.63 per cent while the latter recorded 1.62 per cent annually (Sivanandan 1994).

In recent years, however, the growth in production was significantly better. The SDP from agriculture grew at a compound annual rate of 3.81 per cent during 1981-82 to 1995-96 as against 3.10 per cent for all-India. The index of production for all crops stood at the average of 144.93 during 1994-97 with the base of triennium ending in 1979-80. The indices of area and productivity were 104.62 and 120.67 respectively (Sawant 1997;GKL 1998). Below we give a brief look into the crop-wise growth in production and productivity.

Foodgrains

Kerala has always been a food deficit state, and the situation has deteriorated considerably over the years. The per capita production of foodgrains declined from the average of 64.5 kg during 1960-63 to 63.0 kg in 1970-73, and then by 1993-96 it was down to only 32.8 kg (Table 4.1). The trend in production and productivity since 1970 is presented in Table 16.1. There was a continuous decline in foodgrains production from the annual average of 13.63 lakh tonnes during 1970-73 to 8.36 lakh tonnes during 1995-98. The area under foodgrains was down to 4.63 lakh ha from 9.35 over the same period. The growth in yield rate was also nominal. It rose to the average of 1,903 kg/ha during 1990-93 from 1,460 kg in 1970-73, but in the last three years (1995-98) it was down to only 1,797 kg.

The relative position of Kerala among the states was distressingly poor. The per capita production was the lowest, and constituted only 16 per cent of the national average during 1993-96, declining from 33 per cent in 1970-73. The situation on productivity was, however, not so gloomy. It was significantly higher than the national average, the latter being 1,552 kg/ha. During 1993-96, only three states had higher levels of productivity (Table 4.1).

In foodgrains, the production of cereals had declined by 27 per cent between 1977-80 and 1994-97, with a fall in area by as much as 41 per cent and in productivity by 24 per cent in this period. In pulses also, there was a similar decline in area, but the growth in productivity was higher, at 38 per cent, and therefore, the fall in production was less, by 21 per cent (GKL 1998). The area under pulses declined from the annual average 33.7 thousand hectares in 1970-73 to 21.5 thousand hectares in 1994-97. The yield rate increased to 1,047 kg/ha in 1993-96 from 363 kg/ha in 1970-73.

Table 16.1

Trend in Production, Yield and Area under Foodgrains in Kerala

Year/Period	*Foodgrains*			*Rice*		
	A	*P*	*Y*	*A*	*P*	*Y*
1970-73 (a.a.)	934.6	1363.4	1460	875	1342	1530
1980-83 (a.a.)	841.4	1331.2	1580	796	1306	1643
1983-84	776.7	1231.8	1590	740	1208	1630
1984-85	764.7	1279.8	1670	730	1256	1720
1985-86	719.0	1262.5	1760	678	1173	1730
1986-87	696.7	1157.2	1660	664	1134	1710
1987-88	636.8	1061.0	1670	604	1037	1720
1988-89	611.3	1037.4	1700	577	1007	1750
1989-90	613.0	1099.0	1790	578	1074	1860
1990-91	593.6	1111.1	1870	559	1087	1940
1991-92	574.4	1083.3	1890	541	1060	1960
1992-93	568.6	1110.4	1950	538	1085	2020
1993-94	541.0	1044.4	1930	508	1004	1980
1994-95	533.8	999.9	1870	503	975	1937
1995-96	501.0	973.6	1940	471	953	2023
1996-97	453.9	852.1	1877	425	832	1958
1997-98	433.2	681.3	1573	404	661	1636
1995-98 (a.a.)	462.7	835.7	1797	433	815	1872

Source: CMIE 1999c.

Note: Area: '000 ha, Production: '000 Tonnes, Yield: kg/ha.

The most important crop in foodgrains was rice, always accounting for more than 90 per cent of the total area under foodgrains. The production here declined continuously from the annual average of 13.42 lakh tonnes in 1970-73 to 8.15 lakh tonnes in 1995-98. The area under the crop was halved over the period, falling from 8.75 lakh ha to 4.33 lakh; the yield recorded a rise of 22 per cent, ignoring fluctuations, from 1,530 kg/ha to 1,872 kg/ha (Table 16.1). Kerala's edge over the all-India average in yield declined noticeably over the years. During 1970-73 its level was 38 per cent higher but in 1995-98 there was virtually no difference; the latter's yield was 1,110 kg/ha and 1,859 kg/ha in the two periods, respectively.

District-wise variation in yield rate was substantial, as evident from Table 16.2. During 1994-97, rice yield stood at the highest of 2,312 kg/ha in Pathanamthitta as against the lowest of 1,237 kg/ha in

Kozhikode. Between 1981-84 and 1994-97, the growth in yield varied between the highest of 42.5 per cent in Thrissur and the lowest at 5.2 per cent in Palakkad. For every district there was a decline in area under rice, and as the growth in yield was not substantial, production also had a negative growth. The fall in area was as much as 74 per cent in Kozhikode and Kannur in this period. In the total production of rice, four districts – Palakkad, Thrissur, Alappuzha and Ernakulam together – contributed 65.0 per cent in 1994-97, rising from 62.2 per cent in 1981-84.

The decline in area under rice was due to a number of reasons. Rice cultivation has gradually sunk into a high cost-low productive regime. The cultivation is not only less remunerative compared to other competing crops but also arduous and risky. There has been an enormous increase in wage cost and widening disparity in the prices of foodgrains and other agricultural commodities. And then there was the plentiful supply of rice through the PDS, and free flow of rice in the open market from other states.

Table 16.2

District-wise Trend in Area, Production and Yield of Rice in Kerala (annual averages)

Districts	*Area ('000 ha)*		*Production*		*Yield (kg/ha)*	
	1981-84	*1994-97*	*1981-84*	*1994-97*	*1981-84*	*1994-97*
Palakkad	1779	1347 (-24.3)	3720	2961 (-20.4)	2091	2199 (5.2)
Thrissur	1102	575 (-47.8)	1485	1099 (-26.0)	1347	1919 (42.5)
Alappuzha	745	468 (37.2)	1377	1018 (-26.1)	1848	2202 (19.2)
Ernakulam	978	568 (-41.9)	1414	988 (-30.1)	1445	1739 (20.3)
Malappuram	768	370 (-51.8)	959	632 (-34.1)	1248	1708 (36.9)
Kottayam	329	234 (-28.9)	684	518 (-24.3)	2081	2215 (6.4)
Kollam	493	236 (-52.1)	810	448 (-44.7)	1643	1901 (15.7)
Wayanad	302	204 (-32.5)	539	449 (-16.7)	1786	2235 (25.1)
Thiruvananthapuram	309	161 (-47.9)	453	290 (-36.0)	1467	1800 (22.7)
Pathanamthitta	-	109 (-)	-	253 (-)	-	2312 (-)
Kannur	646	165 (-74.5)	852	262 (-69.2)	1319	1594 (20.8)
Kasaragod	-	117 (-)	-	203 (-)	-	1745 (-)
Kozhikode	331	85 (-74.3)	371	105 (-71.7)	1120	1237 (10.4)
Idukki	91	48 (-47.3)	175	105 (-40.0)	1921	2182 (13.6)
State	7753	4684 (-39.6)	12847	9332 (-27.4)	1657	1994 (20.3)

Source: CMIE 1996b; GKL 1998.

Note: figures in parentheses are percentage increase/decrease over the period.

Non-Foodgrains

Kerala specialises in some of the important non-food crops. But here also the situation has not been very encouraging. Coconut, accounting for the largest area under non-food crops, did not show any appreciable growth in yield. As may be seen from Table 16.3, the yield per ha annually averaged 5,450 nuts during 1970-73, but in the following two decades it remained at much lower levels; only in the last few years there has been some recovery, and averaged 5,869 nuts during 1995-98. In the neighbouring state of Tamil Nadu the yield rate in the latest period was nearly double its level, being 11,114 nuts per hectare; even the national average stood at 6,958 nuts. Kerala's relative share in all-India production of coconut declined from 66 per cent in 1970-73 to 45 per cent in 1995-98, with a growth in production of only 48 per cent.

District-wise, there was wide disparity in yield rate. During 1988-91, while Thrissur had 6,659 nuts/ha, for Wayanad it was only 1,374. The growth in yield was very low in some of the districts. Between 1981-84 and 1988-91, while Thiruvananthapuram had a growth of 42.8 per cent from 4,216 nuts to 6,024 – in Wayanad it was only 5.9 per cent, the yield in the first period being 1,298 nuts.

The low yield rate of coconut in Kerala is due to a number of reasons. Being a traditional crop, Kerala has the oldest generation of coconut palms in the country. Under the intensive homestead system of cultivation coconut holdings have been subjected to continuous overdraw of productive capacity beyond the recuperative limits of the soil. Another factor is the non-availability of irrigation facility. Not more than 10 per cent of the crop receives irrigation. The root-wilt disease is also an important cause behind instability in production. The disease is rampant in the southern districts of the state.

The next important crop has been rubber, and its growth performance was quite impressive. The production registered an annual increase of 12.1 per cent between 1960-61 and 1974-75, with the area under it rising at the rate of 3.5 per cent and the yield 8.6 per cent. In the following years the growth rate decelerated, as may be seen from Table 16.3. In fact, the yield rate till mid-eighties was lower than the level in 1970-73. However, from early nineties, there was again a significant uptrend; the yield per hectare rose to 1,454 kg during 1994-97 from less than 600 kg till 1985-86. Kerala continues to account for the overwhelming proportion of all-India production; in 1996-97, it stood at 94 per cent.

Table 16.3

Trend in Area, Production and Yield of Selected Non-Foodgrain Crops in Kerala

Year/ Period	*Coconut*			*N. Rubber*			*Pepper*		
	A	*P*	*Y*	*A*	*P*	*Y*	*A*	*P*	*Y*
1970-73 (a.a.)	731	3985	5450	199.6	118.0	591	104	22.0	210
1980-83 (a.a.)	669	3075	4597	262.6	144.2	550	107	28.0	260
1985-88 (a.a.)	729	3299	4533	341.4	201.1	597	132	36.8	276
1990-91	864	4527	5240	407.8	307.5	750	168	46.8	280
1991-92	843	4206	4970	425.8	343.1	1139	178	50.3	282
1992-93	877	5125	5844	428.9	368.6	1203	183	49.7	271
1993-94	882	5197	5890	437.1	408.3	1304	184	49.5	269
1994-95	911	5335	5860	443.3	442.8	1389	187	59.3	317
1995-96	982	5905	6013	449.0	476.5	1443	192	59.9	312
1996-97	1006	5835	5802	450.0	514.5	1530	173	53.8	312
1997-98	1020	5911	5793	-	-	-	174	55.5	319
1995-98[a] (a.a.)	1003	5884	5869	447.4	477.9	1454	180	56.4	314

Tapioca			*Banana*			*Cashewnuts*			*Coffee*		
A	*P*	*Y*	*A*	*P*	*Y*	*A*	*P*	*Y*	*A*	*P*	*Y*
301	5246	17427	48	363	7563	101.6	114.0	1122	36	15	432
243	3897	16280	49	311	6350	140.3	80.7	575	59	23	390
174	3030	17465	54	382	7020	131.0	86.1	659	67	24	400
146	2803	19134	66	492	7400	115.6	102.8	888	84	22	260
142	2658	18733	65	502	7664	112.1	104.6	933	84	31	466
135	2629	19518	68	520	7648	109.0	95.6	877	84	36	431
131	2602	19860	67	523	7745	106.7	87.5	820	82	43	655
131	2578	19680	72	573	7967	103.4	95.5	924	82	39	589
119	2500	22008	73	592	8121	103.3	82.8	801	86	25	290
142	2588	18228	73	611	8308	100.5	78.4	781	93	38	410
133	2842	21383	75	629	8405	-	-	-	93	39	420
131	2643	20540	74	611	8278	102.4	85.6	835	91	34	373

Arecanut			*Cardamom*			*Tea*		
A	*P*	*Y*	*A*	*P*	*Y*	*A*	*P*	*Y*
87	53.7	583	48	1.3	27	37.7	48.4	1283
61	52.7	530	54	2.7	53	35.8	50.3	1410
59	52.3	557	61	2.7	43	34.7	52.7	1517

Contd...

Contd...

65	66.5	690	62	2.8	40	34.7	60.7	1750
63	65.1	1030	44	3.5	79	34.7	66.8	1925
64	70.7	1106	43	2.4	56	34.5	54.4	1578
69	79.5	1150	43	4.4	136	34.7	67.8	1954
72	105.8	1460	44	4.7	145	36.8	68.4	1859
76	91.2	1190	44	5.4	122	36.8	64.8	1762
73	80.1	1100	43	5.4	125	36.8	62.0	1684
76	94.0	1235	43	5.4	126	36.8	69.6	1891
75	88.4	1175	43	5.4	124	36.8	65.5	1779

Source: CMIE 1999c; GKL 1998, 1997j.
A: Area in '000 ha; P: Production in '000 tonnes, except for Coconut where it is million nuts; Y: Yield in kg/ha, except for Coconut where it is nuts/ha.

Note: a: in case of rubber and cashewnuts, the average is for 1994-97; the figures for the latest year are provisional.
In case of discrepancies between the data, government source has been used.

Pepper is another important crop in Kerala, and production here had a significant growth until recent years. It rose to the maximum of 60 thousand tonnes in 1995-96, from the annual average of 22 thousand tonnes in 1970-73, but in the last two years it was at a significantly lower level. Over the entire period of nearly three decades, there was a growth of 156.4 per cent, the production in 1995-98 averaging 56 thousand tonnes. In the increase of production, the contribution of area increase was larger than that by growth in yield. The former recorded a rise of 73.1 per cent as against 49.5 per cent by the latter. In the all-India total production, here also Kerala occupies a monopoly position, as much as 97 per cent of the total during 1995-98. A large portion of the output is exported; in 1995-96, it was to the extent of 41 per cent. There is ample scope for raising the yield rate of Pepper, as has been pointed out by the Taskforce on Field Crops (GKL 1997j).

In cashewnut, another important export earner, the situation is quite depressing. The production averaged 114 thousand tonnes during 1970-73 but this level could never be reached again, and in 1995-98 it stood at 85.6 thousand tonnes. The yield per ha declined similarly from 1,122 kg to 835 kg over the period. The area under cashew dropped noticeably in recent years due to the pressure from rubber. It has been estimated that about 50 thousand ha of cashew plantation are in the declining phase of productivity due to their old age (GKL 1997j). Land is a major problem in the cultivation of cashew. The land ceiling laws limit its cultivation to small and marginal holdings, the owners of which are not economically sound.

In tapioca, which is considered the poor man's cereal substitute, there was a substantial growth till mid-seventies. Between 1960-61 and 1974-75 production increased at the annual rate of 6.5 per cent, with the area rising by 2.9 per cent and yield at the rate of 3.5. The following years, however, noticed and absolute decline in production. As evident from Table 16.3, the level in 1995-98 was half that in 1970-73. The area under it was down to 43.5 per cent of the earlier level, and the yield recorded a rise of 17.9 per cent. Kerala's relative share in all-India production declined to 45 per cent from 90 per cent, over the period. The sharp fall in area under the crop is due to its replacement by rubber, whose prices had an enormous rise over the years.

In coffee, with a substantial acreage devoted to it, there was wild fluctuation in production. On the whole, however, a growth in production is discernible. The annual average rose to 34 thousand tonnes in 1995-98 from 15 thousand tonnes in 1970-73; the maximum production reached in any year was 43 thousand tonnes in 1993-94. The yield rate, on the whole, showed a decline, while the area under it recorded a noticeable rise. The production of tea has also registered some increases over the years although the area under it stagnated or declined. In fact, the yield has also stagnated in recent years, as may be seen from Table 16.3.

Cardamom has registered a significant growth in production in this period of nearly three decades. It stood at the annual average of 5.4 thousand tonnes in 1995-98 as against 1.3 in 1970-73. This was a product exclusively of growth in yield as the area under it showed a decline. Arecanut has also on the whole recorded an increase in production. Ignoring fluctuations, it rose to the annual average of 88.4 thousand tonnes in 1995-98 from 52.7 in 1980-83. This was a product of both yield and area increases, mainly the former. The performance of ginger was appreciably better. The production increased from the average of 22 thousand tonnes during 1970-73 to 50 thousand tonnes in 1995-98, that is, by 127 per cent. This was largely a product of yield improvement, from 1,863 kg/ha to 3,739 kg/ha; the area under the crop increased from 12 to 14 thousand ha.

Among fruits and vegetables, banana had a substantial acreage, and increased from the average of 48 thousand ha in 1970-73 to 74 thousand in 1996-98. But the growth in production over the whole period was only 68 per cent -- from 3.63 lakh tonnes to 6.11 lakh tonnes. This was because the yield improvement was nominal, from 7,563 kg/ha to 8,278 kg/ha. Kerala's relative position among the states was very poor. In the latest period, the all-India average of yield rate stood at 26,159 kg/ha, and in the neighbouring states also it was much higher than Kerala's.

Causal Factors

Behind the poor performance of agriculture in Kerala many factors had operated. The availability of land for cultivation itself was very limited here. The net sown area in 1995-96 stood at only 22.65 lakh ha, which was the lowest among the major states. The per capita area here came to 0.073 ha as against the all-India average at 0.155 ha. As percentage to the reporting area, however, the net sown area was higher than the national average, being, respectively, 58.3 and 46.6 (CMIE 1996c).

The possibility of bringing more land under cultivation is very limited here. The culturable waste was placed at only 90,000 ha in 1992-93, constituting 2.3 per cent of the reporting area; at all-India level the proportion was as much as 4.8 per cent (Table 4.4). The utilisation of this land is also not very easy. More than half of it is in hard laterite zone with undulating terrain. This land has an upper crust of about three to four feet which is very hard and difficult to break, although the soil below is suitable for all types of tree plantation (1997j:39).

As regards augmentation of land through higher cropping intensity, probably there is still substantial scope. The gross cropped area as percentage to the net has stagnated at 135 in the last two-and-half decades. Although this is higher than the national average, being 131.2 in 1995-96, Punjab had as much as 187.3. The extent of cropping intensity depends on a variety of factors like the land tenure system, irrigation facility, provision of inputs, marketing facilities, etc. Below we give a brief look into the situation in some of them.

Landholding Pattern

On land reforms, the progress in Kerala was much better than in most other states. Even in the pre-independence years the feudal relations in production was abolished in a big way in the Travancore region by the erstwhile Maharajas of Travancore. In the Kochi-Malabar region, however, the situation changed only after the independence; in fact, more than two decades after it.

The Kerala Agrarian Relations Act was passed in 1959 by the first communist ministry but it could not be implemented because of the dismissal of the ministry and later due to court rulings. It was only after the amendment of the Act in 1969 that the land tenure system in Kerala began to change.

In January 1970, invoking section 72 of the Act, the Government of Kerala ordered that the entire rights, titles and interest of holdings held by the cultivating tenants be vested in the government and they become owners of their leased-in holdings, subject to the ceiling provisions and the payment of a purchase price. The price was calculated on the basis of a fair rent and way below the market price. Resumption for personal cultivation was permitted only in case of those holding less than two hectares, and that too only for making it upto that size under severe restrictive conditions. By the beginning of February 1980, out of 36,14,836 applications filed or booked suo moto for transfer of rights to tenants, 24,34,310 cases, that is, two-thirds, were approved and certificate of purchase issued in virtually all the cases. As regards the latest position, by January 1999, 28.42 lakh tenants were conferred ownership rights in Kerala, involving a total land of 14.50 lakh acres (Herring 1980; GOI 1999).

The slogan 'land to the tiller', however, cannot be said to have been fully realised. The Congress Agrarian Reforms Committee recognised only the rights of farmers engaged in 'personal cultivation', defined as those putting in "a minimum amount of physical labour and participating in actual agricultural operations", the only exception being widows, minors and the disabled (AICC 1949: 10). Following the Planning Commission's guidelines, the KLRA included 'supervision' in the definition of 'personal cultivation'. This significantly nullified the essence of the slogan 'land to the tiller'. There are a large number of 'absentee' farmers in Kerala. The teachers, the shopkeeper, the lawyer, the government servant and even most politicians have their farming avocations. When some of them got ownership rights as a result of land reforms, a good many of them became supervising farmers rather than tilling owners. Even officially, tenant holdings are still not totally absent in Kerala. The NSSO 48th round (1991-92) found 5.2 per cent of the total number of holdings as tenant holdings, with 2.9 per cent of the total area (GKL 1997b; NSSO 1997).

Moreover, the beneficiaries from the land reform were not primarily the most oppressed agrarian class. This followed mainly from the fact that leasing-in, often in large blocks, was characteristic of large operators, many of whom owned significant amount of land. The tenants as a class, according to the Land Reforms Survey of 1966-67, owned 31.7 per cent of the land they operated. Some were large owners and large operators in the Kerala context (GKL 1976).

With regard to land ceiling and redistribution, the performance was more or less of all-India pattern. At the end of 1979, around 1.60 lakh acres were declared surplus, 75,831 acres taken possession, and 47,873 acres had been distributed. The area redistributed constituted only one per cent of the operated area; the number of beneficiaries stood at 75,483 -- receiving an average of 0.61 acre each. The surplus land was later reduced to 1.38 lakh acres, and as at the end of September 1998 64,922 acres could be distributed to 1,48,423 beneficiaries after taking possession of 95,987 acres. Thus, the land taken possession constituted only 69.3 per cent, and that distributed 46.9 per cent of the declared surplus. This is a very poor performance; at the national level, the proportions were, respectively, 88.3 and 71.9 per cent. The number of beneficiaries constituted 2.68 per cent of all-India total, and the per capita benefit came to only 0.44 acre in Kerala as against the national average of 0.96 acre (Herring 1980; GOI 1999).

The poor performance in land ceiling and surplus distribution was due to a number of reasons. A great deal of the land in large holdings, being tenanted, was redistributed but was not subject to the ceiling *per se*. The 1966-67 survey had reported that in the largest holding size group, larger than 25 acres, 83.71 per cent of the households leased out land; these large owners leased out 63.81 per cent of their owned area. Thus land redistribution in Kerala was primarily via the abolition of tenancy as in case of Karnataka. Had there been no provisions abolishing landlordism, a much larger area would have been subject to the ceiling measures; and consequently, more of the poorest group -- agricultural labourers – would have received small plots.

The impact of the ceiling was limited also because the ceiling was rather high relative to the average size of holding – as much as 20 ordinary acres for a large family against the average operated holding of 1.25 acres. Certain gifts and transfers were also allowed. And then, as in other states, since the abortive Reform Act of 1959, landowners had ample opportunity to rearrange their holdings to evade future ceilings. It is also certain that large owners were engaged in fraudulent practices during the implementation of the 1969 Act to evade the ceiling (Herring 1980).

The slow progress in taking possession of the declared surplus was mainly due to litigations. Of the land ordered taken over till 1979, about 20 per cent (30,385 acres) was invalidated by High Court rulings. There were also 1,998 stay orders affecting around 26,000 acres.

Another 15,000 acres were involved in legal disputes, gift deeds, or were covered by separate confiscatory legislation directed at private forests. After nearly two decades, at the end of October 1996, the situation was as follows: land invalidated by High Court orders 34,616 acres, covered by stay orders 22,575 acres and the extent involved in disputes, forest etc., 18,006 acres (Herring 1980; GKL 1997b).

The poorest group -- landless labourers -- was very little benefited by the land reform measures. The land ceiling was of little value due to the small amount of surplus made available. The option available was to purchase at nominal prices with government assistance hut sites, or kudikidappus, of up to 0.1 acre. This, however, could be done only by those labourers who had a house site on someone else's land. Under the scheme, the owner of the land was allowed compensation at the rate of 25 per cent of the market value, and the purchaser paid half of the price fixed, the balance being paid from the government fund. Till 1979, out of 4,33,106 applications received for purchase, 2,65,829 -- that is, 61 per cent -- were allowed. The latest position is that, till November 1996, 5,33,188 applications were filed, of which 4,266 remained pending (GKL 1997b).

The land reform measures have brought significant changes in the pattern of operational holdings. The proportion of marginal holdings, which was already very high in Kerala, rose further over the years. It stood at 91.6 per cent of the total in 1991-92, rising from 86.2 in 1970-71 (Table 4.5). An overwhelming proportion of the holdings were sub-marginal. Those below 0.50 ha constituted 79.2 per cent of the total, and the average for marginal holdings was 0.18 ha. The average size of holding in Kerala was 0.35 ha in 1991-92 as against the all-India average at 1.34 ha (NSSO 1997). Such a large proportion of uneconomic holdings probably had an impact on the productivity of land. The group farming attempted in recent years has not been much of a success.

Irrigation Facilities

Although Kerala gets plenty of rainfall, irrigation support has a special significance for making better utilisation of the limited amount of land available. The development of irrigation facility is, however, not in keeping with the need, or the resources available. Kerala accounts for only 1.1 per cent of the land area of the country but it has 4.8 per cent of the water resources. The net irrigated area as percentage to the state's cropped area is one of the lowest, as may be seen from Table

4.6. In 1995-96, it stood at only 15.1 as against the national average of 37.6. Not only this, whereas in most other states the proportion increased over the years, here it declined from the level of 20.3 per cent in 1960-61.

The utilisation of the potential has been very low, particularly with regard to minor irrigation. In 1990-91, against the ultimate potential of 11 lakh ha in minor irrigation, only 4.98 lakh was created, that is 45.3 per cent. This was the lowest level of achievement among the major states. In major and medium irrigation, the creation was to the extent of 67 per cent of the potential -- 6.69 lakh ha out of 10 lakh; there were six major states with higher levels of creation (Table 4.6).

Among the districts of Kerala there was extreme of variation in the potential created. For Kannur, it was as low as 1.5 per cent in 1996 and in Wayanad and Idukky 4.9 per cent as against the highest of 51.7 per cent in Thrissur. The utilisation of ground water potential in 1992 varied between 4.93 per cent in Wayanad and Idukky as against the highest of 32.88 per cent in Kasaragod, and the state average at 15.31. (GKL 1997c).

The utilisation again was far behind the creation of facility. The total of net irrigated area in Kerala stood at 3.35 lakh ha in 1956-57, and over the years there has been virtually no change in it -- the average for 1993-96 came to 3.41 lakh ha. The gross irrigated area also had a similar trend -- rising from 4.49 lakh ha to 4.61 lakh over the period. As regards the type of facility, in the total of net irrigated area at 3.42 lakh ha in 1995-96, government canals accounted for 30.1 per cent, followed by wells 21.4 and tanks 14.4 per cent (GKL 1963, 1998).

Among the crops, paddy continued to be the major beneficiary although with a declining trend. In 1991-92, 59 per cent of the gross irrigated area was accounted for by paddy and in 1995-96 it declined to 50.3. The shift is mainly towards commercial crops like coconut, arecanut and vegetables. The gross area irrigated in non-food crops rose to 183 thousand ha in 1995-96 from 129 thousand in 1991-92. It may be noted here that percentage of area under foodgrains irrigated in Kerala declined from 52.9 during 1970-73 to 39.4 in 1992-93; in the latest year, the all-India average stood at 49.6 per cent (Table 4.6).

The investment in irrigation increased quite rapidly over the years, particularly in the recent plans, as may be seen from Table 15.6. But it was predominantly for major and medium projects. In the cumulative total of investment at Rs. 2,090 crores on irrigation till the Eighth Plan, Rs. 1,459 crores, that is, 70 per cent was provided to them; only the balance of 30 per cent went to minor irrigation.

The over-emphasis on large projects is largely at the root of the problem in irrigation facility. Long delays and cost escalations are common problems with them. At the beginning of the Eighth Plan, there were 19 ongoing projects, which included one project started as early as in the Second Plan, six projects in the Third Plan, one in the Fourth Plan, five in the Fifth Plan and six projects in the Sixth Plan. The total investment originally estimated for these ongoing projects was Rs. 198 crores with an ayacut of 3.43 lakh ha (net), giving an average cost of Rs. 5,770 per ha. But as per the latest estimate the anticipated investment for these projects is of the order of Rs. 2,724 crores, that is Rs. 81,093 per ha. The viability of these projects have considerably eroded. To give one example: The Pazhassi project launched in 1962 at an estimated cost of Rs. 4.42 crores, was estimated to cost Rs. 100.00 crores in 1992. With an expected area to be irrigated at 8,130 ha, the cost per ha has risen to Rs. 1,23,000 from Rs. 5,437.

For many projects the original assumptions are no longer valid due to the shift in cropping pattern from food crops to commercial crops taking place throughout Kerala. The new cropping system with less water demanding crops would enable the existing irrigation network to support more areas with the same quantity of water. The design of the dam, the layout of the distribution system and the management of water would require a new orientation and fresh appraisal.

The implementation of projects continued to be delayed despite certain measures taken in recent years. The Eighth Plan had a target of bringing 1,48,000 ha under irrigation but only 33,626 ha, that is, just 23 per cent, could be achieved. A special project fund, Rural Infrastructure Development Fund, was created in this period for time bound implementation of projects but then also the time schedules could not be maintained.

The progress in command area development was also very slow until recent years. The cumulative total of area benefited by field channels construction stood at 147.6 thousand ha till March 1997, of which 56.6 per cent were constructed in the Eighth Plan; on the construction of field drains the figures were respectively, 12,073 ha and 48.4 per cent, and on land levelling and shaping 1,132 ha and 94.1 per cent. The cumulative total of area covered by warabandhi stood at 1,23,316 ha, of which a third was done in the Eighth Plan. The CADA activities are carried out in 14 projects with a cultivable area of 1,80,000 ha (GKL 1998).

As regards minor irrigation, despite its suitability for Kerala's situation, did not get any priority in the earlier plans; only since the Seventh Plan it was given some attention. The cumulative total of area under minor irrigation up to March 1997 came to 2.03 lakh ha (net), of which only 0.74 lakh ha – that is, 36 per cent – was achieved by the end of the Fifth Plan. The schemes undertaken were primarily on surface water.

Groundwater development in Kerala gathered momentum only from early 1980s, and so far only 15 per cent of the potential has been tapped. Number of pumpsets/tubewells energised – although these are not solely for groundwater – increased from 14 thousand in 1968-69 to 3.05 lakhs in 1995-96. In relation to the all-India total, these constituted respectively, 1.3 per cent and 2.7 per cent. In the latest year, Kerala had 9.9 pumpsets per 100 ha as against around 6 at the national level (Table 4.7). An important reason behind the sub-optimal utilisation of groundwater is the paucity of technical manpower and infrastructural facilities. During the Eighth Plan, Rs. 28.75 crores were spent on the development of groundwater resources.

Use of Inputs

The use of modern inputs in Kerala's agriculture is relatively low. In the most important crop, rice, the area under HYV seeds has remained almost static. In 1975, it covered 167.7 thousand ha and in the following two decades this level could rarely be exceeded. In the last one decade the maximum area covered was 175.1 thousand ha in 1992-93 and the average for 1994-97 came to 164.9 thousand. HYV paddy seeds distributed increased from 1,675 tonnes in 1991-92 to 4,598 tonnes in 1994-95 but in the following two years it was at lower levels.

Kerala's relative position among the states in adopting HYV seeds was the worst, as may be seen from Table 4.7. Between 1987-90 and 1992-95, the aggregate of area under HYV here declined from 223 thousand ha to 180 thousand, whereas at the all-India level there was an increase by 16.2 per cent. In relation to the gross cropped area, the area under HYV was only 5.7 per cent here as against 35.3 per cent at the national level.

In the use of fertilisers also the situation was not much better. The total consumption of chemical fertilisers increased from the annual average of 5,121 tonnes during 1956-59 to 65,298 tonnes during 1970-73 and then to 1,98,924 tonnes in 1994-97. The per hectare consumption, as evident from Table 4.7, rose to the highest of 84.4 kg in 1990-91 but in the following years it was at a much lower level; the average for

1995-98 came to only 66.5 kg. The growth in consumption came mainly after mid-seventies; until then, for one decade it stood almost static at 21 kg.

The relative position of Kerala has worsened considerably over the years. Till mid-seventies, its level of fertiliser consumption was higher than all-India average, but in the nineties it became significantly lower. The all-India average consumption per hectare stood at 79.7 kg during 1995-98, rising from 17.1 in 1975-76. Most of the major states had higher levels than Kerala's.

On the use of organic manures no noticeable improvement appears to have come, despite some attempts in recent years to popularise them. Raising of green manure crop in the summer fallows of command areas was encouraged, and some attempts made to promote compost making in homesteads and local bodies. The soil testing service continues to be narrow-based, and therefore, much diversification in manure use could not be achieved.

In plant protection measures, the use of plant protection chemicals has shown a vacillating trend in recent years. In the first four years of nineties it averaged 756 tonnes, declining from 1,074 during 1986-90, but in 1994-95 again it touched 1,381.4 tonnes. This pattern is atleast partly due to the policy of restricting their use only to situations where pests and diseases cannot be controlled through biological means. The area under biological control declined from the average of 214.0 lakh ha in 1991-94 to 172.1 lakh ha in the following three years.

Looking to the type of chemicals used, the use of fungicide increased from 304 tonnes in 1980-81 to 344 tonnes annually during 1991-94 but in the following three years it jumped to 979 tonnes. The consumption of insecticides and weedicides declined. The former was down to 218.41 tonnes in 1996-97 from 616 tonnes in 1980-81, and the average for last three years came to 257.8 tonnes. The use of weedicides declined from the annual average of 25.88 tonnes in 1991-94 to 15.04 tonnes in the following three years. The consumption of rodenticide stood at 16.42 tonnes during 1994-97 and 14.28 tonnes in the preceding three years (GKL 1998).

As regards the extent of mechanisation in Kerala's agriculture, on the basis of electricity consumption, it appears to be the least mechanised. In 1993-94, per capita consumption in agriculture here came to only 8.66 kwh as against the all-India average at 79.62 kwh. For irrigation, the total consumption of electricity came to 329 million units in

1996-97, constituting 4.69 per cent of the aggregate of consumption in the state.

To look at the use of some of the machine-operated implements: The use of plant protection equipment was quite extensive here. In 1987, Kerala had 37.99 equipments per thousand ha, rising from 11.74 in 1972; the all-India average in these two years were respectively, 13.61 and 3.27. As regards use of pumpsets, on electric sets, Kerala had 80.00 number per thousand ha in 1987 as against the all-India average at 33.18. On diesel sets, the numbers were respectively 17.77 and 85.66. The use of tractors was naturally very low here – only 0.86 per thousand ha as against the national average of 5.42. On power tiller also the situation was similar.

On bullock-operated implements too Kerala's position was not good. Number of iron plough per thousand ha came to only 33.7 in 1987 as against the all-India average at 65.1. In wooden plough these were respectively, 63.4 and 316. Number of seed drills in use was 21.7 in Kerala as against 47.5 at the national level (Deb 1997).

An important reason behind the low level of mechanisation is the extremely small size of holdings in Kerala, as noted earlier. The proportion of large holdings (10 ha and above) in 1991-92 was only 0.01 per cent as against 1.33 per cent at the national level (Table 4.5). However, the high wage rate was a factor promoting mechanisation. The daily wage rate here in 1972 was Rs. 20.32 as against the all-India average at Rs. 14.46; in 1987, these were respectively, Rs. 24.90 and Rs. 16.60.

Provision of Bank Credit

On the provision of credit to agriculture, Kerala's relative position was appreciably better cooperative credit institutions in particular are playing an important role. The Kerala State Cooperative Bank Ltd. is operating with 14 district cooperative banks and 1,591 PACS. Its working capital in 1996-97 stood at Rs. 848.9 crores, rising from Rs. 449.7 crores in 1991-92. The loans outstanding in these two years were respectively, Rs. 522.2 crores and Rs. 279.7 crores. The share of agriculture in it was, however, no more than a fifth (GKL 1998).

The PACS had a membership of 115 lakhs and a resource base of Rs. 6,469 crores at the end of June 1996. However, only 703 of the societies are operating on profit as against 844 on loss. The total loans disbursed by PACS averaged Rs. 1,486.5 crores during 1995-97, and the proportion of borrowing members constituted 27 per cent. A disturbing feature in the operation of PACS is that the credit for agricultural purposes is declining. In the last two years it averaged only Rs. 524.5 crores, that is, 35.3 per cent of the total.

The relative position of Kerala in the provision of credit by the PACS was very good, as may be seen from Table 4.8. Loans per hectare of gross cropped area in Kerala increased from Rs. 373 in 1981-82 to Rs. 4,918 in 1992-93 and these were respectively, 3.8 times and 14.6 times the all-India average. In 1995-96, however, the difference was down to 12.3 times, the per hectare loans being Rs. 6,559 in Kerala and Rs. 535 at the national level. The amount outstanding at the end of March 1994 was Rs. 1,840.49 crores, constituting 16.3 per cent of the national total. In the loans outstanding, the share of those with holdings upto 2 ha was 55.1 per cent as against 29.6 per cent at the all-India level (RBI 1999: II). This is a significantly better share even if one considers the larger proportion of such holdings in Kerala.

For long-term credit, there is Kerala State Cooperative Agricultural and Rural Development Bank at the apex level, with 44 primary agricultural development banks at taluk level as members. During 1994-97, the primary banks provided loans to the extent of an annual average of Rs. 12.95 crores, and in the preceding three years Rs. 11.95 crores. The loans were mainly for the purpose of land development, construction of godowns/cattle sheds, barbed wire or stone fencing and plantation/horticulture. In the last three years, the first three items accounted for 85 per cent of the total, with the first one alone accounting for 36 per cent (GKL 1998).

The scheduled commercial banks also performed relatively better here. Short-term agricultural advances per hectare came to Rs. 1,259 in 1993-94, which was eight times the national average at Rs. 154. In 1996-97, the SCBs advanced a total of Rs. 515.98 crores to farmers in direct finance, covering both short and long term loans, and this constituted 6.7 per cent of all-India total. The total of agricultural advances outstanding in March 1996 stood at Rs. 1,259 crores (covering both direct and indirect finance), constituting 4.6 per cent of all-India total. This is a relatively low figure and it is partly indicative of better recovery performance in Kerala. It is necessary to note, however, that in the aggregate of advances by SCBs in the state, the share of agriculture was relatively low, only 14.6 per cent, and it was lower than the level in as many as nine of the major states (Table 4.8).

In the provision of credit by the SCBs, as in case of the PACS, the share of marginal farmers was relatively much better in Kerala. In the total of short-term direct finance outstanding to farmers at the end of

June 1997, the share of those with land upto 2.5 acres was 58.2 per cent in amount and 72.4 per cent in number of accounts; the proportion at the national level were respectively, 31.4 and 41.5 per cent.

The advances from RRBs to agriculture was relatively low. Loans issued per hectare stood at only Rs. 501 in 1996. However, in relation to other states, here also the performance was the best; the all-India average of per hectare loan came to only Rs. 187. Similarly, as in case of the SCBs, in the aggregate of advances outstanding from RRBs the share of agriculture was low. At 43.7 per cent, it was lower than the all-India average and exceeded by as many as nine of the major states.

The NABARD played a significant role in providing agricultural credit. The cumulative total of refinance provided by it till March 1997 to Kerala stood at Rs. 1,292.3 crores, constituting 3.9 per cent of all-India total. The amount provided annually rose to Rs. 184 crores in 1996-97 from Rs. 85 crores in 1991-92. In the cumulative total disbursed till March 1993, plantation and horticulture accounted for the largest share of 29.9 per cent, followed by minor irrigation 22.9. In the last three years, 1994-97, their shares were respectively, 20.1 and 15.0 per cent. The non-farm sector is getting an increasingly large share of the total refinance in recent years. During 1994-97, the average share for it came to 40.0 per cent as against 29.5 in the preceding three years (NABARD 1993,1998).

The aggregate of credit flow to agriculture in Kerala, covering both production and investment credit, increased from Rs. 530.40 crores in 1988-89 to Rs. 1,333.40 crores in 1996-97; the growth in per hectare credit was from Rs. 1,743 to Rs. 4,347, that is 149 per cent. The production credit per hectare, however, had a growth of only 136.6 per cent in this period, from Rs. 1,310 to Rs. 3,099 (GKL 1997d).

Although the provision of bank credit to Kerala's agriculture is appreciably better than in most other states, there remains much to be done yet. According to a calculation by the NABARD, the credit gap in lending to the primary sector in relation to the requirement (as per potential linked credit plan for districts) is estimated at Rs. 447.56 crores. The gap varies between the highest of Rs. 74.4 crores in Ernakulam district and the lowest at Rs. 6.1 crores in Alappuzha (GKL 1998).

Marketing Facility

Organised marketing support is of critical importance in Kerala as the cropping pattern is dominated by cash crops and industrial raw materials and the production is concentrated in the small farm sector. Mobilising marketable surpluses from millions of tiny holdings, completing primary processing and transporting them all require organised efforts. But the existing infrastructure and facilities are very inadequate for the purpose. Farmers often do not get a remunerative price for their produce. Although cooperatives are operating fairly actively they do not have any effective control on the market forces.

In the case of commodities which have recorded significant increases in production, such as rubber and coconut, its favourable impact on the income of the farmers has been largely nullified in recent years due to the steep fall in their prices. Coconut prices touched a low of around Rs. 2,500-3,000 per thousand number during 1994-95 and 1995-96 while the prices of rubber plummeted to Rs. 25 per kg in 1997 from Rs. 60 in 1995-96. These two crops together occupy more than 60 per cent of the net sown area and provide livelihood to nearly two-thirds of the agricultural workforce.

The agencies functioning in the cooperative sector for marketing agricultural produce do not have a volume business large enough to make any decisive impact on the market. To look into the magnitude of operation of some of these agencies: The Kerala State Cooperative Marketing Federation, operating with 117 primary agricultural marketing cooperatives, deals with copra, rubber, arecanut, cardamom, other spices, and fertilisers. The level of procurement in 1996-97 stood at only 1,223 tonnes of pepper (2.3 per cent of production), 16 tonnes of cardamom (0.38 per cent of production), 45 tonnes of ginger, 5 tonnes of cloves and 2,637 tonnes of other commodities.

For dealing exclusively with rubber, there is the Kerala State Rubber Marketing Federation, with 37 member societies. It has seven sales branches and 13 purchase depots. It procured 37,079 tonnes of rubber in 1996-97 as against 42,756 tonnes in 1991-92, constituting respectively, 7.2 and 12.5 per cent of total production. Although there were attempts for increased procurement and quality improvement, the Federation could not protect the producers from the recent steep fall in prices.

For copra, there is the KERAFED with 898 PACS as members. Its objective is to bring an integrated development of coconut through procurement, processing and marketing of coconut and its products. The procurement of copra by KERAFED was only 8,379 tonnes in 1996-97 and 4,069 in the preceding year. The sales of copra in these two years were, respectively, 941 tonnes and 3,798 tonnes, of coconut oil 4,905 and 7,673 tonnes and coconut oilcake 2,721 and 375 tonnes (GKL 1998). The prices of coconut and its main product, coconut oil, often fluctuate widely. The organisation does not have the required facilities for procurement, storage, processing and sale.

The price movement which is of critical importance in encouraging or discouraging production of a commodity, has been often unfavourable for certain commodities. For food crops as a whole, the increase in prices was of a lower order than the average for all agricultural commodities. The wholesale price index for the former stood at the annual average of 470 during 1982 to 1984 as against 894 for the latter, with the base of 1952-53 = 100. In recent years, however, the gap has narrowed; during 1994 to 1996 these were respectively, 1,575 and 1,690. For the most important crop, rice, the situation was very much worse. The indices in the two periods were respectively, 389 and 1,094. The highest growth in prices were recorded by fruits and vegetables. The indices in the two periods were 811 and 2,916, respectively. Among non-food crops, plantation crops had the worst performance. The indices in the two periods were only 493 and 1,406 (GKL 1998: Appendix 3.8).

II
Allied Activities

Animal Husbandry

Kerala has a diverse livestock wealth and about 10 per cent of the state domestic product is derived from this sector. Milk, meat and eggs produced here meet about two-thirds of the animal protein consumption requirement. It also serves as the major supplier of two major inputs to crop production, viz., draught power and manure.

However, livestock development in Kerala on an organised pattern received attention only from the beginning of the Third Plan. Adoption of scientific methods on an intensive scale began to be emphasised from then on. Some significant changes came over the years, but the growth in number of livestock was low. The total of livestock (excluding poultry) increased from 47.29 lakh in 1961 to 53.18 lakh in 1977, 55.01 lakh in 1987 and then a nominal rise to 55.71 in 1996 (GKL 1998). Thus, a growth of only 17.8 per cent over the period of three-and-half decades. The poultry population, however, had a noticeable growth. Even in the last nine years it increased by 50 per cent. Below we make a brief analysis of the pattern of growth in important livestock species and their output.

Cattle and Buffalo Development

In the livestock population, cattle and buffalo are the most important in terms of output. However, the growth in their numbers over the years has been very low; the latter in fact recorded an absolute decline. Number of cattle increased from 21.85 lakh in 1951 to 27.53 in 1961, 30.06 in 1977 and 34.24 lakh in 1987; in 1996, there was a marginal declined, to 33.96 lakh. Among the major states, Kerala's was the worst performance. Between 1972 and 1987, as may be seen from Table 4.9, while Kerala registered an increase of only 19 per cent, for all-India it came to 56 per cent. In the all-India total number, Kerala's share declined from 2.2 to 1.7 per cent.

The buffalo population had a sharp decline over the years. In 1996, it stood at only 1.65 lakh as against 3.29 in 1987, 4.72 in 1972 and 4.88 lakh in 1956. No other state recorded an absolute fall. Kerala's share in all-India total number stood at 1.0 per cent in 1972 and declined further to 0.4 per cent in 1987.

The fall in bovine population, however, could not affect the milk production due to two favourable changes. The proportion of females in both cattle and buffalo increased remarkably and there was also a rapid growth in number of crossbreds. In the total number of cattle, percentage of females increased from 72.7 in 1972 to 85.2 in 1987 and 88.7 in 1996. In adult cattle, the female/male ratio rose to 5.74 in 1987 from 3.32 in 1972. In no other state the ratio was so high. In buffaloes, the percentage of females increased from 43.0 in 1972 to 60.5 in 1987 and remained at almost the same level in 1996. Here, however, the proportions are much lower than the all-India average. The growth in number of female buffaloes between 1972 and 1987 was only 34 per cent in Kerala as against 110 per cent at the national level (Table 4.9).

As regards crossbred, their number increased from 13.55 lakh in 1977 to 17.02 in 1987 and 22.86 in 1996. Their proportion in total number of cattle rose to 67.3 per cent from 45.1 over the period. The percentage of females in crossbred was as much as 88.4 in Kerala in 1987 as against the all-India average at 65.4. In the all-India total number of crossbreds, Kerala's share stood at 14.9 per cent, next only to Uttar Pradesh.

Milk production in Kerala recorded a rapid growth. From 2.8 lakh tonnes in 1971-72 it rose to 9.1 lakh in 1980-81, 17.8 in 1991-92 and 23.8 lakh tonnes in 1996-97. The annual average growth in the last two decades was 9.3 per cent as against 4.7 per cent at the national level. Per capital milk production increased from 13.1 kg in 1971-72 to 69 kg in 1994-95, that is, a growth of 427 per cent; at the national level it was only 71 per cent in this period. No other state could register such a rapid growth.

This, however, does not mean that there was no scope for further increase in production. The average milk yield per animal per day is presently 5.6 litres compared to the potential of eight to ten litres (GKL 1998: 39). The biggest obstacle in realising this is the weak feed and fodder base. Development efforts so far have focused disproportionately on herd improvement and health care. Production of green fodder has been introduced only in recent years. Kerala is deficient also in concentrate feeds which make up for 60 to 70 per cent of the cost of milk production. Nearly 80 per cent of the feed requirement in the state is met by supplies from the neighbouring states. The reduction in paddy areas has brought a sharp fall in internal supply of straw from rice fields.

The area under fodder increased from 2,980 ha in 1991-92 to 7,739 ha in 1996-97, and the production of fodder from 89.4 thousand tonnes to 274 thousand in this period. The production of fodder seed, however, declined sharply. In the last three years, 1994-97, the annual average came to 31.3 tonnes as against 62.3 tonnes in the preceding three years. For cattle feed, there are two plants with capacity of 500 tonnes per day, but it remains unutilised to a large extent due to organisational problems.

Poultry Development

Poultry rearing is done extensively in Kerala as a backyard enterprise and is considered highly suitable for the resource poor rural population as a subsidiary economic activity. The birds mostly thrive on surrounding resources and kitchen waste, and therefore, are not burdensome for the rearer. Almost 90 per cent of the poultry population is found in small backyard farms.

The growth in number of poultry has been substantial over the years. It increased from 67.95 lakh in 1956 to 101.48 lakh in 1966, 138.49 in 1977, 188.42 in 1987 and 268.33 lakh in 1996, that is, nearly a four-fold rise over the entire period. The proportion of ducks in it varied between 3 and 5 per cent. In mid-eighties, nearly 55 per cent of the layers in the state were improved birds. The average production level in the traditional backyard farming system is 100 eggs per bird per year and for improved variety 200 eggs.

Total production of eggs in the state increased from 943 million in 1977-78 to 1,605 million in 1991-92 and 2,069 in 1996-97; the annual average for 1994-97 came to 1,921 million. About two-thirds of the production was from improved birds. In the all-India total production of egg, Kerala accounted for 7.55 per cent in 1993-94. The per capita production here stood at 61 in this year as against the all-India average of 28, and the highest at 109 in Punjab (Table 4.10). As regards broiler production, the state's performance has not been significant, although it is developing quite rapidly. In 1988-89, total production came to 80 lakh birds, equivalent to 8,000 tonnes of meat. The aggregate of poultry meat production reached 34,000 tonnes in 1996-97 as against 24,000 in 1991-92.

The potential for developing poultry is enormous. Nearly 60 per cent of the eggs produced are presently consumed by the rearing households, and more than 400 million eggs are brought from outside the state every year. Even then the per capita availability of eggs is far less than the norm of minimum 180 eggs per individual per year recommended by the World Health Organisation. The backyard poultry production can be greatly increased with proper infrastructural facilities by way of hatchery support and rearing units for day-old chicks.

The government's efforts at developing poultry has been negligible. During the Eighth Plan, the total expenditure on it came to Rs. 2.23 crores, constituting 15.5 per cent of the aggregate on animal husbandry (GKL 1997a: II). The Kerala State Poultry Development Corporation was established in 1989, particularly for taking up area specific egger development programmes and providing market tie-up, but the corporation remained dormant until 1996-97. The functioning of departmental poultry farms is also far behind expectation. Chicks hatched out in them rose to 9.21 lakh in 1994-95 from 6.37 in 1991-92 but in the last two years it averaged only 3.73 lakh (GKL 1998).

Fisheries Development

Fisheries play a crucial role in the economy of Kerala. Over 3.3 lakh fishermen spread over 222 coastal villages depend on it as their main source of income and livelihood. As per 1991 census, the total fishermen population in Kerala is 9.99 lakh, of which 7.75 lakh are in the marine sector. Fish is also an important source of protein in the diet of Kerala people. Fish consumption here is about four times the national average.

The fisheries resource base in Kerala comprises of 36,000 sq km of marine water-spread within 200 metres depth range -- 13,000 sq km inshore and 23,000 offshore – and about 3,600 sq km of inland water spreads. It has been estimated that the maximum sustainable yield of Kerala's inshore waters is 5.7 lakh tonnes, and the total marine resource potential of the coast around 10 lakh tonnes. The inland water-spreads comprise of 2.43 lakh ha of brackish water area, 3,300 ha of fresh water ponds and tanks, 30,000 ha of reservoirs and 85,000 ha of rivers and streams.

The growth in fish production was, however, not in commensurate with the resources available. The aggregate of fish output in Kerala increased from the annual average of 3.57 lakh tonnes during 1984-87 to 5.73 lakh tonnes during 1991-94, that is, a growth of 60.5 per cent. Although this growth rate is higher than the national average, there were six major states with a much higher level. Kerala's share in all-India production in this period increased marginally from 12.4 per cent to 13.0 (Table 4.11). In the total production of fish in Kerala, the marine sector accounted for more than 90 per cent.

Marine Fishery

A number of measures was taken for development of marine fishery in Kerala. The first important step was the launching of the Indo-Norwegian project in the fifties under which mechanised boats were introduced in Kollam. The government also distributed 1,400 mechanised boats – of which 1,200 were trawlers – to fishermen through cooperatives. In the early sixties, nylon nets were introduced in place of cotton. In late sixties, the emergence of prawn fishery as a lucrative export trade gave a significant boost to capital investment in marine fishery. The plan expenditure on fishery rose to Rs. 28.8 crores during 1966-67 to 1979-80 as against only Rs. 4.1 crores during 1956 to 1966. Motorisation of artisanal crafts from the beginning of 1980s brought a decisive change in the traditional sector. Between 1981 and 1986 about 7,200 country crafts were fitted with outboard motors; in 1990 it rose to 9,914 and in 1995 to 15,336. Number of processing and freezing plants increased to 409 in 1990 from 117 in 1970. Construction of fishery harbours and landing centres was also given attention. The expenditure on fishery in the Sixth, Seventh and Eighth Plans, totalled Rs. 162.72 crores, the last one accounting for 69 per cent of the total. (GKL 1998, 1997e).

The trend in marine catches since early fifties is presented in Table 16.4. The production fluctuated significantly from year to year but on the whole the growth was substantial. The annual average of production reached 5.57 lakh tonnes in 1994-96 from 1.44 in 1951-53, that is, a growth of around four times over the period of four-and-half decades. The rate of growth was faster in the first two decades than in the following two-and-half, the increase being respectively, 162.5 per cent and 47.4 per cent. In value term, the growth was much faster. It increased from Rs. 28.36 crores in 1970-71 to Rs. 82.22 crores in 1980-81, Rs. 453.75 crores in 1990-91 and Rs. 867.86 crores in 1994-95, that is a growth of 31 times over the period of two-and-half decades.

The relative share of Kerala in the all-India total production of marine fish has declined noticeably over the years. Its share rose to the highest of 34.99 per cent of the total quantum in 1970-72; but this level could never be reached again in the following years, and the average for 1994-96 stood at 23.78 per cent. In export also Kerala's relative share declined. It was down to 23.3 per cent in 1994-97 from 38.5 in 1982-85, with a six-fold rise in value of export – from Rs. 143.52 crores to Rs. 869.36 crores; the growth at the national level in this period was ten times -- from Rs. 373 crores to Rs. 3,733 crores.

The marine fishery in Kerala faces some disturbing trends. A serious matter of concern is the over-exploitation of inshore areas. Unregulated use of crafts, gears and adoption of a capital-intensive technology has resulted not only in depletion of marine fisheries resources, but also reduced the accessibility of traditional fishermen to the marine resources.

The number of crafts in the marine fishing sector of Kerala was estimated at 33,338 in 1980-81, but by 1995 it rose to 5,31,648. The number of motorised fishing crafts also increased at a fast pace, as noted earlier. The Kalawar Committee, set up in 1984, had recommended limiting the number of motorised canoes to 2,200-2,700 and mechanised trawlers to about 1,145 in the inshore waters (Kalawar 1985). But a census in 1991 showed that around 10,000 motorised crafts were in use. The Balakrishnan Nair Committee of 1989 had recommended banning of ring-seine in Kerala, but the above mentioned census found 2,259 ring-seines being used for fishing. In 1995, there were 2,15,287 trawl nets and 2,13,502 ring-seines in operation in the Kerala coast. Trawl gear, on an average, contributed 46 per cent of the total landings in recent years and ring-seine 34 per cent; only 5 per cent of the landings was from non-mechanised (traditional) sector (GKL 1998, 1997e).

The introduction of mechanised fishing has no doubt led to the widening of area of operation and increase in the time spent in the sea. But the increases in number of crafts, and gears have not brought adequate increase in production; in the last six years, it stagnated at around 6 lakh tonnes (Table 16.4). This clearly shows overcapacity and tendency towards overexploitation in the inshore area. There is need for strict regulation in the number, and area of operation of different types of fishing crafts.

Table 16.4

Trend in Marine Fish Production in Kerala

(in lakh tonnes)

Period/Year (Calendar)	*Quantity*	*Period/Year*	*Quantity*
1951-53	1.44 (26.51)a	1989	6.18 (29.03)
1970-72	3.78 (34.99)	1990	6.63 (30.66)
1980-82	2.93 (21.39)	1991	5.64 (25.39)
1983	3.86 (25.39)	1992	5.61 (24.63)
1984	3.93 (22.11)	1993	5.75 (25.60)
1985	3.33 (19.17)	1994	5.68 (24.07)
1986	3.36 (19.66)	1995	5.32 (23.54)
1987	2.83 (17.14)	1996	5.72 (23.73)
1988	4.69 (26.41)	1994-96	5.57 (23.78)

Source: GKL 1998.

Note: a: figures in parentheses are percentages in relation to all-India total.

Inland Fishery

Inland fishery in Kerala did not receive any attention until recent years, and consequently vast areas of waterspread remained unutilised. Even reliable data on production over a long period are not available. Whatever information is available shows that production has been gradually rising from 1960 onwards. From 6,385 tonnes in mid-sixties it rose to 28,000 tonnes by mid-eighties, 36,342 tonnes in 1990-91 and 52,105 in 1996-97. The annual average of production came to 50 thousand tonnes in 1994-97, rising from 26 thousand in 1980-83. In value term, the growth was quite rapid. It increased from Rs. 1.18 crores in 1970-71 to Rs. 10.93 in 1980-81, Rs. 58.29 in 1990-91 and Rs. 130.90 crores in 1995-96, that is, a growth of 111 times over the entire period (in current prices).

In the total catch, five varieties -- prawns, etroplus, tilapia, murrels and catfish -- accounted for the overwhelming bulk; during 1994-97 their share averaged 66.8 per cent, with prawns alone accounting for a quarter. As much as 80 per cent of the inland fish production comes from backwaters.

The inland fisheries which is basically a subsistence activity in Kerala, has been facing a number of challenges. Unbalanced developmental activities and high level of pollution area the two major problems. In Kerala, there are 30 reservoirs but fish rearing has been taken up in only 12 of them. The development of reservoirs was given attention only in the Eighth Plan. Five projects have been selected on a pilot basis for cultural activities on scientific lines. The utilisation of brackish water also received attention only since 1989 with the launching of the Kerala Fisheries Development Project for Prawn culture. About 65,000 ha of water was identified for immediate prawn culture. However, till March 1995, an area of only 160 ha could be taken up for development. There are six Brackish Water Fish Farmers' Development Agencies and 14 Fish Farmers' Development Agencies in the state. These agencies have so far brought an area of 877.81 ha under prawn culture, and another 2,400 ha under other fish culture.

The availability of fingerlings continues to be very inadequate. There are only eight fish hatcheries in the state with a total production capacity of 250 lakh fingerlings a year. This is only one-fourth of the total requirement. The nurseries available are also very inadequate. They number only 10, and most of them are not put to optimal capacity utilisation. The major variety raised in them is carps.

A different type of problem that needs a mention here is the very low growth in income of fishermen. The growth in fishery has virtually left them untouched so far as income growth is concerned, particularly in recent years. During 1980-81 to 1994-95, per capita income in the fisheries sector stagnated at around Rs. 1,000 whereas that of the state income grew at the rate of 2.8 per cent – from Rs. 1,508 to Rs. 2,113 (GKL 1998). Earlier, according to an estimate, during 1969-70 to 1982 for those using non-mechanised craft there was a continuous decline in income from Rs. 630 to Rs. 420 (at 1960-61 prices) (Kurien 1994). The poor housing and habitat condition of the fishing community bear testimony to their deplorable level of living. A recent survey found that 42 per cent of the fishing families live in huts with thatched walls and roof. In 93 per cent of the villages beaches are used as toilets (GKL 1998, 1997g).

An important reason behind the low income of fishermen is the lack of their control over the marketing of fish. The fishermen's share of the consumer rupee for the different varieties of fish has been estimated to range from as low as 18 per cent for white baits in the Kozhikode region to 74 per cent for sharks in the Trivandrum region.

The variations are due to the number of intermediaries between fishermen and consumer and the market power of the fishermen.

The most important point on the 'fish chain' is the point of the first transaction, the seashore. The nature of transaction and the composition of the buyers here determine how much the fishermen will get. An assessment of the quantum of fish sold through fair auctioning revealed that in a quarter of the villages in the state only a negligible quantity was thus transacted and in another quarter less than 50 per cent; only in 38 per cent of the villages over 75 per cent of the fish were auctioned (GKL 1997e: 44).

Forestry

Kerala has a relatively large forest area. Although the estimates of forest area vary from source to source, according to the Forest Department, on the basis of legal status, it is presently 1.122 million ha, constituting 28.9 per cent of the state's total land area. This is the third largest proportion, after Orissa and Madhya Pradesh, among the major states. The per capita forest area in Kerala is, however, only 0.04 ha as against the all-India average at 0.11 ha. This recorded forest area includes the area diverted to non-forestry purposes. Excluding the diverted area, the effective forest area is only 0.94 million ha, constituting 24.2 per cent of the geographical area. Of the total forest area, 83.2 per cent constitute the Reserve Forest (GKL 1997f).

The density of Kerala forest is by no means optimum, despite the protection measures. In 1995, 81.5 per cent of the total forest area was considered dense – that is, with crown density above 40 per cent. The balance, largely open forest, was with a density of 10 to 40 per cent. As regards the forest type, tropical moist deciduous accounts for 43.6 per cent of the total, tropical wet evergreen forests 37.0 per cent and plantations 16.4 per cent.

The area under plantation increased from 97 thousand ha in 1979-80 to 160 thousand in 1997. Teak presently accounts for 47.5 per cent of the total area, followed by mixed plantation 21.4 and eucalyptus 18.4 per cent. The increase in area under plantation was nominal in the last few years. But some of the species which accounted for a very small share of the total, had a significant growth. Soft wood which contributed less than a thousand ha till 1995-96, suddenly jumped to 3,312 ha in the following year. Similarly, the area under bamboo increased from 646 ha in 1991-92 to 2,114 ha in 1996-97.

The output of forest produce in Kerala is on the whole declining.

Production of timber (round logs) increased from 78,691 cubic metres in 1993-94 to 1,23,501 cum in 1994-95 but in the following two years it stood at less than half this level. Production of firewood declined to only 30 thousand tonnes in 1996-97 from 83 thousand in 1994-95. The sandalwood production was down to 1,03,523 kgs from 2,18,424 kgs in 1993-94.

There are, however, significant standing volumes of wood available from homestead areas in the state. Small farmers operating multi-tier holdings plant coconut, rubber and timber trees often mixed together. The estimated total number of trees in these homestead is 440 million, of which trees below 10 cm girth account for 43 per cent. This works out to a total growing stock of 134.130 million cum, of which 44.983 million (33.5 per cent) is commercial volume and the balance fuelwood growing stock (GKL 1997f, 1998).

As regards resource use, consumption of industrial wood in Kerala is estimated at around 2.5 million cum, of which 47.9 per cent comes from home gardens, 29.7 per cent from estates, 13.7 per cent from imports and the balance of 8.7 per cent from state forests. Imports, especially of higher quality species, have increased steadily in recent years as the supply from Kerala's own resources is reduced. The forest department does not take much interest in improving their plantations as they have to supply mainly to two large companies at much below the market price. In the supply of fuelwood also the role of the forest department is low. The total supply of fuelwood in Kerala is estimated at about 17 million cum, 89 per cent of which comes from the household sector. The household sector's consumption is estimated at 63 per cent of total (GKL 1997f, 1998).

The revenue from forest to the state exchequer has risen significantly in recent years. Till the beginning of Eighth Plan the total revenue from the forestry sector was in the range of Rs. 32 to 48 crores per annum but during the Eighth Plan it rose to Rs. 128.26 crores; it may be noted that during 1957-58 to 1961-62 the annual average revenue from forests stood at Rs. 3.52 crores (GKL 1963, 1998).

The plan expenditure on forestry and wildlife was, however, relatively insignificant. In the Eighth Plan, the outlay fixed for it was Rs. 90.75 crores, constituting only 1.66 per cent of the grand total. The plantation activities in this period covered raising of 8,460 ha and maintenance of 18,559 ha. In the new raising, fast growing species accounted for 52.5 per cent of the area and teak 35.1 per cent. There is also a commitment of Rs. 137 crores under non-plan account for afforestation over a period of ten years from 1993-94. Till March 1997, 22,100 ha had been completed under this programme (GKL 1997a: II: 425, 1998: 48).

The forest resources of Kerala are faced with many problems, as in case of other states. The quality of natural forests has undergone drastic changes adversely affecting the ecological functions of the forest. Overexploitation has resulted in a rapid depletion of forest. The encroachment on forest land has also been huge -- as much as 28,588 ha has been lost due to it. The efforts at compensating the losses through proper afforestation programmes have been negligible. The government policies were often not favourable to protection and development of forest.

The pricing policies, especially in respect of pulpwood industries, which is provided subsidies of about Rs. 20 crores annually, is not only a disincentive to private investment and production but also discriminates against the weaker sections like tribals (GKL 1998). Prices of raw materials need to be fixed keeping in view the increases in general price level. Many restrictions on felling and transit of forest products also discourage planting of forests on private lands. The forest department do not have a strategy for forest sector worked out with stake-holders of forestry. There is no arrangement to coordinate inter-sectoral activities, and effective monitoring of the activities.

17

Industrial Growth and Structural Change

The history of industrial development of Kerala dates back to the year 1881 when the first manufacturing unit on a factory basis was started at Quilon to make clothes. Shortly after that a coir factory was started at Alleppey. Palghat and Calicut also witnessed the emergence of some industrial units by the end of the century. In the twentieth century, a particularly notable period was the ten-year prior to independence. Nearly 40 industrial units were established in the state of Travancore in this period.

In the post-Independence period, during the First Plan very little emphasis was given to industrial development. In the subsequent Plans, however, a large number of industrial units were established. But Kerala continued to be relatively backward industrially. The contribution of manufacturing sector to SDP averaged 14.2 per cent during 1994-97 as against the national level of 21.3 per cent. Earlier, during 1960-63, also the proportion for manufacturing in Kerala stood at almost the same level, being 14.7 per cent. The compound annual growth rate during 1991-92 to 1996-97 came to only 3.9 per cent here as against 9.0 per cent for all-India (at constant 1980-81 prices) (RBI 1998, 1999). The growth of industrial production as a whole was, however, not so depressing. The index of industrial production stood at 255.49 in 1995-96 with the base of 1980-81=100. Below an analysis of the sectoral pattern of growth is attempted.

Factory Sector

The factory sector in Kerala had a very gloomy performance. The growth in value of output here was only 127 times between 1960 and 1994-95 – from Rs. 73 crores to Rs. 9,350 crores – as against 148 times at all-India level, from Rs. 3,504 crores to Rs. 5,17,987 crores. The relative share of Kerala in all-India total rose to 3.0 per cent in 1977-78 from 2.1 in 1960 but in 1994-95 it was down to only 1.8 per cent. The net value added to output has also on the whole shown a decline, as evident from Table 5.1.

The value of fixed capital increased very slowly here. Between 1960 and 1994-95, there was a growth of only 155 times as against 216 times at the national level. The growth was particularly low in the sub-period of 1977-78 to 1994-95, being respectively, 7 and 14 times. In the preceding period, Kerala's growth was higher than the national average. On capital-output ratio, the situation was relatively better. In the latest year, it stood at 0.46 as against 0.54 at the national level. Similar was the position in relation to net value added.

In the provision of employment by the factory sector, Kerala's performance was very poor. Over the entire period of three-and-half decades, it increased by only 167 per cent as against 213 per cent at the national level; the relative share in total employment declined from 4.5 per cent to 3.9. The productivity of employees was also very low. In all the three time-points considered it was much lower than the all-India average, and the disparity has widened in recent years. In 1994-95 the value of output per employee was only 46.6 per cent of the national average as against 76.4 per cent in 1977-78. The low productivity can be explained only partly by the low level of fixed capital. Fixed capital per employee here increased by ten times between 1960 and 1977-78 but the output per employee in this period recorded a rise of only seven times. In the following years, however, the latter had a marginally higher growth than the former.

Structural Change

The industrial structure of Kerala is quite narrow. As evident from Table 17.1, more than 80 per cent of the industrial output from the factory sector was contributed by seven industry-groups even in recent years. However, within this group some important changes have taken place. In 1989-90, rubber, plastic etc., alone accounted for 35 per cent of the total value of output, but after six years, in 1994-95, its share was only 11.6 per cent. Of the remaining six, industries, five had raised their shares considerably. For food products it rose to 23.8 per cent from 15.0, and of basic chemicals from 14.0 to 18.9 per cent. In employment, food products alone contributed 42 per cent of the total in 1994-95, rising from 29.7 per cent in 1989-90. This was followed by beverages and tobacco with 10.3 and 11.9 per cent, respectively. In the total fixed capital of factory sector, electricity alone accounted for 44.6 per cent in 1994-95, and another 31.2 came from basic chemicals, food products, rubber etc., and cotton textiles combined. In 1989-90, the proportions were respectively 40.5 and 35.0 per cent.

Table 17.1

Industrial Structure of Kerala (Factory Sector)

Industry	*% share of total (1994-95)*			*Fixed capital per employee (Rs. '000)*	
	Output value	*Employ-ment*	*Fixed capital*	*1989-90*	*1994-95*
Rubber, plastic etc.	11.6 (34.9)[a]	4.8	6.4	329	163 (-50.5)[b]
Food products	23.8 (15.0)	41.8	6.9	7	20 (185.7)
Basic chemicals	18.9 (14.0)	6.1	11.9	174	239 (37.4)
Electricity	7.1 (4.6)	6.8	44.6	354	797 (125.1)
Machinery and equipment	6.7 (7.9)	4.1	4.0	96	118 (22.9)
Paper etc.	6.6 (4.6)	3.5	5.0	108	175 (62.0)
Cotton textiles	6.4 (4.3)	5.5	6.0	55	133 (141.8)
Non-metallic min. prods.	3.0 (2.1)	5.4	4.4	45	100 (122.2)
Beverages and tobacco	2.5 (2.3)	10.3	0.7	6	8 (33.3)
Metal and alloys	4.0 (3.7)	1.4	3.9	125	351 (180.8)
Transport equipment	1.5 (1.0)	1.2	3.2	265	326 (23.0)
Metal products	1.0 (1.2)	1.0	0.5	59	60 (1.7)
Wood and its products	1.4 (1.0)	3.0	0.7	14	29 (107.1)
Jute textile	2.5 (0.8)	0.9	0.3	17	49 (188.2)
Textile products	0.6 (1.0)	1.2	0.3	17	31 (82.4)
Repair of capital goods	0.4 (0.3)	1.5	0.1	9	9 (-)
All industries	100.0 (100.0)	100.0	100.0	88	122 (38.6)

Output per employee (Rs. '000)		*Net value added to output*	
1989-90	*1994-95*	*1989-90*	*1994-95*
2145	6445 (-69.9)[b]	0.22	0.15
115	151 (31.3)	0.17	0.15
431	825 (91.4)	0.25	0.25
102	276 (170.6)	0.54	0.49
319	437 (37.0)	0.26	0.28
266	498 (87.2)	0.25	0.27

Contd...

Contd...

146	308 (111.0)	0.30	0.21
71	149 (109.9)	0.28	0.32
44	65 (47.7)	0.34	0.44
503	775 (54.1)	0.19	0.24
188	337 (79.3)	0.09	0.50
176	263 (49.4)	0.12	0.20
57	121 (112.3)	0.17	0.17
243	775 (218.9)	0.08	0.15
154	142 (-7.8)	0.32	0.21
37	76 (105.4)	0.79	0.81
226	265 (17.3)	0.24	0.24

Source As in Table 13.1.

Notes: a: figures relate to 1989-90.
b: percentage increase/decrease over the period.

To look into the position of some of the technical coefficients: The fixed capital per employee increased for almost all the industries; an important exception was rubber, plastics etc. In the latter, it was halved over the period of six years – falling from Rs. 3.29 lakhs in 1989-90 to Rs. 1.63 lakhs in 1994-95. The output per employee had a sharper decline, from Rs. 21.45 lakhs to Rs. 6.45 lakhs. The highest growth in fixed capital per employee was in jute textile, followed by food products, metal and alloys, cotton textiles, electricity and non-metallic mineral products. The productivity of workers, however, did not increase in commensurate with it in a number of industries. In food products, for example, fixed capital per employee was nearly trebled over the period, but the output per employee increased only 31 per cent. Similarly, in metal and alloys, these were respectively, 181 and 54 per cent. On the other hand, in repair of capital goods with no increase in fixed capital the output per employee rose by 105 per cent, and in metal products by 1.7 and 49.4, respectively.

The net value added to output declined in a number of industries. The electricity industry, with highest amount of fixed capital, recorded a fall from 0.54 to 0.49 and in food products with the largest share of employees from 0.17 to 0.15. The highest growth in value added was in case of transport equipment -- the ratio rising from 0.09 to 0.50. The capital-output ratio in some of the industries with large share of fixed capital registered a significant rise. In food products it rose to 0.14 in 1994-95 from 0.06 in 1989-90, in rubber etc., from 0.15 to 0.22 and in basic chemicals from 0.40 to 0.42.

Spatial Distribution

Spatially the industries were highly concentrated in a few districts. In 1982, as evident from Table 17.2, Kollam alone accounted for 40.7 per cent of total employment in the factory sector, followed by Ernakulam 14.1 per cent; another 30 per cent came from Kozhikode, Kannur, Thrissur and Thiruvananthapuram combined. Thus, these six districts together accounted for 85 per cent of the total employment. There has not been much reduction in concentration over the years. The share of these six districts declined to 75 per cent in 1996, with Kollam's falling to 33.2 per cent. The combined share of four districts, Wayanad, Kasargod, Pathanamthitta and Idukki, on the other hand, was only 4.3 per cent in 1996. The growth in employment in some of the districts with low share was not appreciable.

Table 17.2

District-wise Growth in Registered Working Factories in Kerala

Districts	*No. of Factories*[a]		*Employment (in '000)*	
	1982	*1996*	*1982*	*1996*
Thiruvananthapuram	371	881 (137.5)[b]	20.5	31.7 (54.6)[b]
Kollam	883	1132 (28.2)	123.5	137.6 (11.4)
Pathanamthitta	-	459 (-)	-	6.8 (-)
Alappuzha	604	1160 (92.1)	17.1	24.9 (45.6)
Kottayam	669	1181 (76.5)	9.4	18.9 (101.1)
Idukki	159	263 (65.4)	4.6	7.4 (60.9)
Ernakulam	1567	2504 (59.8)	42.9	60.4 (40.8)
Thrissur	1001	2109 (110.7)	22.5	35.2 (56.4)
Palakkad	907	1892 (108.6)	12.0	27.2 (126.7)
Malappuram	340	899 (164.4)	4.1	11.7 (187.6)
Kozhikode	1175	1751 (49.0)	24.1	26.5 (9.8)
Wayanad	-	130 (-)	-	1.7 (-)
Kannur	1423	1457 (2.4)	22.7	22.2 (-2.1)
Kasargod	-	188 (-)	-	2.0 (-)
Total	9099	16406 (80.3)	303.6	414.4 (36.5)

Source: GKL 1984, 1998.

Notes: a: for both the years, data refer to December-end.
b: percentage increase/decrease over the period.

In terms of number of factories, four districts – Ernakulam, Thrissur, Palakkad and Kozhikode – together accounted for half of the total in 1996, and slightly higher in 1982. The factories in Kollam were of large size; its share in number of factories being only 6.9 per cent in 1996.

Small-Scale Industries

Small-scale enterprises play a very important role in Kerala's economy. According to the 1961 census, this sector provided employment to 8.47 lakh persons, constituting 83.1 per cent of the total workforce in industry (GOI 1963). However, it did not receive adequate attention from the government. Not to speak of other aspects, even the plan expenditure on it was quite low. In the Third and Fourth Plan together, the total expenditure on VSI came to Rs. 8.06 crores. It was only since the Fifth Plan the expenditure on this sector was raised substantially. The outlay for it increased from Rs. 8.49 crores in the Fifth Plan to Rs. 25 crores in the Sixth Plan, Rs. 44 crores in the Seventh Plan and Rs. 150 crores in the Eighth Plan. However, even in the latest Plan it constituted only 2.7 per cent of the grand total outlay, and 18.5 per cent of that on industry and minerals. Below we give a brief look into the pattern of growth in different segments of this sector.

Modern SSIs

After two decades of development efforts, the relative position of Kerala's modern SSI did not appear satisfactory. The first census of small scale industries brought out the following picture: In 1972, Kerala had 5,618 working SSI units, constituting 4.45 per cent of all-India total. In gross value of output the share was 4.44 per cent and in total value added 4.30 per cent. All these are not totally disappointing if compared with the population share of Kerala. But for Punjab, a much smaller state, the proportions were much higher. It had 9.35 per cent of all-India total output and in value added 7.56 per cent (GOI 1976).

The employment provided by this sector in Kerala was relatively much better. At 1.26 lakh persons in 1972, it was 7.7 per cent of all-India total as against 7.47 in Punjab. The productivity of Kerala's employees was, however, very low. The output per employee in this year stood at only Rs. 9,141 as against the all-India average at Rs. 15,744 and the highest of Rs. 22,082 in Maharashtra. The value added per employee was only Rs. 2,860 as against the national average at Rs. 50,872. This is explained largely by the low level of fixed capital per employee. It stood at only Rs. 3,484 in Kerala – lowest among all the states – as against the national average of Rs. 6,380. The capital-output ratio was, however, lower than the all-India average, being 0.38 and 0.41, respectively (GOI 1976).

On the latest position, comparative data are not available. However, it is apparent that the organised SSI sector has made a significant progress over the years. Number of SSI units rose to 36,342 at the end of March 1986, 64,675 in 1990 and 1,60,544 at the end of March 1997, that is a growth of 4.4 times in the last 11 years. In relation to 1979-80, when the cumulative total number stood at Rs. 16,951, the growth is 9.5 times (GKL 1992, 1998).

Total of investment in SSI stood at Rs. 1,922.69 crores at the end of March 1997, the value of goods and services at Rs. 6,330.11 crores and the employment at 8,39,596 (GKL 1998). The output per employee came to Rs. 75,395 and fixed capital at Rs. 22,900. The capital-output ratio stood at 0.30. All these are significant improvements over the situation found by the 1972 census.

As regards the district-wise distribution of SSI units, it is more or less in the same pattern as in case of the factory sector. In the total number of units at the end of March 1997, six districts, namely, Ernakulam, Thiruvananthapuram, Thrissur, Kottayam, Kollam and Alappuzha, together contributed 64 per cent, and including Palakkad and Kozhikode it was 79 per cent. In the value of output, Ernakulam alone provided 26.3 per cent, and another 37.8 came from Thrissur, Alappuzha, Thiruvananthapuram and Kannur combined. On the other hand, four districts – Kasargod, Wayanad, Idukki and Pathanamthitta – together contributed only 5.6 per cent of the total. In employment, Kollam accounted for the largest number, followed by Ernakulam. Their combined share was 28.8 per cent. The value of output per employee was only Rs. 26,245 in Kasargod as against the highest of Rs. 1,53,035 in Ernakulam (GKL 1998: Appendix 6.19).

Khadi and Village Industries

The performance of KVI in Kerala was quite depressing, as may be seen from Table 17.3. Over a period of one-and-half decade, 1981-82 to 1996-97, the value of output increased only five times, from Rs. 26.98 crores to Rs. 135.07 crores, and in employment (full time) a negligible 41.7 per cent, from 92 thousand to 1.30 lakh persons. The part-time employment, however, increased at double this rate – rising from 39,875 to 73,485. The output per employee had a growth of 253 per cent, from Rs. 2,940 to Rs. 10,389 (considering only full-timers).

The relative position of Kerala among the states is also not satisfactory. In 1993-94, it accounted for only 3.45 per cent of all-India total production, declining from 4.13 in 1982-83. The growth over the period was 249 per cent here as against 317 at the national level. In employment, it was respectively 12.6 per cent and 55.2 per cent and consequently, Kerala's relative share in total employment declined from 4.9 per cent to 3.5 over the period. The output per employee continued to be significantly lower than the national average (Table 5.4).

In the total production of KVI, as evident from Table 17.3, six industries -- village oil, lime, blacksmithy and carpentry, village pottery, cottage match and village leather – together accounted for 55 per cent in 1996-97 as against 41.1 in 1981-82. Among these industries, lime recorded the highest growth, followed by blacksmithy and carpentry. There was a nearly 13-fold rise in value of lime production, but in employment it was only 172 per cent. Village oil, the highest contributor to production, had a three-fold rise in production and 42 per cent in employment. Some of the minor items had recorded a rapid growth in production. For example, fruit processing and preservation had a 70-fold rise over the period, and it accounted for 3.2 per cent of total production in 1996-97 as against 0.16 in 1981-82. Non-edible oil and soap also had a 25-fold growth in production.

In employment, four industries, namely, khadi, cane and bamboo, bee-keeping and gur-khandsari, recorded absolute declines. In the first one by 44 per cent with a 151 per cent rise in production; in cane and bamboo by 39 per cent despite a nine-fold rise in production. The single most important provider of employment in KVI was fibre and screwpine. In 1996-97, it accounted for 47.0 per cent of the aggregate of full-time employment, declining from 57.7 in 1981-82. In production, its share was down to 5.5 per cent from 16.9. Thus, a large proportion of the workers in KVI are having very low productivity. Part-time workers constituted 36.1 per cent of the total in 1996-97. More than half of it was provided by bee-keeping, palmgur and fibre and screwpine.

Table 17.3

Trend in Khadi and Village Industries of Kerala

Industry	*Production (Rs. Lakhs)*		*Employment (Number)*[a]	
	1981-82	*1996-97*	*1981-82*	*1996-97*
A. Khadi	158.81	398.53 (3.0)	14437	8087 (6.2)
B. Village Industries				
Village oil	500.58	1609.13 (11.9)	575	815 (0.6)
Village pottery	162.56	1125.24 (8.3)	7374	18254 (14.0)
Fibre and screwpine	456.14	738.79 (5.5)	52961	61151 (47.0)

Contd...

Contd...

Blacksmithy and carpentry	99.80	1240.81 (9.2)	1669	7014 (5.4)
Handmade paper	8.41	155.00 (1.1)	246	888 (0.7)
Gur-khandsari	142.09	252.90 (1.9)	1272	1164 (0.9)
Palmgur	66.74	221.02 (1.6)	300	1018 (0.8)
Beekeeping	249.71	111.14 (0.8)	3000	1980 (1.5)
Village leather	112.85	1067.60 (7.9)	894	2394 (1.8)
Lime	105.59	1332.91 (9.9)	1897	5153 (4.0)
Non-edible oil and soap	20.14	518.80 (3.8)	52	405 (0.3)
Cottage match	127.50	1079.81 (8.0)	2480	3707 (2.9)
Cane and bamboo	35.72	329.82 (2.4)	2436	1488 (1.1)
Processing cereals and Pulses	440.12	644.40 (4.8)	1752	6012 (4.6)
Fruit process. and preservation	6.11	434.30 (3.2)	27	1348 (1.0)
Polyvastra	4.38	55.62 (0.4)	367	888 (0.7)
Total KVI	2697.82	13507.21 (100.0)	91742	130012 (100.0)

Percentage Growth		*Output per Employee 1996-97[b] (Rs.)*
Production	*Employment*	
150.9	-44.0	4928
221.1	41.7	197439
590.2	147.5	6164
62.1	15.5	1208
1143.3	320.3	17690
1743.0	261.0	17455
78.0	-8.5	21727
229.8	239.3	21711
-55.5	-34.0	5613
846.5	167.8	44595
1162.2	171.6	25867
2476.0	678.8	128099
746.9	49.5	29129
823.8	-38.9	22165
46.4	243.2	10719
7008.0	4892.6	32218
1169.9	142.0	6264
400.7	41.7	10389

Source: GKL 1984, 1998.

Note: a: only full time.
b: based on full time only.

The output per employee was highest in case of village oil, at Rs. 1,97,439, followed by Rs. 1,28,099 in non-edible oil and soap. Their combined share in employment was, however, a paltry 0.94 per cent. The largest employer, fibre and screwpine, had the lowest output per employee only Rs. 1,208, which is 11.6 per cent of the average for all KVIs in the state.

Household Enterprises

Household enterprises play a very important role in Kerala's small enterprise sector. In 1961, they accounted for 57.7 per cent of total number of workers in small enterprises. For the latest situation we refer to the NSS 45th round, covering the period July 1989 to June 1990 (NSSO 1995c). Total number of household enterprises in Kerala was found to be 5.76 lakhs, constituting 3.68 per cent of all-India total. In the total number, the share of rural areas was 83 per cent as against 76 per cent at the national level.

The enterprises in rural areas, as in other states, are weaker than those in urban areas. The proportion of NDMEs – that is, those having at least one hired worker but not more than five – was only 12.6 per cent in rural areas as against 26.8 per cent in urban areas. The average value of fixed assets per enterprise was found to be only Rs. 5,947 in rural areas as against Rs. 14,218 in urban areas. Both of these figures were lower than the all-India average, as may be seen from Table 5.5. In value of plant and machinery, however, Kerala's position was better not only in relation to all-India but also as compared to other southern states. In the value of working capital used also Kerala had an edge over the all-India average.

The household enterprises in Kerala provided employment to a total of 9,74,686 in 1989-90, of which 7,72,183, that is 79 per cent, was in rural areas. The proportion of part-timers in the total was 13.8 per cent in rural areas and 9.3 per cent in urban areas. The value of output per enterprise was found to be Rs. 15,751 in rural areas and Rs. 24,357 in urban areas. In value added to output also urban areas were in a better position. It was 45.0 per cent in urban areas as against 37.5 per cent in rural areas.

As regards the industry-wise distribution of enterprises, in rural areas, three groups of industries – beverages etc., wood and wood products and coir – together accounted for 65.4 per cent of total number of units. Their share in employment was, however, only 54.5 per cent. In the provision of employment other important industries were food products, textile products and repair services, with a combined share of 26.7 per cent. The value of output per enterprise was the highest in machinery etc., except electrical, at Rs. 1.36 lakhs, followed by food products, transport equipment, non-metallic mineral products and basic chemicals. The ratio of gross value added to output was more than 70 per cent in four industries repair of capital goods, repair services, cotton textile and beverages etc. The lowest proportion was in leather, at 5 per cent.

In urban areas, six industry groups – coir manufacture, repair services, food products, textile products, wood and wood products and beverages etc. – together accounted for 76 per cent of total number of enterprises. Their share in provision of employment was 73 per cent, with the first two contributing 32.6 per cent. The value of output per enterprise was the highest in basic metals, at Rs. 1.94 lakhs, followed by transport equipment, rubber etc., electrical machinery etc., and food products. The ratio of value added was above 60 per cent in six industry groups – repair services, repair of capital goods, electrical machinery etc., transport equipment, coir etc., and machinery other than electrical; the lowest was in basic metals at 11.7 per cent.

Kerala's industrial situation overall is quite gloomy. It comes out more vividly if we give a look to the position of some of the traditional industries and the health of the public sector.

Traditional Sector Industries

Coir, handloom and cashew are the three important traditional industries in Kerala providing employment to a large number of people. Coir industry provides employment to about 4 lakh people, 3.5 lakh of which are in the spinning sector and the rest in product sector. Out of the total coir workers, 84 per cent are women. About 35 per cent of coir yarn and 90 per cent of coir products of the country are produced in this state (GKL 1998, 1997h).

The industry is, however, faced with a severe marketing problem. The export of coir stood at 76,076 tonnes in 1961-62 but steadily declined to only 24,672 tonnes in 1985-86. In the following years there were considerable improvements but could not reach the earlier peak. In 1996-97, it stood at 45,540 tonnes. In the domestic market also the industry is facing a slump. There are 679 coir cooperative societies, of which 165 are dormant and 69 have not yet started production. There are only 63 societies working on net profit. The membership of primary societies and manufacturing societies totalled 7.51 lakh in 1996-97 but they could provide direct employment to only 0.76 lakh workers. The quantum of fibre produced by primary societies declined from 2,125 tonnes in 1995-96 to 1,962 tonnes in 1996-97, and of yarn from 94,180 tonnes to only 11,203 tonnes. This was due to a variety of reasons like non-availability of raw material and lack of working capital.

Measures taken for modernisation of the coir industry are very inadequate, and whatever little has been done is not spreading at the desired rate. The traditional husk retting, fibre extraction and spinning operations are carried out in the most unhygienic conditions. Because of the unhygienic process and the drudgery involved, the younger generations are reluctant to take up work in this industry. Moreover, the traditional retting process being a source of pollution to the rivers and lagoons, environment consciousness is another deterrent factor. There are indications that in the near future the industry will have to manage with mechanically extracted fibre from green husk.

The utilisation of husk in the state is only 31 per cent. To solve the problem of raw material scarcity, the utilisation rate has to be at least doubled in the near future. Moreover, much greater attention needs to be given to the product sector. At present, only about 20-25 per cent of the coir yarn is converted into products.

The position of handloom industry, which provides direct employment to two lakh persons, is also not much better. Production of handloom cloth in the state was estimated at 104.86 million metres in 1988-89 but in the following years it was at much lower levels; the average for last two years came to 92.37 million metres. Total number of handlooms in the state was 75,913 in March 1997, of which 61,589, that is 81 per cent, were in the cooperative sector. Total number of cooperative societies this year stood at 753, of which 135 were factory type and the rest cottage type. In the factory sector, 17 societies were dormant, two under liquidation and five were yet to start working. In the cottage sector, 60 were dormant, 77 under liquidation and 15 yet to start working.

Number of weavers in the cooperative sector was 1,04,570 but employment generated in 1996-97 stood at only 574 lakh mandays. Their production in this year was 70.35 million metres, constituting 74.11 per cent of total production. In the value of production, at Rs. 301.69 crores, their share was 81.4 per cent. In the corporate and unorganised sectors, there were 8,205 weavers, and the employment generated in 1996-97 stood at 36 lakh mandays. The productivity in this sector was higher than that in the cooperative sector; quantum of cloth produced per loom annually came to 1,676 metres in the former as against 1,161 in the latter in 1996-97.

For procurement and distribution of handloom fabrics there are two organisations: in the cooperative sector, the Kerala State Handloom Weavers' Cooperative Society (Hantex), established in 1961, as the apex marketing organisation; and the Kerala State Handloom Development Corporation (Hanveev), functioning since 1968, outside the cooperative fold. The former, with 435 primary societies as members, had a production of 6.96 lakh metres valued at Rs. 2.01 crores in 1996-97, and the sales turnover at Rs. 26.83 crores. The society is not able to procure even 25 per cent of the total production in the cooperative sector. Moreover, it is saddled with a huge stock of various varieties of cloth. The member societies are still producing slow-moving items. The corporation, with 32 clusters of producers, is also functioning very poorly. Although the licensed capacity is 6,500 individual weavers the actual utilisation was below 25 per cent. The number of active weavers dwindled year after year. The accumulated loss of the organisation rose to Rs. 5.71 crores in 1996-97 (GKL 1998: 76).

The cashew industry comes next in terms of employment. There are about 379 cashew factories in the state, nearly 90 per cent of which are in the private sector. The Cashew Workers Apex Cooperative Society (CAPEX) and the Kerala State Cashew Development Corporation (CDC) are the major agencies engaged in the development of cashew industry. The CAPEX has 10 factories under it with employment of 6,000 persons. Its performance has been very poor in recent years. The procurement of raw nuts decreased from 6,258 tonnes in 1995-96 to 1,869 tonnes in 1996-97, and the export earnings from Rs. 26.49 crores to Rs. 6.53 crores in this period. The CDC is also in a similar position. It has 36 factories and provided employment to around 23 thousand persons in 1996-97. The corporation is not in a position to utilise its capacity fully, and is incurring substantial losses every year.

A major problem with the industry is availability of raw nuts. It is estimated that approximately 5 lakh tonnes of raw nuts are required for providing 200 days of employment to those engaged in the industry. But the state's contribution is only one lakh tonnes per annum. About two lakh tonnes are procured from the neighbouring states. But there also more cashew factories are coming up and it will be difficult to procure from these states in future. The prospect of raising production of raw nuts in the state is also not very bright, as noted in Chapter 16.

Public Sector Enterprises

The state of public sector enterprises in Kerala is quite depressing, probably more so than in many other states. Looking to central enterprises first, the investment itself was relatively low here. In the all-India total of central investment (gross block) Kerala's share declined from 3.24 per cent at the end of March 1975 to 1.76 in 1985 and 1.28 per cent in 1995. The growth in investment here was only 14 times – from Rs. 202 crores in 1975 to Rs. 2,906 crores in 1995 – as against 36 times for all-India, from Rs. 6,242 crores to Rs. 2,27,349 crores. At the end of March 1995, there were 19 companies operating in Kerala with total employment at 26,865. Their sales and other income totalled Rs. 4,093 crores, that is, Rs. 15.23 lakhs per employee. Five of the companies under the National Textile Corporation were running on loss and were under BIFR (GKL 1997i).

As regards state public sector enterprises, they numbered 44 at the end of March 1997, 20 of which were fully owned by the government and the remaining with majority shares. Among the government companies, seven out of the 15 reporting for 1996-97 had made profits. In government majority companies, out of the 14 reporting, nine had earned profits.

Industry-wise, the chemical sector with 12 enterprises accounted for the largest investment. However, the investment here decreased from Rs. 351.25 crores in 1992-93 to Rs. 253.53 crores in 1994-95, and employment from 7,331 to 7,216. There were six profit making and two loss making units in 1994-95. Half of the total number of units were with negative worth and two were under BIFR. The electronic sector came next with capital invested at Rs. 232.71 crores in 1994-95 and employment at 3,751. There were eight loss making units this year, with the total loss at Rs. 38.49 crores; only two units made profit. The sector as a whole had negative net-worth totalling Rs. 43.52 crores. In the engineering sector, there were 11 units with capital invested at Rs. 199.86 crores and employment at 3,536. Eight of the units were making losses, with total loss at Rs. 20.30 crores in 1994-95; excepting one, all were making cash losses. Seven units had negative net-worth and for the industry as a whole it was negative to the extent of Rs. 55.59 crores. In electrical equipment, with five units, capital invested totalled Rs. 159.65 crores and employment stood at 4,395. Two units were making losses, and the industry had negative net-worth.

That the industrial environment in Kerala has not been favourable is evident from certain other data also. The per capita paid-up capital in private corporate sector of Kerala stood at only Rs. 908.90 at the end of February 1998 as against the all-India average at Rs. 2,104.69 and the highest of Rs. 4,341.12 in Maharashtra. Kerala's share in all-India total of paid-up capital declined from 2.29 per cent at the end of March 1957 to 1.96 in 1974 and 1.42 in 1998 (GOI 1997c, 1998b).

Causal Factors

The industrial growth of a state depends on a variety of factors, as noted in Chapter 5. Here we discuss briefly the situation on three of the factors: trade unionism, availability of infrastructure and provision of bank finance.

Trade Unionism

Behind the poor industrial performance of Kerala, generally militant trade unionism is considered an important factor. During the seventies there was much labour unrest in the state that led to strikes and frequent agitations. Along with the increase in number of political parties, the number of trade unions also increased. With this the inter-union rivalry and friction increased and made the management task more burdensome. Number of mandays lost in Kerala due to industrial disputes stood at 2,055 thousand in 1978 and rose to 3,770 thousand in 1979, constituting respectively, 7.25 and 8.60 per cent of all-India total. The ratio of number of disputes to number of factories was always higher in Kerala than in the neighbouring states. In 1960, for Kerala it was 0.104 as against 0.032 in Tamil Nadu and 0.023 in Karnataka; in 1970, these were respectively, 0.122, 0.043 and 0.031; and in 1984, 0.023, 0.020 and 0.009 (Thampy 1994). In recent years also the situation has not improved much. During 1993-97, the average number of mandays lost due to strike and lockout came to 2,382 thousand. Number of disputes arising annually in this period averaged 5,970 (GKL 1998). The ratio of number of disputes to number of factories stood at as much as 1.63 in 1993-94.

It is largely due to the militant trade unionism, wages in Kerala increased at a higher rate than the productivity. During 1970-71 to 1982-83, wages per worker in the SSI sector increased by 244 per cent whereas value added per worker rose by only 94 per cent. Share of wages in value added averaged 37.9 per cent in Kerala during 1980-83 as against 29.3 at the national level. In the neighbouring states wages were lower than in Kerala, and increased at a lower rate than in value added. Between 1970-71 and 1982-83, the growth rates in Tamil Nadu were respectively by 190.6 and 292.7 per cent. In Karnataka also the situation was similar (Thampy 1994). This naturally attracted entrepreneurs to the neighbouring states.

It was not only that the wage rates were high in Kerala, welfare expenditure on workers was also high. For example, in case of head-load workers there are provisions for bonus, holiday wages, educational aid, group insurance, etc. The employer has to pay 25 per cent of the worker's wage as a levy for the welfare scheme (Pillai 1996).

Infrastructure

The overall infrastructural situation in Kerala was relatively much better than in most other states. An infrastructural development index prepared by using 13 indicators gave Kerala a score of 155.1 for 1992-94 (with all-India=100). This was the second highest, next only to Punjab (Table 1.1). This, however, included a number of items which are not directly relevant for industrial growth. A particularly important item of infrastructure for industry is the availability of power, and therefore, below we give a brief look into the trend in its position.

The power situation in Kerala was very satisfactory till early eighties. But since mid-eighties it became quite problematic. Prior to 1982 the major power cut in Kerala was only in 1965-66. During 1977-78 to 1981-82, the state was selling on an average 800 MU of power to neighbouring states. This was short-lived, and in 1982-83 power cut had to be imposed due to the failure of monsoons. Thereafter it became almost an annual feature, and soon demand began far outstripping the supply. Net import of power per annum rose to 1,254 MU at the end of March 1989 from net exports to the extent of 250 MU in March 1985. In recent years, the deficit has increased further; imports rose to 3,296 MU in 1997 (GKL 1991, 1998).

New projects could not be taken up in time due to environmental and other reasons. The Silent Valley project, which the state wanted to take up in the late seventies, was denied clearance on environmental considerations. The Pooyankutti project which was suggested as a substitute is still to be cleared. The projects under implementation also got unduly delayed and the costs escalated. The Kakkad project where work commenced in April 1978, could not be commissioned even in 1998, and the latest cost estimate is Rs. 146.0 crores as against the original estimate of Rs. 18.6 crores. The Eighth Plan had the target of creating an additional 439 MW but only 32 MW could be added. The actual expenditure on power programme, however, touched Rs. 1,796.43 crores against the target of Rs. 1,300 crores (GKL 1998).

While expansion in generation capacity was marginal, that in distribution could not be held back. Total number of consumers in the state rose to 49.23 lakhs in March 1997 from 37.03 lakhs in 1992 and 22.17 lakhs in 1985. Although electricity reached all villages of Kerala by 1979, about 60 per cent of the households have been electrified so far. The per capita consumption of electricity in the state was 224.18 kwh in 1996-97, which was the lowest among the neighbouring states and far below the national average, being 314 kwh.

The major problem of power development in Kerala is the sole dependence on hydre power which is subjected to the vagaries of monsoon. The state's efforts to diversify the sources have not been much, and there are inherent difficulties also. Its geographical location with respect to coal bearing regions is extremely unfavourable making transportation of coal most expensive and difficult. The oil and gas exploration in the Kerala coast have not led to any significant discoveries. Only recently, in 1996, construction of a thermal project, the Kayamkulam project, has been taken up by the NTPC. Some steps have also been taken to promote thermal power projects in the private and joint sectors.

On the availability of transport, however, Kerala's position is very good. The road density per thousand sq km stood at as much as 3,650 km in 1995-96, which was five times the national average, and highest among all the states. The proportion of unsurfaced roads was, however, very high -- as much as 69.6 per cent as against the national average of 44.5. As regards railway route length, it stood at 27.02 km in 1997-98 as against the national average of 19.01. Vehicle density per sq km stood at 34.86 in 1996-97, which was more than three times the national average (CMIE 1998a, 1999e).

The infrastructure for industry covers a variety of facilities, and recently the government has set up the Kerala Industrial Infrastructure Development Corporation with statutory powers to look after them. The corporation, launched in 1993, is presently implementing the following projects: Export Promoting Industrial Park Kakkanad, Ernakulam; KINFRA-International Apparel Park, Menamkulam; Techno Industrial Park, Calicut; Integrated Infrastructure Development Centre, Menamkulam; and Integrated Industrial Township, Palakkad.

Provision of Finance

In the provision of finance, both for working capital and long-term purpose, Kerala's relative position was far from satisfactory. The growth in scheduled commercial banks' credit to SSI in Kerala was always lower than that at the national level. Between June 1968 and December 1983, as may be seen from Table 5.7, the outstanding advances had risen only 11.6 times in Kerala as against 28 times at the national level. In the following 12 years, ending in March 1995, however, the gap narrowed the growth being respectively 5.3 and 5.4 times. In the aggregate of advances to SSI at the national level, Kerala's share declined from 9.8 per cent in 1968 to 4.0 in 1983 and 3.9 in 1995. In number of units assisted, however, Kerala's position was much better than in most of the states. In the total number of units assisted in the country, its share rose to 7.4 per cent in 1995 from 4.7 in 1983. Thus, the amount of assistance per unit was very low in Kerala.

As regards long-term financial institutions, here also Kerala appears to have been largely neglected. The cumulative total of per capita assistance from all FIs till March 1997 stood at only Rs. 1,364 in Kerala as against the all-India average of Rs. 2,587. Kerala's level was only 39 per cent of Tamil Nadu's and 43 per cent of Karnataka's. In recent years, the position has worsened considerably. During 1992-97, the per capita assistance for Kerala stood at only Rs. 155 as against Rs. 347 for all-India and Rs. 446 in Tamil Nadu.

The flow of assistance was particularly low from all-India financial institutions. The cumulative total of per capita assistance from them till March 1997 was only Rs. 1,136 as against the all-India average at Rs. 2,501 and the highest of Rs. 6,841 in case of Gujarat. Tamil Nadu also received three times the Kerala's level. The provision from the KSFC was, however, not so depressing. At Rs. 293 per capita cumulative, it was higher than the all-India average though much lower than in the neighbouring states. The recent trend is also similar. The assistance from the KSIDC, functioning since 1961, was much lower. However, the relative position was similar. The per capita cumulative assistance came to Rs. 112 as against the national average at Rs. 103 (Table 5.8).

The assistance to SSI from the term-lending institutions was relatively much better in Kerala. From the national financial institution, SIDBI, the cumulative total of per capita assistance till March 1997 came to Rs. 301, which could be exceeded by only three of the major states and was much above the national average. The assistance from the SFC was, however, relatively low. The cumulative total till March

1994 came to Rs. 422.8 crores, constituting 3.6 per cent of all-India total. The SSIs' share in the aggregate of assistance from the SFC was 63.1 per cent in Kerala as against 70.5 per cent at the national level. In the neighbouring states also the SSIs received higher proportions. The more recent trend appears to be still worse. In 1996-97, in the total of assistance disbursed by KSFC, the share of SSI was only 48.3 per cent -- Rs. 91.12 crores out of Rs. 188.61 crores.

In the recent years, almost all the states are vying with one another to make their respective states attractive for industrial investment. Kerala has also effected a number of policy and institutional changes. These include tax and duty concessions, increase in investment subsidy, sharing cost of market and feasibility studies and providing entrepreneurs all required clearances from a single window. The response to these changes, however, has not been appreciable. During August 1991 to March 1998, the investment proposed for Kerala as per entrepreneur memorandum was Rs. 5,728 crores, constituting only 0.94 per cent of all-India total. Not only this, the implementation was also very slow here. Investment worth Rs. 237 crores, constituting 4.14 per cent of that proposed, has been implemented so far. The proportion implemented at the national level is 18.68 per cent (RBI 1999: I). A state biased towards working class has certain in-built difficulties in attracting industries, particularly when the neighbouring states follow a more pro-industry policy.

18

Towards Poverty Alleviation

We have noted in Chapter 2 that Kerala's success in removing utter poverty has been remarkable, particularly since late seventies. Presently only two states -- Punjab and Haryana -- present a better picture. However, there are still 20.73 lakh families living below the poverty line. Poverty removal requires, as has been noted earlier, not only general economic growth but also specific programmes in that direction. We have noted in the preceding chapters that the economic growth in Kerala has not been satisfactory. The poverty reduction came largely because of inflow of income from outside the state, higher wages and welfare expenditure, and the implementation of certain specific programmes for the weaker sections.

The object of this chapter is to look into how the programmes for weaker sections were implemented? The attention is focused, as in case of the relevant earlier chapters, primarily on the wage employment programmes, self-employment programmes, the PDS and nutrition programmes.

Wage Employment Programmes

The importance of wage employment in Kerala may be gauged from the fact that the proportion of labour households in rural households increased from 42.1 per cent in 1964-65 to 49.3 per cent in 1983. These proportions were much higher than the all-India average, being respectively 25.4 and 37.3 per cent. Even in recent years the situation has not improved much. According to the 1991 census, agricultural labourers constituted 32.46 per cent of total main workers in rural areas of Kerala as against 30.09 per cent in all-India (Unni 1997; GOI 1993).

Special employment schemes were introduced in Kerala, as in other states, from early seventies. But, the unemployment situation continued to be much worse here than in most other states. In 1983, according to the NSS, person rate of unemployment (full unemployment plus marginal underemployment) in Kerala stood at 52 in rural areas which was the highest among all the states; in 13 of the states it was less than 30. Even person rate of full unemployment was as much as 15.20, the highest among all the states; in 13 states it was less than 5 (NSSO 1987).

The employment created through rural employment programmes were meagre. The NREP and RLEGP together created an annual average of 113.3 lakh mandays during 1981-84 and increased to 184.4 lmd in 1985-88. The annual average of expenditure on them stood at Rs. 1,583.8 lakhs in the first period and Rs. 5,022 lakhs in the second period (GKL 1986, 1991). Thus, the cost per manday increased from Rs. 13.98 to Rs. 27.23 over the period. Below we give a brief look into the magnitude and manner of implementation of two of the currently running programmes-the JRY and the EAS.

Jawahar Rozgar Yojana

Under the JRY, launched in 1989, till 1996-97 a sum of Rs. 586.86 crores was spent for employment generation, that is an annual average of Rs. 73.36 crores. The annual spending rose to Rs. 88.88 crores in 1995-96 but declined to only Rs. 72.71 crores in the following year, and the target for 1998-99 was fixed at a meagre Rs. 44.79 crores. The employment generation over the eight-year period till 1996-97 totalled 1,161.46 lmd, and stood at the highest of 213.79 lmd in 1989-90 and the lowest at 101.01 in 1994-95. For 1998-89, the employment target under JRY has been fixed at 69.8 lmd (GKL 1998). The decrease in the size of the programme since 1996-97 is partly due to the shifting of intesified JRY to the EAS.

The comparative position of Kerala on JRY may be seen from Table 6.1 in chapter 6. Kerala's share in all-India total of spending under the scheme till 1994-95 came to only 2.45 per cent, that is, much below its population share. In the total of employment created, it was 1.88 per cent. The growth in resource utilisation between 1989-90 and 1995-96 was only 34.9 per cent here as against the all-India average at 61.3 per cent. The cost per manday created averaged Rs. 44.96 in Kerala as compared to Rs. 34.54 at the national level.

The proportion of workers from the weaker sections was very low here. The share of SC/ST in total number of mandays created was only 38.2 per cent and of landless workers 16.5 per cent as against 55.6 and 45.5 per cent respectively, at the national level. However, the proportion of SC/ST in the state's population was also low here, being only 11.0 per cent as per 1991 census as against 24.3 for all-India. Similar was the situation with regard to landless families due to better implementation of land reform measures. From the angle of annual income, however, the weaker groups appear to have been better represented here. The first concurrent evaluation of JRY had found that in Kerala those with income upto Rs. 3,500 constituted 8.13 per cent as compared to 5.41 per cent at the national level.

As regards the nature of assets created, wells, roads, sanitary latrines and houses were the major ones. Number of wells constructed over the entire period totalled 23,228, of which 78 per cent were under the Million Well Scheme, 15.6 per cent under drinking water wells and the rest irrigation wells. Road construction totalled 13,544 km, and declined from as much as 3,532 km in 1989-90 to 802 km in 1996-97. Construction of sanitary latrines numbered 12,453 at the highest in 1996-97 and at the lowest 4,313 in 1994-95; the total number over the entire period was 52,045. Number of houses constructed under JRY totalled 1,54,187, and increased continuously from 6,349 in 1989-90 to 29,952 in 1996-97 (GKL 1998).

To look into the comparative position in some of the areas: Kerala's share in the all-India total number of wells constructed under the MWS till March 1995 was 1.46 per cent, and in the expenditure 1.59 per cent. Cost per well came to the average of Rs. 37,599 here as against Rs. 34, 557 at the national level. In construction of houses under the IAY, Kerala's share in all-India total number constructed during 1985-86 to 1994-95 was 5.64 per cent, 1,15,760 out of 20,50,667. The average cost per house came to Rs. 16,020 here as against Rs. 12,079 at the national level.

As regards the quality of assets created, Kerala's position appears to be significantly better than many other states. According to the first concurrent evaluation carried out during January-December 1992, the proportion of good/satisfactory assets was 82.62 per cent as against the all-India average at 73.80; the proportion of poor quality assets were respectively, 0.24 and 8.13 per cent.

With regard to wage component in total expenditure also Kerala's position was better than in many other states. The wage/non-wage ratio was found to be 56.44 here in 1992 as against 53.47 at the national level. This however, could not increase the number of beneficiaries as the wage rates were much higher in Kerala. For unskilled workers, it was Rs. 34.78 for male and Rs. 27.39 for female as compared to Rs.

22.80 and Rs. 21.21, respectively, at the national level. For skilled workers also it was higher than the all-India average. Despite this, the wages paid in Kerala were much lower than the local off-season rates.

A major deficiency in the implementation of JRY in Kerala was that the maintenance of muster rolls was very poor. The concurrent evaluation found it non-available in 51.16 per cent of the cases; at the all-India level, the proportion was only 15.85 per cent. This was a serious deficiency because it enabled manipulation of the employment figures. Regarding discussion of the Action Plan in Gram Sabha meeting also Kerala's situation was very poor. The meetings were found to be held in only 0.75 per cent of panchayats as against 60.71 per cent at the all-India level. Thus, the violation of guidelines was widespread in Kerala.

Employment Assurance Scheme

The EAS, launched in October 1993, was also of small size. In 1993-94, it generated a total of 2.60 lakh mandays, constituting 0.53 per cent of all-India total. The programme was in operation in 21 blocks of seven districts. In the following year, 1994-95, the scheme generated 27.64 lmd, constituting 1.0 per cent of all-India total. In 1996-97, when the intensified JRY was merged into it, the programme was extended to 60 more blocks. The employment generated, however, increased only marginally, to 28.76 lmd. The expenditure on the programme increased nominally in these years, from Rs. 19.01 crores in 1994-95 to Rs. 20.63 crores in 1996-97. In 1998-99, however, the fund available for the programme rose to Rs. 63.42 crores. The cost per manday was naturally high here as the wage rates were high. In 1994-95, it stood at Rs. 68.79 as against the national average at Rs. 45.10 (GKL 1998; GOI 1995a, 1996c, 1999).

The expenditure on EAS continued to be heavily concentrated in a few districts. In 1996-97, six districts -- Idukki, Thiruvananthapuram, Wayanad, Kottayam, Kannur and Malappuram -- together accounted for 82.9 per cent of the total; for idukki alone it was 26.6 per cent. In the total of employment generated, their share was 84.4 per cent. The cost per manday created was lowest in Ernakulam, at Rs. 42.29, but the employment generated here was only 0.41 lmd. The highest cost was in Pathanamthitta, at Rs. 78.00 per manday, and the employment generated stood at 0.02 lmd. The average cost per manday this year was Rs. 71.75.

As regards the rate of progress in completion of works, in 1996-97, for example, 1,997 works were taken up but only 714, that is, 36 per cent, could be completed. In Idukki, where the largest number of works were taken up, the completion rate was 51.2 per cent, 311 out of 608. In Pathanamthitta, on the other hand, 19 works were taken up and none could be completed.

Overall employment creation through various public works was also very low in Kerala. According to the NSS data, per thousand number of households, participation in public works stood at only 42 in Kerala in 1987-88 as against the all-India average of 64. In 1993-94, these were respectively 49 and 59. Even this performance of Kerala was, however, the best among the southern states (NSSO 1998a).

In the earlier chapters on poverty alleviation we have spoken of the role of wage rates in raising the weaker sections above the poverty-line. In case of Kerala this appears to have played a big role. The wage rates increased noticeably over the years. For paddy field workers, the average daily wage rate increased from Rs. 11.13 for male in 1980-81 to Rs. 35.77 in 1990-91 and Rs. 92.18 in 1996-97. For female, the rates in these years were respectively, Rs. 7.91, Rs. 21.11 and Rs. 60.52. Among skilled workers, for carpenter the wage rate rose to Rs. 128.54 in 1996-97 from Rs. 54.47 in 1990-91 and Rs. 19.82 in 1980-81; for mason, the rates were respectively, Rs. 127.81, Rs. 53.98 and Rs. 19.78 (GKL 1998: 22-23).

Self-Employment Programmes

For the weaker sections, important self-employment programmes in operation were the Integrated Rural Development Programme, the TRYSEM and the DWCRA. Below we give a brief look into the magnitude and impact of these programmes in Kerala.

IRDP

This programme was launched in the state in 1978-79 in 58 selected blocks, and extended to 5 more in the following year. Presently it is implemented in all the 152 blocks in the state through the DRDAs. This is a 50 per cent Centrally sponsored credit linked scheme for identified poor families, as noted in the relevant preceding chapter. Families with annual income below Rs. 11,000 at 1991-92 prices are assisted under the programme. However, those with income below Rs. 8,500 are assisted first. A substantial part of the total outlay is earmarked for families belonging to SC/ST, women and physically handicapped. A group approach has been introduced recently for making the programme more effective. Table 18.1 presents the trend in progress of the IRDP.

Table 18.1

Trend in Assistance under the IRDP and its Sub-Schemes in Kerala

Year/ Period	IRDP				TRYSEM				DWCRA		
	Subsidy (Rs. lakhs)	Loans (Rs. lakhs)	Per Capita invest-ment (Rs.)	No. of families (in '000)	No. Trained	Expendi-ture (Rs. lakhs)	Expend. per trainee (Rs.)	% employed	Groups formed (no.)	Expenditure	
										Total (Rs. lakhs)	Per group (Rs.)
VI Plan total	4513	13116 (190.6)[a]	3463	509.0	25787	128.85	500	56.8	81	18.88	23309
VII Plan "	7461	5629 (109.5)	4745	486.6	26472	602.54	2276	71.2	803	65.82	8197
1990-92 "	3316	5030 (51.7)	7022	118.8	12783	380.91	2980	69.8	443	70.68	15955
VIII Plan "	9749	20654 (111.9)	11763	242.6	29218	1147.77	3928	80.5	3304	574.82	17398
1992-93	1485	2251 (51.6)	7369	50.5	7919	222.85	2814	68.3	241	41.10	17054
1993-94	1798	2646 (47.2)	8275	53.7	5549	247.29	4456	73.9	551	77.92	14142
1994-95	2173	3987 (83.5)	13307	46.3	5854	281.32	4805	90.9	753	105.78	14048
1995-96	2009	5239 (160.8)	16717	43.4	4860	237.66	4890	87.8	797	147.95	18563
1996-97	2286	6531 (185.7)	18108	48.7	5036	158.65	3150	87.5	962	202.07	21005

Source: GKL 1998.

Note: a: percentage in relation to subsidy.

The first noticeable thing is that there has been a sharp decline in the number of beneficiaries. As against 5.09 lakh families assisted in the Sixth Plan, in the Seventh Plan it was down to 4.87 lakh and in the Eighth as low as 2.43 lakh. Sectorally, schemes in the primary and tertiary sectors got a much higher preference than those in the secondary sector. The share of the primary sector varied between 40 and 43 per cent and of the tertiary sector 34 to 36 per cent. The fall in number of beneficiaries was partly due to the policy of making larger investment per capita so that the family is in a position to cross the poverty-line. It was also because of the emphasis on the ability of the recipient to utilise the fund properly.

Number of beneficiary families could have been increased by raising the allocation of fund to the programme. But there was no such attempt. The growth in fund allocation was not in keeping with the objective of raising per capita investment. The total of expenditure on subsidy increased from Rs. 45.13 crores during the Sixth Plan to Rs. 97.49 crores in the Eighth Plan, that is, it was a little more than doubled. Per capita investment, on the other hand, was more than trebled in this period, rising from the average of Rs. 3,463 to Rs. 11,763. The growth in per capita investment actually came from the third year of the Eighth Plan, and stood at as much as Rs. 18,108 in the last year, rising from Rs. 7,369 in the first year. The mobilisation of bank loans was also very low in some of the years. Loan as percentage to subsidy was as much as 190.6 in the Sixth Plan but this level could never be reached again, and it was as low as 47.2 in 1993-94.

In comparison with the performance in other states also Kerala's is not satisfactory. In the all-India total of fund utilised on IRDP, Kerala's share declined from 2.55 per cent in 1990-91 to 2.35 in 1994-95 and 2.28 in 1997-98. In the total number of families benefited, however, its share rose to 2.59 per cent in 1997-98 from 2.09 in 1994-95 and 2.10 in 1990. The representation of SC/ST among the beneficiaries was relatively low in Kerala. As may be seen from Table 6.2, in 1997-98 Kerala had only 35.2 per cent as against the national average of 46.4.

The programme had a very limited impact on poverty reduction, particularly in the earlier years. It was not only due to inadequacy of financial assistance but also because of wrong identification of families. According to a study by the State Planning Board, in 1983 around 23 per cent of the households selected were ineligible ones (Kannan 1995). Marketing of the products produced by IRDP households was also a real bottleneck until the launch of Kerala Rural Development and Marketing Society in 1986. However, the sales picked up only since 1992-93, and touched Rs. 54.82 lakhs in 1996-97 (GKL 1998: Appendix 10.6).

TRYSEM and DWCRA

The TRYSEM as a component of IRDP, as noted in chapter 6, aims at imparting training to rural youth to enable them to take up self-employment ventures. Successfully trained youths are assisted to start their own enterprises with loan and subsidy under the IRDP. The expenditure on the programme has increased noticeably in Kerala over the years. Whereas during the Sixth Plan only Rs. 128.85 lakhs were spent on the programme, in the Seventh Plan it rose to Rs. 602.54 lakhs and in the Eighth Plan to Rs. 1,147.77 lakhs, that is, nearly a nine-fold rise.

In the number of youths trained, however, the growth was insignificant. It increased from a total of 25,787 in the Sixth Plan to 26,472 in the Seventh and 29,218 in the Eighth Plan. The cost of training per youth rose sharply over the years. In the Sixth Plan, it averaged only Rs. 500 per youth but in the Eighth Plan rose to Rs. 3,928; in fact, it touched as much as Rs. 4,890 in 1995-96.

The placement of the trained youth was also not satisfactory. A large number remained unemployed for a long period. The proportion unemployed in the Sixth Plan was as much as 43.2 per cent of those trained. In the following plans it declined and stood at 19.5 per cent in the Eighth Plan. The percentage of youth getting self-employed continued to be very low and showed a declining tendency. During the Eighth Plan it was only 25.1 per cent of the total number trained as against 32.1 in the Seventh Plan (GKL 1998: Table 10.5).

Looking to the relative position of Kerala among the major states, in 1995-96, the fund spent on the programme constituted only 2.5 per cent of all-India total. In the number trained, it was still lower, being 1.8 per cent. It is necessary to note that while the expenditure was 142 per cent of the allocation, on the physical target there was a shortfall of 20 per cent. The percentage of self-employed in Kerala this year was 29.6 as against 31.7 at the national level. The proportion remaining unemployed this year was, however, the lowest in Kerala – only 12.2 per cent as against 52.3 at the national level. The coverage of SC/ST was as much as 87.8 per cent of the total number as compared to 47.7 per cent for all-India.

Overall, there appears to be a great mismanagement of the scheme. If properly managed, it could be an important instrument for reducing unemployment among the rural youth. Given the level of literacy and the extent of unemployment among the youths, there was no reason for it becoming a failure to the extent it did.

The other sub-component of IRDP, the DWCRA, meant for women and children, had a much better performance. Number of groups formed increased from only 81 in the three years of Sixth Plan to 803 in the Seventh Plan and as many as 3,304 in the Eighth Plan. Th expenditure on it rose to Rs. 574.82 lakhs in the Eighth Plan, from Rs. 65.82 in the Seventh and Rs. 18.88 lakhs in the Sixth. The aggregate of expenditure over the 15 year period came to Rs. 730.20 lakhs and the number of groups formed 4,631, with 80 per cent of them functioning.

The average cost of groups formed varied widely. While it was as much as Rs. 23,309 in the Sixth Plan, in the Seventh it came to only Rs. 8,197. In the following years, at the minimum it was Rs. 14,048 in 1994-95 and at the highest Rs. 21,005 in 1996-97.

Public Distribution System

The rationale for PDS in Kerala arose as a result of the food deficit nature of the state. The PDS was started in 1964 covering the entire population, excluding those who produced enough for their own consumption. Over a period of time, the scheme established itself and now has two components: One is informal rationing through a network of ration shops, and the other is a system of fair price shops for selling essential items. The importance of the latter is marginal since the quantity distributed is only around 10 per cent of that distributed through the former.

The number of families with ration cards increased from 41 lakhs in 1961 to 50.06 lakhs in 1991 and 59.5 lakhs in 1998. Total population covered by rationing stood at 301.85 lakhs in January 1998. On an average, there is one retail outlet for every 400 households. There were 14,236 retail ration shops in 1997, of which 1,069 were cooperatives.

The effectiveness of a PDS to reduce poverty depends on a number of factors like, availability of essential commodities on a regular basis, affordability in terms of prices vis-a-vis the open market, the share of these items in the total purchase, spatial coverage of the PDS and physical access to the shops. Although the PDS in Kerala is still constrained by a number of factors, including the inability of the state to obtain greater allotment of rice from the Centre, very low quality of rice and highly inadequate distribution of cooking oil, probably the above-mentioned factors are much better met here than in most other states. This will be evident from the analysis below.

The total quantum o rice and wheat distributed in Kerala through the PDS increased from the annual average of 11.91 lakh tonnes during 1975-77 (three years) to 16.25 in 1987-89 and 18.02 during 1995-97. The quantum of rice distributed in these years were respectively, 9.33, 14.71 and 13.80 lakh tonnes. The per capita distribution of rice-plus-wheat increased from the average of 43.4 kg during 1975-79 to 67.8 kg in 1990-91 and then declined to around 62 kg in 1995-97. On the basis of total population of respective states, the per capita PDS of foodgrains averaged 51.39 kg during 1973 to 1989 in Kerala, which was the highest among all the major states. In the neighbouring state of Tamil Nadu it was 24.38 kg and in Karnataka 19.48 kg (Geetha and Suryanarayana 1993). With regard to PDS per poor population also Kerala's position was generally the best among the major states, as may be seen from Table 6.4.

Recently, under the revamped PDS, a scheme for supply of rice at concessional rates to 42 per cent of families below the poverty-line has been introduced in Kerala, although the government of India scheme covers only 25 per cent of the population. Under it, common rice was supplied at the rate of Rs. 3.90 a kg in January 1998. The subsidised 'A' grade rice was priced Rs. 6.50 and the non-subsidised at Rs. 7.50 a kg. Total of foodgrains allotted under the new system stood at 17.76 lakh tonnes in 1996-97, declining from 23.85 lakh tonnes in the preceding year. In the all-India total of allotment under the PDS, however, the share of Kerala increased from 9.33 per cent to 10.77 per cent. The relative share of BPL families in the total allotment to Kerala is very low. In 1996-97 it was only 10.4 per cent as against 42.7 per cent at the national level (Mooij 1999).

Nutrition Programmes

For alleviating the problem of malnutrition in Kerala two Programmes were particularly important. First, there was the Special Nutrition Programme (SNP) for pregnant women and pre-school children, and secondly, the school meals programme for children in the primary schools. The coverage of SNP became significant only since the early eighties. Total number of beneficiaries rose to 5.18 lakhs in 1981-82 from 3.00 lakhs in 1979-80. Since 1984-85, however, the Integrated Child Development Scheme (ICDS) began playing the major role in it. Number of beneficiaries under the SNP declined to only 0.15 lakh this year, whereas for ICDS – a Central Government programme – it increased to 7.70 lakhs from only 1.93 lakhs in the preceding year. During 1988-91, total number of beneficiaries covered by both SNP and ICDS annually averaged 7.60 lakhs, with the latter contributing 95 per cent (Kannan 1995).

The ICDS is providing 300 calories and 8.12 gms of protein per beneficiary in the age-group 0-6 years, and 500 calories and 25 gms of protein per day to pregnant woman and nursing mother. These are provided for about 300 days in a year. There were 120 ICDS projects in 1997 in the state, of which 111 were rural, one tribal and the rest urban projects. There were 15,605 anganwadis in the state benefiting 10.32 lakh children and women. There were also 39 non-ICDS blocks covering 1.23 lakh beneficiaries, served through 913 feeding centres. They provide the same type of benefits as the ICDS (GKL 1998).

The programme for feeding school-going children has a much longer history. However, on a Kerala-wide scale it was started in 1961. The full commodity support for the programme came from a voluntary relief organisation, Cooperation for American Relief Everywhere (CARE) till the end of 1970s and partially till the mid-'eighties, when it stopped the support. Since then the programme is continuing with support and financial assistance from the state government. The objective of the programme is to provide approximately 410 calories and 15 gms of protein, which would account for one-fourth of the normal daily requirement of a child. There were 11,370 centres in 1997 for providing mid-day meals. Number of beneficiaries from the programme rose to the highest of 32 lakhs in 1987-88 and in other years it fluctuated between 13.80 lakhs in 1990-91 and 23.75 lakhs in 1996-97. As a proportion of school-going children (LP/UP), the coverage varied between 56 per cent in 1990-91 and 79 per cent in 1989-90. The cost of providing a meal came to Rs. 144 per child per year in 1997 (GKL 1991, 1998).

There were in addition two associated programmes of nutrition, viz., Applied Nutrition Programme and Composite Programme for Women and Pre-School Children. The ANP provided education in nutrition, child care, family planning and production of nutritionally valuable foods, in addition to supplementary feeding to pre-school children and pregnant and lactating mothers. Number of beneficiaries under it stood at 4.80 lakhs in 1984-85 but declined drastically to around one lakh in the following years. Under the composite programme, child care centres and other facilities were built. The number of beneficiaries from the programme annually averaged 1.24 lakhs during 1985-91 (Kannan 1995).

The impact of all these programmes on the problem of malnutrition is probably not much. Surveys conducted in recent years showed a high degree of malnutrition among school children. On preschool children it was observed that 47.4 per cent suffered from mild form of malnutrition, 32.9 per cent from moderate form and 2 per cent suffered severe form of malnutrition (GKL 1998: 121).

Minimum Needs Programme

The MNP received much less attention in Kerala as the social sector is highly developed here. As a separate head of expenditure, it was there only in the Sixth Plan. A total of Rs. 134.97 crores was spent on MNP in this plan, and it was proportionately higher than in the neighbouring states of Tamil Nadu and Karnataka. In the total expenditure under MNP, the highest proportion went to rural water supply, at 27.0 per cent, followed by rural roads 22.3, elementary education 16.6, housing 13.4 and nutrition 10.7 per cent. While the expenditure on housing exceeded the approved outlay by 105 per cent and that on rural roads by 78 per cent, in case of rural water supply it was 19 per cent short of target.

Although there was no MNP in the following plans, this did not mean that the situation was perfect everywhere. Particularly with regard to water supply and housing, there is much that remains to be done. At the end of November 1997, only 52.3 per cent of the rural population had access to protected water supply. District-wise, there was wide variation in the provision. In Kozhikode and Kannur less than a fifth of the total population were covered. In piped water supply, the coverage was less than 5 per cent in six districts and the maximum was 12.3 per cent in Thrissur. In terms of habitation, in April 1997, 11.7 per cent were yet to be covered and 16.4 per cent had partial coverage, with supply of less than 10 lpcd.

As regards housing, it is estimated that a total of 10.9 lakh houses, 20 per cent of the total in Kerala, are thatched huts of semi-permanent nature. Out of these, 5.5 lakh units are substandard and not fit for human living. Moreover, 5 per cent of the existing houses are required to be demolished and reconstructed. This situation prevails despite the existence of a number of housing schemes for the weaker sections.

The problem is that the schemes were not big enough to meet the situation properly. Till mid-eighties, there was negligible attention to the problem. Up to March 1986, a total of only 67,447 houses were constructed under the NREP and RLEGP, Kudikidappukar Housing, Fishermen Housing, Huts/Houses for Rural Workers and House Sites to Rural Landless Workers combined. In the last one decade, however, the progress was faster. Till March 1997, a total of 2,24,190 houses were constructed under the JRY, Fishermen Housing Scheme, House Sites to Rural Landless Workers, Huts/Houses for Rural Workers and Kudikadappukar Housing, with the first one alone accounting for 75 per cent of the total (GKL 1998: Appendix 9.77).

Other Measures

There are a variety of other measures also to benefit the weaker sections. The social security measures are quite extensive in Kerala. There are as many as 30 schemes covering the poor aged agricultural workers, widows, destitutes, handicapped, khadi workers, coir workers, cashew workers, handloom workers and so on. In 1997, Rs. 107.33 crores were spent on various major pension and welfare fund schemes for the benefit of 12.06 lakh persons. The amount provided to each beneficiary is, however, negligible. For example, under the agricultural workers' pension scheme, introduced in 1980, only Rs. 100 is provided per month to those above 60 years of age and having a family income below Rs. 15,000. Similarly, under the Kerala Fishermen's Welfare Scheme, introduced in 1987, Rs. 85 is provided to those above 60 years.

There were special measures for scheduled castes and scheduled tribes covering a wide area comprised of education, health, housing and other social welfare schemes. Special component plan for the SCs and Integrated Tribal Development Project for STs were introduced from the Fifth Plan. But, in the process of implementation, most of the schemes got diluted and those genuinely deserving were often neglected. In case of the special component plan, for example, the outlay was to be fixed on the basis of the SCs, share in the total population, but it was found to be significantly lower. A review of the programme also revealed that the schemes were often not relevant to the local needs and there was a high degree of leakage (GKL 1998: 124).

Forces against the weaker sections are too strong even in a communist stronghold state like Kerala. We may cite here the government's manner of handling the land alienation problem of the tribals.

In the tribal areas of Kerala, non-adivasi migrant settlers have grabbed large areas of the land belonging to adivasis through deceit and cunning. A rapid survey in Wayanad district in 1976 revealed that out of 298 cases, 71 were grabbed by force, 67 for measly sums and the rest for a small amount (Bijoy 1999: quoted). A legislation passed in 1975 provided that all transactions of adivasi land during the period 1960 to 1982 become invalid and are to be restored to the original owners. The Act was silent on the loss incurred by the adivasis due to the grabbing of their land by the settlers.

This Act, however, could not be implemented. Even the rule operationalising the Act came a full decade later, in 1986. It is estimated that 8,553 applications for restoration of lands totalling some 10,177 hectares were filed till the last date of receipt of applications. The government did not make any real attempt to implement the Act, except for some stray and insignificant actual restoration. The applicants were to prove prior ownership of lands applied for. The RDOs were empowered under the Act to summarily determine the validity of the applications. Naturally, the fact that adivasis, due to their ignorance of the complex laws and procedures, invariably could not get their land rights recorded, made it easy for the RDOs to reject a large number of applications. What remained was just 4,524 valid applications for some 7,640 acres. Even this the government was unwilling to restore. A High Court order came in October 1993 directing the government to "dispose off the applications pending before them within six months". The government appealed for more time again and again. In 1996, the court declared that the government has "no will to implement the legislation" (Bijoy 1999).

The 1975 Act was repealed by another Act passed in February 1999. As per the new Act, only land in excess of 2 hectares will be restored, and for alienated land upto 2 hectares alternate land would be given elsewhere. This is applicable to land alienated between January 1960 and January 1986. The 1975 Act had prohibited land transactions since 1982, but the present Act exempts land alienated during 1982-86 up to 2 hectares. That the government is for the land-grabbers is transparent.

VI

Summing Up

19

Summary and Conclusion

I

Economic development must aim at reducing the disparities in levels of living, for stark poverty and riches can never coexist for long without producing disorder and violence. India's development efforts, therefore, aimed to provide the semi-starving millions with a standard of living that would make for peace and harmony everywhere. The Directives Principles of State Policy of our Constitution as well as plan documents bear testimony to this. Section 39 of the Constitution is unambiguous about the right of everybody to "an adequate means of livelihood" and avoiding "the concentration of wealth and means of production to the common detriment". It also speaks about "free and compulsory education for all children" and opportunities for children to develop in a healthy manner. Special attention was to be given to the "educational and economic interests of the weaker sections of the people".

But what came about ultimately over the last half-a-century was largely a negation of all these assurances. Almost by design the masses of the population were kept in darkness and extreme of poverty. Illiteracy continues to be overwhelming; more than half the female population of the country is still illiterate, not to speak of functional literacy. The size of population living below the poverty-line is staggering. On the other hand, a small segment of population is wallowing in riches. Reduction of regional imbalance in development was paid only a lip-service. The already developed areas continued to receive a disproportionate share of the resources, both material and human. Inter-state disparities in development continued to be glaring. The rural areas, with an overwhelming majority of the population, were also deprived of the due share of attention. In general, they continue to lack the bare minimum of facilities required for a living.

All these were largely because of the nature of people that came to power after independence, and the political framework chosen. The leadership fell into the hands of people brought up under feudal or a capitalistic system and it was unexpected of them to bring a socialist type of economy. Ostentatious living became the order of the day. The parliamentary system and the federal structure were also limitations. However, the Union Government cannot be fully blamed for the inter-state or intra-state disparities in development. The states enjoyed considerable power and could do much if they wanted to. The resource endowment differed but its effect could be minimised with appropriate actions from the government.

In the given framework and influences, how the South Indian economies performed? Comparisons have limitations, but in general, the South Indian economies performed better than the national average. On per capita income, each of them had lower level than the national average, but in reducing the proportion of population below the poverty-line, their performance was much better than in many of the major states. In the social sector also, on the whole, they did better than the national average. On the life expectancy and the infant mortality rate, each of the southern states is in a better position.

The performance among the southern states varied greatly. The worst performer, by and large, was Andhra Pradesh with the largest population. The per capita income here was the lowest among the southern states. Its level of consumer expenditure (MPCE) was lower than the national average in both rural and urban areas. In reducing illiteracy Andhra's record was the worst, literacy rate being less than even the national average. In improving life expectancy also, its performance was poor, being lowest among the southern states, although above the national average. Regional disparities continued to be very wide. The percentage of urban population in 1991 was less than 15 in four districts as against the state average of 27. The female literacy rate was less than 20 per cent in two districts as against the highest of 64. Andhra had, however, the lowest percentage of population below the poverty-line in 1993-94.

Kerala, the smallest state, showed the best performance. Its MPCE in rural areas was the highest among the southern states in 1992. Among all the states, only Punjab and Haryana had higher levels. The proportion of population below the poverty-line was much less than the national average. The per capita income was low but it was made good by large remittances from abroad. Its performance in the social sector was best among all the states. The literacy rate here was as much as 90 in 1991. In the development of infrastructure its position was next only to Punjab. The regional disparities in development, however, continued to be high. The per capita income varied between Rs. 1,369 and Rs. 3,617 in 1996-97 among the districts.

Tamil Nadu had a very dismal record in poverty alleviation. Until recently, the proportion of population below the poverty-line was higher than the national average, and even now it is highest among the southern states. The MPCE in rural areas was less than the national average in 1992 and the rural-urban disparity was very wide. All these despite the state being the most industrialised in the south. The position of the social sector is, however, quite good. The literacy rate in 1991 was 63 per cent, the third highest among all the states., Inter-district disparity in development is too high. Per capita power consumption in 1993-94 varied between 20 units in Pasumpon and 2,302 units in Nilgiris.

Karnataka's performance was also not satisfactory. Despite having the highest per capita income among the southern states in recent years, the proportion of population below the poverty-line was high. The MPCE here was less than the national average, and lowest among the southern states. In the social sector, however, the situation was significantly better than the national average, and also in relation to Andhra among the southern states. The position of infrastructure, as a whole, was quite depressing. The inter-district disparity in development was also very high. The human development index of the most backward district was only 22 per cent of the highest in 1996.

The differences in the broad parameters of development have their origin in the pattern of resource mobilisation and deployment, the sectoral pattern of growth, and the sincerity with which the poverty alleviation programmes were implemented. The findings on all these are stated below for each of the states separately.

II

Given the extent of backwardness, there was need for huge deployment of funds, and this required utmost efforts at resource mobilisation. But Andhra's performance here was very poor. The aggregate of budgetary resources mobilised increased only 47 times over the long period of more than three decades, 1965-68 to 1994-97, as against 60 times for all states together. The per capita receipts in Andhra Pradesh stood at only Rs. 1,962 annually during 1994-97 which was substantially below the all-states' average and lowest among the southern states.

In the total receipts, the revenue receipts had a relatively high growth, and its share rose to 71 per cent in 1994-97 from 56 in 1965-68. The latest proportion was, however, the lowest among the southern states. Moreover, in the total revenue, the proportion contributed by the central transfer was high here – as much as 40 per cent in 1994-97 against the average of 33 per cent for all states.

The growth in OTR was very low here. Over the entire period, it increased 60 times as against 67 times for all states. The per capita tax collection came to only Rs. 625 in 1994-97 which was less than the all-states' average, and lowest among the southern states. In non-tax revenue, the position was slightly better. The growth in ONTR was much higher than in other southern states although less than the average for all states.

As regards capital receipts, in the last two decades, it had a relatively rapid growth. Between 1975-78 and 1994-97, it multiplied 21 times as against 14 times in revenue receipts. The composition of capital receipts changed substantially in recent years. The contribution from recovery of loans rose to as much as 33 per cent in 1994-97 from only 5 per cent in 1985-88. The share of loans from the Centre, on the other hand, declined from 51 per cent to 39. The contribution from internal debt also declined.

As the resource mobilisation was low, the level of expenditure also could not be high. The per capita total expenditure here was the lowest among the southern states. Moreover, the revenue expenditure had a rapid growth and its relative share rose to 80 per cent in 1994-97 from 58 in 1965-68. This was, however, not an unusual situation. In the latest period, the proportion was still higher in other southern states and also in the all-states' average. In the revenue expenditure, the proportion of development expenditure declined, as it increased by only 18 times in the last two decades as against 21 times in non-developmental. In the non-development expenditure, interest payment accounted for 42.7 per cent in 1994-97, rising from 31.4 in 1975-78. The latest proportion is highest among the southern states.

The growth in capital disbursement was very low as a large proportion of the capital receipts went to meet revenue expenditure. In the last two decades, capital disbursement increased only nine times as against 18 times in revenue expenditure. Moreover, the proportion of development expenditure in it showed a decline. Naturally, the plan expenditure could not grow as per requirements, and this affected the growth of the economy. The per capita plan expenditure of Andhra was generally lower than the all-India average.

As regards the growth of different sectors, the agricultural situation in Andhra has not been satisfactory. In the production of foodgrains its position worsened considerably over the years. During 1993-96, the per capita production here averaged only 168.3 kg as against the national average of 207.7 kg. And this was despite a noticeable improvement in yield rate. The area under foodgrains declined substantially over the years. In the most important crop rice, the growth in production slackened considerably in the last one-and-half decades. In non-food crops, which occupy half of the state's total cropped area, also the situation was not good. The most important crop groundnut, had a dismal performance. There was wide inter-district disparity in most of the crops.

Behind the low growth, apart from natural factors, the human deficiencies also played a big role. In the provision of irrigation facility, inputs, credit, marketing facility and land reform measures there were many shortcomings. The proportion of irrigated area was only 38.8 per cent in 1995-96, which was nominally higher than the all-India average. District-wise, while Nellore had 80 per cent of the cropped area irrigated in 1996-97 for Adilabad it was only 12 per cent. On the use of inputs, while the area under HYV seeds was low, the consumption of fertilisers increased quite rapidly. The per hectare consumption of fertilisers averaged 134.5 kg in 1995-98, which was the second highest among the states. On the provision of bank credit, Andhra's situation was better than most other states.

In the allied sectors also the performance was not appreciable. In animal husbandry, the growth in bovine population was relatively low. However, increase in milk production was substantial due to a favourable buffalo-cattle ratio in females. Between 1971-72 and 1994-95, the per capita milk production here increased 123 per cent as against 71 per cent at the national level. In poultry, the performance was much better. The per capita egg production stood at 59 in 1993-94, which was more than double that at the national level. The scope for further development of animal husbandry was substantial. There were wide inter-district variations in bovine density and in poultry development. In fishery, the growth in production was not in keeping with the resource base and Andhra's relative share in all-India production declined. The marine fish landings had a very slow growth due to inadequacy of infrastructure and low level of mechanisation. The development of inland fishery also did not receive adequate attention, despite there being ample scope for growth. The contribution from forestry was also low, despite having a relatively large proportion of forest area. In the state's NDP, forestry's contribution varied between 0.25 per cent and 0.59 per cent. Proper maintenance of forests hardly received any attention and unauthorised exploitation continued unabated until recently.

On industrial growth, Andhra's record was very dismal, particularly in recent years. The contribution of manufacturing to the state's NDP was only 10.2 per cent during 1994-97, which was less than half the level for all-India. Sectorally, the growth of the factory sector was quite impressive. The value of output registered a 338-fold rise over a period of three-and-half decades, and Andhra's relative share in national total rose to 7.3 per cent from 3.2. The movement in some of the technical coefficients was, however, not satisfactory. The gross output per employee remained significantly below the all-India average. The net value added to output was also very low. The growth in fixed capital per employee was not adequately reflected in the value of output. The position of small-scale industries, as a whole, was quite depressing. The growth in production of KVIs was very low, and Andhra's relative share in all-India total declined. The household enterprises were also in a poor situation. The value of fixed assets per enterprise was much lower than at the national level. The output per enterprise in rural areas averaged only Rs. 7,200 in 1989-90. On inter-district disparity in industrialisation, the situation was very depressing. The value of output per employee in the factory sector varied between Rs. 11.45 lakhs in Visakhapatnam and only Rs. 30 thousand in Nizamabad.

There were many reasons behind the poor industrial situation. The position of infrastructure as a whole was very unsatisfactory. The index of infrastructure development in 1992-94 was only 96 in Andhra as against 144 in neighbouring Tamil Nadu, with all-India=100. The availability of power was quite problematic in recent years, and this was mainly due to delay in completion of projects. District-wise, there was wide disparity in every type of infrastructure. On the availability of bank finance Andhra's relative position was poor, particularly with regard to SSI units. In the all-India total credit to SSI in 1995, Andhra's share was only 5.8 per cent as against 13.0 per cent in Tamil Nadu.

With regard to term finance to industry also the situation was similar. The per capita assistance from all financial institutions was much less than the national average. The role of promotional institutions set up by the government, particularly those meant for SSIs, was very unsatisfactory.

As the agricultural and industrial growth were very low, particularly for the backward districts, the government had to take some special measures for poverty alleviation. The schemes, however, came very late, and then also adequate funds were not provided for them. Moreover, the programmes were rarely managed in a way as to give benefits to the more needy. In the most important employment scheme, JRY, there was large-scale violation of the guidelines and the mandays created were insignificant. The self-employment programme, IRDP, was also of not much help. Identification of wrong families, fictitious purchase of assets and non-utilisation of the assets purchased were quite common. The management of the PDS left much to be desired, although there has been considerable improvement in recent years.

III

Tamil Nadu's performance in resource mobilisation was better than in many other states. The per capita budgetary resource mobilised averaged Rs. 2,290 in 1994-97, which was higher than in ten of the major states. The rate of growth in resource mobilisation was, however, relatively low, and its share in all-states' total declined to 6.6 per cent from 8.4 in 1965-68. In the aggregate of receipts, the proportion of revenue receipts increased significantly over the years, and stood at 79 per cent in 1994-97; there were only three states with higher levels of contribution. The per capita revenue receipts here was much higher than the all-states' average and highest among all the southern states.

In the revenue receipts, the contribution from central transfer was relatively low, less than the all-states' average. The state could collect a much higher level of tax revenue than most other states. The proportion of tax revenue in total revenue stood at as much as 84 per cent during 1994-97, rising from 66 per cent during 1965-68. Tamil Nadu's was the highest proportion in the latest period. In the tax revenue, the proportion of OTR was 79 per cent in 1994-97, much above the average for all states, and highest among the southern states.

In non-tax revenue, however, Tamil Nadu's performance was very poor. Not only the proportion in total revenue was the lowest among all the states, the rate of growth in collection was only half that for all states. The contribution from central transfer was also high. The proportion of ONTR in NTR declined from 65 per cent in 1975-78 to 49 in 1994-97. There was ample scope for raising the collection from ONTR.

The growth in capital receipts was very low. It increased by only 27 times over the entire period of three decades as against 46 times in the total receipts; for all states, the capital receipts had multiplied 52 times in this period. Loans from the Centre was the single largest contributor here, as much as 45 per cent of the total in 1994-97. This was followed by recovery of loans and internal debt. Although the growth in capital receipts was low, the per capita outstanding liability in Tamil Nadu stood at as much as Rs. 2,352 in 1997.

As regards expenditure, the proportion of revenue expenditure in the total was very high -- as much as 85 per cent in 1994-97, rising from 65 in 1965-68. This high growth in revenue spendings led to a large revenue account deficit. In the revenue expenditure again, the proportion of development expenditure had a sharp decline in recent years. In the last two decades, the non-developmental spendings registered a 19-fold rise, with interest payment recording 26-fold.

The capital disbursement was relatively low as a substantial portion of the capital receipts went to meet revenue deficit. Over the entire period of more than three decades it increased only 19 times as against 45 times in the aggregate of expenditure. Moreover, the development expenditure in it was not high, a large proportion being disbursed by way of loans, and repayments to the Centre. Consequently, the plan expenditure remained very low. The per capita plan expenditure in Tamil Nadu was lower than the all-India average in five of the plans. This affected the development of different sectors.

The growth of agricultural output in Tamil Nadu was generally very low. Per capita foodgrains production in fact recorded an absolute decline, and in recent years stood at much below the national average. The acreage under foodgrains declined continuously, and the growth in yield rate was also low. The performance in non-foodgrains was, however, much better. Groundnut, with the largest acreage, showed a substantial growth in production due to a sharp rise in yield rate in recent years. Coconut also registered a rapid growth. In cotton, however, the performance was poor; there was a nominal growth in yield rate over the period of nearly three decades. District-wise, in most of the crops there were wide variations in yield rate.

The low agricultural growth was due to a variety of reasons. But the availability of cultivable land itself was very unfavourable in Tamil Nadu. The per capita availability in 1992-93 was only 0.15 ha, which was lower than in all but two states. The cropping intensity also did not show much improvement and remained much below the national average. On irrigation facility, for the state as a whole the position was not bad, but there was wide inter-district disparity. In 1995-96, net irrigated area constituted 49 per cent of the cropped area, which was exceeded by only three of the states. Among the districts, however, the variation was between the highest of 81 per cent in Chengalpattu and 25 per cent or less in three districts. The state faces a number of problems in the area of irrigation. On the use of inputs, the position with regard HYV seeds and fertilisers is quite good; it is the fourth largest user among the states in both the inputs. On the availability of bank credit also Tamil Nadu's position is one of the best. In every area, however, there were wide inter-district disparities, and this points towards the potential for growth.

In allied sectors, Tamil Nadu's performance was quite good. In animal husbandry, milk production had a rapid growth and the state's relative share in all-India production rose to 6.3 per cent in 1994-95 from 4.1 in 1971-72. The per capita production, however, continued to be less than the national average. In poultry, Tamil Nadu's share in all-India total of egg production stood at 12 per cent in 1993-94, next only to Andhra Pradesh. The production was, however, heavily concentrated in one district, Salem. In fishery, Tamil Nadu had a very low growth in recent years, and consequently, its share in all-India production declined from 14 per cent in 1984-87 to 12 in 1991-94. Major portion of the fish production came from the marine sector; in recent years it was to the extent of three-fourths. The growth in inland fishery was very small and the potential remained largely unexploited. As regards forestry, the proportion of state's area under forest is relatively low – only 16.5 per cent. Even this, however, could not be protected well, despite 84 per cent of the area constituting reserved forests. The increasing pressure of population led to deforestation and widening gap between demand and supply of various forest products. The measures taken over the years were far behind what was required. The violation of regulations on maintenance of forests was rampant.

As regards the industrial sector, the growth in production was impressive. In the factory sector, Tamil Nadu's share in all-India total value of output rose to 11.6 per cent in 1994-95 from 6.4 in 1960, with a growth in output of 270-fold. In the latest year, there were only two states ahead of it. The trend in some of the technical coefficients was, however, not satisfactory. The net value added to output recorded a decline and the capital-output ratio increased noticeably. The industrial structure changed substantially in recent years. In the total value of output, cotton textile which was already at the top raised its share further, whereas food products, paper etc., and metal and alloys recorded declines. In the SSI sector also Tamil Nadu had a very good position. In KVIs, it accounted for 14 per cent of the all-India total value of output in 1993-94. Tamil Nadu's main problem was the concentration of industries in a few districts. There was also the neglect of rural areas. In household enterprises, the share of rural areas was only 56 per cent as against 76 per cent at the national level.

Tamil Nadu's position on the availability of infrastructure was very good. The index of infrastructure development stood at 144 in 1992-94, with all-India=100. The power generation had a rapid growth, and per capita power consumption multiplied 20 times between the First Plan and the Eighth Plan. Among the districts, however, there was extreme of variation. In 1993-94, Pasumpon had only 20 kwh against the state average of 347 kwh. On the provision of bank credit the situation was very good, although highly concentrated in a few districts. In 1995, the state accounted for 13 per cent of the aggregate of credit outstanding to SSIs from the SCBs. The provision of term finance from financial institutions was also very good. The beneficiaries were, however, disproportionately from the large-scale industries. Even the SFC's attention to the SSIs was relatively low.

Tamil Nadu's neglect of backward districts and the rural areas had its impact on the poverty situation. However, even the specific poverty alleviation measures were not managed properly. In case of the wage employment programme – JRY, there was large-scale violation of the guidelines, and the beneficiaries came to a large extent from those above the poverty-line. The self-employment programme – IRDP – also suffered from many deficiencies, and the number of beneficiaries declined in recent years. Under the TRYSEM, the placement of trained youth was very disappointing. Until recently, the PDS also did not benefit the poor much.

IV

Karnataka's efforts at resource mobilisation were substantial although the aggregate of collection remained small. The aggregate of per capita receipts here averaged only Rs. 2,161 in 1994-97, which was much below the national average. The growth in total receipts was low and its relative share in the aggregate for all states declined. An encouraging feature is, however, that the proportion of revenue receipts in the total was very high here, as much as 80 per cent in 1994-97 and it was highest among the southern states. The per capita receipt was significantly above the national average. And this was despite a very low level of central transfers. The share of central transfer in the state's total revenue stood at only a quarter in 1994-97, which was less than in ten of the major states.

In the revenue receipts, tax revenue played a very important role. Its relative share rose to 78 per cent in 1994-97 from 54 in 1965-68. The growth in receipts was highest among the southern states. The per capita tax collection was much above the all-states' average. In non-tax revenue, Karnataka's performance was depressing. Over the entire period of three decades, it increased only 30 times as against the average of 52 times for all states. The proportion of ONTR was, however, not bad. At 62 per cent in 1994-97, it was highest among the southern states and much above the all-states' average. There was ample scope for raising both the OTR and ONTR.

In capital receipts, Karnataka had a very low growth. Over the entire period of three decades, it increased only 28 times as against 52 times for all states. Moreover, a very large share came as loans from the Centre – as much as half of the total during 1994-97. The recovery of loans, on the other hand, had a sharp decline, to as low as 9 per cent in the recent years from 23 a few years back. The small savings, registered a noticeable growth and contributed 12.6 per cent in 1994-97 as against 5.1 in 1975-78.

As regards budgetary expenditure, although the growth was relatively low, the per capita level in 1994-97 stood at much above the all-states' average. In the aggregate of expenditure, the share of revenue expenditure was as much as 83 per cent in 1994-97, rising from 60 per cent in 1965-68. In the latest period, there were many states with lower proportions. Moreover, in the revenue expenditure, non-developmental spendings showed a higher growth. In the last two decades it multiplied 20 times as against 17 times in development expenditure.

The capital disbursements had a very low growth in Karnataka. In the last two decades it increased only seven times as against 23 times for all states. However, the development expenditure grew at a much higher rate, and the relative share rose to 65.1 per cent in 1994-97 from

38.8 in 1975-78. The proportion going as loans by the state as well as on repayment of loans to the Centre had a sharp fall in recent years. The plan expenditure in Karnataka had a relatively high growth, but even then the per capita level remained much below the national average.

As regards the sectoral pattern of development, the growth of agricultural production was significantly better here than in most other states. In recent years, it had grown at more than double the rate for all-India. Among the crops, foodgrains, however, did not perform well, particularly in recent years. The per capita production of foodgrains in Karnataka stood at the annual average of only 179.7 kg during 1993-96 as against the all-India average of 207.7 kg. The most important crop, jowar, had a sharp fall in area and the growth in production in the last two-and-half decades was a negligible 6.9 per cent. In non-foodgrains, cotton had an impressive growth in yield rate, and despite a sharp fall in area in recent years, the production increased substantially. The production of groundnut also increased noticeably and its relative share in all-India production rose to 13.0 per cent in 1994-97 from 10.9 in 1970-73. This was, however, largely due to acreage increase. Safflower and coconut also registered a rapid growth in production. District-wise disparity in yield rate was, however, very wide in most of the crops.

There was ample scope for improvement in Karnataka's agriculture. The utilisation of land left much to be desired. The cropping intensity here was much less than the national average and lowest among the southern states. This was largely due to lack of irrigation facility. The irrigated area as percentage to the state's cropped area stood at only 22.1 in 1995-96; there were only two states with lower proportions. Part of the reason behind this is of course the low irrigation potential of Karnataka. But utilisation of even the available potential is not high.

As regards the use of different inputs, Karnataka's position was not at all satisfactory. The proportion of area under HYV seeds was much lower than that at the national level. In consumption of fertiliser also the situation was not good. The per hectare consumption averaged only 79 kg, in 1995-98, slightly less than the national average. In mechanisation of agriculture, the use of pumpsets here was the lowest among the southern state. On the provision of credit, the situation was very poor. And then, in every area there was extreme of variation across districts.

In the allied sectors, Karnataka did not perform well. In animal husbandry, the per capita milk production remained low, despite a relatively high growth. In poultry, the level of egg production was exceeded by as many as six states in 1993-94. There was ample scope for developing the animal husbandry. In fishery, Karnataka's position was very depressing. Its share in all-India production of fish declined from 7.4 per cent in 1984-97 to 5.6 in 1991-94. An overwhelming proportion of the total came from the marine sector. The inland fishery hardly received any attention until recent years, and the production increased by only 37 per cent over a period of one-and-half decades. The condition of forests was also very unsatisfactory. The proportion of forest area here is relatively low, but even this could not be maintained properly. A large area has been lost to different purposes like hydroelectric projects and direct submersion. The denudation of forest areas continued unabated and the commercial return from forest declined sharply over the years.

On industrial growth Karnataka's overall position has not been satisfactory, particularly in recent years. The proportion of SDP derived from manufacturing was much less than at the national level in recent years. However, the growth of the factory sector over a long period was quite impressive. Between 1960 and 1994-95, the value of output increased by 267 times, and the relative share in all-India production rose to 4.7 per cent from 2.6. The trend in value of some of the technical coefficients was quite encouraging. The net value added to output despite showing a decline, was the highest among the major states. The capital-output ratio also declined. The position of SSIs was, however, very much worse. The growth in output of the KVI sector was very low and consequently, Karnataka's relative share in all-India total declined from 6.5 per cent in 1982-83 to 5.0 in 1993-94. The household enterprises were also relatively weak here. And then, irrespective of sectors, the industries were heavily concentrated in a few districts. Number of employees in the factory sector was as low as 2,300 in Kodagu in 1994-95 as against more than two lakhs in eight districts.

Although industrial growth depends on a variety of factors, the infrastructural situation of Karnataka has not been at all satisfactory. The index of infrastructure development stood at only 96.5 in 1992-94, with all-India=100. The electricity generation fell far short of the requirement in recent years, and even after imports from the neighbouring states there was huge deficit. The total of installed capacity here was only half the level in Tamil Nadu. In the provision of bank credit, the SSIs were largely neglected. In the aggregate of credit to industries by the SCBs the share of SSIs declined from 32.7 per cent in 1988-89 to only 20.5 per cent in 1994-95. The provision to artisan and village industries was very small.

On poverty alleviation Karnataka's efforts were very inadequate. Not only that the development of backward regions did not get proper attention at the right time, even the specific poverty alleviation measures were not managed properly. The implementation of JRY suffered from many deficiencies and the benefit to weaker sections was relatively low. The IRDP also had many loopholes. As in the other states, wrong identification of families and supply of substandard assets were quite common. The role of after-care support or monitoring was not given any importance. In case of the TRYSEM, the performance on placement was very poor. The PDS also did not give the due share of attention to the poor.

V

As in the other southern states, in Kerala also the growth in budgetary resource mobilisation was not satisfactory. Over the period of more than three decades – 1965-68 to 1994-97 – it increased only 49 times. The per capita collection in the latest period was marginally less than the all-states' average. However, in the aggregate of receipts, revenue receipts constituted as much as 76 per cent in 1994-97, which was much higher than the all-states' average.

In the revenue receipts, tax revenue contributed 81 per cent in 1994-97, rising from only 58 per cent in 1965-68. In the latest period, there were only two states with higher contribution. In the tax revenue, the proportion of OTR was generally a little more than three-fourths, much higher than the all-states' average. The per capita tax collection in Kerala averaged Rs. 1,120 in 1994-97, which was 59 per cent higher than the all-states' average.

In non-tax revenue, Kerala's performance was very depressing. The growth in collection over the entire period was only 23 times as against 74 times in tax revenue. The state's own collection of NTR stood at only 48 per cent in 1994-97, which was lower than in as many as ten major states. The growth in collection was very low from a number of items.

The growth in capital receipts was relatively high in Kerala, higher than in all-states' average. However, its relative share in the state's total budgetary receipts declined. In the composition of capital receipts, loans from the Centre played a relatively small role in recent years. Internal debt and small savings provided a very large share. Their combined contribution in 1994-97 was 55 per cent, rising from 25 in 1975-78.

As regards budgetary expenditure, it was relatively high in Kerala. The per capita came to Rs. 2,246 in 1994-97, much above the all-states' average and lower than only five of the major states. However, an overwhelming proportion of the total went to revenue account – as much as 85 epr cent in 1994-97, rising from 68 per cent in 1965-68. In the revenue expenditure again the non-development expenditure had a faster growth than development expenditure. The former had 21-fold rise in the last two decades as against 12 times in the latter. In non-development expenditure, interest payment constituted 41 per cent in 1994-97.

In capital disbursement, the proportion of capital outlay fluctuated rather widely, and averaged 52 per cent in 1994-97. Loans and advances by the state was the next important item and had a rapid growth in the last two decades – the relative share rising from 20 per cent to 32 per cent. Repayment of loans to the Centre constituted only 14 per cent in 1994-97, declining from 39 per cent in 1985-88. The growth of plan expenditure in Kerala was substantial but the per capita level generally remained less than the all-India average.

As regards the sectoral pattern of growth, neither agriculture nor industry performed well. The position of agriculture is very depressing. Between 1977-80 and 1994-97, the agricultural production increased by only 45 per cent and productivity by 21 per cent. The per capita production of foodgrains was halved over the last three-and-half decades – from 64.5 kg during 1960-63 to 32.8 kg in 1994-97. Kerala's per capita was only 16 per cent of the national average in 1993-96. This was primarily due to a rapid fall in area under foodgrains; the relative position on yield rate was quite impressive. In non-foodgrains also the situation was not encouraging. The most important crop, coconut, did not show any appreciable growth in yield, and its relative share in all-India production declined from 66 per cent in 1970-73 to 45 in 1995-98. In cashewnut and tapioca also the situation was very depressing.

There are many reasons behind the poor performance. The availability of land itself is very limited in Kerala. The per capita net sown area in 1995-96 was only 0.073 ha, which was less than half the all-India average. The culturable waste available is also very limited. As regards irrigation facility, only 15 per cent of its cropped area is irrigated. The utilisation of the potential has been very low, particularly with regard to minor irrigation, and there is extreme of inter-district disparity. The use of modern inputs in Kerala's agriculture is also relatively low. The position on HYV adoption is the worst. Fertiliser consumption per hectare was only 66.5 kg in 1995-98, much less than the national average. On the provision of credit to agriculture, however, Kerala's position is very good. The credit outstanding from PACS was 16 per cent of all-India total in March 1994.

The growth of the allied sectors was much better in Kerala. In animal husbandry, milk production had a rapid growth due to a very favourable change in female/male ratio. In poultry, the per capita egg production in 1993-94 was more than double the national average. In fishery also Kerala's position is very good. During 1991-94, it accounted for 13 per cent of all-India total production, which was the second largest. In the total catch, marine fishery accounted for more than 90 per cent. The marine fishery, however, faces some disturbing trends. There has been overexploitation of inshore areas and unregulated use of crafts and gears had reduced the accessibility of traditional fishermen. Regarding inland fishery, until recent years it did not receive any attention. In forestry, although Kerala has a relatively large forest area its return is on the whole declining. The forest resources are faced with many problems, as in case of the other states. Over-exploitation has resulted in rapid depletion of forests but the afforestation programmes are very inadequate to compensate for the loss.

As regards the industrial sector, its contribution to the state's income is very low. During 1994-97, only 14 per cent of the SDP came from manufacturing. The performance of the factory sector here is very depressing. The growth in value of output over the long period since 1960 was only 127 times, which is much less than the national average and lowest among the southern states. Kerala accounted for only 1.8 per cent of the all-India total value of output in 1994-95. The productivity of the employees is very low. In 1994-95, the value of output per employee was only 47 per cent of the national average. The industrial structure of Kerala is very narrow and the traditional industries face many problems. District-wise, there is extreme of variation in the size of the factory sector. The position of SSI sector is also not satisfactory. The KVIs' relative share in all-India production declined from 4.1 per cent in 1982-83 to 3.4 in 1993-94 and in employment from 4.9 per cent to 3.5. The household sector is also relatively weak here.

Behind the poor performance of Kerala's industries many factors are responsible. But overall, it is the unfavourable industrial climate that is primarily to be blamed. Kerala has to contend with the more pro-industry policies of the neighbouring states, particularly Tamil Nadu. Militant trade unionism here is generally considered a very unfavourable factor. It is largely due to this the wages and other benefits to workers are high here. As to infrastructure, although the overall position is very good, in recent years power situation has become quite problematic. A major problem in power development here is the sole dependence on hydro-power, which is subjected to the vagaries of monsoon. In the provision of finance from commercial banks and financial institutions Kerala's relative position has been very poor. In the aggregate of credit to SSIs from the SCBs, the state's share in 1993-94 was only 3.9 per cent, declining from 9.8 in 1968.

On poverty alleviation, so far as the specific measures are concerned, the Kerala government did not give any special attention to them. Under the JRY Kerala spent only 2.45 per cent of all-India total and created 1.88 per cent of total employment over the entire period till 1994-95. The implementation of the scheme suffered from many deficiencies, as in case of other states. The IRDP was also not managed properly and the number of beneficiaries declined continuously. The operation of the TRYSEM was not satisfactory. A large number of trained youth remained unemployed for a long time. The PDS and the nutrition programmes were, however, managed much better in Kerala than in most other states. In reducing poverty, the high wages and social security measures played a big role here. The government's sincerity towards poverty reduction was, however, not beyond question. The manner of handling the land alienation problem of the tribals is just one example.

VI

Finally, a few words need to be added on development in general and on each of the South Indian states. For economic development of the right type, that is, that which serves the long-run interest of everybody, it is of overriding importance that education and character building gets the highest priority. A socialist pattern of society can be built only by people oriented that way, and not by those with crude capitalist and feudal mentality. Nor is it possible to have a self-reliant development with people devoid of nationalist feelings. Character building is however, easier said than done. It requires a strong, resolute government.

In the context of Indian economy, or South Indian economies for that matter, this may appear simply a pious wish, given the character and inclinations of the present ruling class. But even within the limitations, much can be done. The right thinking people need to assert their existence and organise people's power so that the evil forces are compelled to mend their ways. Things must change otherwise violence and disorder will be the order of the day.

Next to education, in every development effort, health facilities should get the utmost importance. If these two things are there, even a relatively small income can make for a happy living. The term 'health facilities' needs to be used in a broader sense, to include not only curative measures but also preventive ones. Preventive measures, however, encompass a variety things like availability of drinking water, sanitation and environmental improvements and personal hygiene, and it is greatly influenced by the quality of education provided.

In the context of south Indian economies, each of them needs to give much greater attention to education and health facilities than given hitherto. Andhra Pradesh is the most backward state in these respects, and therefore, must allocate the highest amount of fund for these purposes. Karnataka's position is also not much better, and therefore, needs to provide the highest allocation to them. Tamil Nadu and Kerala too cannot afford to neglect these sectors. In case of Kerala, the need is particularly of giving attention to the backward communities and regions, and on qualitative improvement. It may also be noted that the fund allocation is not everything, what is more important is how the fund is spent, for whom and for what type of education and health facilities.

The most important, and probably the most difficult task is giving the right amount of attention to rural areas. So far a great injustice has been done to the majority, living in rural areas, by neglecting their development. The rural areas were deprived not only of fund but also of human resources. As the economic growth was very limited, all quality people were compelled to leave the rural areas. The education system also played a part in this driving out process. There is now need for a reverse flow of resources, both human and material, from urban to rural areas.

At the same time there should be a determined attack on the structures and processes responsible for the poverty of the rural masses. Presently, all the major determinants – the policy environment, the markets and modernised agriculture – tend to bypass the poor rather than work towards their development. President K.R. Narayanan, in his address to the nation on the eve of the fiftieth anniversary of the Republic, lamented that the decade old liberalisation has completely ignored the poor and needy.

On industrial growth, it is high time that we become conscious about its cost. The craze for higher and higher living standard and a variety of non-essential goods must be severely curbed. In our unending crave for ostentatious living we have already damaged much the quality of air, water and sunshine, the basic elements of sustenance for all creatures. To mention only one area of action urgently needed: We must make utmost efforts to raise the proportion of forest area to one-third of the total, as laid down by the Nation Forest Policy as early as 1952. Karnataka and Tamil Nadu in particular, need to give much greater attention to their forests as the proportion of the forest area in them is very low.

Above all, there is need for a severe curb on population growth. The quality of life of the masses cannot be improved much if we go on increasing the size of population. Natural resources are not unlimited that we can go on exploiting them indiscriminately for the rapidly rising population. Andhra Pradesh and Karnataka, in particular, should take stringent measures for curbing the population growth. In the decade 1981-91, Andhra's population increased by 24.20 per cent, higher than the national growth, and Karnataka's by 21.2 per cent.

Bibliography

Books

All India Congress Committees (AICC) 1949. The Congress Agrarian Reforms Committee Report, New Delhi.

Andhra Pradesh State Electricity Board (APSEB) 1998. Power Development in Andhra Pradesh (Statistics) 1996-97, Hyderabad.

Centre for Monitoring Indian Economy (CMIE) 1992. Basic Statistics Relating to the Indian Economy, Vol.2, States, September.

—1996a. India's Social Sector, February.

—1996b. India's Agricultural Sector A Compendium of Statistics, July.

—1996c. India's Industrial Sector, January.

—1997a. Approach Paper to Ninth Five Year Plan, February.

—1997b. Profile of States, March.

—1998. Agriculture, September.

—1998a. Infrastructure, December.

—1998b. Banking and Finance, December

—1998c. Public Finance, May.

—1999b. Public Finance, February.

—1999c. Agriculture, September.

—1999d. Energy, March-April.

—1992e. Infrastructure, December.

Dandekar, V.M. and N. Rath 1971. Poverty in India, Poona.

Deb, Kalipada 1982. Foreign Resources and Development in India, New Delhi: Heritage Publishers.

—1986. Rural Development in India Since Independence, New Delhi: Sterling.

—1988. Indian Banking Since Independence The Challenges And Response, New Delhi: Ashish.

—1997. The Challenges of Rural Development Five Decades of Indian Experience, New Delhi: MD.

George, P.T. and V.B.S. Rao 1979. Land Reforms: Production and Productivity: A Study in Andhra Pradesh, National Institute of Rural Development, Hyderabad.

Government of Andhra Pradesh (GOA) 1960. Statistical Abstract of Andhra Pradesh 1957, Directorate of Economics and Statistics, Hyderabad.

—1972. Statistical Abstract 1969.

—1986. Statistical Abstract 1983.

—1997. Statistical Abstract 1994.

—1999. Statistical Abstract 1997.

—1981. Sixth Five Year Plan (1980-85), Hyderabad.

—1986a. Seventh Five Year Plan 1985-90.

—1993a. Eighth Five Year Plan (1992-97).

—1993. Public Sector Undertakings in Andhra Pradesh Performance Review 1989-92, Directorate of Economics and Statistics.

—1995. Hand Book of Statistics Guntur District 1994-95, Guntur.

—1996. State Report on Live Stock Census 1993, Directorate of Economics and Statistics.

—1998. Economic Survey 1997-98, Finance and Planning Department, Hyderabad.

Government of India (GOI) 1961. Third Five Year Plan, Planning Commission, New Delhi.

—1963. Census of India Paper No.1 of 1962, 1961 Census Final Population Totals, Registrar General and Census Commissioner, New Delhi.

—1963a. Annual Survey of Industries 1960, Summary Result for Factory Sector, Central Statistical Organisation (CSO), New Delhi.

—1972. Infant Mortality in India, Office of the Registrar General of India, New Delhi.

—1975. Economic Survey 1974-75, Ministry of Finance, New Delhi

—1975a. Livestock Census, 1972, New Delhi.

—1976. All-India Report on the Census of Small Scale Industries, Development Commissioner, New Delhi.

—1979. Study of Crash Scheme for Rural Employment (1971-74), Programme Evaluation Organisation (PEO), New Delhi.

—1980. Annual Survey of Industries 1977-78, C.S.O., New Delhi.

—1980a. Evaluation of Food for Work Programme, Final Report, P.E.O., New Delhi.

---1983. Census of India 1981, Series 1 India, Paper II B (i) Primary Census Abstract, General Population, New Delhi.

—1985. Economic Survey 1984-85, New Delhi.

—1986. Census of India 1981, Series 10 of Kerala, Paper-3 of 1981.

---1992. Report on the Second All India Census of Small Scale Industrial Units, Development Commissioner, New Delhi, August.

—1993. Census of India 1991 Series 1 India Paper-2 of 1992, Final Population Totals: Brief Analysis of Primary Census Abstract, New Delhi.

---1991. MRD Annual Report 1990-91, Ministry of Rural Development, New Delhi.

---1995. Health Information of India, Central Bureau of Health Intelligence, New Delhi.

—1995a. MRD Annual Report 1994-95, New Delhi.

—1996a. Economic Survey 1995-96, New Delhi.

—1996b. Family Welfare Programmes in India Year Book 1994-95, Ministry of Health and Family Welfare, New Delhi.

—1996c. MRD Annual Report 1995-96, New Delhi.

---1997. Annual Survey of Industries 1994-95 Summary Results for Factory Sector, CSO, New Delhi.

—1998. Economic Survey 1997-98, New Delhi.

---1998a. Rural Labour Enquiry Report on Consumption Expenditure of Rural Labour Households (50th Round of NSS), Chandigarh.

---1999. Annual Report 1998-99, Ministry of Rural Areas and Employment, New Delhi.

---2000. Basic Rural Statistics, March, 1999, Ministry of Rural Development, New Delhi.

Government of Karnataka (GKT) 1972. Economic Development of Mysore 1956 to 1969, Bangalore.

—1981. Sixth Five Year Plan 1980-85, Bangalore.

—1982. Karnataka Annual Plan 1982-83, Bangalore.

—1982a. Karnataka State Gazetteer, Bangalore.

—1985. Seventh Five Year Plan 1985-90, Bangalore.

—1990. Draft Eighth Five Year Plan 1990-95, Bangalore

---1991. Draft Eighth Five Year Plan 1992-97, Annual Plan 1992-93, Volume I, Bangalore.

—1991a. Annual Report 1990-91, Department of Rural Development and Panchayat Raj, Bangalore.

---1992. Trend in Area, Yield and Production of Principal Crops During 1960-90, Directorate of Economics and Statistics, Bangalore.

—1994. Karnataka State Gazetteer Decennial Supplement (1983-93), Bangalore.
—1996. Karnataka At a Glance 1995-96, Directorate of Economics and Statistics, Bangalore.
—1997. Economic Survey 1996-97, Department of Planning, Institutional Finance, etc., Bangalore, March.
—1997a. Panchayati Raj in Karnataka, Department of Rural Development and Panchayat Raj, Bangalore.
—1997b. Annual Plan 1997-98, Vol. 1, Department of Planning, Institutional Finance, etc., Bangalore.
—1997c. Annual Report 1996-97, Department of Rural Development and Panchayat Raj, Bangalore.
—1998. Ninth Plan 1997-2002, Bangalore.
—1998a. Economic Survey 1997-98, Bangalore.
Government of Kerala (GKL) 1963. Kerala 1962 An Economic Review, State Planning Board (SPB), Trivandrum.
—1969. Kerala 1968 An Economic Review, Trivandrum.
—1973. Fifth Five Year Plan 1974-79 A Draft Outline, SPB, Trivandrum.
—1976. Land Reforms Survey Report (1966-67), Trivandrum.
—1984. Economic Review 1983, Trivandrum.
—1986. Economic Review 1985, Trivandrum.
—1991. Economic Review 1990, Trivandrum.
—1992. Economic Review 1991, Trivandrum.
—1994. Statistics for Planning 1993, Department of Economics and Statistics, Trivandrum.
—1997. A Review of Public Enterprises in Kerala 1996-97, Bureau of Public Enterprises, Thiruvananthapuram.
—1997a. Ninth Five-Year Plan 1997-2002 and Annual Plan 1997-98, SPB, Thiruvananthapuram, August.
—1997j. Report of the Taskforce on Field Crops, SPB, Thiruvananthapuram.
—1997b. Report of the Taskforce on Land Reforms and Agrarian Institutions, SPB, Thiruvananthapuram
—1997c. Report of the Taskforce on Ground Water Development, SPB, Thiruvananthapuram, June.
—1997d. Report of the Taskforce on Agricultural Financing, SPB, Thiruvananthapuram, June.
—1997e. Report of the Taskforce on Fisheries and Aquaculture, SPB.

—1997f. Report of the Taskforce on Forestry and Wild Life, SPB, December.
—1997g. Report of the Taskforce on Livelihood Secure Fishing Communities, SPB, June.
—1997h. Report of the Taskforce on Traditional Industries, SPB.
—1997i. Report of the Taskforce on Public Sector Industries, SPB.
—1998. Economic Review 1997, SPB, Thiruvananthapuram.
Government of Mysore (GOM) n.d., Fourth Five Year Plan: A Draft Outline, Planning Department, Bangalore.
Government of Tamil Nadu (GOT) 1972. Tamil Nadu: An Economic Appraisal 1971-72, Evaluation and Applied Research Department, Madras.
—1982. Sixth Five Year Plan 1980-85, State Planning Commission (SPC), Madras.
—1993. Eighth Five Year Plan 1992-97, SPC, Chennai.
—1997. Tamil Nadu- An Economic Appraisal 1995-96, Chennai.
—1998. Ninth Five Year Plan Tamil Nadu, SPC, Chennai, July.
Haque, T. and A.S. Sirohi 1986. Agrarian Reforms and Institutional Changes in India, New Delhi: Concept.
Industrial Development Bank of India (IDBI) 1995. Report on Development Banking in India 1993-94, Bombay.
—1998. Report on Development Banking in India 1996-97, Mumbai.
International Institute for Population Sciences (IIPS) 1995. National Family Health Survey (MCH and Family Planning) India 1992-93, Bombay, August.
Khadi and Village Industries Commission (KVIC) 1983. Annual Report 1982-83, Bombay.
—1994. Annual Report 1993-94, Bombay.
Kurien, C.T. 1981. Dynamics of Rural Transformation A Study of Tamil Nadu 1950-75, Madras: Orient Longman.
Nadkarni, M.V. et al 1989. The Political Economy of Forest Use and Management, New Delhi: Sage.
National Bank for Agriculture and Rural Development (NABARD) 1987. Statistical Statements Relating to the Co-operative Movement in India 1981-82, Part I, Bombay.
—1989. Statistics on Regional Rural Banks, September.
—1993. Annual Report 1992-93, Mumbai.
—1998. Annual Report 1997-98, Mumbai.
—1984. Statistical Statements Relating to Co-operative Movement in India 1978-79, Part II, Non-credit Societies, Bombay.

National Council of Educational Research and Training (NCERT) 1998. Sixth All India Educational Survey, National Tables, New Delhi.

National Sample Survey Organisation (NSSO) 1957. Report on Landholdings (3), Report No. 36, Eighth Round 1953-54, New Delhi.

—1977. Unemployment at a Glance, New Delhi.

—1987. Report No. 341, Thirty-eighth Round, June.

—1995a. Key Results on Employment and Unemployment, Report No. 406, Fifth Quinquennial Survey, Fiftieth Round (July 1993-January 1994).

—1998. Debt and Investment Survey, NSS Forty-Eighth Round (January-December 1992), New Delhi, August.

Reserve Bank of India (RBI) 1970. Report on Currency and Finance 1968-69, Bombay.

—1983. Report on Currency and Finance 1981-82.

—1991. Report on Currency and Finance 1989-90.

—1996. Report on Currency and Finance 1994-95.

—1997. Report on Trend and Progress of Banking in India 1995-96, Mumbai.

—1998. Report on Currency and Finance 1996-97.

—1998a. Statistical Tables Relating to Banks in India 1994-95, Mumbai.

—1999. Report on Currency and Finance 1997-98.

Articles in Books

Kurien, John 1994. "Kerala's Marine Fisheries Development Experience", In ed. B.A. Prakash, Kerala's Economy Performance Problems Prospects, New Delhi: Sage.

Pani, Narendra 1984. "Reforms to Pre-empt Change Land Legislation in Karnataka", In ed. A.R. Raja Purohit, Land Reforms in India, New Delhi: Ashish.

Pasha, Syed Ajmal 1996. "Problems and Prospects of Uncultivated Lands and the Livestock Economy of Hyderabad-Karnataka Region", In ed. Abdul Aziz and Sudhir Krishna, Regional Development Problems and Policy Measures, New Delhi: Concept.

Prahladachar, M. 1996. "Industrial Development Status and Prospect", In ed. Abdul Aziz and Sudhir Krishna, ibid.

Samuel, M. Johnson 1996. "Infrastructure for Regional Development", In ed. Abdul Aziz and Sudhir Krishna, ibid.

Shyam Sunder, S. and A.N. Yellappa Reddy 1986. "Pressure on Our Forests", In ed. Cecil J. Saldanha, Karnataka: State of Environment Report, Bangalore.

Sivanandan, P.K. 1994. "Performance of Agriculture in Kerala", In ed. B.A. Prakash, op. cit.
Thampy, M.M. 1994. "Development of Organised Small-Scale Industries: Some Issues". In ed. B.A. Prakash.
Thimmaiah, G. and Abdul Aziz 1984. "The Political Economy of Land Reforms in India". In ed. A.R. Raja Purohit, op. cit.

Articles in Journals

Ambirajan, S. 1999. "State Government Subsidies The Case of Tamil Nadu", Economic and Political Weekly (henceforth EPW), April 3-9.
Baruah, A.K. and Parmod Kumar 1979. "Why do Voters Not Vote", EPW, 22-29 December.
Bhalla, G.S. and D.S. Tyagi 1989. "Spatial Pattern of Agricultural Development in India", EPW, June 24.
Bijoy, C.R. 1999. "Adivasis Betrayed: Adivasi Land Rights in Kerala", EPW, May 29-June 4.
Geetha, S. and M.H. Suryanarayana 1993. "Revamping PDS: Some Issues and Implications", EPW, October 9.
Hara Gopal, G. and C.H. Bala Ramulu 1989. "Poverty Alleviation Programmes IRDP in An Andhra Pradesh District", EPW, September 2-9.
Herring, Ronald J. 1980. "Abolition of Landlordism in Kerala A Redistribution of Privilege", EPW, June 28.
Janakarajan, S. 1993. "In Search of Tanks: Some Hidden Facts", EPW, June 26.
Jhabvala, Renana 1998. "Minimum Wages Based on Worker's Needs", EPW, March 7-13.
Kannan, K.P. 1995. "Declining Incidence of Rural Poverty in Kerala", EPW, October 14-21.
Krishnaji, N. 1975. "Inter-Regional Disparities in Per Capita Production and Productivity of Foodgrains A Preliminary Note on Trends", Special Number.
Krishnan, T.N. 1992. "Population, Poverty and Employment in India", EPW, November 14.
Mathew, E.T. 1999. "Growth of Literacy in Kerala State Intervention, Missionary Initiatives and Social Movements", EPW, September 25.
Mooij, Jos 1999. "Dilemmas in Food Policy About Institutional Contradictions and Vested Interests", EPW, December 25-31.
Moses, Brindavan C. 1983. "Noon Meal Scheme", EPW, January 22.
Neelakantan, M. 1994. "Jawahar Rozgar Yojana An Assessment through Concurrent Evaluation", EPW, December 3.

Nihila, Millie 1993. "Development Process and Status of Women Tanning Industry in Tamil Nadu". EPW, October 9.

Panini, M.N. 1999. "Trend in Cultural Globalisation From Agriculture to Agribusiness in Karnataka", EPW, July 31-August 6.

Parthasarathy, G. 1995. "Public Intervention and Rural Poverty Case of Non-sustainable Reduction in Andhra Pradesh", EPW, October 14-21.

Pillai, S. Mohanan 1996. "Social Security for Workers in Unorganised Sector Experience of Kerala", EPW, August 13.

Pinto, Ambrose 1999. "Andhra Pradesh Politics of Opportunism", EPW, September 4-10.

Prakash, B.A. 1998. "Gulf Migration and Its Economic Impact: The Kerala Experience", EPW, December 12-18.

Rajan, S. Irudaya and A. Jayakumar 1992. "Impact of Noon Meal Programme on Primary Education An Exploratory Study in Tamil Nadu", EPW, October 24-31.

Rajan S. Irudaya and P. Mohanachandran 1998. "Special Statistics: Infant and Child Mortality Estimates-Pat I", EPW, May 9-15.

Rao, B.V. 1988. "Poultry a neglected Sector", Survey of Indian Agriculture 1988, The Hindu, Madras.

Rao, M. Govinda 1992. "Proposals for State-Level Budgetary Reforms", EPW, February 1.

Rao, P. Jaswantha 1998. "Andhra Pradesh Tribals' Struggle Against Land Alienation", EPW, 17-23 January.

RBI Fiscal Analysis (RBIFA) 1967. "Finances of State Government: 1967-68", RBI Bulletin, August.

—1968. "Finances of State Governments: 1968-69", RBI Bulletin, May.

—1978. "Finances of State Governments: During 1974-75 to 1978-79", RBI Bulletin, September.

—1979. "Finances of State Governments: 1979-80", RBI Bulletin, September-October.

—1987. "Finances of State Governments: 1979-80", RBI Bulletin, October.

—1988. "Finances of State Governments: 1988-89", RBI Bulletin, October.

—1991. "Finances of State Governments: 1990-91", RBI Bulletin, April.

—1992. "Finances of State Governments: 1991-92", RBI Bulletin, April.

—1993. "Finances of State Governments: 1992-93", RBI Bulletin, March.

—1998. "Finances of State Governments: 1997-98", RBI Bulletin, February.

Reddy, P. Prudhvikar 1998. "Trends in Agricultural Wages An Inter-regional Analysis in Andhra Pradesh", EPW, March 26-April 3.

Sarangi, Satinath and Gary Cohen 1995. "Andhra Pradesh A Tale of Two

Industrial Estates", EPW, June 17.

Sawant, S.D. 1997. "performance of Indian Agriculture with Special Reference to Regional Variations", Indian Journal of Agricultural Economics (IJAE), July-September.

Sen, Abhijit 1996. "Economic Reforms, Employment and Poverty Trends and Options", EPW, Special Number.

Sharma, H.R. 1994. "Distribution of Landholdings in Rural India 1953-54 to 1981-82 Implications for Land Reform" EPW, March 26.

Simhadri, S. 1997. "Andhra Pradesh River Water Politics in Drought-Prone Telangana", EPW, September 13-19.

Thangaraj, M. 1995. "Trend in Fragmentation of Operational Holdings in India: An Exploratory Analysis", IJAE, April-June.

Thippaiah, P. and R.S. Deshpande 1998. "Analysis of Market Infrastructure, Prices and Terms of Trade: A Case Study of Karnataka", IJAE, July-September.

Unni, Jeemol 1991. "Regional Variations in Rural Non-Agricultural Employment An Exploratory Analysis", EPW, January 19.

----1997. "Employment and Wages Among Rural Labourers: Some Recent Trends", IJAE, January-March.

Vasavi, A.R. 1999. "Agrarian Distress in Bidar Market, State and Suicides", EPW, August 7-13.

Visaria, P. *et al* 1993. "Literacy and Primary Education in India 1980-81 to 1991", Journal of Educational Planning and Administration, January.

Vyasulu, Vinod 1995. "Management of Poverty Alleviation Programmes in Karnataka An Overview", EPW, October 14-21.

Vyasulu, Vinod and B.P. Vani 1997. "Development and Deprivation in Karnataka A District-Level Study, EPW, November 15-21.

Other Sources

Agro-Economic Research Centre (AERC) 1986. Report of the Study on National Rural Employment Programme in East Godavari District of Andhra Pradesh, Waltair, May (mimeo.).

Centre for Monitoring Indian Economy (CMIE) 1999a. Monthly Review of the Indian Economy, July.

Government of India (GOI) 1964. Agricultural Situation in India, November (Periodical).

—1999a. Agricultural Situation in India, May.

—1997a. Company News and Notes, May (periodical).

—1998b. Company News and Notes, June.

—2001. Kurukshetra, April.

Kalawar, A.G. et al 1985. Report of the Expert Committee on Fisheries in Kerala, Bombay (mimeo.)

National Sample Survey Organisation (NSSO) 1990. Sarvekshana, April-June.

—1993. Sarvekshana, October-December.

—1995b. Sarvekshana, January-March.

—1995c. Sarvekshana, July-September.

—1997. Sarvekshana, January-March.

—1998a. Sarvekshana, April-June.

—1998b. Sarvekshana, January-March.

Sen, Amartya 1994. "Market, Social Opportunities and Economic Development", D.T. Lakdawala Memorial Lecture, Centre for Development Studies, Thiruvananthapuram, June.

The Hindu (Chennai) 1999. 13 January (Newspaper).

The Statesman (Calcutta) 2000. 'President smells a time bomb in reforms', 26 January.

---2000a. 'Presidential Govt., Economic Reforms on Review Agenda', 30 January.

—2000b. 'Joint Fund to Meet Bandit's Demand', 28 August.

Index